Amiri Baraka & Edward Dorn

RECENCIES Research and Recovery in Twentieth-Cecntury American Poetics
MATTHEW HOFER, *Series Editor*

This series stands at the intersection of critical investigation, historical documentation, and the preservation of cultural heritage. It exists to illuminate the innovative poetics achievements of the recent past.

Other titles in the Recencies series available from the University of New Mexico Press:

Amiri Baraka and Edward Dorn: The Collected Letters edited by Claudia Moreno Pisano

The Shoshoneans: The People of the Basin-Plateau by Edward Dorn and Leroy Lucus

Amiri Baraka

&

Edward Dorn

The Collected Letters

Edited by

Claudia Moreno Pisano

University of New Mexico Press | Albuquerque

LIBRARY OF CONGRESS CATALOGING-IN-PUBLICATION DATA
Amiri Baraka and Edward Dorn : the collected letters / edited by Claudia Moreno Pisano.
     pages cm. — (Recencies: Research and Recovery in Twentieth-Century American Poetics)
  Includes bibliographical references and index.

 ISBN 978-0-8263-5391-7 (cloth : alk. paper) — ISBN 978-0-8263-5392-4 (electronic)
1. Baraka, Amiri, 1934– —Correspondence. 2. Dorn, Edward—Correspondence.
I. Moreno Pisano, Claudia, editor of compilation.
 PS3552.A583Z48 2014
 811'.54—dc23
 [B]
                            2013015141

Book design and composition by Lila Sanchez
Text composed in Minion; Display type is Calibri and Courier

For my family

Contents

Foreword

From the Archive Out

The inauguration of Recencies is a most welcome addition to the field of possibilities in contemporary literary studies and yet another indication that new pressures are being brought to bear on our conceptions of recent cultural history. By creating a space for older work to be seen anew, the series further formalizes an important shift in recent scholarship. The early idea for Claudia Moreno Pisano's extraordinary project to collect the letters written between poets Edward Dorn and LeRoi Jones/Amiri Baraka came at the very beginnings of what would become Lost & Found: The CUNY Poetics Document Initiative, an innovative pedagogical/publishing venture founded in 2009 under the auspices of the Center for the Humanities at the Graduate Center of the City University of New York. With an emphasis on "extra-poetic" work by poets—further conceptualized as representing the actual thought and research of writers in face of the academic, ideological, and political straight-jackets of the Cold War—Moreno Pisano's choice to focus on these letters, and through them the friendship of two major figures of late twentieth-century North American culture, has proven revelatory in ways we can only begin to enumerate.

I say *only begin* because many more such projects await, in the form of research and scholarship, that will fully establish the enormous scope, and the often heroic character, of writers associated with what came to be called the New American Poetry or, perhaps more accurately, "unofficial" verse culture. The recent but significant turn away from literary theory and toward textual scholarship focusing on the immediate past is the first stage in making available what Ed Dorn would call "the data" and establishing the very terrain upon which we might more soberly account for the explosion of the kind of radical poetic, formal, artistic, and intellectual creativity and restlessness that the work of Baraka and Dorn represents. Moreno Pisano's work, then, is a model of such "data" collection—and one worth emulating.

By taking past innovation in textual organization and commentary (I think of Ralph Maud's work on *The Selected Letters of Charles Olson* but many others as well) and adding a dense but seamless layer of social and political commentary in her enormously useful headnote sections, Moreno Pisano manages to embed her stance toward the material in a running narrative that contextualizes the work for both then and now. Because she has also taken into account the further trajectories of Baraka and Dorn, beyond the dates of these letters, we are given great insight into some of their later practices. In her opening commentary on letters from 1959–1960, for example, Moreno Pisano refers to a 1972 interview conducted with Dorn in which he speaks of the importance, for a writer, of "getting assignments." Given that, at this point, neither Baraka nor Dorn have an audience to speak of, she proposes the letters themselves "to serve as this kind of assignment," as "Dorn and Jones are proving themselves to one another, testing the limits of their poetry and ideas, and doing so against worthy partners."

The extent to which so many major ideas and forms of the time were explored in letters cannot be overstated and constitutes a primary site for the exploration of the curious inversion of the "public" and the "private" during the Cold War, reaching, perhaps, an apotheosis in the surveilled letters written by imprisoned activist George Jackson. When Dorn characterized the United States in the early 1960s as a "permissive asylum," his prescience met head on with Baraka's experience, the kind of experience limned in one of his earliest texts, "Suppose Sorrow Was a Time Machine," in which the story of his grandfather's forced migration due to racism is told through an "enlightenment" that can only become obscure, through the vibrations of time travel in which, as in Baraka's masterpiece *Blues People*, "emotional validity" is what everything must be tested against.

We are only beginning to come to grips with the still ongoing legacies of the Cold War and the National Security State, particularly as it has affected not just the horizons of our political life but designs of and on the imagination itself. In one ripple effect, the 9/11 Commission Report concludes that "we believe the 9/11 attacks revealed four kinds of failures: in imagination, policy, capabilities, and management." Section 11.1 of the Commission's chapter on imagination states the following: "Considering what was not done suggests possible ways to institutionalize imagination. . . . It is therefore crucial to find a way of routinizing, even bureaucratizing, the exercise of the imagination." Against the expected "Orwellian" scenarios often presented by liberal thought, it might make more sense *not* to divorce something like the 9/11 Commission Report from the general culture, to see it as following and not leading, as confirming what has already taken place.

In this sense, making available this kind of primary material gives us a conduit to begin deinstitutionalizing our imaginations, to return to possibilities both thwarted and realized but certainly imagined. One of the prime pedagogical principles in the Lost & Found project is to put aside labels of schools and movements and conventional literary histories, such as exist of the period, and "follow the person." By following Amiri Baraka and Ed Dorn, guided by Moreno Pisano's sure hand, we are presented with an alternative universe tracing the formation of 1960s North American thought and culture in ways almost impossible to find elsewhere. Naturally, primary materials are messier than codified studies, but they open worlds usually foreclosed by decorum, disciplinary stricture, dictates of fashion or relative worth, and a host of other containment methods.

Finally, it is well worth considering what it might mean to view Baraka and Dorn (and others associated with them) in light of global decolonization. Both Baraka and Dorn fed on the foundational ideas of Charles Olson, the primary North American post–World War II thinker who broke with both institutional academic and political opportunities in order to be a poet and pursue knowledge in radical and new forms but also to be part of a political project, part of an effort to propose and initiate new structures. Dorn's initial encounter with Olson came as a student at Black Mountain College, as the recipient of Olson's "program" of study, in the form of "A Bibliography on America for Ed Dorn." This would remain a foundational source for his continued study of the dispossession of Native peoples on this continent. For Baraka, the connection was more as an interlocutor and publisher of key texts by Olson and as someone from whom Olson knew he had things to learn. Baraka's work, in part, was shaped by exposure to African American scholars working far from the mainstream, outside reigning conceptual strictures. Baraka's encounter with Sterling Brown, for example, while studying at Howard University, led to an immersion into music as history, music as the embodiment of African American and American historical experience. These tributaries of historical methodology would have a major impact on the work of both Baraka and Dorn, and it is in these letters and in their relationship that we can see traces of these complex sources begin to have their long-lasting impact.

Making the inaccessible available and bringing unread texts to light is part of the necessary work of refinement, part of constructing a storehouse of materials and resources that can allow us to see our more recent history anew, with fresh eyes, and make better use of it. The resistances mounted by Baraka and Dorn are unyielding, resulting in forms and works both harsh and beautiful at the same time, forcing readers into the spaces their consciousnesses forged. Thanks to the work of Claudia Moreno Pisano, we now have some access into the early sources of that space.

AMMIEL ALCALAY

Preface

Amiri Baraka, *Ed Dorn & the Western World*

Ed Dorn & the Western World is the keynote speech delivered by Amiri Baraka on March 4, 2008, at the Ed Dorn Symposium hosted by the University of Colorado, Boulder, originally published by Skanky Possum & Effing Press, Austin, 2008.

I first came upon Ed when I was putting out the magazine *Yugen* from Greenwich Village, a few months after I got thrown out of the US Air Force. This marked a remarkable sequence since I had joined the Air Force—Error Farce I later called it—after getting thrown out of Howard University.

The magazine sought to bring some unplanned newness to a literary scene that was dominated then by so called new criticism. The *Sewanee, Kenyon, Partisan, Hudson* and so forth reviews for whom poetry was something that could only be written if preceded, riddled, and packaged with strings of Latin, Greek, quotes which most readers I'm sure did not understand.

These were the last days of the Pound-Eliot influence on a younger generation that took that poetry for granted but did not think they had to climb into it and pull the coffin lid down. The review people however used the Pound-Eliot paradigm as a broken umbrella to keep out the world, but wanted no part of the outright excesses that some focused attention to the real world would surely provide.

Eliot had been embalmed in Anglo Christianity and Pound had been tried as a fascist sympathizer and locked up in the loony bin. Ginsberg and I journeyed to DC to see him. Ginsberg was admitted; I waited outside. You had to have an appointment.

Ginsberg said that he had to get the monkey of talking to Pound in the real world off his back. He comes out and says Pound told him he was sorry he had succumbed to the suburban prejudice of Anti Semitism, and this seemed to put Allen's mind at rest. Though I taunted him asking how could he deal so easily with the abuses in the *Cantos* &c.

I say this because for my generation that stuff with Eliot and Pound, though we had admired them earlier, was part of the reason that we came to think and write the way that we did, because we were putting both restraints of their excellence as well as the simplemindedness of their social backwardness behind us.

It was Ginsberg who I wrote to at Git le Couer in Paris when I moved to the lower East Side asking him was he for real on a piece of toilet paper. He replied he was but he was tired of being Allen Ginsberg. He used a better grade of toilet paper.

He also sent me lists of poets who I should contact and ask for poems, he also sent me some of his own. The list was actually a menu for what would some years later form the core of *The New American Poetry*, edited by good friend Don Allen.

The magazine thus began as a loose amalgam of new young writers, eclectic and fresh. By *Yugen* 4, which features a cover by Black Mountain's Fielding Dawson, there was a less eclectic but still diverse grouping of poets, but now with a more conscious attempt to work with writers from what I had now perceived as different schools. There were the Beats, Ginsberg, Corso, Kerouac, Burroughs; The San Francisco School, Whalen, Snyder, Duncan, Lamantia & younger ones like Loewinsohn and Meltzer; The Black Mountain folk Creeley, Olson, Dorn, and their acolytes Finstein, Oppenheimer, Sorrentino, Early, and the New York School, O'Hara, Koch.

And while the first issues of *Yugen* included several Black poets, Allen Polite who had been my high school hero and 1st mentor in Greenwich Village, and Tom Postell, a surrealist from Cincinnati who went into Bellevue, from the third issue on all the poets except LeRoi Jones were white.

I had thought to bring those various schools together in a sort of United Front against the tired academic poetry that dominated the establishment reviews.

Interestingly enough, I wrote a defense of the so called Beat Generation in *Partisan Review*, in answer to Norman Podhoretz who most recently has been one of Bush's Certified nincompoops. So you see it was not just a few of the New American Poets who became "Political" as a silly man has written recently criticizing Dorn.

During the *Yugen* run which went to 8, I began publishing separate volumes under the rubric of Totem Press, and then in collaboration with the 8th street bookstore, Ted and Eli Wilentz, we began Totem/Corinth Press and published some of the most important young writers of the time. Ginsberg, Kerouac, Snyder, Whalen, Sorrentino, Oppenheimer, O'Hara (w/ a cover by Larry Rivers), Loewinsohn, di Prima, and Ed Dorn's first volume, *The Newly Fallen*.

What was most impressive to me about the work was Ed's breathing lyricism, not vatic or from the pulpit of some chosen emotional "I," but a simple saying, some heartfelt observation. As disciplined as we were then by Olson and Creeley, since the poets I ran with every day downtown and got wittily wired with were indeed their sworn posse, it was Dorn's "What I see in the *Maximus Poems*" that intrigued me. That here was one of the insiders, a Black Mountain voice who spoke of a way into *Maximus* and a self determined way beyond. Remember Fee Dawson and Joel

Oppenheimer used to crash in my house on the far west side regularly, I mean crash. Painter, Basil King, Sorrentino, Finstein—all BM troops—and I used to swallow tons of ale at the Cedar Tavern, along with O'Hara, Kline, de Kooning, Norman Bluhm, Bob Thompson.

I had published Olson's "Projective Verse" as a separate volume and "Proprioception" in the magazine. I had gone to Gloucester to see Charles a couple times and talked into the mornings about America and indeed about the "Western World." So his prescription of a poetry that reached beyond the bounds of literary obsession were hard in my thinking. He was talking about a poetry that used history and place as an engine to wrest meaning from the present. To see how now got to be now and where was it going and where had it been.

At the time, these were the most important theoretical directions that I took seriously to heart. Plus the general celebration of Williams was important. Ginsberg never failed to lecture me and everyone else on the critical meaning of Williams's variable foot and use of the breath phrase and the need for American speech as poem. This is where the poets that I chose to present in *Yugen* came closest to uniting. The need for *A New American Poetry*.

I remembered too that of those four great poets to journey to Europe, William Carlos Williams and Langston Hughes returned with similar use to their work (see Hughes's "The Negro Artist and the Racial Mountain" and Williams's *In The American Grain*. Or *Paterson*). Both emphasize the need to understand "where we're at where we're coming from." Eliot and Pound stayed, literally and literarily in Europe.

So that it was just before *The Newly Fallen* that Dorn and I began to correspond. That correspondence lasted from that time in the early 60's . . . Ed and I wrote back and forth into the 90's. So it is this correspondence which is key to our relationship, changing but stalwart, in the sense that those letters gave us a peculiarly honest forum in which to hear how we sounded to someone we respected, learned from but were never timid about disagreeing with. Some of these letters have already been published by the *Chicago Review*, others are scheduled.

The discourse reflected where we were in our own growth to maturity re-maturity and re-rematurity. The initial discussions had to do with a kind of delineation in our minds of what constituted the "New" in that rhetorical titled anthology. Who we thought important, who we didn't know in that exchange of intelligence. Perhaps who we liked and didn't but we were not, as I recall, gossipy.

We wanted an exchange of information, new facts, new registrations, reinforcement of some stances, permission to abandon others. I know we wrote about Olson and the Black Mountain experience, school, hangers on, aesthetic—what did it mean? There was even an exchange in *Yugen* between Gregory Corso and Gil Sorrentino . . . Corso himself a parody parodying what he thought the limitations of the "Black Mountain approach." He meant the short line, the use of the slash to stop the breath flow. Sorrentino shot back in the next issue, intending to chide

Corso for the lack of discipline in the Beat writing. Neither, it seemed to Dorn and I, were very accurate.

But those discussions were one animating feature of that broad united front against academic poetry death. Sometimes one was surprised at how close we were in our disagreements and how distant we were in our union. But the evaluation of Ginsberg, Olson, Creeley, O'Hara were frequent in my correspondence and in my house those long ago weekends we drunk ourselves or partied ourselves into verbal profundity. I reported these to Dorn very often. The Apple, The Village, The Lower East Side, The Politics Social antics thereof. While Dorn reported from Santa Fe, Pocatello, California, Colorado to his "New York, New York: a wonderful place to live, a poor place to visit."

Our intercontinental conversations changed as our minds did. A silly man could wonder why we changed so. People are always staking me to that ignorant bit of small talk turned question. Why have your views changed . . . you mean since sliding out of Anna Lois Jones' womb? Place had a lot to do with it. Actually Time, Place and Condition as the Marxists insist.

It is a silly question whose only merit is seeking after real information. To wonder at the change itself is nonsense. Let us hope that most of us have had some revelation to change our paths and direction since we got here. Even since we first thought of ourselves as quote intellectuals.

I was fed the myth and reality of Black Mountain up close from some of its most loyal students: Joel Oppenheimer, Fielding Dawson, Basil King who I saw almost nightly. What Dorn thought about Black Mountain and its primary teachers Olson and Creeley I got, actually, in antidote to the aforementioned whose juiced up recollections frequently bordered on the sentimentally surreal. Though they were instructive and important to me (See Fielding Dawson's *The Black Mountain Book*).

But all were urging a clarity to me about what there was of value in the *NAP* that ironically finally made me look beyond it without ever abandoning what I thought was valuable. Olson's insistence on a projection of poetry outside the box of literature into the field of anthropological, archaeological, linguistic, social, political unfoldings wrapped up in what we get from the top . . . not as topical as newspaper but people die everyday because they do not grasp what is in these (to paraphrase Williams).

Interestingly, one difference in the crowd I described was that as the Civil Rights Movement deepened, our minds were changing in conversational contradiction at the same time we remained a crowd. It was Dorn also reporting on his changing vis-á-vis what was in that field in this world to be reported and how was a poem to do that.

So that some of this crowd of poets could say to me poetry and politics don't mix even while paying homage to intensely political poets like Ginsberg or Olson.

One of the things the so called Language poets don't like about Ginsberg is that they call his an "impossible politics"—that was the argument at a poetic gathering in Maine several years ago, when they also said that Black poets' works were oral, their own, one imagines, cerebral. I referred them to DuBois. Amazingly I had to mention the same DuBois in answer to Bellow's question deprecating Black Studies: Who is The Tolstoy of the Zulus?

But the string of literary intercontinental communiqués comes in times of stress, reflection, philosophical need, aesthetic reassurance, or state of the world messages did indeed take us into the field. With the same back and forth of question, answer, rejoinder, question.

The purely literary, which was never purely anything, had to take on the questions that arose for me about the Civil Rights Movement. 1957 I got undesirably discharged from Error Farce, just as the Montgomery Bus boycott was sizzling to some kind of denouement. So by 1958 I was an established young village resident poet. I had even gotten a post card from Langston Hughes greeting my first published poem "Preface To A Twenty Volume Suicide Note" published in *The Naked Ear* in Taos, New Mexico with a post card written as all his letters were in green ink saying, "Hail, Leroy, from Harlem . . . I understand you're colored!" from Langston Hughes. And with *Yugen* magazine proof to Hail the double consciousness, Black and American.

In 1958 when the boycott was successfully ended the racists blew up Dr. King's House. When the black folks arrived with rifles raised in the air shouting, "Dr. King, what shall we do?" His answer, "If any blood be shed let it be ours." That pushed me and a great portion of my generation away from King.

In 1959 Fidel Castro entered Habana, while Oppenheimer, Finstein, Sorrentino, and Dawson sat in my living room and put together a little pamphlet called "For You" Jan 1 1959 to Fidel Castro. Though Sorrentino who had written a coy little poem to Fidel told me he hated men in uniforms.

You bet the Cuban revolution set off a torrent of discussion with the poetry community which I was part of. The back and forth between Dorn and I was also reflective of that torrent. Ed questioning what the real significance of Fidel Castro was. What did it really mean to the Cuban people. And what could it mean to us here. Though he was never dismissive, nor was Charles Olson, who even wrote a poem about his exchanges with me vis á vis Cuba, which he read publicly in San Francisco.

They were both open but both with critical analysis of Latin American history and politics and the United Snakes' likely reaction to it. The fact that Fidel had done that, that those *Barbudos* had overthrown an ugly satrap of US imperialism had to be celebrated. But for those people who somehow saw poetry as a relief or distancing from politics it brought a sullen kind of cynicism. And Fidel was not yet a declared Communist.

The amazing imbalance of thought from the other poets in our crowd who some-how thought that they were "freer" than what Fidel and company proposed by lib-erating Cuba from a henchperson of US Imperialism. And that somehow poetry made them freer.

One of the astonishing confirmations of the backwardness of the post modern movement (what do dat mean?) is that such contagious propounders of this crev-ice, actually a denunciation of post enlightenment modernism, is that groups like the language poets are steadfastly politically reactionary, which I guess is con-firmation that they are post or pre modern indeed. (The Maine exchanges about Ginsberg's politics and the mode of Black poetry confirmed that for me.)

Dorn never thought that poetry excluded him from politics it gave him a way to get inside politics and carve it to the bone. This was an aspect of Dorn from "What I See In *The Maximus Poems*," and even in the lilting lyricism of *The Newly Fallen*.

In 1960 I went to Cuba for the 1st anniversary of the July 26 Movement triumph in Cuba. The first celebration which saw thousands of invited guests from all over the world, including de Beauvoir, Sagan, Sartre, Robert Williams, Harold Cruse, Julian Mayfield. I wrote an essay, "Cuba Libre," which won an award and that was discussed in our letters as well as back and forth from Olson.

The sense is that I had made a step, that I had taken some action, that the field was real life not just a poetic allusion. But that there were real life dangers, both physi-cal and philosophical—ideological—that should be discussed. But it was Olson and Dorn who did not back away from the discussion. As some who thought that my headlong flight into Revolutionary rhetoric was somehow heresy.

But that was the openness I treasured, the lack of fear at heading into areas that many of our free and open crowd thought out of bounds. And this movement into the rush of political challenge was leading me where America and the world was going in real life. 1960 I had gone to Cuba, 1960 was the first national appearance of Malcolm X on the television special "The Hate That Hate Produced."

It was Malcolm X who seemed, in contradiction to Dr King, by saying, "You treat people like they treat you. If they treat you with respect, you treat them with respect, but if they put their hands on you, send 'em to the cemetery!"

So that now as I was taken by Black Nationalism, our letters flew back and forth trying to analyze the real from the illusory. What was to be done here and now by us all? Where was the black poet LeRoi Jones headed and where were my erstwhile friends headed as well. Would the community of poetry and poets be spared the rising fire of the Black Liberation Movement?

It was Malcolm X's murder that sent me hurtling out of Greenwich Village, denouncing even some of my best friends it seemed. What it was is that as Fanon said, the integrated intellectual of an oppressed nationality when he discovers him-self to be so integrated into the theoretical oppressor community develops a self criticism that makes him denounce what were his heretofore day to day social context and associates, even becoming for a time super black or super native, but then if he is consistent there is some hope that that pose can be dismissed and the mindset of actual revolution take its place.

What Dorn wanted to know was if there was some actual dialogue left for us that did not include us denouncing each other. Dorn said he would not be a European American, to be an American is enough psychical punishment. Ginsberg insisted upon that dialogue as well over the years, disagree though we did. But Ed wanted to know what it was that made me so furious with what I had taken up with for so many years. Which was Poetry! Was there nothing of value in what we had discussed and agreed upon? Of course there was, but it was necessary for me to get away from the Village and the alienation which made me so ashamed as I stood in the Eighth St Book Store when Leroy Lucas (whom Ed collaborated with on a book about Native Americans) ran into the place in the middle of a book party shouting that they had just murdered Malcolm X.

I was inconsolable. Ed could understand that but what were the actualities of such a situation? What would I, what could I do, and what could he make of it himself to be involved and at what level and to what end? Was this Liberation which I now shrieked about an exclusive Black province—isn't there an intellectual and ideological alignment that includes the willing?

That is what Ed Dorn asked throughout the development of his work. Is there a genuine alignment of progressive concerns? Is there an attention so rigorous that it makes us common workers for some as yet unclearly stated alternative to all this. The pettiness of the evil around us and in us to whatever degree we cannot fend it off, is not actually petty at all. If it is petty we are safe in our germ free sanitized intellectual niches of not so quiet self regard. We are safe because we will not question, we will not work to actually change what might be simple annoyance or unjust criticism, or oppression or torture or death.

What is this Place? And what has it made us? Where does it come from? We are shaped by what it has made us as we shape what it is ourselves. It was Sékou Touré saying the same thing essentially as Olson. I was moving from one locus to another but prepared as much by what I had gleaned as by what I was entering. It was Wittgenstein who taught me Ethics and Aesthetics are one.

So our discussions became at one point the most closely read report from a front from which I willingly had fled. You treat people like they treat you. I could handle that with Dorn because he spoke openly and to the point. He was a man, I said once, who would rather make you an enemy than lie to you. So we could keep up our dialogue, though for a period. So that even after I had fled uptown to Harlem, denounced white folks one and all and opened the Black Arts Repertory Theater School which sent four trucks a day throughout Harlem all summer of 1965 with drama, poetry, music, painting trying to 1) create a poetry that was black in form and content 2) bring the arts out of the elitist dens of ambiguity and into the streets 3) create an art that fought for the liberation of black people, my dialogue with Dorn went on.

One story told to me by a friend of O'Hara's had this poet rushing in to tell Frank, "LeRoi Jones has said he wants to kill all white people. O'Hara's rejoinder (probably without putting down his drink) Well he won't start with us!"

Dorn's comments just after that period when he was interestingly in England as he says in "The Outcasts of Poker Flats" with a pained comic outer view of Ed Sanders and his newly released *Fuck You: A Magazine of the Arts* which seemed to sum up the entire craziness of the period, "To begin with, since we are in a foreign country (and who isn't) let's take it right out of the mail."

After excoriating with delight archness Sanders' commendable project and summation he goes in part iv to "In another ecclesiastical area the poet and playwright LeRoi Jones has shifted into the most absolutist position of all" (and you should read the rest of this) "The absoluteness of LeRoi Jones position is correct." He says, "THE WHITE MAN IS OBSOLETE," which sounds right. . . . (*Views*)

In another statement of the period Dorn writes in "The Poet, The People, The Spirit" which is about a conference in which his book with Lucas, *The Shoshoneans* was discussed, he says, "I was not actually asked to attend the Berkeley Conference of the summer of 1965, but went as a substitute forced on the organization of the conference by LeRoi Jones, who had begun to withdraw from such contact. And that's how I went as an Indian." (*Views*) It was just such statement of Ed's views that kept us within writing distance.

What it meant is that Dorn did indeed understand my leap into Black Nationalism. He says of the works *Dutchman, The Slave, The Toilet*, "he outlined what I think must have been for him the prolegomena to a transfer back into a world he was of but had not been part of. Harlem is not his native ground. When Malcolm X was assassinated there was clearly no other intellectual leadership equal to Jones in those ranks . . . The Negro people do not have just one white enemy in America. There are hundreds of different kinds of white men all in their phantasmagoric masks and not just white men—Red men, Brown men, Yellow men green men there are white Negroes not just the ones Norman Mailer because he fancies marijuana had in mind."

So that it was not just Jones journeying through the land of Blackness to become Baraka up through Harlem with the accrued awards of friends pointing guns at his stomach, threats from uptown gangsters, and religious organizations, home to rebellion split open head and knocked out teeth, there had been deep change in Dorn, but one that had been always sharp in observation, perception is poetry he said, brilliant in rationalization, and the use he made of it in poetry and in practice. The journey away from the states was to me, his own way of signaling the breakup of our camp. That the big Greenwich Village of our younger days which stretched from

Black Mountain to the Lower East Side to Gloucester to Buffalo to San Francisco and the well advertised bongo playing Road of the Kerouacs had become dysfunctional. The era of Good Feeling, Ginsberg called it, had passed. My own move uptown and then back home was my own way of co-signing this occurrence.

About the West, for Ed the outward motion in the poem placed before him by Olson, his own discursive self education from that model, what polis is, can only lead to politicks what moves that people in its quest for what DuBois called "true self consciousness" is both incisive and constantly revelational.

After very accurately describing "Malcolm had just begun to make headway through the terrible delicate discriminations between MLK, Elijah Muhammed . . . LeRoi Jones has been unable to assure that leadership for various and complex reasons." What Dorn has gleaned from our conversations and instinctively put together on his own is that my (and his by his understanding of my need) movement was not stopping at Black Nationalism and, what he would soon be faced with discussing was this brothers movement into Marxism.

But the West for Dorn was not just the western part of the United States but that is how he got to the bigness of the whole West. That Western World that Europe claims and has never been. "Leave England headed West" I wrote, "You arrive in Newark." For Dorn the West the journey out first from Gloucester then ultimately from Idaho was in space and time. From history to the history of the future. What is past and what is passing.

It was the elemental America that the West symbolized, yet it was the pushing past the old from those original thirteen states. Dorn born at the edge of the East and the beginning of the West, of a heroic farm and working class people doomed by their own ability to sustain themselves with less than they need. Listen to this great later poem "Tribe," a long echo of what could be dug from even the first pages of *The Newly Fallen*, that there is a loyalty to that back story, tribe indeed, all the way back to Odin, of those poor hopeless white people for whom hope is a scam, a stolen election, cheap merchandise advertised as Holy. Their belief that democracy is a place where they live but have not often explored.

You see I could feel that, even to that which could never be defended among my own tribe, but that we had lived on the edge of disaster and been told that we had survived, but into what and as what? So it was I felt always with Ed, we must know ourselves to step away and analyze ourselves and then step back, climb within our own mythology to cleanse it of mendacity. Only Dorn and Tennessee Williams could use that word like those electric swords in Star Wars, but with actual life effect.

The Way West as the great summation of *Gunslinger* and the other trekking poems to find a heroic paradigm which could be studied, analyzed, turned forward and upside down, made mythological enough to say something about reality was just what it seemed. A searching. Searching for the real West. Searching for the real America.

Searching for the real heroic engagement with the meaning of it all. Himself, our-selves included.

But there is no clearer delineator of the sum than Dorn. We all admire Robert Creeley for the precision of his line, the incisive twist of his verse, which some have even called Cubist. Dorn's reviews of Creeley indicated that not only did Ed understand what Creeley was doing, and was much admired of it, as we all are. But he understood where Creeley had chosen to REMAIN. And so wound around and around near the end, satisfied with his rare music, eloquent locution and inverted use of world and word.

Why some silly man cannot use Dorn's later work is that it is not only eloquent in word and skilled in construction, but that his meanings begin to be so clear to him that they become as quick as Billy the Kid's response that he make his nephew a whistle, Billy draws and fires the exact hole in the exact reed to make the whistle. "How can you hit the target without aiming," the young boy asks, "I'm always aim-ing," says Billy the K.

So that Dorn who is aiming for years and years now can spin and plug a hole dead center in whatever target. It is the politics at question in the silly man's mind that is squishy with the compromise of self satisfied mediocrity. We hold these truths to be self evident is a bulletin. The Bullet the Boston Tea Party.

The traditional lyric is the elevation of the singular I to the world as the attention of the world. It is the usual concern of young poets not yet able to see the connection of that I to the world. One of those links, of course, is study the other experience. For whom do you write Mao asks in *Yenan Forum*, what do you celebrate what do you put down, what do you love, what do you hate, the work carries all of this. Art, Mao said, is the ideological reflection of the world in the mind of the artist.

But there are artists for whom there is no world but themselves and whatever lit-tle inarticulate eating and shitting and sleeping and copulating have to say to them that is good, bad, perfect, execrable or whatever. There are also, again, (see my essay "why most poetry is boring, again," in the *Poetry Project Newsletter*) poets quite at home in what Dorn called "the very permissive asylum" the US has become. Cer-tainly if they have tenure and tidy little birdcages in which they can make poo poo on a removable floor and have it published.

The moving out to investigate the real West, the Westness of us, that is the real openness, newness, freshness, innovation of America the promise is to finally see that this promise has been the threatened future of this world of European inven-tion and discovery, colonialism and capitalism and imperialism and always war and this Afro Asian Latino world of submission and imprisonment and defeat. But it has been that tribe of Dorn's that has also slipped outside the well advertised virtues of this hell and to include them in the torture must make Dorn then search outside the given, outside the relentlessly stated lie of American democracy to see that America and its place in the world for what they actually are.

That early lyricism always carried the sting of contrast to what surrounded it, in metaphor or in contemplative portraits of the subject. But as I moved more directly into political activism and away from the icy literary world, I grew impatient with a mere infatuation with language. That language that I still admired was to signify action, a move away from the given, the static, the dead.

It is DuBois who said, one cannot actually love beauty without loving truth. So that is the warp that challenges the words of the post moderns (what dat mean?) that to shy away from truth is to misunderstand beauty. Truth and Beauty said Keats and the Doctor are our only pledges.

The Wild Dog kept me posted and the News polemic *Rolling Stock*, I looked forward to. I was at Naropa just before the great poetry war. I remember Duncan and I humorously challenging Allen who had changed into a suit and tie he bought from the Salvation Army at the urging of Trungpa. I had asked one of Trungpa's minions why it was that Tibetan music only had three notes. So it was not so shocking when the news broke about Trungpa's insisting that Bill Merwin and his lady friend undress for his dizzy metaphysic. Nor was it any shock that Dorn was screaming so loud it could be heard in the East that there was a scandal of idiots at Naropa. I know he vowed never to set foot in the place again. How far we had gotten away from our poetry community's desired unity of purpose. Allen in the clutches of drunken Buddhists and myself in the clutches of drunken judges who sentenced me to three years without parole in the Newark rebellion. And Ed still trying to be heard as some voice of analytical reason or reasonable analysis. But now growing less metaphorically lyrical, with a language that continued to hone itself to a fantastic gleaming sharpness. So I could feel his words again at the point of actual conflict with this thing that threatened to digest us one way or another.

Dorn's diction, his placement of words, the stunning vocabulary, the music that came from such precision always was in evidence till the very end. To challenge that is silly, man. The poems after *Gunslinger* bring another aspect of Dorn's work into full function, his humor. A satirical arsenal that was so funny so true so funny because it was so true. Bulletin Bullet to that bulls eye right between the eyes of the willingly blind.

Hello, La Jolla made me fully aware of Dorn's work again. *The Selected Poems*, the prose stunts in *Views, Yellow Lola* and then the great work of socially loaded poetry *Abhorrences* which I began to share. I think now that it must have been Dorn's influence not quite conscious to me that had something to do with the *Low Coup* that I began to put out. Or that we had come to similar conclusions that what had to be said could be said just as the Japanese had discovered many moons ago. There was a contemporary use for Basho's brevity. Though we substituted satire, pun, a savaging politics to blow up the superficial, the fake, the wholly disgusting ignorance which is American social life and political shenanigans.

The reason a silly man could not grasp the explosive poetics that such gun slinging truth makes is that many of these sacred cows Dorn blows away the silly man rides to work on everyday to school to the bank and back to the old bullshit ranch.

What we miss in Dorn is an actual gladiator poet at the very top of the number. We had fought against fools and liars all our poetic lives, at whatever level of consciousness. We need Dorn right now when the stupidity and backwardness that warped the '50s (McCarthy time we had to get past the Korean debacle turned into VietNam and the deaths of Kennedy, Malcolm, King and Kennedy). We had to become hard and action focused not only to produce but to survive. And now here we are at the bottom of the Sisyphus Syndrome again, both truth and beauty at risk, dizzy little pimp nerd professors and assholes in waiting want to make poetry the servants of cowards and right wing pundits disguised in strophes again.

If Fascism, as Dimitrov said, is the rule by terror what Bush has done, with his top down Bush-it-is rule with the fear of terror which is the reverse trench coat of the same fascist tactic. So that now the suspiciously oily Texas smell of 911 and the non hunt for Bin Laden has led instead to Afghanistan, Palestine, Iraq, Lebanon, with sights pointed at Iran, North Korea and China. Not so ironically this "Axis of Evil" which has been coined by the Assholes of Evil in DC are all colored and this is the tumult in which the Homeland security Heimat-Sicherheit has pushed a clumsy fascism directly down our throat. And poets are urged to quiet down and become more literary less understandable, less confrontational as the nation struts toward Nazi-hood.

This has frightened many people who have grown sophisticated in their acceptance of the Fridgidaire that follows any progressive period. So that while the *New American Poetry*, The Black Arts Movement tried to roll the stone of American art culture democracy and equality up the mountain of would be American dream, the rock has been rolled back down Sisyphus style so that like Lenin poets like Dorn who fought against the rule of the dead and who developed a highly personal poetic style as his vehicle as well as the rest of us who fought against the sterility of literature disconnected from American reality, was called the old man by the economists, that is, dudes just wanting to get paid, or get tenure or get published in the safety of their weak metaphors and poorly hidden conservatism rather than pulling down the stale icons of minority rule and majority frustration and transform the system. We must not only talk about Dorn we must read him. We must read the poets of the *New American Poetry* and The Black Arts Movement, not just in those anthologies, *The New American Poetry* and *Black Fire* but dig up their later works which are mostly out of print as the publishers are now letting great works go out of print or made hard to get while they wholesale restock the American bookshelves with garbage as iridescently dull as Eisenhower's oatmeal the harbinger of McCarthy.

Acknowledgments

I would like to thank, first, Ammiel Alcalay for not only introducing and sharing a tremendous body of knowledge but for serving as staunch believer in and facilitator for my intellectual pursuits. Without the support, advice, and enthusiasm of those closest to these letters, Amiri Baraka and Jennifer Dunbar Dorn, this project would not exist. I thank them both for their permission to take these letters out of the archives, as well as for their patient work in helping me transcribe particularly difficult-to-read letters and their willingness to answer my many queries along the way.

The original letters reside in two archives: the Amiri Baraka Papers at the Charles E. Young Research Library at the University of California, Los Angeles; and the Edward Dorn Papers at the Lilly Library at the University of Indiana. I would like to thank and acknowledge the many librarians and archivists who helped me, answering my questions and making available to me these collections.

Tremendous thanks and appreciation to David Parsons, Jerry Watts, David Greetham, Basil King, Martha King, David Southern, Dale Smith, Joseph Richey, Elsa Dorfman, Josh Schneiderman, John Harkey, Kyle Waugh, Justin Rogers-Cooper, and all of my colleagues and professors at The Graduate Center. I would also like to thank everyone at the University of New Mexico Press, especially Matt Hofer and John Byram for their encouragement and support, and copyeditor Mark Bast for his incredibly helpful suggestions, ideas, and patience.

Introduction

From the end of the 1950s through the middle of the 1960s, Amiri Baraka and Edward Dorn fostered a friendship primarily through correspondence. Though many of the original letters have been lost over time, those that do exist testify to the complicated and intense friendship of these two self-consciously avant-garde poets. Bonding around their commitment to new and radical forms of poetry and culture, Dorn and Baraka also created an interracial friendship at precisely the moment that the civil rights movement was becoming an undeniably powerful force in national politics. The major premise of the Dorn-Jones friendship as developed through their letters was artistic, but the range of subjects in the correspondence shows an incredible intersection between the personal and the public, providing a schematic map of what was so vital in postwar American culture to those living through it. The early 1960s found both poets just beginning to publish and becoming active, public figures.

The two poets were younger contemporaries in a world that was watching the establishment of the Beat Generation and its already famous writers and friends: Jack Kerouac, Allen Ginsberg, William Burroughs. This correspondence offers a vivid picture of American lives—connecting, remarkably, around poetry—during a tumultuous time of change and immense creativity. Among those writers and poets who frequented the art worlds of Jones and Dorn, other correspondence friendships were also created, taking their place among many: Charles Olson and Frances Boldereff; Robert Duncan and Denise Levertov; Neal Cassady and Jack Kerouac; Kenneth Koch and Frank O'Hara, to name a few. Reading through these correspondences allows access into personal biographies, and through these biographies, profound moments in American cultural history open themselves to readers in a way not easily found in official channels of historical narrative and memory.

For Jones and Dorn, their personal correspondence became a key source of information, aesthetic feedback, mutual advice, and trust. The economic hardships that came with a self-chosen avant-garde life, and for Dorn, isolation in small towns, created a sense of urgency, freely exhibited here in these letters. The stark honesty and sometimes raw, shocking authenticity that developed in their dialogue was a treasured ideal, given the rigid social and political circumstances of Cold War America that surrounded them and so deeply influenced their respective artistic visions.

" "   " "

Edward Dorn (1929–1999) was born in Illinois during the Great Depression, and his stark, impoverished childhood would mark him forever. Intellectually hungry and dissatisfied with the status quo, Dorn engaged in sharp, critical inquiry using language as a means of knowledge, investigation, and understanding in an attempt to push into motion what he knew was a too-often complacent country. Dorn spent his life writing, teaching, and editing as he traveled between North America and England. After having lived in places as varied as Washington state, San Francisco, California, and Santa Fe, New Mexico (where Dorn was living when he and Jones began corresponding), Dorn accepted a part-time teaching position at Idaho State University in Pocatello, Idaho. Dorn's time in Pocatello saw him through the end of his letters with Jones; they would not write again until the mid-1980s, when Jones (who had by then long been known as Amiri Baraka) wrote to Dorn praising his and wife Jennifer Dunbar Dorn's little magazine/newsletter, *Rolling Stock*. Eclectic and witty, *Rolling Stock*'s motto was "If it moves, print it!" In 1965, through the English poet Donald Davie, Dorn was offered a position as a Fulbright lecturer at the University of Essex in Great Britain. He remained there until 1970, after which he returned to the United States, continuing his struggle to maintain a living while writing poetry and teaching part time. In 1977 he accepted a teaching position at the University of Colorado, Boulder, where he stayed until the end of his life.

From an early poem like "On the Debt My Mother Owed Sears Roebuck," dealing with the particular realities of North American poverty, to a later work like *Gunslinger*, which takes on American identity and history in the form of an epic western, Dorn's poetry continually pushes poetic language into the darkest corners of experience. Dorn spent several years studying with the influential poet Charles Olson, a major twentieth-century American poet and thinker and rector for a time of the experimental and progressive Black Mountain College. Both Jones and Dorn would count Olson as a major force in their poetic lives, powerful for both his poetry and his ideas about poetry, put forth in essays and speeches throughout his life. By the late 1950s Olson had already established his reputation as a Melville scholar, won two Guggenheim Fellowships (the first in 1939, the second in 1948), and then abandoned all formal channels of academia until given a highly unusual and brief teaching position at the University of Buffalo, State University of New York, in 1963, setting his poetic and social radicalism against the growing confines of Cold War America. Dorn worked with Olson both in and out of the experimental Black Mountain College, where in 1955 Olson created "A Bibliography on America for Ed Dorn." The bibliography was a syllabus of sorts, written in the form of an essay, a list, and a graph all in one. It was an entry into the larger world of America that dealt with everything from sociology, politics, and geography to poetry and literature.

Born in Newark, New Jersey, in 1934, Amiri Baraka has spent his life as a poet, music critic and historian, dramatist, and activist. Reared in a stable working-class household, Jones excelled academically in the public schools of Newark and subsequently was awarded a scholarship to attend Howard University in Washington, D.C. At Howard, Jones found himself alienated from the institution's bourgeois mobility education ethic. He rejected these aspirations and flunked out, subsequently joining the United States Air Force (the Error Farce, as he later called it), where he received a dishonorable discharge after being falsely accused of Communist affiliations.

By 1958 Jones had ventured to Greenwich Village in New York City, where he became an integral participant in the bohemian poetry, theater, and music scenes. A prolific writer, Baraka has been publishing and performing for nearly his entire adult life, beginning his path as public artist and intellectual amid the creative foment of New York City in the 1950s and '60s. Still known then as LeRoi Jones, he wrote poetry and prose—everything from essays about Cuba, modern art, and Black Nationalism to liner notes for jazz albums, as well as a full-length history of jazz in America, *Blues People: Negro Music in White America*—and worked to establish two small magazines, *Yugen* (with then-wife Hettie Jones, née Cohen) and the *Floating Bear* (with poet Diane di Prima), as well as a small press, Totem.

In the mid-1960s, Jones rejected the Village scene and moved uptown to Harlem, where he would begin the process of changing his name, a public indication of his private journey into a deeper black identity. Baraka experienced much of his evolving political and poetic consciousness in his letters with Dorn, an able and willing partner in the navigation of the twentieth century; this was a friendship that would continue to influence Baraka's ideas and actions even through his growing black militancy and separatism. In 1965, after the death of Malcolm X, Baraka established the Black Arts Repertory Theatre/School (BARTS) in Harlem. The idea for BARTS had begun some time before, and the building was found and bought before Malcolm had died; at his death, the transition became final. Baraka has since returned to Newark, continuing his work in the arts and as an activist.

"" ""

Having seen several poems of Dorn's in various small literary magazines, in 1959 Jones began by writing to him with praises and a request for poems for his own magazine, *Yugen*, edited with Hettie Jones. This was the first little magazine to include many of the various writer groups that would come to comprise what became known as the New American Poetry, groups that came to be labeled the Beats, the New York School, Black Mountain, and the San Francisco Renaissance. Donald Allen's seminal book, *The New American Poetry*, was published in 1960 by Grove Press, making its poets available to a larger audience for the first time. The collection issued from a body of poets presenting alternative forms of knowledge and testimony to those in society at large and in the culturally conservative Cold War–era structures of the academy.

Despite the positive impact of this volume, however, the arrangement of the poets into various groupings codified these writers into categories far more rigid and inflexible than the actual aesthetic fluidity of the real-live poets. Baraka was adamant that *Yugen* would not reproduce either Allen's decisions about labels or the decisions of mainstream poetry editors. Baraka struggled, as well, against the university system in North America, which felt problematic to many artists and intellectuals. The rise of government funding and the blossoming of sponsored research came with what many felt to be an untenable obligation to uphold the systemic ideals of the postwar affluent society.

The letters between Dorn and Jones show serious attempts at extrication from these prevailing ideologies. The realities of the Cold War, of both urban and rural poverty suffered by untold numbers of Americans, of racial tensions and the rising civil rights movement, of the social and political conservatism that had risen out of the ashes of World War II victories—all of these things existed in tandem with the deep belief in prosperity so fervently promoted by postwar America. While the dominant images skewed toward a prosperous white middle class, this was never the full reality. Allen Ginsberg's 1955 seminal poem *Howl* illustrated this very point, as did another much lesser known poem, Edward Marshall's "Leave the World Alone," also written in 1955 and included in Donald Allen's *The New American Poetry.* Avant-garde and experimental art, music, and poetry would reflect the conflict, fear, and elation of the futuristic, space-traveling sixties.

The correspondence between Jones and Dorn took place in this context of conflicted ideas and realities in the United States. The letters became the primary ground for a wide range of discussions, from quotidian observations of being snowbound without enough heat or being overdressed on an overly warm spring day to the hashing out of experiences, fears, and anxieties directly related to the sociopolitical culture of the early 1960s: bar fights around race matters, an aggravated police presence around fears of agitation and protests. With self-publishing and -production of art as a branch of self-governance, we might say that the many little magazines and broadsheets, the chapbooks and public readings created and organized by the poets themselves, are all part of this reconfiguring of democratic ideals and definitions of the citizenry.

A look at the complete set of letters finds them formative and showing signs of what is to come later: by 1965, knowledge, beliefs, actions, friendships, and alliances had shifted drastically, setting the stage for a highly tumultuous late 1960s. The correspondence between Dorn and Jones takes the reader from a time when the norms of cultural ideology held Americans squarely in a superficial postwar ease to the uncovering of darker truths and the veneer of consumer culture beginning to fray. Dorn and Jones understood the poem as an act of the intellect, a public action that carries with it responsibility. Narratives are created both personally and in confrontation, and for those who write, public formation is often linked to personal narrative, creating a complicated public identity, a thing difficult to define but crucial to understand. Seen side by side, the poetry and the letters of Dorn and Jones give us entry into multiple scenes of knowledge.

Corollary to the new poetic forms coming out of the 1950s and '60s was free jazz. Breaking away from traditional musical constraints like the melodic line, the four-bar standard, and chord sequences, musicians like Thelonious Monk, Ornette Coleman, John Coltrane, and Cecil Taylor began to open up the sound of jazz. The opening of both musical and poetic line went beyond technical aspects, signifying important cultural and political views as well. As the civil rights movement gained greater and greater urgency, the ugly underside of American culture and politics was revealed, and many jazz artists would be part of the fight to change their status as black artists. The struggle to gain tighter control over their own work, taking that work out of the hands of the large, exploitative music companies, was close to LeRoi Jones's own work and mission.

Jones would both write for and produce the vehicles—small magazines and a small press—for distribution on his own terms. In this context, friendships, like that of Jones and Dorn, were developed that took on the qualities of an alternate media. In 1950, Neal Cassady penned a thirty-thousand-word letter to Jack Kerouac that became known colloquially as the "Joan Anderson" letter. It was passed out among the poets and fervently talked about; in a letter to Allen Ginsberg, Kerouac says,

> Yes, publish Neal's Joan Anderson, it's a masterpiece and was the basis for my idea about prose . . . that dense page where he breathlessly drew a diagram of the toilet window is the wildest prose I've ever seen and I like it better than Joyce or Proust or Melville or Wolfe or anybody. (*Selected Letters* 464)

In another letter to Ginsberg, Cassady himself says,

> All the crazy falldarall you two boys make over my Big Letter just thrills the gurgles out of me, but we still know I'm a whiff and a dream. Nonetheless, tho I blush over its inadequatcies [*sic*], I want you to realize the damn thing took up the better part of three straight Benzedrine afternoons and evenings. So I did work hard at it and managed to burn a little juice out of me. (*As Ever* 104)

Here the letter writing is itself prose, an artistic creation of its own. This is particularly true given the lack of publishing venues, as witnessed by Kerouac's own delayed publishing history; while *On the Road* was written in 1951, it was not published until 1957. Charles Olson's epic, *The Maximus Poems*, begun as letters to his friend and fellow Gloucester poet Vincent Ferrini, followed the same kind of trajectory. We can go even further back to see this tradition being practiced by early American poet Emily Dickinson, who also sent poems as or in letters.

Letters collapsed far distances and long periods of time apart for many, an easy and inexpensive way to create and continue vital conversations outside of anyone's control, fully one's own. At a time when both Dorn and Jones were struggling to be published and to be heard, the letters themselves became part of their art and their means of fighting back. Sometimes this was to the detriment of both poets, as their often brutal sarcasm, homophobic derisions, and frequent misogyny are used to express deep anger and frustration. For two young writers with a tremendous desire to have their work read and shared, they often responded to rejection and insults (of which they faced a great deal) with vitriol. Despite all their real beliefs in radicalism in art, culture, and politics, both fell often into the standards of the language of the day: the slurs they flung were hateful and far too typical of the time. Being young, angry, and rejected brought out a certain degree of wildness; the language of the letters reveals a sense that they wanted to be as offensive to the world as they felt the world was to them. Unfortunately, the targets are far too frequently women, about whom they were decidedly conservative, and homosexuality in both men and women.

At a time when homosexuality was still considered grounds for institutionalization and the landmark Stonewall riots were still several years away, men and women who identified as gay stood to suffer personally, politically, economically, and culturally. Despite the relative progressivism and freedom present at the time in New York City, homosexuality could and did still carry a stigma, and the possibility of violence and derision toward anyone identifying as gay was a very real factor in people's lives. Jones (more frequently than Dorn, though Dorn often echoes this homophobic language) takes up this violent language quite often as his own, despite the fact that he lived in New York City and counted numerous close friends who identified as gay, including Frank O'Hara, John Wieners, and Michael Rumaker. Jones's work sometimes dealt with his seemingly contradictory feelings about homosexuality; 1965's *System of Dante's Hell* explored the borders of sexuality, queer and straight. Coupled with the homophobic barbs peppered throughout the letters is an often even more aggressive vitriol toward women, particularly women in positions of power or authority and women (in Jones's case) with whom he had had sexual or romantic relationships.

During this period of correspondence, Jones was married to Hettie Jones, his editorial partner on *Yugen*, a writer and poet in her own right, with whom he had two daughters. In her autobiography, *How I Became Hettie Jones*, she describes her position as wife and mother while also being a writer; ultimately, she could not write while married to Jones, especially after they began having children. Jones expected, shockingly to Hettie, a wife who would raise his children and support his own writing career, a traditional model of marriage in which Hettie had not expected to find herself. Throughout their marriage, there were infidelities on both sides, but as Hettie describes it, her participation in any affair was considered far more transgressive; again and again she found herself in a decidedly non-feminist, unequal marriage with a man she loved deeply. Hettie would bear the brunt of LeRoi's growing radicalism and turn toward Black Nationalism throughout the '60s; as Hettie was not black, Jones drew away from her, eventually leaving her with their daughters in 1965 after the assassination of Malcolm X.

For a time during his marriage to Hettie, Jones maintained an affair with the Brooklyn-born poet Diane di Prima, with whom he had a child. In 1961, di Prima and Jones released the initial issue of their coedited poetry newspaper, the *Floating Bear*, published by themselves, pasted up by hand and copied on a mimeograph machine. The little magazine functioned, in essence, as a poetry newsletter, printed quickly and inexpensively and spread widely to fellow poets and fans. During the same year, di Prima, in partnership with other poets and artists, founded the New York Poets Theatre in the East Village. Di Prima maintained an independence as a poet, as a mother, and in her hard-won work in the 1950s and '60s that many women were unable to maintain. Di Prima's autobiography, *Recollections of My Life as a Woman: The New York Years*, details her life as a young poet, describing her move from a strict Italian American household in Brooklyn to wilder, more radical, bohemian enclaves in Manhattan (and, eventually, California).

«» «»

Fueling each poet was a sense of art as not only a valid but a necessary means of grappling with and understanding both the beautiful and the horrific in the world. The letters then become both reflection and place of creation, the ground upon which to experiment. Dorn believed any major institution of power, whether it be the United States, the former Soviet Union, or Cuba, could never be trusted or assumed to have any benevolent qualities. Baraka, on the other hand, at least in the earlier years of his activism, believed the state could be changed to make it work in favor of the subjugated. Baraka, of course, was not alone in his ideas about the capacity for citizens to change the state. The stance is part of a larger discourse on the role of intellectuals—and artists—in society. In his correspondence with Dorn, Jones expressed this idea of hope and possibility for change. However, as the '60s wore on, his radicalism would lean ever more toward breakage rather than repair; the later letters to Dorn show his growing anger and frustration.

Baraka channeled this artistic and political sensibility into the independent, collaborative magazines *Yugen* and the *Floating Bear* and Totem Press, an independent small publisher (in conjunction with Eli and Ted Wilentz's Corinth Press). Baraka was, with these projects, key in providing space for numerous artists from several different strands in the late 1950s and into the 1960s. These included Dorn, Charles Olson, Denise Levertov, and Robert Duncan, artists who would all later be published in Donald Allen's highly influential *The New American Poetry*. Baraka published two of Dorn's poetry collections, *The Newly Fallen* (Dorn's first book) and *Hands Up!* through Totem Press in conjunction with Corinth Press and saw several of Dorn's poems into print in both *Yugen* and the *Floating Bear*.

Most importantly, the two little magazines became focal points for midcentury artistic ferment, publishing new highly outspoken and radical poets from all over North America. This publishing space helped break down the geographical and human isolation in which so many of these poets found themselves, which is part of the story of Dorn and Baraka's friendship itself. In Pocatello, Idaho, without much money and the mobility that comes with it, Dorn was far from most large cities or centralized locations for artistic production. These magazines served as roving spaces, bringing people to one another when physical travel was not possible. Dorn himself had a hand here beyond poet, acting on numerous occasions as liaison between various poets and publishers, including Baraka, and later helping to found and edit his own small magazine, *Wild Dog*. With the doors of the major publishing houses and even small or independent presses like Grove, William Morrow & Co., and New Directions difficult to get through, the "do-it-yourself" approach was vital.

In the summer of 1965, when Dorn and Jones's letters had tapered off but their friendship was still strong, the Berkeley Poetry Conference took place, a major event in American culture, gathering together more than half of the poets from Donald Allen's anthology. The conference was significant in part because it brought so many older radical poets to one of the key locations of the '60s youth counterculture in all its myriad expressions, political and nonpolitical. The year 1965, though, would prove to be the precipice over which many things fell. Irreparably shaken by the murder of Malcolm X, Baraka declined his invitation to participate in the conference. This was not lost on Charles Olson, who made note of Baraka's conspicuous absence at the event by noting in his own speech Baraka's key role in his own publishing life: "Every one of those essays, by the way, is published by LeRoi Jones alone, in *Yugen*, *Floating Bear*, and *Kulchur*."

Baraka found himself facing a wall with the death of Malcolm. He asked Dorn to go to Berkeley in his place in a short, contradictory letter that relinquished his place—"I don't really feel like making that"—while also espousing Black Mountain as a "useful concept" in the formation of the Black Arts Repertory Theatre. Dorn obliged, in his own ever-provoking way: "I was not actually asked to attend the Berkeley Conference of the summer of 1965, but went as a substitute forced on the organization of the conference by LeRoi Jones, who had begun to withdraw from such contact.

And that's how I went as an Indian." From there, Dorn and Baraka went parallel but separate ways into places forged by thinking that had been working itself out through the previous years. This switching of places, as it were, at Berkeley signals a moment when Dorn and Baraka were still visibly close but shows signs of the coming breach to be brought on by Baraka's very public and near-complete break with his former life. After this final letter in 1965, the friendship between Jones and Dorn would suffer separation but never total loss.

With Dorn in England for the next five years and Jones (soon now to become Amiri Baraka) in Harlem and then Newark, the two nevertheless kept abreast of one another, each supporting the other's decisions despite any trepidation they might have had. Writing from England in 1965 in a piece called "The Outcasts of Foker Plats," Dorn would show his support: "[T]he poet and playwright LeRoi Jones has shifted into the most absolutist position of all. With his early plays he outlined . . . what must have been for him the prolegomena to a transfer back into a world he was of but had not been wholly part of. . . . The absoluteness of LeRoi Jones' position is correct." After having undergone various social, artistic, and political stances (Village bohemian, black nationalist, Marxist) Baraka at present maintains a deep interest in reclaiming this part of his intellectual life.

If we think of a text as defining political boundaries and providing historical continuity, as Dorn's friend and colleague Gordon Brotherston describes it in *Book of the Fourth World: Reading the Native Americas Through Their Literature*, these letters constitute the history of these men and their times better than many other forms of documented history. These letters display many facets: the razor-sharp intellect, the deep bonds of allegiance, the vitriol of inherited attitudes in deep transition. As both historical and autobiographical lens into two key writers at the very pulse of the turbulent cultural and political happenings of mid-twentieth-century America, these letters reveal an extraordinary snapshot of American identity and history.

" "   " "

A Note on Methodology

I came to awareness of these letters in 2005 after Summer 2004's *Chicago Review* fell into my hands; the issue is dedicated entirely to Edward Dorn, and along with poems, essays, and reminiscences, there are a handful of Dorn's letters to and from various friends and acquaintances, many of whom are poets and artists. The correspondence between Jones[1] and Dorn in particular caught my attention; filled with clear expressions of friendship, the letters were also filled with social, political, and poetic commentary. Wanting to read more, I began my search. The *Review* includes

---

1   A note on name usage: all references to Baraka during this period of correspondence, 1959–1965, are indicated with his name from this period, LeRoi Jones.

a brief listing of the various letter archives, and I reached out to Amiri Baraka and Jennifer Dunbar Dorn (Edward Dorn's widow), both of whom have been of great help to me in finding and decoding the letters. The letters are archived in two university libraries: Amiri Baraka's letters to Ed Dorn are at the Lilly Library at the University of Indiana; and Dorn's letters to Baraka are at the Charles E. Young Research Library at the University of California, Los Angeles. I traveled to both libraries to make photocopies and scans of all the letters as well as envelopes, photographs, drawings, and included poems and began the process of transcription and annotation. Though this is a fairly contemporary correspondence from less than fifty years ago that would in theory seem decodable, the body of work yet does present many methodological and ideological issues, from the minutiae of correcting and maintaining spelling and punctuation, to offering a critical analysis in relation to what is at stake in the realm of literature, culture, and politics.

My editorial approach aims to place the letters in a broad historical context. With literally hundreds of letters written to and from each poet throughout his life, this act of letter writing extends the idea of poetic authorship into what is often considered ephemera but can be seen instead as fully integral to our understanding of twentieth-century American poetics. Models for this edition are found in seemingly different projects such as Charles Olson's *Call Me Ishmael* and Susan Howe's *My Emily Dickinson*. These are two books of textual scholarship and history that aim, if not to overthrow, to at least disrupt the status quo of preconceived notions in American letters. Olson read Melville's editions of Shakespeare in order to read his marginalia, allowing Melville's words to give us a greater understanding of his own books. Howe grappled with Emily Dickinson's poems and letters, which have been in edition upon edition greatly altered from their original forms; Howe's goal was to unravel Dickinson's complicated publishing history.

While the letters between Dorn and Baraka are on the whole unpublished and therefore unedited until now, the time in American history from which they come has been edited, ad infinitum, not always for the better. Ralph Ellison, in an essay on New York City's jazz club Minton's Playhouse, talks about memory and how it travels:

> [T]he very effort to put the fragments together transformed them—so that in place of true memory they now summon to mind pieces of legend. They retell the stories as they have been told and written, glamorized, inflated, made neat and smooth, with all incomprehensible details vanished along with most of the wonder—not how it was as they themselves knew it. (qtd. in Kelly *Thelonious Monk* 62)

With the presentation of this correspondence, I hope to add a layer of knowledge to American poetics and history. There is the sense, as Howe worries over in her study of Dickinson, that suppressed deeply enough, recovery of knowledge will slip entirely out of reach. This gathering of ephemera, marginalia, conversations—the extra-poetic pieces—works toward a goal of greater transparency, a path through the tangle of American experience.

The letters are full of misspellings and typos; heady enthusiasm for the conversation at hand often keeps grammar at bay. What gets corrected and what is left alone? In general, most "mistakes" have been left as is to give the reader the clearest sense possible as to how the letters were actually written and received. William Carlos Williams, model for many twentieth-century poets, maintained that there is indeed an American idiom, a way of speaking that is particular to Americans, and he worried about the flattening and deadening of those idiosyncrasies. To this end, the transcriptions in this edition aim to hew closely to the original text, with the caveat that perfect transcription is never possible and that the editor's hand is always visible.

I have tried to maintain the appearance of the originals as closely as possible, re-creating the sometimes irregular spacing, paragraph, and layout choices Dorn and Jones used in their type- and handwritten letters. That said, minor editorial corrections have been made. Stray punctuation and missing or extraneous letters have been silently corrected. Many of the letters, particularly on Dorn's side, are handwritten; there are several words and phrases that are unreadable. I have been in contact with both Jennifer Dunbar Dorn and Amiri Baraka to clarify as much as possible, but places where transcription remains unfeasible I have marked with brackets [. . .]. As a corrective to my corrective of the letters, several scans of original letters are included to give readers a truer sense of how the correspondence appeared.

Tied to the matter of corrections is the issue of dating—many of the letters are not dated at all or are improperly dated. Envelopes are infrequently included with the original materials; where dates are unclear, then, I have arranged according to content; any errors in sequencing are my own. Any letters dated by archivists and librarians or any indications by me of possible date discrepancy rather than by the poets themselves have been noted by the date enclosed in brackets [ ]. Additionally, there are several references to enclosures found with the original letters, usually of poems, pictures, or newspaper clippings. In almost every case, these have been lost or misplaced; rather than noting every case where this is true, I have left these spots silent in the annotations.

Letters

I

1959–1960

*T*he LeRoi Jones–Edward Dorn correspondence begins with a request, from Jones in New York to Dorn in Santa Fe: "I'd like to have a couple of poems." The poetry is the starting place, the central point around which these artists' lives revolved. The letters from these first two years make clear how quickly the two poets realized their friendship, levels of ease in conversation belying their short acquaintance. They began to share their poetry, to share admiration and argument around these poems, to quickly make connections for each other with the many poets in their many circles of friends.

The correspondence has a definite ebb and flow, letters flying back and forth as quickly as once or twice a day while sometimes several weeks pass without a word. The letters work along many lines, from solidifying friendship to contact against loneliness to development as a writer. In a 1972 interview, Dorn said that getting assignments, so to speak, as you mature as a writer is incredibly important. Assignments are something you want and need in order to keep growing: "[I]n fact, the more you mature as a writer, the less you want to invent your own products and the more you want to be given them, to show what you can do" (Views 16). In a very real way, the letters serve as this kind of assignment—the audience, the response, and give and take of a written conversation is part of the thrust of the writing itself. Dorn and Jones are proving themselves to one another—testing the limits of their poetry and ideas and doing so against worthy partners. "LeRoi was, when I lived in Pocatello, my main correspondent in the East and I wrote him a lot—weekly, at least, sometimes a couple times a week. . . . [I]t was more than friendship" (Interviews 21).

In these first two years Dorn and Jones began their process of observing, worrying, and grappling with the unfolding of the late '50s into the early '60s: "So this was a time of transition. From the cooled-out reactionary '50s, the '50s of the Cold War and McCarthyism and HUAC, to the late '50s of the surging civil rights movement" (Baraka Autobiography 189). Here are conversations from the ground.

13

« »   « »

The list of poets and little magazines in Jones's letter sets the stage for the heart of the Lower East Side poetry scene in New York City. In 1959 Jones and his wife Hettie were already editing, writing for, and printing Yugen, *and there were often parties and gatherings in their home attended by the many poets, painters, and actors living in and visiting New York. Hettie Jones notes,*

> *From a quick first look at* Yugen *4 you'd say Beats, as the three Beat gurus— Kerouac, Corso, and Ginsberg—were represented. Except the "New consciousness in arts and letters" was more inclusive. Like Basil King, Joel Oppenheimer, and Fielding Dawson, the poets Robert Creeley, John Wieners and Charles Olson were out of Black Mountain College, where Olson was the last rector. Frank O'Hara, like the painters he knew, was a poet of the "New York School." Gilbert Sorrentino lived in Brooklyn, Gary Snyder in Japan, Ray Bremser in a Trenton, New Jersey, prison. (74)*

The Allen G. *in this letter is, of course, poet Allen Ginsberg (1926–1997), a great facilitator in mixing circles of artists, introducing everyone he knew to one another. That sometimes worked the other way around though: it would be Jones who first introduced Ginsberg to Langston Hughes. Jones and Ginsberg began their own friendship when Jones moved to the Lower East Side: "I wrote to [him] at* Git le Coeur *in Paris when I moved to the Lower East Side asking him was he for real on a piece of toilet paper. He replied he was but he was tired of being Allen Ginsberg. He used a better grade of toilet paper."*

Dear Ed Dorn,   26 Oct [1959]

I've been reading quite a lot of your verse recently (I'd read it before in Ark, Moby . . . Measure & Evergreen) . . . but I hadn't drawn all those separate threads together. Recently tho, with that Igish poem in Migrant and the mass of poems I saw at Don Allen's . . . I finally realize what a strong thing you have (a strong separate voice &c.) Anyway, I'd like to have a couple of poems for YUGEN. (I was very much impressed by yr 6th, 7th & 8th . . . also the lg mother poem.) Don tells me he's using some of them in his ant'y . . . but it'd be alright to put them in the magazine. But I thot it'd be better to ask for anything you wanted to send &/or for permission to use those poems I saw at Don's. Whatever you think! We have some kind of loose deadline for the next issue (6) . . . say about the 2nd wk in Nov. (but that's stretching pretty close). At any rate, I hope you'll send me something . . . or let me hear about the other poems. Thanks and take care.

best, LeRoi Jones

—Oh, I heard a reading of yrs on a tape Allen G. had . . . really marvelous! A funny scene, that was, with Allen, Peter Orlovsky,[2] Joel Oppenheimer,[3] Paul Blackburn,[4] Ed Marshall, Gil Sorrentino[5] & Diane di Prima . . . all squatting on the floor (+ wife & I) all singing yr hosannahs. . . . . . a funny age??

Lj

Charles Olson's Projective Verse *was a small treatise on the nature of poetry and language, originally published in 1950 and reprinted by Jones's Totem Press in 1959. This essay proved to be a powerful influence on the many poets who read it, opening up the restrictions, regulations, and boundaries within which mid-twentieth-century American poetry found itself confined. Olson talked about the poem's connection to the breath, recognizing the poem to be a living entity integral to the world at large rather than a function of staid academic rigmarole. Poets responded wholeheartedly to Olson's decree that "verse . . . if it is to be of essential use, must, I take it, catch up and put into itself certain laws and possibilities of the breath, of the breathing of the man who writes as well as of his listenings."*

It seemed to Dorn, though, that many poets didn't quite understand what Olson meant. In a 1977 lecture at the Naropa Institute called "Strumming Language," Dorn said, "I never thought that his discussion of the breath was

---

2   Peter Orlovsky, 1933–2010, American poet and actor. Orlovsky was prominent in the many radical poetic and theater circles of the mid-twentieth century and was Ginsberg's lifelong partner.
3   Joel Oppenheimer, 1930–1988, American poet. Oppenheimer studied at Black Mountain College with Charles Olson and was friends with Dorn. Oppenheimer would become the first director of the important and influential St. Marks Poetry Project in New York City, in 1966.
4   Paul Blackburn, 1926–1971, American poet. Citing Ezra Pound as a major poetic influence, Blackburn would come to be associated, and become friends, with many of the Black Mountain poets. He was also included in Donald Allen's *The New American Poetry*.
5   Gilbert Sorrentino, American writer, 1929–2006. A native of Brooklyn, New York, Sorrentino's work often reflected the specific linguistic and cultural markers of the Brooklyn in which he grew up. Friends with Dorn as well as the Joneses, he traveled throughout the Southwest with his wife. Sorrentino served for a time as the editor of *Kulchur* and later became an editor at Grove Press. Sorrentino lived in New York teaching, writing, and editing, as well as publishing the small magazine *Kulchur*, until 1982, when he took a position as professor at Stanford University.

meant to be taken as a way you could write poetry. I always thought it was meant to suggest to you that you could get involved physically with the poem in a way that, up to that point, hadn't actually been suggested. . . . But, for anybody who thought that it was meant to function *in a way that a VW manual will tell you how to set the valves, I just never took it that way."* Projective Verse *found its way into the many circles and schools of poetry burgeoning in the '50s and '60s and continues to be a key text for understanding the history of American poetry.*

Dear Ed Dorn: 5:XII:59

Finally looked at those poems of yours again, & I think 6th & 7th "Communications" wd do us best this time. Both, very fine. Your clear & marvelously exact images are really good news. That communication about that large woman or such I really dug, but space is always the kicker in this small shot business. But anyway, I'd like to use a couple more for the next Y⁶ (after one this month). #7 (if we can hold). #6 as I see it ought to make it later on in December. Or maybe we'll get pushed into the sixties. (Wow, isn't that straight out of some science fiction hash . . . THE SIXTIES . . . I mean, where are the goddam anti-gravitators &such. Maybe we lived too soon anyway. Poo)

Saw Olson last wkend. Spent 3 days up there in froze Gloucester. But lovely to see Chas again. We (totem pr) just finished doing Proj Verse (reprinting the original article plus a supplementary letter from Olson) last night it arrived. Salud! When I get the whole batch in I'll send on a copy.

Ok, well . . . NY cold & blue (like the negroes sing) eery like . . . but this is only time sensible person shd live here. Autumn & winter (well, ok, spring too) but summers are out. No woods or anything, but staring all day out at Hudson can be a real kick . . . anyway, you take care &c. & when you think of it send a poem or two??

best, LeRoi Jones

John Wieners (1934–2002) was a Boston-born poet, connected by art and friendship to many circles of poetry, including the San Francisco Renaissance and the Beats. He studied at Black Mountain with Charles Olson and poet Robert Creeley in the mid-1950s. Wieners edited and published three issues of Measure, *an important small magazine. An active fighter in the gay liberation movement, a political activist, and involved in several publishing cooperatives, Wieners also struggled throughout his life, suffering through institutionalization in a psychiatric hospital by the hands of his family as a young poet. His struggles caused great pain for his friends and fellow poets: "[He] was a gem who flickered in and out of our lives. Our hearts. John's story was tragic, but familiar, too. His Boston Catholic family had had him committed for*

---

6 *Yugen.*

*being gay, and using dope, and maybe junk, now, all those shock treatments later, he
was more than a little crazy" (Di Prima Recollections 273). Jones laments Wieners's
state in this letter to Dorn.*

*Irving Rosenthal (b. 1930), who Jones notes here as a possible help to John Wieners,
was an editor for the* Chicago Review *and a writer himself, a great supporter and en-
thusiast for the emerging poetry of mid-twentieth-century America. He was willing to
publish what others wouldn't, including the first chapter of William Burroughs's* Naked
Lunch *in the Spring 1958 issue of the* Review. *The printing of this chapter of a book
even Allen Ginsberg claimed was certainly too risqué to find a publishing home in
the United States at the time caused great upheaval and no small backlash. An article
titled "Filthy Writing on the Midway" in the* Chicago Daily News *ended up with the
resignation of Rosenthal, Paul Carroll, and three other editors of the* Review *after the
administration refused to publish the Autumn 1958 issue, in which would have been
printed the second chapter of* Naked Lunch *along with a slew of Beat, San Francisco
Renaissance, and other new poets. Rosenthal and the rest would go on to found* Big
Table, *an independent magazine of poetry and the arts; they took the unpublished material from the Autumn issue of the* Chicago Review *for their first issue of* Big Table.*

Dear Ed Dorn,   19:I:60

Sorry for long silence but I've been on my back, suffering from evil combination of
debauchery, bad lungs & probably malediction. Also, I don't remember whether
I sent those books I mentioned or not, so I'm sending them now (under separate
cover).

Thanks for letting me see that poem (The Pronouncement) . . . really liked
it. Your materials move right . . . or you handle them like statements about
things (rather than filmy abstractions of the floppy tie school of poets &c.)
Yass, if we could always keep talking about things, rather than just writing, cd
stretch our materials (& our gruesome limitations: each is only where he is, no
quick materialization to other lives: I mean, we can only write about what we
know . . . which, you bet, is a definite limitation. "KNOW thyself." OH what bullshit.
LOSE thyself works just as well I'm certain. Anyway, all lovely poem, & I'd like to
see any you want to send . . .

Magazine (#6) is slow because of my flabbiness. Physically & mentally. I move
faster now . . . & prospects are good for early February. This one is larger, 52 pages,
& is painful process to do.

Oh, I also included a book of Max Finstein's[7] in pkg . . . thot you'd be interested in.
John Wieners was by here a couple of weeks ago. Stayed with us for week or so. He's

7   Max Finstein, American poet. Finstein was a friend of Jones and many of the poets and artists in
his circles.

in terrible shape. Sullen silent . . . never saw him like that before. Very disturbed (??) And that's a terrible way to try to say it. Disturbed??? Like who isn't? When John left N.Y., he went up to his parents in Boston. His mother apparently flipped and called up the mental hospital people. They came & from what I get from Irving Rosenthal, they carried John off in straight jacket. He's got to stay in that place at least 40 days, cause his mother signed him in. Seems so bleak . . . but Ivg wants to get some kind of writ to get John out under his care. Hope so. Otherwise very bleak.

Big Table 4 sounds, for the most part, like a good idea; tho I differ with P. Carroll[8] in that Gawd knows there's too much good poetry around now to confine it to some SPECIAL issue. Shit, why ain't he (Carroll) just publishing and a publishing. He cd pack that goddam expensive thing with good poems each time it comes out . . . instead of degenerate frenchmen and their even more degenerate melican[9] imitators. HoHum. But I hope he's got something of yrs in this special one too. I know you've got something (?) in #3.

NY still cold & silent. Tho we all "drink to our extinction." Creeley[10] reviewing some Totem books for Evergreen. Which is good, tho Creeley had asked Rago[11] at Poetry . . . but Rago had already sent books out (to some creep, I bet).

Ok, & you take care of yrself, & let me hear when you get enough time.

best, roi jones

3/1/60

Dear LeRoi: Sorry I haven't answered your letter but I have barely managed to drag my ass around thru the snow, and there is a lethargic pall or something like that, overhanging these outlands. It snows daily, the white element disappears and the dark is thus at a low seeking to be white. I was saddened to hear abt J. Wieners. Have you subsequently heard any more about him? Was that man forgot his name, able to do anything for him. I wrote Olson to see if he had gone to see him, or knew anything abt him, but he apparently misunderstood me and wrote news abt M. Rumaker;[12] there are so many of us in the nut house. Now

---

8   Paul Carroll, American poet, 1926–1996. Carroll was at this time editing and publishing *Big Table*.
9   The word *melican*, according to Baraka, "was a send up of WW2 US war films, how they had the Asians speak" (personal correspondence). However, according to Diane di Prima, *melican* is a send-up of Ezra Pound (personal correspondence).
10   Robert Creeley, American poet, 1926–2005. Associated most frequently with Black Mountain College, where he both studied as an undergraduate and then taught as a professor, Creeley was a figure of great importance in mid-twentieth-century radical poetry. Dorn studied with Creeley at Black Mountain College; the two were to become friends out of this experience. Creeley called Dorn "the defining poet of Olson's effect—the one who did hear most particularly. Charles spoke of him as having an 'Elizabethan ear' years ago and marveled at his grace" (qtd. in Clark *Charles Olson* xx).
11   Henry Rago, American poet, 1915–1969. Rago edited *Poetry* magazine from 1955 until his death in 1969.
12   Michael Rumaker, American writer, b. 1932. Rumaker studied at Black Mountain College in the early 1950s, later penning a memoir about the school and its poets, including Robert Creeley and Charles Olson, called *Black Mountain Days*.

the mistakes are evident. / How do you feel? I hope spring, with her lewd flowing tresor is nearer to hand there than she is here. Altho the relief of the seasons is a short lived deceptive thing. It was curious to hear I had a poem in la grande table,[13] I haven't seen it yet and am not at all sure I remember which one it was. I think Creeley must have sent it to Carrol for me. This is meant to keep a letter in mind, which I will write as soon as I am up to it. There is a brilliant English poet, Charles Tomlinson[14] in town but he ignores me. Later, Ed.

Always a staunch supporter of Dorn's writing, Jones sent his work to various venues where there might be an opportunity for publication. This initial "sell" to Joyce Glassman at William Morrow would eventually prove to end in frustration. Such forays into more established publishing houses frequently failed, not only for Dorn and Jones but for so many of the poets around them. These dead ends, though, helped to draw out the poets' sense of urgency and fierce belief in one another, thereby tightening the many poetic communities deemed "outsider" art. Despite the differing writing styles, conflicting theories and beliefs, disagreements and arguments, and friendly and unfriendly feuds within the circles of these "outsider" poets, a resilient sense of affiliation bound them.

Joyce Glassman—now Joyce Johnson—is known for Minor Characters *(1983), the groundbreaking memoir of her life and relationship with Jack Kerouac, as well as her biography of Kerouac,* The Voice Is All: The Lonely Victory of Jack Kerouac *(2012). At the time when Jones approached her on behalf of publishing Dorn, she was an assistant at the commercial publisher William Morrow. Though she appears to have worked as best she could to help Jones, Dorn, and others get published, Glassman was not an editor with final decision-making authority. Nevertheless, she was the recipient of a great deal of unfortunate animosity from Jones, who took these rejections to heart and who may not have been familiar with the acquisitions process at commercial publishers—or did not care. Throughout the correspondence Glassman is the target of some of Jones's more vicious misogynist vitriol.*

Ed,   [Mar ? 1960]

Joyce Glassman thinks that piece of yours in Yugen "is great!!" and wants, if possible, to see the other fictionprose&c pieces, like the ones I'm using in the ant'y. I cdn't show her those because I already handed them in. If you had copies, tho. Might be something, I mean just based on what you got going already. Long shot, but she brought it up so I figure it's worth trying. I mean, like "wow" is what

---

13   *Big Table.*
14   Charles Tomlinson, British poet, b. 1927. Tomlinson studied at Queens College, Cambridge, with poet Donald Davie. Davie would later become an influential figure in Dorn's life, bringing him to England as a Fulbright scholar at the University of Essex.

she sd, and she's supposed to be halfassed hip (having been the girlfriend, for brief periods of, Kerouac, Dawson,[15] Oppenheimer, Rumaker . . . until the last few years she's been hanging out w/ painters (but amazing how much people "on the scene," so to speak, are ignorant of. But anyway send that material to Joyce Glassman c/o Wm. Morrow, Inc. 425 Park Ave. So. NY16, NY. If you cd do this soon, the ball, in whatever direction, cd begin to move.

Otherwise, I'm still way under the weather . . . sore throat for 3 weeks! now & really grumpy and in my trouble making bag these days. Loud and incautious. But some work . . . poems . . . appear from time to time, so all is not completely threw.

I just remember now you said "Woolf at Eastlake's expense" or something? I liked *Bronc People* . . . also a story that was in a few Evergreens ago *3 Heroes And A Clown*. But I did really dig those things of his a great deal. Also, a story I read long time ago called *Little Joe*. I haven't read Woolf's Fade Out, but I have liked the stories I've read (all you western cats hung up on "bureaucracy," the hideousness of? As Woolf in "Cougher," "Bank Day," &c. seems to come back to that. Which, I'm aware, *is* valid. And probably you can see no heavy foot stance in Eastlake?? Wow, how come we always argue about lowly prose writers, anyway. But, O.K., for now, just a note I got to go to school and blow my nose.

Love to everyone, from the 4 drippies

Roi

William Eastlake (1917–1997), whom Jones and Dorn are discussing in these letters, was an American writer whose novels and stories were often westerns. While Jones generally enjoyed Eastlake's work, Dorn roundly disliked it, his novels in particular. Dorn's keen sense of American realities and his knowledge of the West led him to disparage Eastlake's heavy-handed "Indian" talk as romantic and false. The West, and the American Indian, were subjects close to Dorn, ones that would appear in his writing throughout his life. He said, "The American West is the place men of our local civilization travel into in wide arcs to reconstruct the present version, of the Greek experience. Not Greek directly of course. American. But there is where you will find the Stranger so dear to our whole experience" (Views 58).

This criticism of Eastlake's "fucking pseudo-myth of the Indian translated talk" can be seen leading to The Shoshoneans (1966), a poetic-journalistic walk through Shoshoni lands with photographer Leroy Lucas. The Shoshoneans attempts no "translation" of the Indian but rather watches, listens, and records. Writer Douglas Woolf (1922–1992), unlike Eastlake, on the other hand, found an admiring reader in Dorn, who devoted a remarkable essay to Woolf, "The New Frontier," published in Kulchur

---

15   Fielding Dawson, American painter and writer who studied at Black Mountain College, 1930–2002. Fee, as he was often called, traveled in many of the same circles Jones did, and he would contribute artwork to some of Jones's publishing ventures, including for the little magazine *Yugen*.

in 1963. Woolf's first novel, The Hypocritic Days, was published in Palma de Mallorca by Robert Creeley's Divers Press in 1955, and he remains a major but very neglected writer. Dorn's concerns in his essay on Woolf focus on themes that would come up in The Shoshoneans, as he finds Woolf "tapping on a fundamental reality and extracting the truth" from it.

[Undated]

Mr. Jones—it's that Eastlake, in those novels does have a heavy foot down—the fucking pseudo-myth of the Indian translated talk—it's a little "Old Testament" no? Besides I dig his stories too. And besides we're not always arguing abt "lovely" prose writers. We—you & me, talk of lots of other things & besides, I agree w/ everything you say, almost.

Nice stationery, no? We're both sorry you've been so ill. All of you ran into the same "organism" how about that shit? That's what the bastards call it.

Hegel is a nice poem. Is that part of a collection . . . the moving logic of it down to its feeling in the last lines. Um. You're doing well indeed.

Just a note to say I got cosmonoughts—message, poem & letter—that was a nice statement they made. I wonder if our own redoubtable assholenought said anything to the "people." I was interested in the statement you mentioned of sometimes in Nomad. I don't get that mag. I don't see how I can. But I've heard of it. Someday perhaps I will get to see it. Have you been digging what the airforce is trying to do to that air [. . .] they extorted a confession of murder here in IDAHO? That is some wild shit—that colonel should be hung. If you don't know abt say I'll send clips. Love & etc Ed

Near the beginning of Call Me Ishmael, Charles Olson's sharp and unconventional study of Herman Melville and Moby Dick, he writes, "I take SPACE to be the central fact to man born in America, from Folsom cave to now. I spell it large because it comes large here. Large, and without mercy. It is geography at bottom, a hell of wide land from the beginning" (11). As a reader of cultural geographer Carl O. Sauer (1889–1975), Olson saw physical space as integral to who people are and the works they create. Counter to the narrow boundaries then defining the field of geography, Sauer advocated a multifaceted approach, incorporating fields like anthropology and history, and in 1941 said that "human geography and history . . . [are] different approaches to the same problem, the problem of cultural growth and change." This growth and change happens across the wide spaces of nation, the particulars of any one place pushing and shaping those who live or pass through, and those who have been through take their spaces with them as they create and move on, widening the net. The U.S. boundaries of the North American continent run roughly three thousand miles east to west, a significant distance to name as one place. The true effect is that it is both one place and not one place at all, a nation filled with many.

Dorn notes this point as happening from the beginning of Western expansion out of Europe and into the American continent, this differing conception of space and people in The Shoshoneans: *"What the European found here was a collection of cosmologies he thought was a continent" (85). A place so large is bound to be filled with small, out-of-the-way pockets where it is easy to be lost and disconnected, and for anyone without the means or time to travel easily, the loneliness can run deep. While Jones lived in New York City, one of the largest poetic and artistic hubs in the United States, Dorn at this time lived in Santa Fe, New Mexico. He would later move to an even smaller town, Pocatello, Idaho, to teach. The geographical isolation made this correspondence that much more urgent. There is the great need for contact with other poets and artists, the desire to send poems and for poems to be sent fueling a connection across great space. Dorn talks here about the pleasure of having other poets, in this case Robert Creeley, come through his relatively isolated space.*

Dear L.J.:   4/12/60

I never wrote that letter I said I was going to. Time has come to be little cakes for me here, which I eat and then fall out. I have been working practically everyday and I am one of those "typical" people which work, "takes everything out of." Etc. But it is a bore to say, and be, as ever. The goddamn weather is springlike, but tonight hail. That's the way with mountain weather. Have you ever lived in the mountains? It can be wild. Here, as you may know it is 7,000 ft. Right here in Santa F. That's ha.

From what I heard from Creel, and then Judson Crews[16] in Taos, it is pretty well settled that he, C, is going to be in T, for the summer. Then someone gave me the enclosed clipping from the Albuquerque paper, and I send it along for kicks. It will be needless to say very fine to have someone passing thru at last, and I guess he will get here sometime in june.

In your last letter you mentioned John Wieners had been thrown in the bug-house. Have you had anymore news about him, and did the man, whose name I can't remember, help him out, ie, was he able. I would appreciate hearing.

Also I heard from someone in NY, I guess that girl, Maxine Shapiro, that she had read some of my poems in a Yugen. Are they then those you talked about printing from Communications? I wonder if you would mind sending me a copy, if it is true.

How are things treating you there. Fine, I hope. And people too. I am now trying to get a bunch of prose together for a man at Scribblers[17] who solicits I guess. It is always a pain for me because I can't spell, nor damn well type too good. But. If I hit it lucky it might mean some loot being prose. So, there is no real excuse for a tired letter, save the guts to send it. the best to you and yours.

Ed

16   Judson Crews, American poet and publisher, 1917–2010. Crews published several little magazines, including *Poetry Taos* and the *Naked Ear*; in this capacity he would publish both Jones and Dorn as well as fellow poets such as Robert Creeley and Diane di Prima.
17   The publisher Scribner.

[Apr. 29 ? 1960] Fri

Ed,

another note to say . . . i'd like to use that poem THE PRONOUNCEMENT, along with any others you care to send for Y7!

mas bad news re all those fellowships. Creeley got turned down for his Guggenheim . . so did Olson & Allen Ginsberg. I hear tell that Jean Garrigue[18] got one tho. Ah, yes

There are 6 cats standing out on my back fence yowling right now. I wonder if it'll rain. Dinner time.

Best, Roi

The term guggers *refers to the Guggenheim Fellowships, awards given annually to working professionals in a wide variety of fields, including artists. Though poet Charles Olson had been awarded Guggenheim Fellowships on two occasions, one in 1939 and one in 1948, these awards were given for poetry he had written before he became the avant-garde Charles Olson who mentored Dorn and Jones. At that time, Olson was still working in more formal arenas of academia (he attended Wesleyan and Harvard, taught English at Clark University, and studied under prominent American studies scholar F. O. Matthiessen, among other endeavors) and politics (for example, working for the American Civil Liberties Union, the Foreign Language Division of the Office of War Information, and the Democratic National Committee).*

By 1960, Olson had long since abandoned any semblance of the poetic or political mainstream. Instead, he was now fully immersed in his radical form of poetics, writing poetry that was undoubtedly too far outside the mainstream to merit an establishment fellowship like the Guggenheim. Dorn accentuates the conservatism of the Guggenheim selection by juxtaposing Olson's actual rejection against a fictitious Guggenheim being awarded to "mad-hatter" Edward Teller, the physicist noted for the creation of the hydrogen bomb: brilliance on behalf of mass murder was deemed more worthy than brilliance on behalf of art. It should be noted, however, that Dorn as well as Olson evidently had doubts about the possibility of anyone winning three Guggenheim awards in one lifetime.

The 92nd Street Y (part of the wider YMHA organization), a cultural community center in New York City, regularly hosted a series of poetry readings in the early 1960s. These events were curated by various poets to introduce newer and unknown poets. On this occasion, fellow poet Denise Levertov (1923–1997) was chosen as host for one of the Y's reading series; she asked Dorn to read, bringing Dorn to New York for the first time. This occasioned one of the rare instances Jones and Dorn would spend time together in person. Levertov was a British-born American poet, deeply influenced, the longer she was in America, by William Carlos Williams and the Black Mountain

---

18   Jean Garrigue, American poet, 1912–1972. Garrigue, who spent many years as a professor, was awarded a Guggenheim Fellowship in 1960, a prize coveted by Jones, Dorn, and many of their poet friends.

ethos. In the 1960s she served as the poetry editor for the Nation. *An active protester against the Vietnam War, Levertov in 1968 would join the War Resisters League.*

5–9-60

Dear L: If you want Pronouncement, fine. I had sent it months and months ago to a jerk named Gilbert Nieman (Dr.) in Puerto Rico, something like interamerican school for something, probably the Americas, and he said in effect nothing abt. it. There were other things too, but I remember this pronouncement was among the group. Now, if on that basis, because I suppose honestly, remotely, virtuously, horribly, decisively I can't offer it as virgin so to speak, you like want it, then ok, is what I mean.

In the mean time. I will send something else by the end of May which was when you mentioned as a limit I think. It will be sooner as possible. I am quite hung now because of prose I have promised to get out. I am also a very sloppy dispersed worker anyway, and it is always more difficult than it should be.

I also deplore as you must the way guggers went this time. I had been asked by Olson to write for him, which I did. I gave it all I had, which was possibly too much, no vanity intended. But he has had *two* prior. And as he expressed his misgivings before asking again, "I don't know that they ever pass the porridge three times" OK. I imagine if you were mad-hatter edward teller, they might. Or Jean G.

I will, see seventh seal[19] if it comes. And it might. There is an art theatre in Albuquerque, 60 miles ride south.

Swell. The weather here is very nice now. The desert, which doesn't change much, is brighter. We sit outside when we can at a table. I wish you and your wife and kids were here for a beer. Creeley ought to be along any time now. I knew he hadn't either and felt bad, as with Olson about it. Both of them could have used it so handily, Olson, if possible, more. But why make such lousy loot relative.

One other possible very remote happy note. Denise Lev. has been chosen as one of the choices for the Y introductions series, and her first choice, of three, all of which are supposed to stick, is me. So next fall I could get a free ride to the Apple. In which case it would be great meeting you but actually it is *so much* a hope [. . .], it might as well at this point be forgotten. But it could do for me if it did materialize. more later, Ed

In 1960, Jones traveled to Cuba to witness firsthand the impact of the Castro-led revolution on the lives of Cuban people. The trip was sponsored by the Fair Play for Cuba Committee, an organization of pro-Castro Americans intent on challenging the negative news reports on Cuba generated by the U.S. State Department. Jones was

---

19   *The Seventh Seal* (1957), directed by Ingmar Bergman.

*part of a delegation that included the writers Harold Cruse, John Henrik Clarke, and
Sarah Webster. Robert Williams, a figure who had obtained a great deal of notoriety
for his advocacy of armed self-defense against marauding whites in Monroe, North
Carolina, was also part of the delegation. Jones has often said that this journey to
Cuba was the key event that caused him to let go of his previous self-definition as a
politically disengaged bohemian writer. As a result of the trip, Jones began to lose the
insularity toward the world that was often typical of life in the United States during
the 1950s and early 1960s. Instead, he developed a more critical attitude toward the
projection of United States power around the globe.*

*The struggles for self-determination of colonized peoples in Asia, Africa, and the
West Indies began to take on a heightened importance. Jones's growing awareness of
the centrality of the United States in the protection and maintenance of European
colonial empires would generate a smoldering anger in him that would not become
full blown until years later. Jones was initially attracted to the youthfulness and image
of vitality of John Kennedy, only to become disillusioned by Kennedy's actions in the
throwing of U.S. military weight around in pursuit of, supposedly, peace. Kennedy's
America was, of course, deeply entrenched in the larger world. But American culture
made it very easy and desirable to remain within the comfort of the close by and the
well known until major events and catastrophes—or near catastrophes, as in the
case of the Cuban Missile Crisis—forced the issue. Jones's reaction, his turn toward
politicization and action, was not atypical. Even a glimpse of the outside—and this
was a period rife with revolutions, declared independences, wars, and civil unrest
from so many formerly or about to be formerly colonized nations—inspired everything from rage and disbelief to hope and idealism in countless Americans.*

*In the year following this letter, 1961, President Kennedy would establish the Peace
Corps, problematic in its typical America-as-savior ideology but a hugely popular
program for young people to step foot into the world. This spark of hope that true
change could be effected, that governments could be erected that would be faithful to
their people, drove much of Jones's thinking in this period (and would continue to do
so even much later), despite his more cynical and angry sensibility regarding institutional systems of all kinds. Dorn and Jones would argue over these ideas, sometimes
quite harshly, over the next few years. Dorn, ever the hard realist, balked at the belief
that the institutions of government, state, and country could be looked to for anything resembling hope. Dorn's thinking in the matter ran more to "fuck 'em all," and
he would say as much to Jones whenever he felt Jones was being unrealistic.*

Dear Ed,   IX:17:60

Sorry for agitated silence, &c. but I've just recently come back from Cuba. And
it takes time to redispose one's self to what it was had got me here in the first
place. Get the responses back in order. Especially after that virtual head opening I

got from that quick look. Sehr erstaunlich,[20] i.e. beautiful is what I got. But that's more than a letter's worth. But the family and I go back to Habana in October for a few weeks, or if I go alone, probably with Allen G. and Joel Oppenheimer, we're going to try to get over to Guatemala to see Creeley after Habana . . . then up through Mexico. So maybe we'll get into N.M. It's a wild thought right now, I mean, everything'll have to break perfectly, &c. Money . . . passports to Guat. C.A. all that. But with some luck it ought to work.

Saw "Pronouncement" in the Nieman mag you mentioned. A strange shot, the whole parcel. A sort of complete *review*, or revue, as it looked to me. Still there were quite a few readable things. Sorry, tho, abt the poem. But still wish I had some things of yrs. Still there is some time. The trip bombed all kinds of schedules I had. Now, trying to get some things together, especially my org. idea for the issue. What it was aiming to be. So far, the best things are articles, essays, pronouncements. Poems by few people. I thot I needed this knd of thing, here, at sort of a juncture. junction. To clear the air. No more *collections*. Certainly that big Grove ant'y put an end to any need for collections. We now, or at least from windy vantage pt. of editor type, need to see where we are/ have gotten, &c. So. The essays, and the rest. I wanted several, at least, of yr poems for that reason. Just one or so is more collecting. Too random now. The scene is certainly outlined . . . time to fill it in. And then, you don't have a book. A larger raison. So I wd think that what wd do you most justice is some larger selection of yr works. Whatever is "at hand." Let me know, or if it is not sensible, I mean from where you work. Let me know about that too.

Di Prima's Elephant[21] promises to be a very good mean. It shd have been around long ago. They have much good material, & if she can keep it swift, that certainly is what's lacking . . . certainly in lieu of any large graciousness on the scene. Meaning that Evergreen is not even interesting anymore, and I'm afraid Paul Carroll[22] will never get himself together. Something like my own shot is in another category, of course. That necessary starkness can oppress, especially its editors. Di Prima at least will be an honest, hopefully constant, newspaper-letter to keep everybody on. But we, I mean the bunch of yng poets loose now, still need some fat girl to soak up everything & everybody w/ some promise of loot. Where?? Anyway, there's a lot for me to do now, even to stay around healthily.

Man here, raising the rent to horrifying level. I lost my job. All kinds of grim things like that. Tho NY is certainly beautiful now. Cool September. It's easier to get on with people in a temperate country. You can exchange pleasantries with

---

20   "Very shocking."

21   Jones is referring to the *Floating Bear*, which would have its first issue in 1961. *Elephant* refers to an earlier magazine idea called the *Elephant at the Door* that di Prima and poet A. B. Spellman had planned to create but ultimately did not. According to di Prima, Spellman did not want to reject anyone's manuscript and therefore did not want to be an editor (di Prima *Floating Bear* vii). The *Elephant* turned into the *Bear* with Jones on board as editor along with di Prima.

22   I.e., with *Big Table*.

the best of them. Have Max and Cissy[23] settled yet. Conflicting reports here, tho I heard from Joel today that they are nearly installed sans furniture. Will you send me their address, or ask Max to write & let me know abt him. Tell him also that we finally got a piano & Hettie & I are grimly at work to re-establish ourselves as the Iturbis[24] of Chelsea. Kellie, our little girl, is more avant-garde.

Anyway, take care of things there and let me know what's going on in that place.

My best to you

Le Roi

A very fine poem of yrs in E.R.[25] Also, did you finally look at Marc's Kulchur??[26] Can you help him out. He sorely needs it.

William Carlos Williams (1883–1963) was a major formative early influence on the development of many of the radical circles of poets of the mid-twentieth century, including those frequented by Dorn and Jones. A physician and poet from Rutherford, New Jersey, Williams was committed to creating and uncovering a distinctive tradition of American poetry. Interested in the American vernacular, Williams brought real, everyday American language into poems, a direct rebuttal to the academic verse of poets like T. S. Eliot or Ezra Pound (with whom he had a lifetime friend/foe relationship). Like Eliot and Pound, Williams had traveled extensively in Europe, but unlike many American artists, Williams returned to the United States both literally and figuratively. He would come back from his travels to Rutherford and Paterson, New Jersey, the towns in which he had grown up, to practice medicine and write poetry.

In his Autobiography, *Baraka would say about Williams that he "wanted American speech, a mixed foot, a variable measure. He knew American life had outdistanced the English rhythms and their formal meters . . . [He saw] the universal in the agonizingly local" (233). Williams worried about "the proper (and deadening) guidelines of the academy for correctness against the exact contours of the idiom as it existed on the tongues of 'a hundred million Americans'" (qtd. in Mariani 717).*

Williams was a great fan of the younger generation of poets, responding with enthusiasm to the New American Poetry. He showed his support in various ways,

---

23   Jones was asking about two separate couples here: Max Finstein and his wife Rena and Joel Oppenheimer and his ex-wife, Cissie. (Cissie had just moved to New Mexico with her and Joel's children following their divorce.)

24   José Iturbi, Spanish pianist, harpsichordist, and conductor, 1895–1980. Iturbi and his family were established musicians, and Iturbi himself would be active until his early eighties. Though in part joking about being famous musicians with the recent purchase of the piano, Jones does here appear to be hoping for a level of artistic recognition and stability that was not yet his.

25   The *Evergreen Review*.

26   *Kulchur*, a little magazine edited by Marc Schleifer. *Kulchur* would be an important small magazine, one with which Dorn was to become regularly involved. Schleifer is today known by S. Abdallah Schleifer, having converted to Islam. He is an expert on the Middle East and is professor emeritus and senior fellow at the American University in Cairo.

even going so far as to include sections of Charles Olson's Projective Verse *in his own* Autobiography *and several poems of Allen Ginsberg's in* Paterson. *Williams's visit to Reed College in 1950 was a great morale booster to three poetry students enrolled there: Gary Snyder, Lew Welch, and Philip Whalen.*

Elsa Dorfman (b. 1937) is a photographer who took portraits of poets, writers, and musicians such as Allen Ginsberg and Bob Dylan in the early 1960s. She also attempted to help publish these same writers through her one-woman-run Paterson Society, named in honor of William Carlos Williams. Reflecting on those days, Dorfman said, "The Paterson Society was ME. I arranged poetry readings in 1959 and 1960 and into say '64 for a variety of writers. And I took a percentage of the money and published some books, namely The Newly Fallen *by Ed Dorn and* Dutiful Son *by Joel Oppenheimer. Actually I gave the money to Leroy, Amiri, and he published them. Those were the days when there were no poetry readings to speak of . . . and I set up tours, etc. I started because I was a secretary at Grove Press and did it to ostensibly have fun and publicize the writers in* Evergreen Review" *(personal correspondence). The money from the Paterson Society enabled Jones to publish Dorn's first book, setting off a flurry of quick letters to work out the details of a hurried deadline.*

Ed,   IX:29 [1960]

Sorry for general sloth, &c. but things have sort of gotten out of hand what with new house, moving, making a living, hunting loot for new Y,[27] makes for gen'ral confusion.

This has to be quick because you needing book now rather than single shots, &c. Well, only reason I lagged on jumping at it was lack of lucre, &c. Now, Elsa Dorfman's "Paterson Society" has agreed to put up bread for about a 40 some odd page book . . . which we're supposed to have OUT by the time you reach disyear town. 20 FEB. (I know, whew! Many expletives!

But I say I'm game to jam it together & work furious w/ printers &c. If you are & you can get some kind of MSS to me (the long thing you spoke of . . . or single short shots . . . whatever you think). I'd say the earlier stuff needed airing more urgent . . . but again that may be too big a shot or not Big enough (ie, format, cheaper than . . .).

Book will be abt size of Whalen & Snyder[28] . . . same general format.

BUT . . . mss will have to be in my hands by 17 DECEMBER or I can't see how in hell it'll make it.

---

27 *Yugen.*
28 Philip Whalen, American poet, 1923–2002; Gary Snyder, American poet, b. 1930. Both Whalen and Snyder were West Coast poets, influential in both the San Francisco Renaissance and Beat poetic milieus and for whom Buddhism was a central tenet of their lives and poetry. Both would spend time in Japan studying Zen Buddhism, and for Snyder, environmental activism would become a key part of his life.

I know it's fast &c. But Ellie just let me hear today, this morning, & I'm quick to get it off to you so I don't pull no leadfoot act on this end. I figured only light was that you had the mss together (I mean largely &c.) already & were just waiting for someplace to hang it.

Well, I don't have to tell you that I've gotta hear quick (queek). SO?

Fast, LeRoi

NEW ADDRESS: 324 E. 14th St., New York 3, N.Y.

Camino Sin Nombre
Santa Fe
12–1-60

Dear L:

Great! Looks like it will be no strain at all for us to get the MS there by the 17th or before possibly. But the chore of selecting from my own work will be a headache, but I will do my best. I just got your letter, so, thinking quickly abt. it right now, I could say I can have it to you by the 10th.

It will be earlier works as you say. None of the things that were in Don Allen's antho—but some scattered pieces here and there in mags. Ok? I take it 40 pages is no hard and fast rule but that 35 or 42 etc will do just as well?

I must say I am very happy Pat. Soc. and Ellie Dorfman are willing to back it. It never occurred to me they would consider me, or did that sort of thing. And very good of you, LeRoi, to rush thru on it! I damn well appreciate that and want you to know it.

Okay. This is just to quickly let you know I will be there with ok ms. Looking forward still to seeing you in Feb. Read your piece in Ev. Rev. Cuba.[29] You were gold and that's good. I would like to hear more abt it in from you when I see you in NY. Ok. Scribner's did you know, took all of Creeley's poems. A fat volume. Oh, I don't know abt that, but a substantial book none the less.

Days here are now cold as a witch's tit. Max and Rena moved to Taos while the Sorrentinos were here. The Sorrentinos are still in Taos before splitting on to San Fran.

I hope you are, or are getting, straight and settled down, regards from here,

Ed

The age of the atom bomb and the threat of nuclear war began, here, finding its way into the Jones-Dorn correspondence. In 1953, President Eisenhower delivered a speech called "Atoms for Peace," launching a campaign to advocate the bomb as an American savior—the bomb would bring peace and comfort, not just terror in the form of mass

---

29   "Cuba Libre," Jones's article about his defining trip to Cuba and meeting with Castro, originally published in *Evergreen Review*.

murder. In 1960, France launched its first nuclear test in the Sahara Desert; the United States submarine USS George Washington *launched a Polaris missile underwater; the* George Washington *began the first patrol of its sixteen Polaris A1s; and the Atlas and Titan missiles were deployed. Atomic testing was commonly known to affect the weather, and the weather frequently worked against the predictions of meteorologists, causing fallout in "unexpected" places. Testing was always promoted as safer than it ever truly was; Jones's comment about the weather speaks to this. In the midst of nuclear threat, Dorn and Jones's poetry would grow and push against the limits of what Jones called "academic poetry death." As jazz musician Max Roach pointed out, "We kept reading about rockets and jets and radar, and you can't play 4/4 music in times like that" (McNally 82).*

Dear Ed,   5 Dec [1960]

O.K., fine . . . let's go. Words from P.S.[30] today & prices I quoted them seem right. Now it's up to you. As soon as you get things hyar I can turn on full speed publisher wheels, &c. Whew!

As you sd . . . from 35 to 42, fine. Shd be lovely. You have any ideas as to what knd of cover you want, &c. I've ideas abt drawing on cover, or can be typographic you say!

Fine news abt Bob[31] . . . you know he damn well deserves it (as even that hundred from POEMS: Chi cd help . . . fatheads, &c.). Anyway so if you can be here as far as mss by few days I can get away I think with plenty to spare. Abombs screwed up weather I think. Warm yestiddy. Thule today. So. You send that stuff I'll write you more as soon as . . .

best, roi

Dec 7, 1941[32]

Dear LR: Whatever you say on cover. I don't think it is worth the gab, 2000 miles of it. I *certainly* have no ideas about it, and as long as you do, and are doing it that's it. You will have gotten like they say the ms. It was a rush because altho it was more or less together, the whole thing had to be retyped, and neither me or mi esp.[33] are great whizzes at accuracy. But I think most of the words are spelled right. Well, would you if you find "time" write and say when you think it will be done, I am kind

---

30   The Paterson Society.

31   Robert Creeley is often referred to as Bob.

32   Dorn is alluding to the attack on Pearl Harbor on December 7, 1941; the year of this letter is 1960.

33   Dorn's wife at the time (his *esposa*), Helene. Helene Dorn and Hettie Jones maintained a strong friendship of their own, writing frequent letters for the next forty years, long after their marriages to, respectively, Ed and LeRoi had ended.

of excited about it now, although, on first proposal it seemed a drag. I had begun to think I would make it all the way sans book.

Edward

Ed,   [stamped 12/30/60]

Things moving smoothly. Cheque from Pat. Soc. Today. Printer sez we shd have the whole thing ready by 20 January. O.K.? Fielding Dawson a dwg for the cover, &c. Happy New Year

LeRoi

II

1961

In 1961, Jones and Diane di Prima published the initial issue of their coedited po-etry newspaper, the Floating Bear. *During the same year, di Prima, in partnership with other poets and artists, founded the New York Poets Theatre in the East Village. The* Floating Bear *and the New York Poets Theatre became central spaces for experi-mental and radical art, free spaces for poets to write plays, writers to act or draw. Part of the experience of this moment was the ability to play with boundaries, cross the lines in the sand: poets published themselves, produced plays, drew, and prac-ticed art in all manner of media. Di Prima says of the time, "It was through the the-atre and music that we caught a glimpse of the power of what we were doing. That it existed beyond the studio, the typewriter, the apartment. Cast a new light on these streets. That it—even briefly—changed the world" (Recollections 147). There is the sense, in this particular period of tremendous world upheaval, that art was integral to living any kind of real life—it was both communication and key to some attempt at understanding. The artistic happenings in American art were happening in spots across the country; poetic and theatrical spaces and bars and clubs for jazz sprouted everywhere as artists grabbed for themselves places in the landscape of new space and forgotten traditions—anything went.*

At the same time, by 1961 the term Beat *was well in use and already being written about as a sometimes repulsive, sometimes admired cultural phenomenon. Rigney and Smith's* The Real Bohemia: A Sociological and Psychological Study of the Beats *both "studied" this wildly diverse group of writers in some real attempt at under-standing it and supported the movement, advertising the fact that it quoted poetry "in extenso." In the midst of the thriving avant-garde scenes around the country, where the artists and writers were often living in poverty if also experiencing creative freedom, the popular commercialization of the Beats was in full force. In 1959 in New York City, it had gone as far as the kitschy and exploitative "Rent-a-Beatnik" service, started by* Village Voice *photographer Fred McDarrah and complete with ads in the* Voice. *This catapult into the mainstream sent the press, young hipster wannabes, and gawkers into the streets of San Francisco, where the poets felt they were being invaded. Poet David Meltzer notes in* San Francisco Beat: Talking with the Poets *that when artistic movements are commodified, they are removed "from historical complexity, [made] safe, [turned] into products and artifacts. The more removed from history's discomfort, the easier it is to imagine and consume history without taking on its weight" (vi).*

Dorn and Jones witnessed the craze and remained outside of it; their letters bear witness to culture and history as they proceeded to develop as both writers and friends.

" "   " "

Though the two men had begun writing in 1959, more than a full year would pass before they met in person. With Dorn and Jones both continually struggling to simply pay rent and buy food, sufficient funds to pay for travel were nonexistent. In early 1961, Dorn was at last able to travel to New York City for a reading at the 92nd Street Y, arranged and organized by fellow poet Denise Levertov. The partial funding from the Y allowed Dorn and his wife Helene to take this rare long-distance trip, though it would still prove to be a financial struggle. This would be the first of only a handful of times Dorn and Jones would have an opportunity to spend any time together in person. Struggling poets with families, traveling would be a luxury for a long time to come still. As Dorn points out in the following letter to Jones's question here regarding a possible visit to Charles Olson, "Loot will be deciding factor dismally enough."

[stamped 2/5/61]

17 inches of snow piled up here!

Ed,

Things still seem to be going well . . . for a change. Anyway, I shd have the finished book by Thurs!

When are you due out here? Where are you staying, &c.?? If nothing else free presents itself we've lots of room, &c. No privacy . . . but space up the yingyang.

Shd I send some copies special delivery . . . or wait till you show up??

How long is the stay?? Think you'll have time to get up to Gloucester to see Charles??[34] O.K., I'll get off . . . Any word from Max?

Best, Roi

---

34   Olson, who spent his life in Gloucester, Massachusetts.

2–8-61

Dear LeR: That sounds fine. Look we don't leave here till 16th Feb. (thurs) if you wld airmail (special delivery don't mean nothing here they bring it in regular mail) 1 copy for me to dig I wld enjoy that. Only if it looks like it will get here by Wed. 15th tho. We will be there in NY abt 2 wks. I want like hell to get up to see chas.[35] Tho loot will be deciding factor dismally enough. The Pat. Soc. is not doing as well as expectations so looks like naught forthcoming there. Y is paying $175 which turns out to be niggardly considering the distance. Max: He was here last night, down from Taos some minor riff w/ Rena. Drunk as a bedbug. He had a mouth-full of bad words for you—like he's starving (he always is, as Creeley says—it's his one goddamn point) and you wldn't send any of his books for sales in Taos. Ok. That's what he sd. Looking very much forward to meeting you. Thanks for offer of space. Thus far we had planned to stay w/ friends. Newtons, down on Greenwich St. I guess we will. Do you have a phone. I'll see. Later—Ed.

*My wife says special does make it so Thurs latest

The Partisan Review *at this time was a mainstay of the New York literary establishment, growing large and like a "lottery," as Robert Creeley put it. It could be, though, still a place for "outsider" poets to publish, so, up to a point, a possibility for exposure and entry into the American poetry scene.* Partisan Review *tended to represent a very particular sort of normalized, academic poetry, well on its way to mainstream popularity. Jones's wife, Hettie, took a job as subscription manager at the* Review *during a particularly hard financial year for the Joneses. This was an ever-present decision to be made, how to live in the most fundamental sense: Who pays the bills? What levels of compromise would need to be made in order to both write and pay rent?*

Some perspective: while the rogue poets were coming to consider the Review *as too middle ground, the U.S. authorities in the form of the military held an entirely different view. During his third year in the U.S. Air Force, Jones was called up falsely on charges of being a Communist, and "among the artifacts the Air Force was amassing as to my offense were copies of the* Partisan Review*!" (Autobiography 176). But there is a tangle of ideology here: the* Review *was financed and partially run by (through Philip Rahv, the editor for a time) the Congress of Cultural Freedom, a CIA covert operation. The Congress was meant to infiltrate the Left, by gathering and convincing artists and writers on the Left that Communism, which in the earliest years of the twentieth century still very much seen as a viable and nonthreatening system, actually was the monstrous body the American mainstream was being pushed into believing it to be. But because the CIA origins of the Congress were not made public until 1967, when Jones was found with copies of the* Review *in his bunk, the Congress of Cultural Freedom was cited as a reason for his supposed Communism, since it was outwardly still known as a "Lefty" organization.*

---

35   Charles Olson.

Ed,   24 Mar. [1961]

Just read your "Notes" and ate most of it up. Think parts of it are marvelous, e.g., "Old Man" . . . "Waiting." Of course they are *random*, or at least their emphasis is dispersed almost as fast as you are aware that there is . . . but as *notes*, or as I see it more substantial, almost going towards "dialogues," and of course the *stories*. But good for all this babble.

Haven't read the thing you sent for Partisan. Hope you some luck there. Creeley calld it, Partisan, "that lottery," which is where it literally is. Funny, I just came from that place stealing books to sell & buy likker . . . which I believe is the final separation of the species. I steal, I doubt if Wm Phillips, &c. wd . . . tho that don't make me nothing . . . but a crook, however I still think that, crookdom, holds more positive action, than those dry old pubes. Like this guy Kazin at some party asked me what I meant by the word "Academic". . . and I was stumped because I didn't want to sound like one . . . so I sd that word was just a word I'd thot up as a euphemism for weakling. I don't think he was properly impressed.

Anyway, Santa Fe sounds cold. And this place is full of 2inch slush from last night, but now it's warm & the sun's melted almost all the ice . . . so we're at least happier.

Your idea to do a thing on Cain's Book[36] sounds good to me. And what I really wanted from someone. I'd asked Rumaker but he sd he cdn't read the book . . . so I wish you would. Of course magazine still shaky, in doubt. But I think something might happen. Anyway, wd be gassd if you'd do that. I guess you just about know my feelings, &c . . . whatever that means . . . but some other clear insight, no matter, is always good.

Do you need any more copies of that F'ing Bare[37] w/ yr long poem in it? If you do . . . let us know. Just got some insane thing from Olson . . . beautiful mashed thots . . . re/ the whole structure of the language. For the bear, too. He called it. "On Grammar . . . a book." It's really something. And, by the way if you have any bare material . . . i.e., poems, discussions, lies, &c. we're hoping you send them. I was even hoping you'd write some kind of travel guide re/ your New York trip. Like for other non-manhattanites to see. Really, some kind of depreciation of yr voyage, I think, wd be pretty wild. Anyway why not try it on, for the bear . . . as I think that's real bear material.

Here, as always, the rush continues. Everybody's got somewhere to go. I met

---

36   *Cain's Book*, by Scottish novelist Alexander Trocchi (1925–1984). The novel describes the coming of age of a heroin addict living and working on a barge on New York's Hudson River. Trocchi published a great deal of his work with Olympia Press in Paris; Olympia was known for its avant-garde and erotic works. Trocchi lived in Southern California in the late 1950s and became involved in the Beat scene there. Jones and Dorn would argue about Trocchi's work extensively in their letters.

37   The *Floating Bear*.

Russell Edson[38] at the bar a few nights ago . . . and I don't think he's half as nice as you say. Perhaps it was me?? Anyway, he told me your name was Edward and not Ed, as I so un-chicly kept mumbling. I think he might be a homosexual.

O.K., Hettie is calling dinner & I've got to eat or I'll be sick.

Hope you feel better and all that snow melts. Write when you can . . . & I'll keep you posted, &c., on anything.

Love to everyone there . . . and take care . . .

Roi

After Dorn's visit to New York City, he penned a short essay about his experience. Jones requested this piece and ultimately published it in the Floating Bear *Issue No. 8. "New York, New York (It's a wonderful place to live but a poor place to visit)" shows all of Dorn's sharp-edged wit and humor, full of pointed observations that flirt with absurdity ("I think a lot of people must live there because they can get good egg-creams"). He is also serious and aware, taking note of how space works: "What I really liked was seeing people unexpectedly on the street I knew and love. It doesn't often happen that way out here, and not altogether principally because I don't love too many people here but more because there aren't enough people here. It's hard to get them to come. And why not? There's really nothing here except a lot of famous space and a little of that goes a long ha way. Whoopee" (Views 48).*

Ed,   11 Apr 5am [1961]

Sitting here listening to beautiful John Coltrane *My Favorite Things* album . . . which you've got to get . . . no matter who has to be bumped off, &c.

Anyway . . . yr notes I want to print in toto or todos, anyway. Whatever so called reservations I have about specific parts of the piece are not as strong as the general impression the thing made on me.

Re/ the thing on Cain . . . I didn't know editors were supposed to agree with everything. Fuckem I say. Just so it's in English. I don't know if my alleged readers are bi-lingual or what . . .

How was ol John Chamberlain[39] when you saw him? Drunk? Funny? Comfortably obscure? Loud? Anyway, rumors here have him all over the damn country. Is he supposed to bring Creeley back East with him? That ought to be

38   Russell Edson, American writer and illustrator, b. 1935. Edson would, in 1974, win a Guggenheim Fellowship as well as several National Endowment for the Arts creative writing fellowships. Though Jones does not expand on why he might not have thought too highly of Edson, it is possible that neither their poetics nor politics quite matched up.
39   John Chamberlain, American sculptor, 1927–2011. Chamberlain studied at Black Mountain College with Olson, Creeley, and Robert Duncan. At the time of this letter he was living in New York and frequenting many of the same haunts as those in Jones's circles.

an insane unternehmung[40] . . . a footnote to On The Road?? Here, lots of people who knew (?) Bob are shuddering visibly at the notion of his return to the apple. They say he will make it dirty, and will not be kind to everyone. Is this true?

We went to another party for you at Basil King's[41] house. This one two days after you'd split. Ah, well . . . you'll make one one day I spose. I'm sposed to go to San Francisco and environs around October for readings, &c., by the same Paterson Soc. Maybe I cd come thru N.M. . . . if I did I'd bring my heat (revolver) with me. I'm deathly afraid of cowboys, &c. And I'm sure they'd be afraid of me.

Wd appreciate the NYC note for Bear. And any kind of short note, spell, or whatever you'd want to send. Creeley sent us a short review of your book for sd animal.

Anyway, before I fall asleep, you take care & give love to Helene and the children . . . We're fine here but still cold.

Easy, Roi

Dear LRJ: 4–13–61

I shouldn't of said that about the Cain thing . . . just thot you wouldn't want to waste print on certain viewpoints you dint etc . . . by the way I will send it off to you about this weekend.

I guess they cld *stand* printing all together, but I, as you, but probably differently, have doubts about parts, I cld never resolve it and yet it always seemed a legitimate thing for me to try to say, but later, perhaps I will have that kind of thing better. I think, in this novel, part of w/ I sent to H., has it better, much. I am frankly much more "ambitious" for the CT (cain thing) and I was thinking maybe the notes are a Bear item but maybe it's all too long, No? I mean it seems extraordinary that I wld take up so much space in Yugen in so short a time, unless you were goin to put off the notes for several issues, because I don't see that waiting on the CT would help much, it, in the sense that the book, and now this other Young Adam are so current, it wld seem a loss to put *that* off. No? But again, I'm not trying to tell you how to run yr life. I will get Coltrane as soon as poss. I always wanted to anyway. Never heard of that one. Brought back from sd apple two delicious Rollins, the one with Limehouse Blues and Doxie on it w/ Teddy Edwards on back, you know. The other with Rollins and E. Coleman.[42] Wow.

---

40   Undertaking, venture.
41   Basil King, British-born painter living in Brooklyn since 1968, b. 1935. King and Jones became fast friends and remain friends to this day. They would spend a great deal of time together in various New York City bars and taverns, including McSorley's Ale House and the Cedar Tavern, talking and, sometimes, fighting as a team against other bar patrons.
42   Sonny Rollins, American jazz saxophonist, b. 1930; Teddy Edwards, American jazz saxophonist, 1924–2003; Earl Coleman, American jazz singer, 1925–1995.

We live in two different worlds. And my ideal. Jesus. B quick, B lovely, B with it. Actually Rollins was the first man in space.

You bring the heat but you won't need it.

If you drop by I will find some way to protect and entertain you. Cld take you up to Taos to see J. Crews which would amuse you a lot I *am* sure. Also, other things. There's Wytter Bynner[43] and WT Scoot.[44] Both hustlers. There's always the only poet in US on govt dole, MF,[45] in Taos.

RE Creeley: Helene makes the offer that anyone scared in NY can take refuge here w/ us in NM. My understanding is, based on letters lately from the ogre himself, is that he and Bobbie[46] are to go from here to Chi where Bob will read, thence to Tuffts or what the hell, somewhere—Vermont maybe, but anyway, thence to apple. They plan to leave the four girls w/ her mother in Albuquerque so that it should be a very nice get-away for them both. LRJ, I am more than confident you will find RC the most deeply sympathetic man you have known, both to yourself and your family and also on general consideration. What can one say more than that. I find him the most consistently engaging man I know, with less exception than you wld believe, and now, knowing you, in the brief but fondly remembered way that I do, I can't think you will feel otherwise about him.

How the myth of Creeley's unmanageability arose I am not too sure. Must been Black Mountain time (ha) but that's getting close to 10 years ago now. I am sure there are lots of people in NY who 'know' him, god yes, they know him, Christ, yes. Actually quien sabe whether they do or not. I know him. I fucking well assure you. We have been in fights in the biggest cities in the US. Very clean and drunk and physical and no bullshit. Not lately tho, and it isn't probably we'll make that scene again, it seems certain I have made my terms with him, and he his with me. Of unkindness he has none at all. Cruelty perhaps a little, like the rest, but you know as well as anyone else there are certain people who require that as a term of any ultimate relationship. He is very different now, I wld say in the last three years, very different. Send me the names of those who shake visibly and I will write them all cards saying "HE'S GONNA GETCHA!!"

Before leaving this theme exhausted let me add that all people do not deserve kindness. Simply because they don't believe it themselves. But, the shorter answer—No, it's not true.

---

43 Witter Bynner, American poet, 1881–1968. Bynner was known to be something of a jokester, having helped to orchestrate a literary hoax by creating a new literary "movement," the supposed Spectrists.

44 Winfield Townley Scott, American poet and writer, 1901–1967. Scott was a local writer (famous for publishing his journals) who had been recorded by Robert Creeley at one point: "Equipped with the station's recorder and tapes, he would engage individual poets in informal conversation and have them read whatever seemed pertinent. Local poet veterans Winfield T. Scott and Witter Bynner were the first targets" (Faas *Creeley* 275).

45 Max Finstein.

46 Creeley's second wife, Bobbie Louise Hawkins, a writer, poet, and painter.

The real point is of course that you come on out here in Oct and maybe we'll kick the shit out of a few cowboys.

OK, as I sd this weekend I will get off to you the CT and also the NY note. Tell H. I dug the note on back of letter (which I also dug she metered on PR meter for which I salute) and hope and pray they want to buy it. Jesse James couldn't want that loot more.

difficult, Ed

Jazz is a frequent point of conversation for Jones and Dorn in these letters. One of Jones's earliest jobs in New York City was as clerk for a jazz magazine called the Record Changer. *The subject of jazz and blues—American classical music—is one in which Jones became fully immersed as he investigated American culture and history as part of his poetics. Friends with many of the avant-garde jazz musicians in New York City, he had direct access to the radical and quickly evolving music scene of the mid-twentieth century. The experience of this music was akin to, and part of, Jones's experiments in poetry. Much of his writing life in the '60s directly dealt with jazz, with numerous reviews in many publications of musicians such as Sonny Rollins, the Cannonball Adderley Quintet, Brownie McGhee and Snooks Eaglin, Jackie McLean, John Coltrane, Cecil Taylor, Muddy Waters, and Dizzy Gillespie.* Blues People: Negro Music in White America, *published by William Morrow in 1963, would be Jones's first full-length book of prose, a study of African American musical traditions from slavery through the early 1960s.*

From his isolated space of Pocatello, Dorn was able to buy jazz records, though he often received records from Jones in New York or brought them back on the rare occasions when he himself visited New York, as he notes here about his recent purchase of Sonny Rollins records. Jazz moved through the country, radiating along various spokes to anyone willing to listen.

5–4-61

Roi: Haven't heard from you for long time. Hope you're not bugged. I sent a dollar w/ this letter for: Hoping you will send a *Newly Fucking* to Kate Thwing, 2222 East 3rd st. Duluth, Minn. She sent me a dollar for a copy but I spent it and didn't have a copy to send. You aren't bugged are you? Jesus, I hope not. I was thinking you'd send a free copy, for me. The rest of the dollar, save postage for that I wld like you to use to send Big Floating Bear to Tom Raworth,[47] a London teahead who makes it. 167 Amhurst Road, Hackney, London, E. 8, Merry old.

---

47   Tom Raworth, British poet and artist, b. 1938. Raworth was early on influenced by Black Mountain poetics. Raworth founded a small magazine, *Outburst*, where he would publish the work of both Jones and Dorn, among others. He also helped found Matrix Press, where he would publish some of Dorn's work as well.

Now, as for you, you mother, I went out immediately and bought *My Favorite Things*, and it is my favorite thing. You are right again. But I like Ornette too. This is out (I mean our) music. I even like the hip pocket trumpet, altho Max, snarlingly, puts it somewhere down.

I called Creeley on the fone last night and found they were there in Alb, just arrived half hour before I called. I guess they will be up Friday, tomorrow, night. He, he said, jettisoned whole kilo of weed in Guat, for lack of room and time to pack it. So, one can't look forward to Everything. I never did anyway. The enclosed also explains orders for newly emerged from SF., ie, like a back-assed moth. My delirium was caused by just taking mushroom tablets pre-picture.[48]

First, Last, And only Haiku

FUCK YOU

    submitted to Floating B.
    by Lin Yu Tang.

There are better reactions I guess but I can make it. Look, why don't you write me, a card of anything. Why not.

5–8-61 Actually, Creel did come up but it was less than satisfactory, why I can't say, I am sorry I wrote such a heated letter in his regard, because it makes a sham of various of the possible ways one may feel. I have a feeling by the way you *did not* dig my [. . .] piece, since you didn't reply.—Ok. Heard from Gil S[49] abt party for "Kultur"—too goddamn much!

All the ideas about new art and new possibilities in artistic expression gave rise to much thought about the complicated and interconnected phenomena of imitation and influence. All new permutations of art necessarily give rise to both specific examples and usages of the form, as well as to even further permutations of the forms themselves. The sticky point is the boundary: What is imitation and what is influence? Can clear lines be drawn? Jones touches on both points in this letter with two different artists, to two different ends. Max Finstein, contemporary poet of Jones and Dorn, is credited with "a few lovely poems" but with too many imitators: "cats that walk, talk, smoke pot, think, & probably fuck like Max." On the other hand, jazz musician Ornette Coleman's free use of the influence of bebop is touted: "Bop & blues I think are the only two complete *musics to come out of Shade music! Completely autonomous!"*

---

48   There was likely a photo enclosed with the original letter.
49   Gilbert Sorrentino.

Dear Ed,   5/10 [1961]

Sorry for the silence. Of course I'm not bugged. Why? One reason I haven't written is that I've been tramping around yr old homeland, Ill. for the dear old Paterson society. Readings at Eureka College (in Eureka, Ill. Quincey College . . . Chi. div of U. of Ill., &c. But I suppose main reason for no letters . . . and no *writing* at all is sorry state of my personal life. Everything seeming to fuck up here . . . altho it's a weird paradox when you think on it . . . since I just got a Whitney Fellowship last week for $2500. But, shit . . . I guess what all those guys've been saying the years about money not being everything . . . &c. must be true. My ass is really dragging. Anyway . . . I haven't told anybody here yet (cept Gil) but Hettie & I are splitting. And I'm really sort of lost. Can't do anything but drag ass & get drunk. (No drugs around house . . . I've been clean for last month since coppers dropped by for abstruse reasons . . . Twice!) My "art," like they say, is suffering . . . in that it's been almost nonexistent. I'd thot that even in this shitty scene . . . Newyork incest friend bullshit . . . that our scene was safe. Above all the other bullshit somehow. But no . . . here it seems even the sweetest and most naïve go down. And me, not so sweet . . . tho I suppose naïve as any of the other hippies around here . . . I go down too . . . harder and ruder than most. Shit, I hate to drag all my old endless anxieties and paranoia out for you . . . but I can't help it. Nothing seems as bright or fixed anymore. No point of reference. I mean, if you can't see the shore the world's all water. Anyway, fuckit. You can still write to me care of the 14th st. address . . . but I'm moving tonight. Another fuckup is new baby . . . due in July. No father from the start. What kind of shit is that? Fuck this dumb town . . . and almost everybody in it. I wonder what my "hero" William Powell (Nick Charles) wd do if he and Myrna Loy fucked up? Anyway, screw it.

Sorry, also, my silence made for doubts about your NY piece. I thot it was great. Really beautiful. Yr note about not getting to personalities . . . glad you didn't. Yrs was terrific. I'll get the personalities. I'm doing . . . projecting really . . . a long character fiction thing called The Platonists about my lovely friends, &c. here in NY. Everybody gets a comic strip name. So far I've casted Smilin' Jack, Downwind, Happy Hooligan, Brenda Starr, & Ignatz Mouse . . . more to follow.

Glad you got to MFT.[50] I think its one of the really huge landmarks in that sport. Trane is too much, but literally. Thot Summertime the highwater mark in tenor playing since Hawk![51] Really. Fuck Max's ideas about music. They (sd ideas) stop in the days when Flip P.[52] was king (whenever that was??). Also, Max's following here . . . and I mean following, i.e., cats that walk, talk, smoke pot, think, & probably fuck like Max have really brought me down on that "influence." You know

50   John Coltrane's *My Favorite Things*.
51   Coleman Hawkins, American jazz saxophonist, 1904–1969.
52   Flip Phillips, jazz tenor saxophonist and clarinetist, 1915–2001.

there's cats here that write poetry like Max Finstein! Wow. I mean, Wow! Ok, he's written a few lovely poems. Tho I'm not that hip on them, and finally think he goes too much to Creeley for impetus (with a little Zuk[53] to keep it mysterious) but for someone to *imitate* Finstein. Agggg! And I do dig Ornette very very much. Also his trumpeter comes over to give me lessons every couple of weeks. My bear note was simply to *place* the two of them. As stylists. As forces, &c. To my mind, going back to Bop (which I sd of Ornette) is genius. Bop & blues I think are the only two *complete* musics to come out of Shade music! Completely autonomous!

With things the way they are here . . . I really wdn't mind coming out West for a time this summer or later. Maybe I can. Or, shit, I don't know what the fuck I'll do. But the *idea*, at least, of going outside the walls seems attractive. Will think on it.

I can imagine what Gil sd about the Kulch function. But we just went up there last night for another demonstration. This time a benefit cocktail party for the Living Theatre (to get to European drama festival or something). This one less shocking because we were ready! Altho I bet Gil writes you about that Queen of Dumbness he talked to. Man, O shevitz! Love . . . Roi the dope

R the D

5–13–61

Dear Roi: Greater NEW YORK . . . METROPOLIS OF MANKIND. That's on a map I have above my desk, natl. geografic, 1935, major shithead doing the photography, a lovely air-shot, but you, you disillusion me.

Anytime it comes down to a Man, of course it is different. Man, that 19th cent term, won't get us anywhere. Or woman. There isn't anywhere, not as place but in area of feeling we can go. I am sorry to hear about all this. And deeply grateful you saw fit to tell me. I love Hettie very much, as much as you, it isn't a pleasure to think about the whole thing. I think I know a little bit of what you are going thru. But perhaps not much. We do, like he said, live in two different worlds, tho that gets to be a pain in the ass too.

Despite what's on record one is rather cruel to think anything. So much is left out. Get on with it. That's a bitter phrase.

Blues Connotations,[54] I am listening to that now. Gil did describe the first party to me, but I haven't yet written to him so of course he hasn't described the other. The money you got, that's good, seems so much. Money, as you said they said, isn't everything. But granting that it comes from such vast sources you shldnt feel that way. Personal problems have very little to do with it now. Think if you were

---

53   Louis Zukofsky, American poet, 1904–1978. Like William Carlos Williams, Zukofsky was an elder poet (radical, avant-garde, Objectivist poet) to whom the younger generation looked up, someone they went to see for both poetic support and friendship.

54   Ornette Coleman's *Blues Connotations*.

splitting broke, all that nag between yourselves over what the rest of the world at large constantly does not make it. This isn't just to say don't kick against the pricks, Please do.

Your letter reassures me in all its bad news. Just to hear from you was very good. It was a strange thing. I had told Max and Rena, you know them, when they asked me, how are Hettie and Roi, they were splitting up when we left, I said, what the fuck are you talking about, looking at the shitty little smugness without which Rena would be faceless, and said they are the happiest two people together I have ever seen. They, Max and Rena, smiled knowingly at one another and I thought, oh fuck it. Which I still do. One is privileged to not be privy to such works. *They* feed on it. It must be very lonely for them in the SW.

Anytime you feel you want to come out to get out of it, do, you can stay here. I am in a bad position. I have I believe succeeded in alienating nearly everyone dear, or in an other sense, important, here in the SW. As I said, or perhaps I didn't, I can't remember, we didn't get on with the Creeleys at all this time when they arrived back. The repetition of a history now approx 8 years old finally pissed me off to the extent I don't give a shit. I mean fuck it, that's done. I can get along without Bob's putting me up, only to put me down down down etc. I only mention this, and indeed to you only, because if you are considering coming west, you ought to realize any relationship with us will have to be predicated on a disapproval from the rest of New Mexico. OK.

I am putting in a poem I wld like your feelings about, but, what the hell would be happy if you'd read. I won't be expecting any quick replies for a while. OK. This weekend I am getting the Cain statement wound up after rewriting and will send. Also for you to see. I suppose Yugen is up in the air?

Anyway, and no matter, give my love to H, to you too, to Kelly, Ed

[Poem on envelope postmarked May 15, 1961]

A POEM FOR CREELEY REPLICAS

If you performed
a satire
of me
what kind
of satire
wd it be?
A mime, slapstick
without a heart
rimed couplet
or verses
& call it art

5–17–61

By the way, I forgot to add—don't knock Flip Philips. He was a Chicago Buster.[55]
I knew him slightly. And, Max never knew anyone save in the mirror of his own
cornea—Ed

[stamped 5/29/61]

Ed—Creeley here tonight? (haven't seen him yet). This piddling note to say send
poems to Prism
3492 W. 35th Ave
Vancouver 13, Canada
c/o Elliott Gose
   They having "special/new forms" issue & want my "appropriate acquaintances"
(?) Anyway you seem rather appropriate

- Roi

6–21–61

Dear Roi Jones have you dropped out somewhere or are you now the secret
worker? I thot maybe I'd get a card from you now and then but I guess not. How's
it now. Read with interest your thing in la bear. Very nice, and to boot confused me
because I didn't imagine you writing something quite like that. Okay. Did you see
Cree in NY. I rec'd a card from him from Cuba, not the one you went to, the other
day, the Eastlake ranch. He sounded down with Pluresy (sp) or something. Maybe
he's reached his Plurality. Nice letter Helene got from Hettie.[56] Baby soon I guess.
How's that all going with you? Okay. I thot I'd like to hear from you but haven't
myself known what to write, maybe you cld bring me briefly back in soon? Like
what's Yugen doing. Or anything else. Had card from Gill S. Why don't you pack
Hett and the new baby and the old one and make it out for a few wks this summer.
Travel is complicated even so and I wldnt blame you if you said, I don't think so. No.
Anyway you look at it I wish you'd show me. Everything swings very cool here in the
likewise Jack Kerouac summer freightcar time. Hear it is hot there—Love, Ed

*The mention of Philip Lamantia (1927–2005) by Jones in this letter broadens the circle
of literary convergences happening during this period. Lamantia was an American
poet, born in San Francisco to Sicilian immigrants, a poet who immersed himself in*

---

55   A Chicago Buster is a play on the word *sodbuster*, a slang term for a farmer. Dorn used the term
Chicago Buster as a way to describe various city people, including Tom Clark, in one of his letters to
Charles Olson (Clark 19).
56   The split between Jones and his wife Hettie was short-lived this time; they did not break for good
until 1965.

Surrealism as he traveled the world, living in various cities in Mexico, Morocco, and Europe. Lamantia was a hub for many other poets, in both literary and physical space. For a poet like Margaret Randall, cofounder and editor of the international little magazine El Corno Emplumado/The Plumed Horn *(1962–1969), Lamantia's Mexico City apartment was key: it was where she met other poets and writers, including Mexican poet Sergio Mondragón, who would become her husband and cofounder of* El Corno. *Randall and Mondragón, like so many other poets, wanted to use the forum of small magazine publishing to open up the literary landscape. She says,*

> *Mexican poet Sergio Mondragón and I met in the fall of 1961 at the home of U.S. Beat poet Philip Lamantia. Philip and Lucille, the woman who was then his wife, had an apartment in Mexico City's exuberant Zona Rosa, an area near the city center where artists and writers congregated at people's homes and in small cafes. . . . This was a time of typewriters, carbon paper, and snail mail service, when even a long distance telephone call was beyond the reach of most young poets. Lamantia's apartment became a meeting place for artists and writers from several countries: Mexico's Juan Martínez and Carlos Cofeen Serpas were often there. Ernesto Cardenal arrived from Nicaragua; this was long before he took his priest's vows. Raquel Jodorowsky visited from Peru. Among the U.S. Americans I remember Harvey Wolin and Howard Frankl. . . . It soon became clear that we needed a forum where we could read new work in the original and in translation, a forum free of the strictures so often imposed by the academies or schools then in vogue. (Randall 1–2)*

July 12 [1961]

Dear Ed,

Sorry to be such a morose and uncommunicative type but have been going over myself with a fine tooth comb, &c., (which sounds like fetishist delight). Anyway, muggy & impossible here. If you go to a beach you meet with the khan's hordes . . . if you stay in the city you perish under radioactive suffocation complexes, or something. But we push (or pull) on. (I sound like Horace Walpole[57] in love.)

What is mostly happening is that I have gotten a lot to do and am very regretful of it. E.G., I'm supposed to do (signed for one already) 2 . . . count 'em . . . 2 books on blues. One on sociological derivation of blues . . . extension of an article in Metronome—and also a book for Macmillan on Lady Blues Singers (complete with free trip to the south to interview families, &c., of Ma Rainey, Bessie Smith, &c.).

---

57   Horace Walpole, fourth Earl of Orford, 1813–1894. Walpole was the author of the Gothic novel *The Castle of Otranto*, a highly romantic, dramatic work.

So all that calls for one definite kind of energy, which I haven't seemed to come into yet. But it seems that I am fast on my way to becoming an eminent musical critic (sez GBS) . . . and it seems that not much to do about it. Hell, I like jazz blues &c. a great deal, and even like writing about them occasionally . . . but I don't want to make a huge production, &c. But also, I don't want to have to go trudging uptown to some job as copy editor or proofreader for Jackoff Funnies . . . hence the books . . . and all the articles.

Magazine still up in the air but I'm confident, for some weird reason, that something will happen shortly and Y8 will ride. You have any loose talk for The Bear? Or, better, POEMS. I liked the Sears Roebuck poem very much, and I just now remembered (?) that I hadn't mentioned it before. (Or have I written since then . . . ? Whew!) Anyway, wish I cd see more of what you doing out there . . . tho I know it's a big drag to re-type mss . . . specially just for general delectation.

You know magazine called *Second Coming*? Well they're mostly commentary, &c. . . . but they can use fiction and they pay well also (75.00). I gave the guy Sam Pitts Edwards your name & told him I wd ask you to send something. Address is 200 W. 107th Street New York 25, N.Y. If you can, send as soon as . . . he's looking around for fiction frantic like he tells me.

Anyway Kellie and I going over to New Jersey today to see my fast talking rich relatives from the South up here for a few days to mock the poorer relations. I will never inherit the Jones Estates in the rolling hills of South Carolina, with an Ofay wife and hairy face, plus one hugely blood shot eye. (It's a still,[58] I think.) But I thot I wd take lil Kellie over and maybe increase her stock . . . (and then years later totter in toothless and beg the little cherub for a few grand so that I might proceed with my whisky habit with dignity . . . &c.)

O.K., don't forget the bear and let us know what's going on out there? (O, Mike McClure[59] was here last week . . . just for a few days . . . really great to see him again. Black tapered pants and black rich jodhpurs this time . . . and heroic demeanor as always. The hugest egotist of us all, I'm afraid. But pleasant like. Also Lamantia is in town. Fastest longest more boringest talker in the East or West. But he's so goddamn enthusiastic about everything . . . you sometimes find yourself actually listening.) End of Hedda Hopper[60] routine.

O.K., again, I'll see you soon I hope. Donno how. Wish to hell we cd get out there . . . but have to wait for capt. midnight in there to break thru . . . EXPLETIVES

Love, Roi

---

58   A sty.
59   Michael McClure, American poet, novelist, and playwright, b. 1932. McClure was influential in the San Francisco poetry and counterculture scenes, known for his political activism in both his art and life.
60   Hedda Hopper, American actress, radio host, and gossip columnist, 1885–1966. Hopper was famous for her gossip column and her very public feud with celebrity columnist Louella Parsons, 1881–1972.

Dear Roi: 7–26–61

Writing from Idaho. Near Pocatello,[61] wow, strange burned hills everybody still got horses, hills with many mine holes in 'em, by the mine hole sat Hiawatha, big with uranium, wheeyu. They drink a lota beer in these parts too, I'll tell ya. And hot, I thot I'd a died. Jeezus Christ, but hot. I thot I'd a died. Lots a mormons. This poem I am enclosing is by a guy I knew here, very young kid, he's written quite a lot, but not for long. I thot you would consider it for Floating Bear, and got it from him, he hasn't published anything before and is wondering how etc etc. Well, I like it, and it certainly seems a legit shot etc. Of course parts of it show he's still learning to write from other writers, and who wholly ever stops that. You say what you think, ok, I mean whether you will or won't. Write to Santa Fe because we'll be back there in four days. And I'll let him know. OK

I am just now going back to Santa Fe to give my notice of leave at that library job. They make it 30 days, illegal, even in Illegal N. Mex. but I can't take the chance of being out of their recommendation file. I guess. Anyway it will give us time to get things together and then back here in mid-sept. I am going to try a winter of discontent, I mean, nothing to do, and hope to get more of the writing gig done. Actually I damn well will and look forward to it very much. The friend I dedicated the book to has a studio on his ranch not far from his own house, can be fixed up, that's where we're going to spend the winter. He is a fine man. Roi, it will be good to get out, I figure to gamble the winter on what I can do, not so much to make it in that vapid sense, but to get the goddamn time, read, fuck around here etc. So that's, this is, where we'll be. Poc. In or by mid-sept. I figure to try for a reading tour in the fall from Ellie, don't know whether or not she'll go for it, but that is on prop. Like they say it will be rough no matter, but I have in mind trying for so called grants or foundation jazz too and I wld appreciate it if you cld suggest any possibilities.

Ok, I'll write again when I get back to SF. Plenty time. Hope things go better there with the blues, and anything else. What's that goddamn Joel up to, I wrote him and he never answered.

                                                        Love to all
                                                        Ed

Dear Ed,   12 July [1961]

    Sorry to be such a morose and uncommunicative type but have been going over myself with a fine tooth comb, &c., (which sounds like fetishist delight). Anyway, muggy & impossible here. If you go to a beach you meet with the khan's hordes...if you stay in the city you perish under radio-active suffocation complexes, or something. But we push (or pull) on. (I sound like Horace Walpole in love)

                What is mostly happening is that I have gotten a lot to do and am very regretful of it. E.G., I'm supposed to do (signed for one already) 2...count'em ...2 books on blues. One on sociological derivation of blues ...extension of an article in metronome- and also a book for Macmillan on Lady Blues Singers (complete with free trip to the south to interview families,&c., of Ma Rainey, Bessie Smith, &c.) So all that calls for one definite kind of energy, which I haven't seemed to come into yet. But it seems that I am fast on my way to becomings an eminent musical critic (sez GBS)...and it seems that not much to do about it. Hell, I like jazz blues &c a great deal, and even like writing about them occasionally...but I don't want to make a huge production, &c. But also, I don't want to have to go trudging uptown to some job as copy editor or proof reader for Jackoff Funnies...hence the books...and all the articles.

                        Magazine still up in the air but I'm confident, for some weird reason, that something will happen shortly and YS will ride. You have any loose talk for The Bear? Or, better, POEMS. I liked the Sears Roebuck poem very much, and I just now remembered(?) that I hadn't mentioned it before. (Or have I written since then!...? Whew!) Anyway wish I cd see more of what you doing out there...tho I know it's a big drag to re-type mss...specially for just general delectation.

                        You know magazine calld Second Coming ? Well they're mostly commentary,&c...but they can use fiction

---

61   Dorn was about to take a teaching position at Idaho State University in Pocatello, Idaho.

Still living downtown, with publishing and writing his primary pursuits, Jones be-
gan foraying into activism more and more regularly. He got himself noticed by the
conservative Mississippi senator James O. Eastland. Eastland was notoriously anti-
Communist, attacking intellectual scholarship and the Supreme Court in one fell
swoop: because scholar Gunnar Myrdal's first name was Karl (á la Marx), and he had
written an influential account of race relations, Eastland "was able to charge, after
Brown v. Board of Education, *that the Supreme Court had dared 'to graft into the or-*
ganic law of the land the teachings, preachings and social doctrines [of] Karl Marx'"
(Whitfield 23). This activism, though, wasn't so simple for Jones; he had, at this time,
definite (dis)illusions about representing black Americans. He was conflicted about
his actions even as he engaged in them: "Do I owe these people that much?" Jones
found himself in a complicated position: married to a white woman (the Jewish Hettie
Cohen, who of her own accord never considered herself to actually be white) and living
among the mixed classes of downtown Manhattan (the Lower East Side, Greenwich
Village), Jones maintained a sense of the complex nature of race and society.

He faced criticism from other black radicals—"So some foul mouthed prick na-
tionalist gets up on a box and denounces me for having a white wife!"—and from him-
self, finding this in-between space a hard one in which to be located. In a letter to Dorn
in November of this year, he went so far as to say, "I mean what's campier than a fuck-
ing black bourgeois soi disant intellectual trying to say what's right for all these poor
coons in the hills of Mississippi," admitting the impossibility of his being able to con-
nect with or know all of the many black communities in America. This conflict would
resolve itself, in 1965, in a hard choice: to walk away as best he could from everything
"white." That stance, however, would be one of many that Baraka tested and contin-
ues to test throughout his life, eventually returning to many of his white friends.

[Sept: 1961]

Hiyou doing there. Wherever that place really is! Is there a Pocatello, Idaho? Really?
Well, I spose so; if there's a Nwk. N.J., then there's right enough in a Po, I. (What is
the abbreviation for Idaho?)

Anyway, things here, besides being unbearably hot, move as they usually do.
Except McClure's living here now. Moved in, lock stock & family, last week. Taking
up residence on our own eastside, for a year, he says.

Me, I'm caught up in usual binds, &c. And now, so busy trying to move stuff
back in. A lot of bullshit went down recently, you must have guessed. Have it
mostly cooled. But now we're broke (I ran through 500 dollars while single.
Lost another 500 dollars on foolish real estate deal. So all my fellowship money
gone . . . Fate tale? . . . and we're like reduced to beatnickdom again. Anyway,
I hope to get on the blues book and git that advance, which wd make us
middleclass again (& put some damnd bottles in the cupboard, which is, after all,
where it all is). Also, now, I'm getting to be a bigtime politico. Uptown (harlem)

speaking on streets, getting arrested. Even made Senator Eastland's list, which is some distinction. "Beatnik poet, radical leftist racist agitator," to quote that dear man. Have a trial coming up next month (after 3 adjournments) for "resisting arrest; inciting to riot; disorderly conduct." All true as hell. My only bitch is that I only got in one good swing before they popped me (but good). What is it all about? Who knows? It's just that I've *got to* do something. I donno. I'm picked. What I wanted (& want) was soft music and good stuffy purity (of intent, of purpose) elegance, even (of the mind). And now I'm fighting in the streets and the cops think I'm dangerous. But what is heavy on my head is . . . Do I owe these people that much? Negroes, I mean. I realize that I am, literally, the only person around who can set them straight. I mean straight . . . not only as to what their struggle is about, but what form it ought to take! I meet these shabby headed "black nationalists" or quasi intellectual opportunities, who have never read a fucking book that was worth anything in their damned lives . . . and shudder that any kind of movement, or feeling shd come down to the "people" thru their fingers. Also, these stupid left wing farts whose only claim to goodness is that they know capitalism is bad! Shit. So where does that leave me? Fuck, if I know. I have people, old men, on Harlem streets come up and shake my hand, or old ladies kiss me, and nod "You are a good man . . . you will help us." And what? So some foul mouthed prick nationalist gets up on a box and denounces me for having a white wife! Brrr.

Anyway, so I'm stretched and turned. Yow. And writing, furiously, I suppose out of fear that all this other thing will close me off. So I sweat and strain and am genuinely scared into putting things onto paper.

Anyway, What's happening wif you? That poem about yr mother & Sears is very fine.[62] Is it spoken for? Can the Bear use it? There are some things in the Crump poem also. Tho it has a tendency to ramble or maybe, overstate. But still let me read it again, it sits pretty firm. Whatever you do, see La Dolce Vita[63] when it gets to Idaho (?). My sister has a little dancing part in it which is pretty funny. (She is also in this movie Cleopatra that Liz Taylor is making.[64] She plays a Nubian (yas) princess whose lover has been slain, & she is forced to dance for the Egyptians . . . so at the end of her dance she throws herself into a pit full of alligators (crocodiles?). So my mother, on learning of this little deal, writes my sister asking her "to be careful." Ah, yes, parental concern is like that of our dear Lord.

Enclosed, the first book. Ahh, well, let's not go into it here. But there's a hard cover edition scheduled too. Have you heard from Don Allen? His new poem book thing?

Love, Roi

---

62   "On the Debt My Mother Owed Sears Roebuck."
63   *La Dolce Vita*, 1960, directed by Federico Fellini.
64   *Cleopatra*, 1963, directed by Joseph L. Mankiewicz.

Sept 21, Pocatello (!) [1961]

Roi—I think it's real. Enclosed pic shows part of it along the famous Portneuf river . . . from where the picture was taken we live up the hill about a mile and a half. Enough out of it to be nice, I mean isn't this whole state out of it . . . turns out Idaho is the least populated state save Alaska, of all. To the consternation of the Cham of Comm. They find fault with everything.

When we got here the rain, man, was tremendous, cldnt fix the very leaky roof of this barn we live in . . . coming from NMex, Creeley bringing up the rear in his VW bus, the canary sitting beside him on the front seat digging the rock&roll radio, Ray,[65] my friend in front, we in middle with dog in back, tres muchachos, etc. A really Oky caravan, blowouts, Ray's pickup setting the tone with our gear flying. Wow. What a harassment. Utah, ugh. Fuck them. The weather has moderated now tho and it isn't such a bad gig. I thot to have all this immediate time, like they, but this piece of course needed much more fixing than I had cond.

Your social radicalism sounds very much to the point, as you'd know I'd feel, envious even, altho I know it is much more other's scene than mine. Keep slugging for whatever fucking reason, and when you run out of reasons, the better.

We're all in good shape here, at last, the kids well into school. I am afraid I had to take a teaching job, freshman english comp, 101, three hours a week, one course, so it won't be discouraging time-wise, I am a little apprehensive about all those goddamn themes tho, 24 studs, once a week, in class etc, you know the scene, meet w/ them first time tomorrow. Far far from any street corner reality.

~~Frump~~, or Crump, si, it is neither here nor there in any *serious* sense, of course. I liked it however, for various reasons, faulty, and true, and passed it on thinking the Bear cld absorb it. As for the Sears poem, fine, I'd like it if you would print it. The list of new things in Bear this time frustrates me, Got your thing ok and Kelley's, both of which I damn well haven't been able to look at, except I knew the title poem of yours and like it, several others too I thought I quickly recognized . . . Raworth tells me he wld very much like to complete his file of Yugen, he is missing #4, do you have any extras of that one? If so, wld you be willing to mail to him? In case you lost it his add is 167 Amherst Road, basement, Hackney, London East 8, Eng. Enclosed is a dollar, good for all debts, the wherewithal for postage, and if it can't be done, can go to said Bear. OK.

The news Roi that you're back is good, to both Helene and I, I don't know for whatever 19th cent reasons, but we had seen you both together and like that, and not knowing anything about contingent scenes were a little displaced by the other part of it. Crazy if you'd give my kindest regards to Hettie, (and to the new kid, altho that's pointless). Will try to get back again soon, when not so damn spread out. Good luck with everything—Love Ed

---

65 Dorn's close friend and supporter, artist Ray Obermayr, b. 1922. Obermayr taught at Idaho State University and lived in Pocatello while Dorn was there at this time.

[Sept ? 1961]

Ed—Somebody may offer me job as *a columnist* for a big liberal newspaper!!!!!
Shd I take it??

Please answer. What do you think?? Will it fuck me up?? But I'll feel guilty if I
don't. I'm not sitting in on anything, anymore. Just a labeled *agitator*.

What do you think??

Answer fast, Buddy

Love—Roi

[Sept ? 1961]

Dear Senator,

Column thing might fell thru of its own oppressive weight. I wanted to do it . . . wd
have, but the fellow making the arrangements was a shyster, pure and simple. He
wanted 50% of my earnings in simple Beau Jack[66] style, what w/ another 10% for
de Lord, I'd be cut up in more ways than the ordinary negro psyche. But I'm going
around him, if possible, Lord might be able to swing the thing heself. In that case
I'd be in, and I mean baby, waaaaaaay in. Dig? 2bills a week for one 2 ½ page col. in
which I cd say almost anything I want to. Like "You readers say you want to help the
arts . . . I dare you to send 1000 to Senator EDorn of Pocatello." Column's newyork
address wd be NYPost liberal motherlumper of the northeastern seaboard (see:
bored). Was to be handled by the Hall Agency which also handles (Dig!) Pogo,
Mr. Mum, Feiffer, Leonard Lyons,[67] and other such intellectual asswipes.

As you say they probably eat that shit up, but I donno. I had a real bag of shit to
lay out for them. If they eat that they really in style. Over television I just saw two
close friends of mine bite the dust at the senate Cuba student hearings. Phil Luce
and Levi Laub,[68] both at my pad, just before the cracker quiz. So I sez to myself, Roi,
I sez, you're nex' you bulgy eyed motherfucker.

Also, now that you mention it, Ringo, there's too many hippies on this scene.
Everybody knows everything. I mean opinion, baby, is rampant. The Kings, Early's,
Hellenbergs, &c. all have opinions based on rechaw of the latest hip mistakes. Oh,
shit, man fuck me. But like last night 3 avant-garde filmes. I'd like to take those
people and do something drastic with them. One film was 30 minutes of a cat (fag)

---

66   Sydney Walker, known as Beau Jack, American lightweight boxer, 1921–2000. He was very popular,
especially during WWII, known for being a powerful, tireless fighter.

67   *Pogo* and *The Satirical World of Mr. Mum* were satirical, politically minded newspaper comic
strips by Walt Kelly (1913–1973) and Irving Phillips (1904–2000), respectively. Jules Feiffer (b. 1929) is a
cartoonist, most well known for his work in the *Village Voice*, for which he won a Pulitzer Prize in 1986.
Leonard Lyons (1906–1976) was a newspaper columnist. His *New York Post* column, "The Lyons Den,"
primarily covered the arts and politics, running from 1934 to 1974.

68   Phillip Luce and Levi Laub were activists at the time; they would go on to become officers of the
Harvard-Radcliffe May 2nd Committee, an organization of students against the Vietnam War. Luce
traveled to Cuba illegally in the 1960s as part of a protest against the newly instituted travel ban.

sleeping nude. Camera would stay in one place, e.g., navel, for 5 (really) minutes. Another flick was all about nature, with naked beatniks flitting thru the leaves.

And speaking of bullshit. Why you let Oppenheimer take the book away from Grove now that they're committed to saying something about it? I talked to Marilyn Meeker, and she said she thought they were sure to take it. Man, it's about time you were published where the fucking books would actually get around and be *read*. Which I take it is your point. All these ego publications, like Oppenheimer and his lovely printer, who it turns out now must read the stuff and decide whether he digs it or not. Bullshit. You shd have left it at Grove until it was turned down, if that was the case! Lovely cat, if he wants to do it, wd do it anytime, no?? Gil was hot for the idea too, until Corinth offered to do it, with a lil' advance, &c. There wd be an advance from Grove too. And you do need the loot. But I'm just sick of *My typewriter just broke!*[69]

your work & other IMPORTANT work being published in these meaningless ego editions. Man, I've got stacks of books in my goddamn closet. All great stuff, &c read by 150 persons. & don't please give me that shit about 150 "ideal" readers— Fuck Literature.

Ron Loewinsohn,[70] another ideal reader! You wanna be the Mina Loy of yr generation???

Duncan[71] is setting up the S.F. reading supposedly, tho I've got no further word. I'm trying to get him here in Spring, to teach a course at the school. But I have to go thru K Koch[72] the poor man's celebrity.

At any rate, w/ this typewriter just [. . .] I'm too pissed off to write anymore. IF YOU AIN'T SUFFERING ENOUGH I'LL SEND YOU SOME CATS OUT THERE'LL REALLY MAKE YOU SUFFER. TRULY, Roi

Sept 27, 61

Roi, Back again, here. Still feel like the man who said let's go, meaning to the scene of the disaster. Are we here. This poem, enclosed, you may probably not like . . . I mean that it may seem another useless and dull plea. Nonetheless I submit the

---

69   The rest of the letter is handwritten.

70   Ron Loewinsohn, American poet, b. 1937. Loewinsohn early on studied William Carlos Williams, later becoming a professor at the University of California, Berkeley, where he had studied as an undergraduate.

71   Robert Duncan, American poet, 1919–1988. Duncan was a major figure in twentieth-century poetics, a teacher at Black Mountain College with Charles Olson and part of the San Francisco Renaissance. Finding his poetic lineage in poets like H. D., Duncan's work and beliefs fit into a Western esoteric, mystic tradition. Duncan was, as well, open about his homosexuality from a young age, a risky stance in the larger mainstream culture of the '30s, '40s, and '50s.

72   Kenneth Koch, American poet and playwright, 1925–2002. Koch was an influential New York poet, active in avant-garde art scenes. A contemporary and good friend of poets like Frank O'Hara and John Ashbery, Koch and Jones knew each other through the New York City art scenes both frequented. Koch's *Fresh Air* was part of Donald Allen's *The New American Poetry*.

mothafucka to you thinking if space allowed it might cage in the Sears bit, or I don't know. Sort of like everybody else has a mother, which is incredible, and even more incredible perhaps that a man wld actually spend time trying out means to say it. Oh well.

Am trying to regain whatever entrance to the art I had, and being neatly shit all over by the gods, like let me write your book of blues, I must have at least a bookfull.

Went up a place today called Bannock Creek, (said here—BANNOCK creek, accent always on the first word, as in SCOUT Mountain, and POCATELLO creek.) I seem always to be doing that. Looking for a spot called something I forgot, didn't find it. All the aspen turning now to a soft crazy yellow. What the hell happened to Sorrentino. Is he really taking over the culture? There were these mountains see, and on' em were the aspens, some not turned so yellow, and the firs which never will, unless of course someone sends out an expert.

Funny now how all that landscape jazz looks like a numbers painting. The modern mind has *really* been conditioned, ain't it?

How's that new babe?—Ed

Dear Ed,   Oct 6, 1961

Here is an item especially for you! I hope you will send them something. The poem you sent me[73] I cd (and have) comment on [. . .], but not here. I wd even like to publish it, in Bear probably, tho I plan to *answer* it (like in Communist publications) not w/ poem, or maybe w/ poem. But I *have to answer* it. A good book for you to read (not to change the subject) wd be *The Soul of Man Under Socialism* by none other than our good friend, Oscar Wilde.[74] It is really a marvelous book, even if it is couched in what must be the most *purple* socio-political terms in history. It cd almost be sub-titled *Capitalism as a Big Camp*.

Thank you for those lovely pictures of Pocatello. It looks mysterious! Anyway, speaking of Mitch Levertov, his wife just took a poem of mine for The *Nation*. Although we exchanged quite a few notes re/ aesthetics & that horseshit. O.K., I hate writing *long hand*. David Poole's *Condition of Rational Inquiry* wd also stand you in good substance for yr long asceticism. That's what the west is, ain't it? Asceticism? I pause, for a reply!

                                                                    Yaws, Roi

Have you heard of new vol. D. Allen is doing? Send anything?

---

73   "An Address for the First Woman to Face Death in Havana."
74   Oscar Wilde, Irish writer and playwright, 1854–1900. Wilde suffered severely for his homosexuality, serving harsh prison sentences in the United Kingdom on charges of sodomy and indecency.

In the spring of 1959, Fidel Castro visited Washington, D.C., on a public relations mission; the United States had become fearful of Castro's intentions by this time, and Castro was attempting to alleviate these fears. While he was in the United States, the New York Times *printed an article about Dr. Olga Herrara Marcos: "A military court sentenced Dr. Olga Herrara Marcos today to death by firing squad. She is believed to be the first woman to be sentenced to death in the history of the republic." Marcos had been found guilty of being an informant to the Batista regime, giving up the locations of the rebels. Shortly after this announcement,* Time *magazine ran a picture of Marcos looking terrified in the courtroom. The events struck a nerve with Dorn, who wrote a poem about it at the time ("the Herrara poem"), "An Address for the First Woman to Face Death in Havana," which disparaged the idea of big nations and alternately pitied and excoriated those who got caught in the machinery. He sent it now, in 1961, to Jones, who promised to "answer" it. Jones "disapproved of the poem; 'counter-revolutionary' was his phrase" (von Hallberg 56).*

In the letter that follows, Dorn responds to Jones's attack, refuting Jones's charge that the poem was somehow counterrevolutionary; he says, "I'm not no fucking counter-anything." Despite Dorn's admiration of Jones's activism, Dorn did not consider himself as an activist at all, noting in his September 21 letter that activism was "much more other's scene than mine." Dorn was more often disgusted with the entire notion of the nation-state, likening "the modern state, revolutionary or not," to a "Grauman's Chinese opening." Grauman's Chinese Theatre in Hollywood opened on May 18, 1927; from its grand opening, the theatre maintained itself as a spectacle for movie openings and star sightings. Suspicious of the spectacle getting in the way of real work, Dorn told Jones, "If the poem is vulnerable to propaganda purposes of your own," then he "wld rather not have anything to do with it."

Poky, Oct 10 [1961]

Come on, back off. I'm not no fucking counter-anything. I'm as truly gassed as anyone, but much more embarrassed than others, at the poor prospects of fellow poets singing the praises of any thing so venal as a State. I am afraid I am not very interested in the "argument" aspects of a statement like the Herrara poem. It wasn't written "against" anything, as ascetic, (was that aesthetics) aside, you ought to know the very word Batista makes me puke. The modern state, revolutionary or not, is run like a Grauman's Chinese opening. Everybody has some scene, a trademark, like a beard, or a fat stomach and bald head, or a wig-type haircut, with big white teeth sticking out of the middle of the smile. Piss on it. The only point I ever had is that when a picture, namely of Mrs. Herrara, Marcos, is printed, showing her puckered up babyface tears, brought forth by the lunatic braggart announcement of her death, it is a matter of *public shame. Sides*, are a bigassed drag. The biggest small-talk of all, like which one are you on? motherfucker. I think

I know what kind of a stupid, scared, caught woman she was. But whatever she did, of what those who murdered her did, or their "reasons," or her "reasons," my limited prospect of the thing is completely correct. And satisfying for everyone. Because there is no embarrassment in sympathy. Aside from the fact that "sympathizers" are always assholes.

Thanks too for the titles, I am always glad to hear of books. Altho I don't plan to use them, ie, in the way you suggest. I don't see the thing as "rational" at all, and perhaps you'd stick to the view that that's the trouble. Whatever the Cuban people are doing, god blesses them, and for however long they can make it. A statement in poem such as I sent you is highly accidental, in the same way junk gathering sculpture is, and gratifying accidents are a really bigger part of the West than that asceticism you mention. If I had seen a picture of a Pre-Castro victim of the same system of organized horseshit, approximately the same thing wld have come out. This is one of the famous limitations of occasional writing. Its alignments are like the ligaments of a starved man, very clear.

If you feel you have to answer it, please do. But if you plan to take a line like: Exhibit 1—an example of a counter-revolutionary hyena getting his kicks—then I wld rather not have anything to do with it. What I am trying to say is, that if you think the poem is vulnerable to propaganda purposes of your own, then I am not sure I want to meet that kind of test yet. Let the National Review[75] worry about that aspect, if that's it.

The Wieners poem is one of the greatest of his, or almost anyone's, isn't it? Ya, wow. By the way did you get to send that Yugen to Raworth? I was wondering; how does the winter hang there now.

Love, Ed

By the way, I am sending Allen that long poem, *part of which*, was printed by Bear. *Landscapes*. If he takes it, which is unlikely, he'll contact you I assume, abt notices [. . .] if there are any *etc*. Like the more I think abt it, can't you read?

---

75   Conservative political magazine.

The tone and meaning of that poem are perfectly clear. I don't mean "just to me"—but wholly. I wish you'd make *as* clear to me what you mean by counter-revolutionary. The issue is the simple one of machination, but which is no more simple than revolution. The only valid relationship I can see between bigassed nations—Russia & USA—and their more pipsqueak imitators is that the bigasses have what the little asses want too—but with this new tack—they say they *need* it. Which is only a part truth. Most of what constitutes the "good" life, *no one needs*. What excitement is there beyond feeding, clothing, and housing anyone? It all ends with the same dull propositions polarized by that big trick "consumption and production." But "leaders" are *all* bigassed in their way. What happens to the so called poor fucking people is a residue of cynicism which is made "classic" by every age—Russia & USA are the twin progenitors of those conditions now. A France or a Germany never made it that big. When I hear Cuba si, USA no,[76] I think—fuck both of 'em. They agree with each other so much. USA has a bigger paw on the rope, that's all.

Oct 11, 1961

Roi—

It gets thick here. Last July my friend Ray Obermayr was having a drink down at a place called the Court Tavern. In walks these performers, part of the company of the Ink Spots who were playing a gig at a place called the Green Lantern. The owners refused to serve them. Ray said, ok, I know a place you can get a drink. He took them over to the Jim Dandy (the JD) which is a colored bar, the only one in Poky. This is a railroad town, you dig, the string runs from Portland to Denver on this particular line, the UP. On that line there's pot, and the lighter forms of shit. It follows the string. The other night I talked to a shade cat who was busted in Burley, if you can dig that, a place of 5 thousand souls. So they get to the JD and have a drink. The local head of the N double[77] hears abt it by this time, a Mr. Wood, porter I guess, who makes a run from here to Denver. OK. They, He, Ray, and two other cats go back over to the Court to test it. (This year a piece of "liberal" legislation was passed in Idaho saying Negroes cld drink and eat anywhere. You know . . . makes a fairer state, but don't use it. In the Court, Wood asked for the test drink and was refused, meanwhile from the bar some cracker cat yells at Ray, are you with these niggers, and Ray says yes, and he hallers niggerlover, then breaks a bottle and comes at all of them. The two other guys cut and that left Ray and Wood. The Cracker cut Wood a big gash on the neck and then the fight was on, with Ray and Wood backed into a narrow corridor going past the bar into the back room.

76 A slogan during the early 1960s lauding Cuba—and Castro—against the imperial power of the United States. It began in Cuba itself and migrated to the U.S. radical left who stood behind Fidel Castro and Che Guevara.

77 National Association for the Advancement of Colored People (NAACP).

The only way they survived it was that not more than two or three or four of the murderers cld get to them in that narrow passage. Wood, an old man, handled himself with professional skill, and Ray used to box, and is tough anyway. So in their way they clobber 'em.

Ray tried in the following days to keep his own bit straight by going to the college president and putting it on the line, thinking he wanted to get it out right off, rather than waiting till the middle of the year to be fired, or better, more likely, having it suggested he leave.

He got quite a few threatening calls, I'm gonna get you, you fucking niggalova. OK. He got a couple today. I guess the whole place is threatened, on edge.

The trial has been going on recently, many hearings. There are two cases. One is against the guy who held the broken bottle. Assault. The other is the civil rights case. In both the tavern people stack the case with witnesses who lied their asses off. It looks now like it will be held that the man never held a bottle.

Court room scene. Real suspender flipping lawyer saying to uh Mr. Obermay, that is your name isn't it, Professsssor Obermayr, uh you do teach at the College don't you, well, now, isn't that interesting, a proooffeesssseer. My My. Uh when did you start subscribing to the Daily Worker, oh you never did, well, uh how long have you been a communist. Oh. Uh, professor, uh, what were the people at the bar drinking, you were there weren't you. Did any of them have Cokes? (the bar was filled etc)

That's the way it went—also like—Prof *Obermayr*, uh, what color were the men who entered the Court Tavern on such and such a date. To which Ray answered, one was medium brown, one was dark brown, and one was pink. (him)

At the time it happened the local press gave it rather shitty angling. The AP called a couple of times from Salt Lake and it looked like enough attention would be forthcoming to make the CR part of it stick. But it got silently dropped. The thing Ray felt about it was simple enough—that it was the only time in his life in which, without thinking too much about it, or even at all, he had *Fought* for better or worse, for something he deeply believed in. No matter how subject *that* is to analysis, it must be true.

The prosecuting attorney is quite uninterested in pushing the case at all,

Oct 11, 1961

Hoi-
It gets thick here. Last July my friend Ray Obermayr was having a drink down at a place called the court tavern. In walks these performers, part of the company of the Ink-Spots who were playing a gig at a place called the Green Lantern. The owners refused to serve them. Ray said, ok, I know a place you can get a drink. He took them over to the Jim Dandy (the JD) which is a colored bar, the only one in Poky. This is a railroad town, you dig, the string runs from Portland to Denver on this particular line, the UP. On that line there's pot, and the lighter forms of shit. It follows the string. The other night I taked to a shade cat who was busted in Burley, if you can dig that, a place of 5 thousand souls. So they get to the JD and have a drink. The local head of the N double hears abt it by this time, a Mr. Wood, porter I guess, who makes a run from here to Denver. OK. They, He, Ray, And two other cats go back over to the Court to test it. (this year a piece of "liber-al" legislation was passed in Idaho saying Negroes cld drink and eat anywhere. You know...makes a fairer state, but dont use it. In the Court, Wood asked for the test drink and was refused, meanwhile from the bar some cracker cat yells at Ray, are you with these niggers, and Ray says yes, and he hallers niggerlover, then breaks a bottle and comes at all of them. The two other guys cut and that left Ray and Wood. The Cracker cut wood a big gash on the neck and then the fight was on, With Ray and Wood backed into a narrow corridor going past the bar into the back room.

The only way they survived it was that not more than two or three or four of the murders cld get to them in that narrow passage. An old man, handled himself with professional skill, and ray used to box, and is tough anyway. So in their way they clobber'em.

Ray tried in the following days to keep his own bit straight by going to the college president and putting it on the line, thinking he wanted to get it out right off, rather than waiting till the middle of the year to be fired, or, better, more likely, having it suggested he leave.

He got quite a few threatening calls, I'm gonna get you, you fucking niggalova. OK. He got a couple today. I guess the whole place is threatened, on edge.

The trial has been going on recently, many hearings. There are two cases. One is against the guy who held the broken bottle. Assault. The other is the civil rights case. In both the tavern people stack the case with witnesses who lied their asses off. It looks now like it will be held that the man never held a bottle.

Court room scene. Real suspender flipping lawyer saying to

because he obviously wants to be elected again. For instance he didn't intervene once when the defense was putting those questions. The technical evasions are many and standard, some of the people involved in the brawl weren't picked up because "they couldn't be found," and you can guess at the size of Pocatello.

So I guess it cld be said to have gotten out of hand. The threats are strange, like all threats are—one needn't believe them, pay attention, yet one must. I guess I am worried abt the whole thing. The N double doesn't seem to have given Wood any help, altho I don't know what they cld do, I just don't know. Of course it is up to the state to "prosecute," and they don't look willing. At all, man.

OK. Tonight I thot I'd write and tell you abt it . . . for no immediate reason, just I suppose hoping you'd have something to say abt it, altho God knows I don't know what, it is just that the whole jig cld be up for him, Ray, you know.

Love, Ed

By the way, I wonder if you know—Bob Creeley's second oldest daughter, a blue-eyed, lovely little girl, was killed in a landslide at Arroyo Embudo,[78] a week ago Sunday. It is a tragedy I can hardly follow.

Idaho, Oct 12 [1961]

LR: That poem. That's awfully good, isn't it. That slow, "contemplative" phrase. I don't "understand it" for anything, but so much is going on, very thickly. I feel I ought to turn around, or something, go out for a walk. I guess I will later. And the surplus verities. They are likewise wild. I don't know how you get such an abstract thing as "the silence of motives" to mean so much. I guess because it does empty. You will get my letter I mailed to you as I picked this out of the mailbox. Wow. The thing with Leslie, Creeley's daughter hangs over us. Very much. We knew her it turns out too well. The way you are haunted by a face, transplanted to every context. Same in death or love, twin poles, an express runs like clockwork back and forth between them. Have been moping around with tears always there. Man, at this point I ache with something. Enough. Anxious to hear from you—love Ed

On Wednesday, October 18, 1961, Jones was arrested at his apartment by FBI agents. He was charged with sending obscenity—i.e., issue No. 9 of the Floating Bear—*through the mail, much as City Lights publisher and poet Lawrence Ferlinghetti had been charged in 1957 for sending Allen Ginsberg's* Howl *through the United States Postal Service. Issue No. 9 contained "Roosevelt After Inauguration" by William Burroughs and a short play by Jones from his still in progress* The System of Dante's Hell; *the charges stemmed from Burroughs's political satire and the overt homosexuality in Jones's play. Though the* Floating Bear *was not sold publicly, "What LeRoi and I had*

---

78   In New Mexico; the eight-year-old Leslie was digging a tunnel in the sand when it collapsed onto her.

failed to take into account was that at least one of the folks on our mailing list was in prison. Harold Carrington, a Black writer in Rahway, New Jersey, never got his copy of Floating Bear # 9. *Instead, a warden who routinely read all the mail, turned it in to the postal authorities." Di Prima herself was also charged, though rather than picking her up at her apartment, they held Jones without setting bail until she turned up so that she would, instead, be forced to turn herself in (di Prima* Recollections *270).*

In this letter, Jones continues his argument with Dorn about the Herrara poem. His note about "bulgarian hats" is a reference to one of Dorn's poems, "Prayer for the People of the World" ("Did America say give me your poor? / Yes for poor is the vitamin not stored / it goes out in the urine of all endeavor. / So Poor came in long black flea coats / and bulgarian hats / spies and bombers / and she made five rich while flies covered the rest / who were suppressed or murdered / or out-bred their own demise.") Jones began articulating here his growing sense that a poem could only function politically and ideologically, where Dorn's idea in the Herrara poem was about the very specific expression of sentiment involved in this woman's life. The ideology was "accidental"; the sentiment would have applied, Dorn implied, no matter what political regime caused it.

[1961 Oct]

Dear Ed,

In all, a terrible week. With the Creeley tragedy at the head of the list, my god, a whole chronicle of uglies in the last week (or news of it). Maya Deren, the filmmaker died at 39 . . . Booker Little, the trumpet player, friday, of leukemia at 23[79] . . . Basil's show cancelled by lying gallery owner, DeKooning booked for socking a guy in the bar . . . & now I add something as you can see from enclosed clipping. Bullshit, all of it. But they want me, I spose, and maybe I just oughta get the fuck out of here??

Your letter stunned me, also aggravated. Idaho too? I didn't think there was enough coons out there to stir up any trouble. Oh, well, one drop makes you whole, or something. Garvey was right. Back to Africa (i.e., the ofays).

Right now we've got to get some kind of civil rights law to handle our

---

79   Maya Deren died on October 13; Booker Little on October 5.

case . . . also round up all literary types to say we're "serious" or some other bullshit. They also picked up my ole caked up waterpipe and, as the stupid muthafucka grinned at me, "we're gonna an-o-lize it to see what you smoke in here." Fuck 'em. He also asked me where I got it, I told him I won it at Coney Island. (1 pt.)

Also, as you can see, the newspapers dragged my poor old bourgeois daddy into it. He's about as true blue american as they come. I sure hope they don't bug him too much. Shit, he's worked for those bastards TWENTY SEVEN years. Oh, well.

Ellie Dorfman asked me to send you 12 copies of the book. They are on their way. Chance it might be reviewed in The Second Coming. Also, I sent it to Denise at The Nation, which might prove something. She just last week reviewed my book, Gil's and Paul's. She was enthralled by Gil, respected Paul, and said I was a comer. (had "promise," as O. Wilde wd say).

If my letter re your poem sounded crusadery and contentious I'm sorry. But I have gone deep, and gotten caught with images of the world, that exists, or that will be here even after WE go. I have not the exquisite objectivity of circumstance. The calm precise mind of Luxury. Only we, on this earth, can talk of material existence as just another philosophical problem. Poets of the middle ages (we go back to St. Hugh, and the number they gave soul and body. Single consciousness, the renaissance . . . and forget that these people with "bulgarian hats" are a Majority. Your body does not hurt you.) I sit for hours reading books of obscure philosophy, magic formulas for bringing back the dead, &c. & have been hungry for four days to make myself a hero! O.K., we are both *good* men, but I think, now, that mere goodness is a limitation . . . just as Christians try to limit Christ to mere Goodness. "Moral earnestness" (if there be such a thing) ought to be transformed into action. (You name it). I know we can think that to write a poem, and be Aristotle's God is sufficient. But I can't sleep. And I do not believe in all this relative shit. There is a right and a wrong. A good and a bad. And it's up to me, you, all of the so called minds, to find out. It is only knowledge of things that will bring this "moral earnestness." We are pushed around by our inferiors! (But then the "accident" of my birth has pushed me into this impasse, I feel guilty everytime I experience some racial slight or bullshit like that, since I begin to whine inside & mumble things like . . . but I'm intelligent, and beautiful, and learned & smart & used to . . . &c. Oh christ fuck shit (as McClure wd say).

The point is that I will not be put in the position of justifying evil. I will not make it relative. I will not allow myself to be used. I am a man, simply. A black man, if you will. And there is a huge monkey of self-hatred goes with that, I don't need to tell you. I feel I am copping out, letting people down, if I say in the face of this ugliness "I am a poet."

If you say of the woman in the poem "The first" woman to die in Habana . . . you know it is strictly "poetic." Not at all true. For the same reasons Fidel did. I tell you a maudlin short story . . . My grandfather, (first man to open a super market in Alabama . . . but run out with fire when he prospered) came to New Jersey and opened another store . . . became a big *Republican* Politician. When he wanted to break with the organization, and run independent for Assemblyman they warned him not to. (A stupid, bullshit job like Assemblyman) O.K., he went ahead and ran . . . and on the night of the election with him winning, on the way home from his office he was hit in the head with a *street lamp*! "It just fell on his head and killed him," they told my grandmother. A Streetlamp! He was over 6 feet and 200 pounds. A huge vital intelligent boot. But when that thing happened, that republican light mashing out his brains, he sat for 5 years in a rocking chair by the stove and spat in a cup, never saying another word. This happened in the 40s. About 3 years ago, the Republicans sent my grandmother 5 Gs for the thing! There is specific evil. With no easy analogies. Eastland is an evil man. I think Castro means to do better. It is some small thing I want. Some goodness I have to see. And these motherfuckers here are going to kill me for it.

Well, Ok I ain't gonna be the James Baldwin[80] of the Beat Generation. I add only that it is still warm here, my babies cry all the time and thanks for the kind words about the poem.

We here looking forward to Creeley. Wish you cd make it out here again. I ain't coming to Idaho without my 45 and 17 nubians.

O.K., love to yrs

Roi

Dear R: Oct 21, [1961]

You hit me rather hard, I deserved it, and am a little ashamed, more, a lot. I'd thot of this more as a technical problem, ie, if I found myself on the same street with you slugging I'd slug too, I don't think I really wld ask what you were slugging abt. I wouldn't, no, never. I never have connected loyalty to anything save love, *ideas*, never, with them, principles also, I am a renegade, they aren't worth a shit and you know it. Christ fuck shit is definitely poetic. An internalized diarrhea that never makes it to a hard, holdable ball of shit. People who write of wind, have, simply crossed the barrier, with some courage there, even, I shld think. But in any case it is the final lapse into uselessness. That wasn't the question. It is emphatically not poetic to say the first woman, the poetic form, has always been, that plural spread, the 20,000ndth. A multitudinous voice. Springs from a rotten center where the world at large which you so put down, is breathed upon so tiresomely . . . but again, the reason I am ashamed is that you apparently have a keener right to that

---

80   James Baldwin, African American writer and critic, 1924–1987. Baldwin's writings most often dealt with class, race, and homosexuality. He was active in the civil rights movement, joining with organizations like the Congress of Racial Equality (CORE) and the Student Nonviolent Coordinating Committee (SNCC). Baldwin also lived for long periods of his life in France.

knowledge than I. I willingly back off from it to some other corner. What I have to say is of course valid. Every man, every woman, who died, dies first, they then are the first ones, one. Any other tack is silly. Unless you of course want to disparage death. The exclusiveness of action is a little difficult to get around. Don't come to me about relativity, I've read Time and Western Man[81] too, or whatever else, and that's all you know of that abstraction, what you've read. In a sighting on right and wrong I am at least as didactic as you.

I get so fucking lonely here, I'd like to tell you this: In NY last spring I thot you the only man who said anything, stood for anything, *anything*, AND STILL DO, (Allen, the other man there has become so iconoclastic with his "world" I yawn (like my mother used to say of carnivals when I wanted to go to one, if you've seen one you've seen them all).

But if you've seen one poet you haven't. Poets are the only fucking people I can stand in this era, everybody else is *not* worth it.

Like Denise likes Gil because he writes lyrics, and since she can't write anymore at all, that makes it. But you are a comer. Uh huh. So it is not so simple minded as doing something or anything. Frankly when I got that blurb from the save Cuva committee w/ Elaine DeKooning etc, I was so fucking embarrassed I didn't know whether or not to sign or not. The fucking stupid lukewarm language, whoever wrote that for all of us liberals was damn near illiterate. Who wants to sign shit like that? But I did because it seemed more the point, your "Fidel's gonna do 'better'" than not. But it is a crappy association. That's indeed the exclusiveness of so called action—you exclude the fire to keep the embers alive. Good God! The laziness of their statement, likewise their action. Those pricks would jump on any ice truck going by. Petty people, like petty rulers, or petty policy makers, piss me off more than big fat billiard heads, I guess.

I guess all I am arguing is that a poet is only ashamed of it if he'd better be something else. That one poor attempt to cut you back, in that poem of mine, The Biggest Killing, is just a prelude to all this I guess. That revolutions are invariably shortsighted enough to determine usefulness, thus starting the assininity of set process all over again. That selfish, exclusive ego again! I don't find it easy to live in *my* body either, altho true it is white and shldnt present too great a problem. Your grandfather is not a single instance, no instances are. Color in that sense is ridiculous. I will not hear any of that in the face of the expendability of 40% of the world's population. Cops even, have this in common with us. When rulers vie in their arrogance for housing and rice and chickens, and nickel, or nylon, at the expense of a mass they know anyway will be automated out very shortly, relativities like "better" become truly time-relative. In that sense the hero is truly dead, in that he is that corrupt, and everybody, deeply and really, is cynical.

81   Wyndham Lewis, *Time and Western Man*, 1927.

But poets are that only outcast force that cannot gain by being chided with plumbing,[82] as I pray John Wieners will not be. It is utterly pointless to think action is a complement to speech. Speech then becomes set and then finally, swallowed. Up. I mean down. Wow, down. And right back out that same plumbing. None of us can help it that this is a sick time. The trouble came about because the mass, a boy with a postmaster father became intelligent, or a gent, or agent, so their goddamn means. The time does not flounder for *them*, they seek uses, their own, only.

It's like that modern French idea that you can only be a true man if you've had an adventure, namely killed someone. And all that complicated horseshit about it ought to be for a "right cause." I mean in this case of Ray's, he is that kind of man altho he did it, pasted a white cracker in the choppers and will have his ass burned for it, he doesn't have any desire to see that bastard go to jail for cutting the coon on the neck. It isn't that way, I mean simple minded, you understand. It is to Fidel. Operatively, right or wrong, better, right *and* wrong can be very goddamn convenient hangers for what the hell you feel about something, and that's *back* to the *World*, and only *poets* know what that's all about. And if you're afraid, for whatever embarrassment, to say you're a poet, then god pity you, you mother, you've really copped. In that sense B Russell[83] is better today than anyone else in that he speaks to all, not some duped up ear with a built in trigger spring. And that angry wet chicken look he has at 90, wow, there's your elegant mind, and man, he hasn't said for one minute he's not *anything*, he's said on the contrary nothing but *fuck you*, which is infinitely more readable than Christ fuck shit. But then you wouldn't put down direct address.

OK. I started out again not to argue because I don't have any argument with you, at all, as I said. Shit, you must think I'm awfully out of it. But I am the one cat who's got straight what poetic is, if nothing else. And I haven't put it down yet. I may, probably will see you in the spring, if they haven't done you in by that time. I have a reading in Jefferson? Missouri end of April, Lincoln College, that's a shade school, and then one at a place called Baldwin-Wallace, which is in Ohio! I don't know how I will make it save by hitch-hike, but I'll be there like they say. Enclosed is the folder from Lincoln and that's ma pitcher. I don't know why I look that way. Habit I guess. The clip you sent w/ yr visage was just as depressing to me as what you said to me because they were both so fucking true. I mean true. Wld it be too naïve to ask is that the end of Bear?[84] Goddamn, and that Burroughs thing was one

---

82   This is a reference to Charles Olson's *Maximus Poems*, "Song 3," in which Olson reminisces about his father standing in the doorway of his house where "the plumbing / that it doesn't work." The "boy with a postmaster father" in this letter is Olson.

83   Bertrand Russell, British philosopher and historian, 1872–1970. Russell was noted for considering himself to be part of various social movements and philosophies while also saying he was not any one of these things in any real way.

84   Di Prima's and Jones's arrests were not the end of the *Floating Bear*; it went on to 37 issues, though Jones himself resigned after issue No. 25 was printed in 1963. Di Prima continued the magazine with various guest editors on both the East and West coasts.

of the best things you printed, perhaps the. Is there anything at all I cld possibly do to help, way out here. I can't imagine it but if there is, say. A letter of protest. Ok, that sounds like shit. But I think Raworth might have good loud London contacts, I will send the clip on to him, and if you think so say to me or him. OK.

Look, I don't want you to think badly of me for all this horseshit I've been sending you, I don't really want to fall out of anything, and besides that, my hangups are not your own. I don't even know why I say that save that I have such a real and living respect for the tight emotional verity of your last letter. I read it in a bar down in Poca and it set me right off the stool. I don't know . . . the point is you are right, and that's it. I don't think I'll let the Marcos poem get out, for all the reasons you enunciate meaning I am too slack at this point to know better. I said some irrelevant things, tho, there, that were true anywhere. But it isn't that much at any rate. I hate it that I took up your time with ground that you're possibly not interested in now. Or possibly ever were.

Oct 22

Had to go out last night in face of raging snow storm . . . wood, all that unhappy jazz, I mean when it catches you, but wild beautiful, even if white weather. Got a card from Creeley saying he wouldn't be getting to Harvard and thus seeing Charles after all, which is sad because he wanted to so much. I keep being brought back to that reality that my body doesn't hurt, it must be you are right, irresistibly. I get sorry all over again for that poem, and the letter I sent. Shit. I know it isn't enough for either of us to be "good," and I ain't even that, not even that. But there must be times when you are. Jesus that was a beautiful letter. And from it I see more than I ever did, of those things. There must be 2000 or 3000 Negroes in Idaho. Funny thing, I was telling that Englishman, TR,[85] about it, and he said essentially, altho I know he'd know less, the same thing you did, Idaho? I thot that shit was restricted to the deep south, the latter you know better of. I mean than. And your poor goddamn grandfather . . . that it has to be a colored grandfather is the sadness, because I get sad when you separate me from yourself with that color shit. Which is a "practical" point. I get excluded for some specious detachment. But then you do too, until the stance is innately real, for instance how long wld the Bear be allowed to go in Cuba? You've been there and may know better, abt that, but I do wonder.

I don't know . . . we may perish here this winter . . . as you may, and admittedly for not half the reason. . . . And if I say I believe you that it is up to you and me, all of the so called minds, to find out, what, I mean how . . . do you say. Shld I get my ass to the so called city where there is no place at all for me (because I am *Not* just another poet sitting in Dillon's). I know it is too true I get sententious where I should make the point. This is an apology.

---

85   Tom Raworth.

The snow deep as hell now abt 2 feet, the sun out, too bright to look anywhere. We're sorta cozy in this little shack, two fires going, plus Coltrane Giant Steps. Be goddamn careful . . . I don't suppose I will get a very quick answer from you, naturally, but keep in mind please I am anxious about the scene there and about you especially. Ok, give our love to Hettie and the baby, Lucia has mentioned you and the baby in letters, so I guess everything is going ok?

Love to all of you—Ed

There is a concern among these poets about the intersection of poetry and politics. Art is necessarily changed, taken out of the hands of the artist once the public receives it: how, then, to manage the manipulation that will take place? Jones says here, "That is, I know finally I will be used," thinking about the Russian writers Isaak Babel, Vladimir Mayakovsky, and Alexander Blok and their increasedly difficult position as writers under Stalin's regime. William Carlos Williams talked about this in 1952 at a talk he gave at Hanover College in Indiana; his biographer Paul Mariani notes,

> *Communists too, [Williams] said, in spite of all their brutal concepts, were really only after a piece of the pie. But they so feared the artist, feared what he might say in showing them up, that they had "cut themselves off from what he might add.". . . Still, if Soviet Russia kept its artists under its thumb—and it did—America did the same out "of fear of the onslaughts of our language upon the secret rigidities of the past—which we fear to attack in order to renew ourselves." (646)*

Jones makes an interesting leap from revolutionary Russian—and, ostensibly, American—poetics and politics to the staid intellectual camp of Lionel Trilling and company in this letter. From Marxist (though anti-Stalinist) to liberal, Trilling and his wife Diana, as well as many others in the intellectual group that came to be known as the New York Intellectuals, occupied a space neither Jones nor Dorn could abide: on the one hand seeming to support leftist or radical positions, while on the other finding favor with the mainstream establishment (including academia).

Howdy,   [Nov 1961 ?]

Still here in grey drizzling "empire city" looking for another house. We have to move pronto. This edifice coming down (to make room for spanking new 15 apartment bldg. with rents of 150 up). So we have to hit the road again . . . where? God only knows. I've been scouring this goddamn town and nothing's turned up yet. One groovy place I found on the other side of town, where we used to live, Hettie didn't like . . . too far from the parks and the popular east side where all our glorious friends reside. Another place, the bitch landlady didn't want to rent to

"Artists" because "they're unstable." The great poet Bob Kaufman[86] is more or less responsible for this since that same lady used to pride herself in having nothing but poets and such as tenants. Kaufman and the S.F. bunch moved in and had such ravings, and dopings, and bustings, plus they got out one midnight owing the lady mucho pan. Anyway, maybe we'll turn gypsy and buy a trailer and live in times square. You'll hear one way or tuther.

I spose our last two letters show that there's still *something* to be interested in; and that, what I always thought it was . . . men. Which I must hope sounds like a truism out there, but unfortunately, here, it is some strange hope for those of us who somehow manage *not* to be friends with everyone. There are so many vilenesses here that want to love you. God. That I respond clearer (certainly cleaner) to anyone who, say, doesn't merely want to be "one of the boys," i.e., any fucking body who's got their own little transistor radio tucked behind their own ear. Really, it's a clown show sometimes. I was talking to Sorrentino about it recently . . . I mean how almost everybody we know (or anybody knows, probably) fit so easily into such predictable behavior patterns. I don't mean like Watson's bullshit rewriting of Democritus and Hobbes to produce—presto— Behaviorism, or Pavlov's aluminum puppies, but even if say most of the people I know weren't ARTISTS and didn't have their thing, their art, to save them from the ridiculous circumstances of existence (and in that hypothesis, no *Models* to base their own lives on . . . i.e., if I write like Olson or Spillane it saves me from certain decisions that should be my own and the assumption then can be that I am Olson or Spillane . . . etc. Remember Allen saying "Who digs Los Angeles is Los Angeles" . . .) For instance, there is a whole coven of Max Finsteins in this place. People who walk like Max Finstein, talk like Max Finstein, and who presumably Are Max Finstein. (One good thing is that Creeley never lived out here for long so most of the Creeleys are strictly literary . . . but somehow that *is* more ugly since it proposes that these Creeleys are more artificial than these Finsteins. Since they must rely on poems alone (which is not to say that a poem is not more powerful than a man . . . certainly in this instance one might be led to think so . . .) But I leave out those of us here who KNOW Creeley and might feel inclined to sit and talk about women with one palm hiding their desired dead eyes. Oh, fuck it. All this abstract sociology. Still I am stuck with it, since so much of my own conduct is based on trying somehow to find and be somebody. That I am egotistic enough to say that sacred character is myself is just another psychological stunt the people at Columbia wd say.

---

86   Bob Kaufman, African American poet, 1925–1986. Kaufman's poetry was highly influenced by jazz, making use of its rhythmic and timing possibilities. As in the often highly improvisational modes of jazz, Kaufman did not often commit his poetry to paper, preferring to compose out loud as he performed. After the assassination of John F. Kennedy in 1963, Kaufman, a practicing Buddhist, took a vow of silence; it lasted until 1973 with the end of the Vietnam War. Kaufman's life was marked, sadly, by poverty, harassment, and addiction.

Of course you're right about that "Declaration of Conscience" paper. It was drafted by Marc Schleifer, who, if nothing else, is at least the world's worst poet. The screwy thing about Marc is that he has been converted to so many religions so many times, but that is my old idealism of litmus paper only being good to register one reaction (process?). He, Marc, used to write "reactionary" (I mean in that old shit flinging sense of being happily wrong) essays in the Village Voice. I first met him when I wanted to punch him in his Ivy League eye for an essay of his in the Voice defending Madison Avenue. (That was his approach . . . a *defense* not so much of the abstraction, but of the actual material filth that that abstraction imposes on us.) "Don't Kill the Butler" was the title. The next time I see him he shows up at our old place with a plan to make Totem Press big business, even offering to kick in monies . . . back Yugen, etc. Wow. "Laziness" and "Lukewarm" your words, both right in that connection.

The difference I make between *The Biggest Killing* and *The First Woman* (excluding the fact that the former is a very *powerful* poem) is that the Woman breaks down into harping and editorial. So much so that any "poetic" is shouted down. *The Killing* was certainly editorial, but it made for its own poetic, only because it was conceived I suppose as a poem *before* it was flat didactic statement.

I know the sense of "use" you mean. And nothing frightens me so much about what I'm doing than that possibility. No, it strikes me, as you thought, as *necessity*. That is, I know finally I will be used. The whole point is, as far as I've gone into it now, will I be able to make my own terms. Mayakovsky's not a half bad poet. In fact, I think he was a very fine poet. And he finally refused to be used *against* his terms. His fucking "Com Party" poems are poems, and will be around when Nick Kruschev is long gone. But the suicide, and Blok's: that is my worry. Or fuck it, to think of Babel whom Stalin murdered and now they heave poor Joe out on his ass. Babel is more used now than he allowed himself to be under Stalin's repression. "The right to write badly," he said. But now that becomes under the Trilling regime, such powerful statement as that, a fucking camp that sterile ex-Trotskyites like Lionel and his dried up wife can use to beat the Soviets with. Vileness. I started out by merely saying to all this group (and to culture ladies with sewed up pussies) Fuck You. And I'll never stop that . . . but now I am committed to more (Is it more? Your question. I hope so. I can't say clearly on that . . . except I hope so).

The black white bullshit is bullshit, make no mistake. Nor do I (I certainly can't afford to). It's simply a matter of accretion of experience. No make that plural/ accretion of experience(s). Damn. It is merely that I have made myself an example of something. Something a great many people detest. And I will not back off because I got away free, so to speak. I mean what's campier than a fucking black bourgeois soi disant intellectual trying to say what's right for all these poor coons in the hills of Mississippi. But the only people who would get the *point*, i.e., the scandalous humor involved in such a situation are people like yourself who don't

give a fuck about that shit in the first place. But what I said before about only a
few people can lend any *clarity* and really forceful statement (as opposed to that
Declaration) to the situation. An incident QED will be the "appearance" I'm making
tomorrow (saturday) on a round table symposium forum type of bullshit with
(or opposing) people from NAACP, CORE, NALB (labor sambos), SCLC (MLKing's
sambos), and several other liberals &c. (Interesting note is that of the groups I just
named, all presumably "Negro" organizations, one *one* SCLC will be represented by
a Negro. All the other speakers are OFays. And that ain't even funny. But what will I
do there? (the topic of discussion Civil Rights, Youth & New York)? But I feel I've got
to be there. I've got to say "All this is a lot of horse shit and if you punks don't know
go fuck off" or something. And on the t.v., right after Gunsmoke. Bilious business.
My issue is that perhaps in Habana there would be no need for The Bear. That is
if such things were handled by people who would bring sensitive and practical
coherence to, say, literature. The Bear is *in lieu* of something better. It is needed,
I think, to fill a void caused by the same things I am bitching about "politically."
The Money Wheel, the commercialism of American publishing, the bankruptcy of
capitalism, and western imperialism, to my mind, are the same bag. The Bear is
more than something someone wants to do, it is, for me at least, something that
one is *forced* to do because the so called normal publishing media are all filled with
Trilling, or Hyam Plutzick,[87] or (to be crudely ironic) . . . Ferlinghetti. And fuck all the
politics anyway, it comes down, stupidly enough, to men again. I would trust you
as a "minister of culture" and would fight a revolution, if it came to that (I hope the
bear, Yugen, Totem, Black Mt., Origin, Measure, &c. constitute some kind of Revolt).
Your point of course is made when I tell you that there is already internal "strife"
over the cultural policies, &c., in Habana. And that the good guys, from our point of
view, i.e., the cats there who say "art shd be just that none of that social realismus
shit" *may not win out*. And the reason they may not will be because some
opportunistic pricks down there refuse to fight the thing out and will suddenly
show up (as one Jose Baraganos, whom I know well, a staunch surrealist poet and
dada nut) proclaiming the virtues of "a peoples poetry." And again I investigate
directly what I feel about it and am stuck with theories again. For instance: When
this country was going thru its flirtation with social justice and an organized left,
in the 30s, the painting of this period and a great deal of the writing was Social
realism. People like Shahn[88] and Levine[89] still in fact remain. Of course guys like

87   Hyam Plutzik, American poet, 1911–1962. Plutzik was an established poet whose book *Horatio* was
selected as a finalist for the Pulitzer Prize in 1961.
88   Ben Shahn, Lithuanian-born American artist, 1898–1969. Shahn studied at Black Mountain and also
worked with Charles Olson at the Office of War Information in the early 1940s. Shahn is well known for
his radical political paintings in the style of social realism.
89   Jack Levine, American Social Realist painter and sculptor, 1915–2002. Growing up in Boston with
Lithuanian Jewish parents, the hard realities of immigrant Boston informed much of his artistic work,
which was known for its socially conscious themes and techniques, particularly satire.

Guston and Motherwell[90] moved out of that thing and into what they're doing now, which is of course much better and definitely more *original*. One can only hope that if social realism replaces the imitation Picassos in Habana, that somehow it will lead to a more original *Cuban* art. Oh, well.

The play (the Dante thing that we got picked up for along w/ Capt. Burroughs tirade) is going well, along w/ one acters by di Prima and McClure. They're starting a regular "Poets Theatre" here, in a little theatre called The Off Bowery Theatre. They've got 3 more plays cast already. The last part of Duncan's Faust Foutu (which is really a fantastic thing . . . my God, I saw Duncan do the first part at the Living Theatre last year . . . it was crazy and really wild. A musical no less . . . and baby, you shd've heard Robert *Sing*.) Also they want to do a play of John Wieners, which Irving Rosenthal is reluctant to let them do because he wants them to get John's permission. (Rosenthal is the caretaker of the Wieners estate.) Of course, John will never answer them, and if he does it will be negatively. I really think they shd go ahead with it. Our Wieners issue of F.B. was done sans permission, but they were poems that John had given to me or di Prima or Frank O'Hara[91] personally some time ago. But anyway Irving wants to be the Max Brod[92] of the Beat generation or something. Have you ever written any plays? I know the people at the OB would be wild to see them. We's all theatrical types here. A play of Joel's is being done by another off Broadway company this weekend. It is not so much a play as it is a pedantic pageant, replete with off stage voices giving out with statements like "THE SIX GUN HELPED WIN THE WEST" or "DOPE: THE DOCTOR'S FRIEND" and then some kind of exposition about said subject. Whew! Have you ever talked to Joel about History. It's like going to a bad private school. O.K., I'm rambling. I'll get off it, let you go out and take a shit or something. Water just cut off in our kitchen for a change so I'll have to make the trek down into the cellar and see what's up. Anyhow I've given the Yugen 8 to the printer finally, hoping that some expected monies will be here soon. Think your "Notes" really a big piece. Glad to print it.

---

90   Philip Guston, American painter and printmaker, 1913–1980. Guston's painting was experimental and surreal; he moved from purely abstract work to cartoonish representations. Robert Motherwell, American painter and printmaker, 1915–1991. Motherwell's work experimented at the leading edge of abstract expressionism and Surrealism.

91   Frank O'Hara, 1926–1966, American poet. O'Hara was a key figure in the New York School of poets and was a contemporary and friend of many of the most cutting-edge, experimental poets and artists. He was also active as an art critic, working at the Museum of Modern Art in New York City. O'Hara and Jones were friends and ran into one another frequently at parties and poetry and art events.

92   Max Brod, Czech Jewish writer, 1884–1968. Jones is referring here to Brod's role in publishing Franz Kafka's work. Kafka had asked that his unpublished papers, which were in Brod's care, be burned upon his death. Brod refused the order, as he had told Kafka he would refuse, and published his work. Jones equates Irving Rosenthal's role in relation to John Wieners as Brod's to Kafka.

Rest of the book will have 6 or 7 poems by Steve Jonas,[93] 6 or 7 poems of George Stanley.[94] Couple of Sorrentino poems, his review of Duncan and Spicer.[95] Creeley's review of Maximus.[96] And few other things. Have to keep issue small because of loot involved . . . as usual.

O.K., take care of all that snow, & love to all your family and Happy Thanksgiving . . . Yeh.

Love, Roi

Dorn's work appeared in the Nation *twice in 1961: they published his poems "Unlike Music" (May 27) and "Hemlocks" (June 17). Robert Hazel's review of* The Newly Fallen, *"Embodied Knowledge," would appear in the magazine on January 20, 1962; Jones sent Dorn a galley of the review with this letter. The review is generally positive—"By and large, Dorn is a careful workman, with acute senses and a subtle mind. His first book is a reward to any finder"—but also quibbles with some of the individual poems, attempting to label the book as "in the Imagist tradition" ("Once in a while he suffers a lapse into the plain literality characteristic of Imagism"), which it wasn't, quite. In poetry, politics, culture, and his own life, Dorn refused labels and was never one to play identity politics of self or art. In his January 12, 1962, letter to Jones, he argued against the idea that his work was Imagist. In response to Hazel's charge that Dorn was using William Carlos Williams's "still-life plums," Dorn said "[T]he point was that contrary to buying that imagist shit I took the plums to be just that commonplace I said it was." The entire critique is problematic, fitting neither Dorn nor Williams, whose life work cannot easily be subsumed under the Imagist label either.*

[Dec 9? 1961]

Dear Poet,

Rec'd this from The Nation this morning. No telling when the magazine will appear w/ the review in it tho. I'll send you one when it does. I know the Nation doesn't get to Idaho.

I'm on my bicycle right now . . . we're supposed to be out of this pad in 6 (count

---

93   Stephen Jonas, African American poet, ?–1970. Jonas lived and wrote in Boston, though not very much is known about his origins. Jonas's poetry was influenced a great deal by Ezra Pound, William Carlos Williams, and, as well, by jazz. As for so many poets, the experimental rhythms, notes, and qualities of improvisation were a force in creating his poetry.

94   George Stanley, American Canadian poet. Stanley was associated with the San Francisco Renaissance; he cites Olson as a key influence in his own work.

95   Jack Spicer, American poet, 1925–1965. Spicer was a contemporary and friend of Olson and Duncan and a key figure in the San Francisco Renaissance. Outspoken and openly gay, Spicer studied and taught linguistics, translating, at one point, the Old English epic *Beowulf*. He was extremely interested in the idea of poetry as dictation, referring to himself as a vessel through which poetry was received from some outside force (Martians, as he liked to say).

96   *The Maximus Poems*, by Charles Olson, a major epic of poetry; at this time it was being published in sections in various small magazines and journals.

'em) days. The 15th. There'll be a large gun battle if they try to throw us out. Gotta purchase a mortar today. Yeh.

O.K., love to all you western hardy pioneer types. It is beautiful outside. Not cold . . . no snow. Tune in next week for next installment of Life w/ the Homeless Joneses.

A River, Roi

"You are there" Dept   [1961]
Ed,

A 'woman' here has offered to sponsor Yugen if I will lay her odd Wednesdays!!

What you think about that, huh, huh? She is only 68 & from what I hear . . . a marvelous fuck!! *What* shall I do?

Yrs, The Latin Lover

Dec 22, '61, Poc

Hi you little shit, whaddya mean comin on so vulgar. Anyway 68 year old women have been diddled before, I'll look for the warmed over naked lunch from you in 12 mos.

Jesus, Xmas. Let's see this is fri, two days before the birth, we went up on the govrm't land to get a tree, a juniper. That's just above us here, up on chink's peak, we walked the kids went, and everything was groovy. This place is dotted with abandoned copper and gold mines and we excursioned into a few, some with little push cars still, tiny gauged tracks etc, a little show here and there, patches, light cover all over in other places, dead deciduous wild rose thickets here and there, up into intimate little draws, the light strong on the ridges above, where the snow, on the north slopes etc, much light, the tiempo very slow, the temperature, oh I dunnow, I guess about 35, brisk, you know.

Last night big moon, "goodbye red moon," I stayed up thru the winter solstice at 12:20, 9:20 I guess your time. Sorta wandered around outside, wrote a bit of shit. etc. Sorta fucked around all night, up on this mountain, and how are you doing in the apple. I been thinking about you, I didn't answer that letter, lassitude overtook me, and you had said all that material concerning those issues, I actually thot of writing to say just that but got very sidetracked. I am circulating again now . . . have something nearly off to Joel, which, if you see I wish you'd say is coming and I hope isn't too late, for Kulch. Creeley has the mumps, I understand from his latest letter, and is in bed. Poor man, poor family, they have taken it on the chest this year. How are you yourself, I been wondering. Have the cops eased off, and did you find an apt? How's that little Hettie and the babes. We think of you often, and wonder those things. I got given a novel, Lord of the Flies, by a cat William Golding, I never heard of. I suppose you ya, have, it looks like an "innerestin paperback."

I am about to set up for a meeting, Native Amer Church, peyote cult, never took it that way w/ real indians. These here are Bannock-Shoshone and according to my swede linguist (who speaks the tongue) friend, they are the most anti-acculturation of all. So it will be hard but not impossible he says. If it comes about I'll tell you all. Fort Hall reservation.

Well, I still look forward seeing you in the spring, April I think or the first part of May. I have agreed to take an extension course in Twin Falls (he was pissing, one eye fixed on pocatello) this next semester, we need the loot bad, it will not be Freshman 101, but Great American Authors or some such horseshit. Emerson Thoreau, Whitman Poe, Crane Whitman, etc. 110 miles away, and travel pay. Wow. Teaching wld be a good racket if it were high-paying instead of simple minded.

O fuck em anyway. I got pretty exhausted last month mostly thru drink. I don't know why I just drank a lot . . . this month has been better I have stuck to a little more business. Brought up some rather decent gage from New Mexico but it is almost gone now, and it come high here. The end of that also. Went down to Salt Lake City last Friday to get Ammon Hennacy[97] who came back with me and stayed here with us over the weekend. He is an old man, maybe you know him, pure in heart but a kind of bore after 21 hours. Endless talker. Pure in heart but sort of a corrupted mind. All that bullshit anarchy I can't quite get with Ok for Spaniards I guess. Ok, latin lover, theys not much more to say here, the wind has been a real bitch the past few days tho now quiet nights and still, but the wind beating against the sides of this shack scared the shit out of us, you cld really feel the structure shake and roll with the punches.

Merry Xmas to all and to all our love, Ed

The American Society of African Culture was established in 1957 after the First International Congress of Negro Writers and Artists, organized by the literary and political quarterly Présence Africaine, *took place in Paris, September 1956. The ferment of mid-twentieth-century radicalism to overthrow the oppression of colonialism of Africans throughout the world found its way into the United States. The American Society of African Culture held various symposia, artist exhibitions, musical performances, and international political and cultural forums. Jones was invited to speak at one of these symposia, "The Negro Writer and His Roots." Houston A. Baker Jr. says about this event that there was "[t]he notion of a mass black readership that becomes coextensive with the appearance of a mass of black Americans, especially in the North. . . . Suddenly, on the American landscape, the black writer discovers a*

---

97   Ammon Hennacy (1893–1970) was an American activist, pacifist, Christian anarchist, member of the Catholic Workers Movement, and a Wobbly.

black readership. . . . [Y]ou have as tangible, functional, object of black American culture THE BOOK. The book, the masses" (Ward 53).

Within the American civil rights movement, parallels to worldwide movements were found and embraced, but as always there were rifts. While agreeing to attend the symposium, Jones attempted to disrupt it at the same time, undercutting the power of black American literature with the declaration that "the mediocrity of what has been called 'Negro literature' is perhaps one of the most loosely held secrets of American culture." Jones took his role as a black man to be the radical one, never pushing for acceptance but, rather, disruption.

Ed,   [Dec ? 1961]

I know it's been a dumb lapse . . . but things here more hectic than usual. I mentioned that we were moving . . . well, we still haven't quite made it. I'm staying at Fielding's . . . he's in N.M. w/ Bob . . . Hettie & Kids in N.J. w. my parents. We'll be in the new (?) place next week sometime. Entire place had to be repaired, &c. all kinds of shit. Mucho loot lost and still we're all spread out in n.e. u.s.

3 hipsters just left here. All heads. Me supplying stuff, and getting bombed with them, for some reason. Too many silences now as bachelor type. And other times, all kinds faded females with legs bouncing religiously open. ( )

I'd rather watch some of the "cats" get on than rub sores on my pecker. Or something. Grim. All ways.

One thing that's good about all this bullshit, if you come in we can put you (you all) up. That wd be a gas . . . Are you certain of the times?? Summer? I lost your last letter in the moving.

Also, along with all the other shit, I'm still trying to get that blues book out. Work, but what else? Here's something I thought you'd like:

> I'm a big fat mama, got the meat shakin' on my bones
> I'm a big fat mama, got the meat shakin' on my bones
> And every time I shake some skinny gal loses her home.
> (Ida Cox)[98]

What's happening West? I hear vaguely how Max is from his doubles. And yr further elucidation on his shoppe . . . which I think is the final extreme of "the american experience" (or dream. As Joel canonizes Sissy for using profanities at the "neighbors." It comes to a very liquid world, with only the color a particular face, or window, or word. Damn it wd be good to have you here in the hot summer. We've a groovy roof now, which I intend, somehow, to fence off, to make safe, and hang out there when it's summerier. But come!

98   Ida Cox, African American singer and performer, 1896–1967.

Funny news: there was some kind of conference "symposium" at a place called American Society for African Culture. Uptown, Rockefeller sponsored coon ranch. And they invited me, along w/ Louis Lomax, Ralph Ellison, John Killens, Loften Mitchell, & others (Baldwin was in Africa sucking some ambassador's dick) to talk about THE NEGRO WRITER AND HIS ROOTS. (Yeh, I know. So I prepared a long formal talk. And then . . . you'll have to get details from Hettie or my mother, they were both there cracking up . . . I laid this shit on them . . . all that guilt and bitterness. The paper was 10 pages. I think it began "The mediocrity of what has been called 'Negro literature' is perhaps one of the most loosely held secrets of American culture." And zoom from there. Their assholes stood open and bled in unison. It was like Bill Burroughs says, 'testy.' They moaned, and called me and mine some terrible names. And then I called them all a bunch of "serious uncle toms" and they pants fell, I mean it was nice. Bag of grass helped the eloquence, yes. So what? Everybody kept saying "but he's a poet." Well.

Turning warm here, and bright. Keeps my nose open eyes peeled. Yugen waiting to come from printer. Need only a little time. Summer shd slow some things. Hettie and I went to see Basie[99] last night. And talked a little to him. Now there's a strange man. He gets very serious if you're really younger than he is. I mean he wants to understand what it is you're doing that's *different* from what he's doing. And bitter that he's heard all his own ideas before. But that awful grin, teeth, hiding two generations of compromise, or eagerness. Who knows which?

If I didn't tell you before the address is 27 Cooper Square, New York 3. We have top floor and 5 rooms and closet. Windows, and stairs to roof go right up out of our kitchen. Right between east side and village, so within bombing distance of both. Also 5spot 50 yards away. James Moody[100] there now.

Well, o.k., send some things for bear, quick. And tell me some other stuff too.

love to everybody, Roi

Oh, we saw a great documentary, with all earliest fight films, couple of weeks ago. Jack Johnson, Sam Langford, Jim Corbett, Fitzsimmons & solar plexus punch . . . Joe Gans, George Dixon, Terry McGovern, etc. But great thing was that the New Yorker quoted beautiful thing of Langford's. When asked why he always threw so many punches to the body, Langford said, "Cause the head got eyes in it."

o.k.

---

99   William Count Basie, American jazz musician, 1904–1984.
100   James Moody, American jazz saxophonist, 1925–2010.

III

1962

In 1962 Dorn's first book, The Newly Fallen, *was published by Jones's Totem Press in affiliation with Corinth Press. After what seemed like endless finagling for money and recognition by publishing houses, there would be tremendous satisfaction at finally seeing this book in print for both Dorn and Jones. For Dorn, who did not have the same literary connections that Jones did by this point, this book set him onto the path of a larger literary landscape, tying together the widely spread ends of small-magazine poetry publishing.*

The Cuban Missile Crisis, building on the disaster of the Bay of Pigs the year before, occurred in October. This year also saw Kennedy playing a terrifying game of "nuclear brinkmanship" (Kurlansky 157) with Nikita Kruschev. World events during this year show up over and over again in the letters of the poets as they attempted to understand and absorb the often horrific events happening around them. Jones, living in New York City, is particularly affected, feeling, as everyone around him did, that the threat to actual human lives was palpable and real. The letters between Dorn and Jones deal with the intellectual conversation of the situation compounded against the true fear for oneself and loved ones in an atmosphere of war hysteria, a hysteria that seemed not hysterical at all to those living through it.

" "   " "

Pocatello, 12 Jan. 62

Dear Roi—Once a "colleague" of mine here on the faculty asked—"Do you pronounce his name *Lee Rwah*?"—Right now abt to have some groovy lunch and listening to Trane—Giant Steps—which I dig even more than tother one *Favorite Things*. Cold as hell—150 miles northeast of here is that place *West Yellowstone* where the other night it was 57 motherfucking *below* 0. But here it hasn't got below 5 below—temperate of it, no?

Got the galley of the review[101]—I guess it is favorable as they say? Too bad the man didn't know how to read Open Road—not that it's that good—but the point was that contrary to buying that imagist shit I took the plums to be just that commonplace I said it was and tried to point out it's a deader world than otherwise because some men do dig the way they look as such—oh well! Thanks for sending and listen you arrogant bastard—we *do* get the Nation in Idaho—the college lib— but I'd be happy to have one of my own. Hope you find a place to snuggle into. More later. Love to all of you—Ed

---

101   Robert Hazel, "Embodied Knowledge," the *Nation* 194.3 (1962): 64–65, a review of Dorn's *The Newly Fallen*.

The connections between art forms, and the movement of artists between these forms, are evident here. Jones by this point was establishing himself not only as a prose writer and poet but also as a playwright. In this letter he expressed his frustration with the avant-garde theater scene in New York City, noting how the politics of friendship played into whether or not a work would be produced. As is so often the case when faced with rejection during this time, Jones's language grew vicious; in this case, homophobic. In this letter Jones notes the changing of hands at the Nation *from Denise Levertov to Paul Blackburn as poetry editor. Blackburn was also an organizer in some of the earliest poetry readings in downtown New York City, an advocate of live performance and the connections between jazz and poetry. Blackburn "used the cafes and bars of Greenwich and its eastern environs to promote live readings vigorously . . . link[ing] poetry to jazz performativity" (Kane 29–30).*

This letter reveals, as well, some of the tensions between changing art forms with more academic approaches to art, poetry in particular. Jones shares with Dorn a review of Olson's Maximus Poems, *which said that, as Jones relayed, "Charles Olson's Maximus poems is the worst book of poetry published in 1961." This was from Robert Bly's the* Sixties *literary journal, which published poetry, translations, essays, and letters. Bly was already deeply entrenched in very traditional forms of academia, winning several mainstream poetry awards. For Jones and Dorn, a poet such as Bly represented everything they were struggling against in poetics. Gilbert Sorrentino published several scathing reviews of Bly's poetry in the little magazine* Kulchur.

[1962]

Dear western man,

What all is happening out there? Tell your bucolic colleague that by all means the pronunciation is Lee Rwah. What else?

We getting ready to cut out from this place next week, I'll send you the new address when we get in. It's a pretty large place, about 6 rooms, but the rent is a lot more than this old run down joint. Where the fuck I'll get 100.00 a month, each and every month, is beyond me, but there's a couple of swinging Puerto Rican cats next door who could teach me mugging. Oh, well, I'll probably have to go on relief like M.F.

A lot of trick shit going on in this burg. Most recent is Joel Oppenheimer's entrance into the world of effort, a la the "theatre." Whew. That filthy play of mine and the cowboy play of Joel's were slated to go up near Broadway (Yes, man, bw) as a package. The producer, some faggot name Wulp, saw both plays, liked them, wanted them in his house, &c. O.K., so then the guy who directed Joel's play calls up Wulp and convinces him that it wd be better to do two of Joel's plays and ditch mine. Yasss. So the cat was convinced. Ahh, says I, weeping, tis the cruelty of small ambition (quoting). Then Joel just drops out of sight, like, with a new group of, what's that word???? Friends. Suddenly he calls the other night and says (and I quote) "Man, somebody's walking around saying you're pissed off at me about . . . &c., Is that right." Me is silenced dead, and walk away with my finger up my ass. O.K., so the whole thing's silly. I know it, &c., but my ass still burns. Not so much about the switch deal, but because Joel (old friend who has thrown up many times on my vests) wd not tell me about the deal when it went down.

Even tho you *do* have access to the Nation, permit me to send you one. Consider it in the nature of a CARE package. As half-assed as that review is, it might be better than the one I expect in Poetry (who, by the way, just took two of my poems. I wonder what happened?) They've sd they'll review the book, so we can look forward.

Denise's tenure as Poetry Editor for The Nation just about up. Paul Blackburn will be the new Jefe. I guess he ought to be writing you about it pretty soon.

YUGEN finally ready to go. Starting to proof read things now. Like that piece of yours very much. When you gonna send something more for Bear? I just got through writing a hateful review of new issues of *60's* which just came out. This issue is dedicated to French poetry (the poets are Nerval, Baudelaire, Mallarme, &c.) Whew. Also, they say, in a review of all 1961 poetry books that "Charles Olson's Maximus poems is the worst book of poetry published in 1961." That's Robert Bly state poet of Minnesota talking. Yeh, like you're bitching about your review. Man, you're lucky.

I leave you w/ another happy note. Some lady came here and wanted to do a poetry thing for a guy on television named Brinkley . . . all about poets &c. They wanted to bring cameras into my house (also Denise's and Gil's, Auden's, Lowell's[102]) and find out how contemporary poets live. They won't come to my house because I said all my family has to be on w/ me. They claim Hettie's appearance wd be too controversial. How's that for the week's largest drag? Woman claimed it wasn't her doing, however. "NBC just wdn't like it," she grinned. I agreed.

Love to all you yrs

Roi

[Feb ? 1962]

Howdy,

I had just about given you up as gone with that herd of ghostly buffalo Vaughan Monroe[103] used to sing about. But I remembered you were on your way up to see Buffalo Bob. Glad to hear you shot your way out of B.C.[104] Did you meet any sideways shits? Poets? Milers? Anthologists? And speaking of the last, I'm really content not to make too much noise. Don can do what he wants, tho, of course,

---

102   Wystan Hugh (W. H.) Auden, English American, 1907–1973. Robert Lowell, American poet, 1917–1977. Auden and Lowell were both well-known, well-received poets.

103   Vaughan Monroe, 1911–1973, American singer, trumpeter, and bandleader.

104   Robert Creeley, in Vancouver, British Columbia.

there's no such thing as an "overlap" clause. Bros. Wilentz[105] unhappy because if Grove paperbook (cheap mass circulated, &c.) duplicates ours too much, it is to be hard cover, and what not, folks will think the Grove is the paper ed. of Corinth. But if they are fixed to the CBQ story, and well they might, I can't do much about it . . . nor do I really give a fuck, personally. It's just as editor, &c. &c., and having to hear rhetoric from Bros. W., &c. Ah's jes a middulman, Cap. But I'll write Don again; my last 3 (count 'em) letters being unanswered. But, fuck all that. What's doin' in Pocatello? I'm sending you a record to cheer things up . . . you shd get it in a while, I'm mailing it manana. It's Ornette Coleman on Tenor. A very hip record. Also, if you are ever in the record buying mood, get this new thing Duke and Coleman Hawkins made together. Really lovely!

Hope, of course, everything goes well with Morrow. But the less I hear of J.G.[106] the better. She's my editor, and we're going over copy, &c. now. She's the dumbest least imaginative bitch since Merle Oberon.[107] But we will pray with you. Got many "favorable comments" on the *Notes*, by the way. From people all over, e.g., Ron Loewinsohn, cat named Prynne from Cambridge U . . . some others. I hope it's time for something to happen! Man, it wd be velly nice to see you all in cool autumn when we can compare welts. Yeh, I hope something does happen, and I hope that ignorant bitch gets off her flabby ass and does something up there. No shit, she is the stupidest woman I've ever met, and thass saying a whole lot baby. But wait and hope. No word at all from Grove about anything. Rosset[108] is in Europe blowing DeGaulle I'd imagine, no telling when he'll get frew. Cold as shit here and I've gone conservative for pretty obvious reasons, not politically, but socially, for sho, staying in all the time, not working, necessarily, just staying close, and with no loot, not even drinking too much. Not sure just what the fuck's happening. But I did go to a wild extraordinary concert last week. Don Cherry, Billy Higgins and Wilbur Ware![109] It was really beautiful. No Shit. Cherry played a long slow gorgeous You Don't Know What Love Is, that floored everyone. He has gotten to be too much. Higgins, is about the finest yng drummer on the scene. And you know Wilbur, high as he was, he came on like big time gang busters. Thing went on in a big dirty loft, and we were carrying our own jugs, and the musicians just went as far out as they could, realizing the extreme empathy, &c. of the audience. Also, as some weird added attraction! There was a cat there, from Copenhagen, a Negro cat, who was

105   Eli and Ted Wilentz, owners of the Eighth Street Bookshop and publishers of Corinth Press.
106   Joyce Glassman (Joyce Johnson).
107   Merle Oberon, actress, 1911–1979. Oberon was a well-known British and Hollywood actress, famous in part for obscuring her past, including her birthplace, which she claimed to be Australia. It was more commonly believed she was born in Ceylon to Anglo parents.
108   Barney Rosset, then owner of Grove Press; he was also editor for a time of *Evergreen Review*. Rosset was a supporter of free speech, publishing then controversial works such as Henry Miller's *Tropic of Cancer* and D. H. Lawrence's uncensored *Lady Chatterley's Lover*.
109   Don Cherry, American jazz cornetist, 1936–1995; Billy Higgins, American jazz drummer, 1936–2001; Wilbur Ware, American jazz double bassist, 1923–1979.

born in Denmark . . . can you dig that? Anyway, the cat's been listening to records, for sho, but he's into something very personal and very swinging. All came to their feet, after a few seconds hanging to see where the cat was going, he straightened out into this weirdweird sound and metre. Like he was huffing and puffing on an *alto*. Or like he wasn't sure whether he was playing Baritone or alto, and dug Harry Carney and Hawk,[110] but really wanted to play like Bird! Can you hear that?? Wow! John Tiinonson I think his name was.[111] I hope sometimes we gets to hear him on some record.

My other business w/ Morrow is going well enough. We already spent the advance. No book in sight yet. Just making notes, reading a few "references," like the collected short essay of Wright Mills, which you shd get for definite. *Power, Politics and People*. Things as "it is our own personal style of life and reflection we are thinking about when we think about politics . . ." from *The Social Role Of The Intellectual*, make the book swing, and very very useful, though for sure you find yourself off from him in some instances. But the general sense is very very good. Don't Don't get those Villejo translations Bly's peddling,[112] unless your Spanish is good enough to get the poem from the bi-ling rendering. Shitty, no-eye translations. Bly is certainly the Eddie Condon[113] of American letters, too bad he doesn't drink. Look, this is just short welcome back to Devil's Island

More Later, Roi

Pocalmeanto tellya
March 30

Dear Roi:

First the biz: here are **4** 5 poems which go with a collection of poems out of the west, ie, I don't know—they are part of a thing I got going for a collection. But I want you most to dig they are on the periphery of the main body, just so me. I'd hope you liked all and printed them. But of course that's not it, I had thot to send many of them and then said to myself the road of excess leads to the palace of wisdom.

Anyhow, that cldn't be groovier about our staying there this summer. I don't think it will be all of us. It is hard to say how it will set between here and summer

---

110   Harry Carney, American jazz saxophonist, 1910–1974; Coleman Hawkins, American jazz saxophonist, 1904–1969.

111   Jones is referring here to John Tchicai, Afro Danish jazz saxophonist and composer, 1936–2012.

112   *Neruda and Vallejo: Selected Poems*, 1962. Robert Bly, through his Sixties Press, released this book of translations.

113   Eddie Condon, 1905–1973, was an American jazz banjoist and guitarist. Condon was a white musician who played early Dixieland-style jazz, a very far cry from the contemporary avant-garde jazz Jones and Dorn were listening to. Jones disparages him by comparing him to the academic poet Robert Bly, who had already set himself against the radical movements with his dismissal of Olson's *The Maximus Poems*.

but it wld seem easier to leave the kids at Duluth, there's a house on a lake there, ie, middle class parents chafing at the bit &c.

Half the time we think let 'em have 'em and good fucking riddance, and then of course think what a gas it wld be for them to dig NY &c. . . . so I think we'll just go by what we take it as at that time. In July, this summer, so grateful either way for your readiness to tolerate us, we may show as two, or we wow, may show as 5.

Back to those poems, if I only had the time to copy them I wish you cld see all, or even I wish you'd say what you think of those I send . . . I am talking for my own purposes. West where I divide it, ie, Illinois, everything west being west of course & likewise same for east.

《 》   《 》

De above was last night, I was rather juiced. A man name of Bernie Garrow, Dr, BG, ie, came up and busted our little party of H, Ray myself just sittin here in the Idaho hills getting very out of it, but when that man came we had to hide the bottle, terrible. He's a nut. He being fired from his "position" at the school. I like him but don't "respect" him you dig, he's a shit, but does groovy things like he ran thru the girls dormitory, Gravesly Hall, stark neckid. The school is too set in its ways to dig it tho, so he's finished. Can't hold any liquor, I rather suspect he might be impotent and thus under what must be a huge frustration, &c. He carries a luger, and generally thinks to be a man, out where men are &c. A sociologist. You'll dig that embellishment, no?

Creeley is coming to visit, 24 of April or so, he says in a letter he thinks to switch to Vancouver, BC, they seem hot for him there &c. It will be good to see him anyway, be here 2–3 days.

Your place sounds very great. Am anxious to get there this summer, talk, see you &c. Do you know anyone at Lincoln U, in Jefferson you'd like me to say Hi to?

I'll write again soon hoping to have something to say, I hate those great lapses— Love to Hettie, kids, and you,

Ed

The anthology Jones refers to in this letter would be published as The Moderns: An Anthology of New Writing in America, *by Corinth Press, in 1963. This anthology was in some ways part of Jones's answer to Donald Allen's* The New American Poetry. *Where Allen presented the newest in American poetic traditions, Jones built upon the idea to present new forms and styles of American prose. As he notes in his introduction to the anthology,*

> *The possibility of a "new American poetry" meant, of course, that there was equally to be sought out, a new or fresher American prose [which] depended*

not a little for its impetus on the revived intellectual spirit that began to ani-
mate American poetry. . . . Consequently there has developed a loose and
deliberately informal rapport between many of the younger American poets
and younger prose writers. (x–xi)

With this connection between prose and poetry, and with the emphasis on poets
who also wrote prose, Jones attempted to collapse some of the restrictive labeling com-
ing more and more into fashion as many of these writers gained wider recognition.
Jones also shifted the literary groupings that Allen used (e.g., Beats, Black Mountain)
to groupings of space. He says, "Urban and non-urban would be the largest incre-
ments of division these writers' divergent concerns display, but in the loosest sense of
those words. I mean them to be loose categories, implying nothing about the writing
except its attentions" (xi).

[April 26 ? 1962]
Thurs morn

High,

Thanks for those poems. They'll go into the Bear straight on. The one about the
Blonde, I especially digged, also the Ginsberg (vs. Pope) one. Reminded of Pope
because it brought to mind a natty little queen professor at Rutgers screaming at
me "An imitation Alexander Pope is better than no discipline at all. Remember that
young boy if a poet you wd be." Ahh, well, how sensational to be wrong and still
be quoted.

But what of the "main body" as you said. How long and how much body?
Another book wd be good. Just had quite a few orders for yrs I suppose on heels of
those reviews. Apparently they *were* good reviews.

But those poems you sent have that feeling of being cut from a fabric. Not
that they are incomplete, but they do point from both sides, towards what,
I suppose, finally is to be gotten. And smooth, very smooth, which is a real
strength for you. Like the work was all in the moving, or the choice made for life
outside the poem. Which brings so much of that energy to bear, inside, which I
am coming to feel is how most of it is done anyway. But when can you applaud
someone their life. Ahh hero.

And I would really like to see all the rest. Maybe when you come East, you'll
have them in a greasy paper bag, along with the lunch. We can eat an talk.

Your speaking of Illinois raised another thing in my mind. Wow. When I
was there, all the stark *terror* that place produced. That flatness beat on me.
("Impinged," Sorrentino would say.) I remember looking deeply into a book so as
not to look out the bus window traveling from Champlain-Urbana up to Chicago.
Yet, I guess the terror, here, (gangs, garbage, bums, hammer of industry, slum,
foreigners, &c.) is something quite *other*; but I have no trouble considering it.

I mean I would rather pass down 13th Street in the middle of fierce Puerto Rican hoods The Dragons, than be lost near Kankakee after dusk . . . or even in the broad daylight approached by some elderly American without no tattoos. Dig?

Literary note: Apparently Grove is now moving to consolidate its gains. They've just agreed to publish books by Selby[114] (Stories and Novel): Duncan (another book poems): Koch (poems) Oppenheimer (those plays!) Me (the dante book). So, what's up? Perhaps they would be cool for a book now. Have you ever tried? I'm not so sure about me showing up on their list, since Knopf is also interested, and I'm just sitting and rockin' since Grove hasn't sent the contract yet. Barney Rosset can go shit if Knopf wants it. He made me wait 3 months any damned way.

But some other news. I'm sending form letters but disregard except for information. I'm editing an anthology of fiction. Maybe called Avant-garde American Fiction or something. Please send me some things. Also, what about the piece Ed Dorn in Santa Fe. Reprint maybe from Migrant also? Anyway please let me know pronto. Advance payment will be bullshit. 1–1.25 a page. This is for Corinth, and they're kind of broke. But the book will be large 350–400 pages. Include about 15 writers. Royalties will be standard. 6% paperback, 10% hard cover. Edition will be 5000 copies (750 hardcover). I want it out by winter. So everybody has to hurry. Is Creeley really moving to British Columbia? Heard that from the Dawsons (Fielding on his way to work in a furniture store, Bon Marche. Man, what love will dew!) O.K. you write me soon, and send love to all those other Dorns.

(Oh, Duncan was through here. He gave a great reading, including a song he delivered in San Francisco C major. After the reading he came down here with other poet types and we had lovely time. W.S. (Bill) Merwin[115] turns out to be a really great cat. I mean he even looks like a poet. I thought have a lofty gut and Italian process. The reading was Duncan and Sorrentino, in that order, due to arbitrariness of Y's system. That didn't do the reading much good because Duncan is so much wider and heavier, that Gil seemed, unfortunately, an anti-climax. Denise did the introductions in New York Concert G. Ahhh well, the city rises.

Love, Roi

At Lincoln U. tell them you know Roi Jones, the poor man's Sammy Davis. (I found out Hettie's Swedish. My!

---

114   Hubert Selby Jr., American writer, 1928–2004. A Brooklyn-born writer, Selby's work offered harshly realistic depictions of working-class and poor sections of Brooklyn, populated most often with down-and-out, often very desperate and suffering, characters. Selby and Gilbert Sorrentino were childhood friends who remained close throughout their lives.

115   William Stanley Merwin, American poet, b. 1927. Merwin was for a time the poetry editor at the *Nation*. He was well known for his Vietnam War poetry (like Denise Levertov, who was also the poetry editor at the *Nation* for a time).

Jones had two poems published in Poetry *magazine in the April 1962 issue: "Balboa, the Entertainer" and "As a Possible Lover," an issue that also featured Charles Olson's "The Red Fish-of-Bones." Dorn says of this event, "Man, at last you're in." Jones would, throughout his life, gain ever wider recognition by the American public, both for his extensive writing and his activism, becoming the subject of debate, admiration, and disgruntled anger. Throughout the '60s Baraka "exemplified those traditional black intellectuals who were trying to navigate the promise of the civil rights movement, the despair that resulted from the popular recognition of its limitations, and the enraged assertiveness that arose among those trying to transcend that movement and its anguish" (Watts xii).*

Dorn's stance, as he noted more than once to Jones, as a decidedly nonactivist nonplayer in the identity politics that would grow more and more important through the mid-twentieth century, served to keep him out of the wider public eye for far longer. Interestingly, Dorn notes in this letter the beginnings of the spreading and acceptance of his American poems in Britain; the invitation from J. H. Prynne to reprint his poetry for an English edition eventually led to Dorn's time as a teacher at the University of Essex. His stature as a poet in England would actually at points be greater than it was in the United States, as England began to "admit the importance of modern American writing," as Dorn notes in this letter. Charles Olson and Robert Duncan had also by this time been published in England, bringing an alternative to the mainstream American vision abroad. There is something larger at work here, as well. Dorn's honesty and style in his telling of American life and, in particular, Native American history has yet to prove really popular in the American imagination. As with Gordon Brotherston (whose work also focuses on Native Americans), Dorn's friend and collaborator, there is a degree of American resistance to certain tellings of its own history.

Pocatello, May 14, 1962

Dear Roi—You suggested printing again that piece *What I See in the Max Poems*, but that won't do. For one thing it has been printed to death by now, and besides part #2 has not been printed yet and indeed isn't quite finished. I have completed some notes, at some length to, say 15 printed pages, on *The Naked Lunch*. So if that sort of thing is usable by you in that Corinth anthology you could look at those to see what you think. Or did you have in mind the Max piece when it was done in part by Gael Turnbull[116] as Ed Dorn in Santa Fe, I don't know. Please clarify. Otherwise I have a story I'll send as soon as you write and I know more.

I saw your groovy poems in Poetry. Man, at last you're *in*. Olson there too. That seems great. I suppose that means they're coming around? *Creeley* seemed somehow to always belong there—likewise Denny. Duncan's poem in Bear I very

---

116   Gael Turnbull, Scottish poet, 1928–2004. Turnbull started Migrant Press, a small British press focusing on modernist poetics. The press published eight issues of its little magazine *Migrant* and was key in introducing poets like Dorn, Olson, Levertov, and Creeley to a British audience.

much liked. He gets better for me all the time—after say, the lovely public address of P.B.W.A.L. by Pindar[117] and now this. He has directed his brilliant attention too long to the world of "literature." Have you come around to those 10th st. people. Card, ie, from Carol Berge,[118] to whom I had once said you, Roi Jones, was a great man, that was in Santa Fe, last year, and she'd said—in effect—shit! ie, your editing her. Ok. I dig. What abt Kelly's poems in Origin? Some seem very good.

I got back from the reading tour 3 days ago—as it turned out I was at Cleveland, Western Reserve, when Madame Denny[119] was at Mich State S. Lansing. Just missed her because I had thot to go there to see relatives at S. Lansing. I went first to Lincoln as you know. The faculty there is mixed light and dark. They seemed straight and relaxed together—all that phony ease of intellectuals I took it, tho really it was good and I liked one shade girl teacher on the English staff—a Miss Berger who had been schooled in Arkansas—one whiteling girl—a Miss somebody else, a graduate of Wisconsin. But the student body was rather out of it—being middle class, rock and rollers from KC and St Louis. They were rather indifferent. Poor kids—get this! There is de-segregation in reverse there and the colored folks are gonna come out on the dirty end—it's like this: School started by the 62nd and 65th colored infantries in 1866, but supported by the state of Missouri. Apparently around the turn of the century more and more whites started attending, not as residents but as day students—the residents are still all the blacks. I talked at some length to one colored boy who was delegated to show me around (a very nice cat from Mass.) and he said the white students were growing in number and are now more than 50%—and shortly will dominate—but won't be part of it, you know attend and demand but don't play ball. And man, in a class I addressed there, those cracker drawls sent shivers up my ass. They sat, sadly, in class in tight little distinct groups and only tittered at each other. It was strange. It is the only case I've seen in which integration of the whites into a negro scene will end inevitably w/ the negroes having to go elsewhere. At Baldwin-Wallace (Remember Harrison Dillard the great hurdler?)[120] it was pretty much a Methodist scene—read in basement of that church, like youth fellowship—the president of the college sat on a sofa near me, and, unbeknownst to me had a copy of my book, with which he followed every move. I have an occasional trick of not reading a line here and there I don't like anymore. I did that once there—at which point he shouted Hey!

117   Robert Duncan's poem "Poem Beginning with a Line by Pindar." Pindar was an Ancient Greek lyric poet (ca. 522–443 BC). Duncan's long poem incorporated materials and drew from several poets and mythologies, including Francisco Goya, Walt Whitman, Charles Olson, and the myth of Persephone.

118   Carol Bergé, American poet, 1928–2006. Bergé was born and lived much of her life in New York City; she was a figure in various poetry circles and worked to promote poetry workshops and little magazines. Bergé published *Center* magazine from 1970 to 1984.

119   Denise Levertov

120   William Harrison Dillard, African American track and field athlete, b. 1923. Dillard won Olympic titles in both sprinting and hurtling. Dillard attended Baldwin-Wallace beginning in 1941.

You left something out! I, bewildered, instantly dug he held my book in his hands and said oh? He said yeh, you left out a line and I think it's the crucial line of that stanza etc. Do you want me to read it? he asked, and I said no, I'll read it. Ai! It was the only true altercation of the trip.

At Cleveland they were very hip. Harvard grads. 10 of em. Structural linguistics and all that shit. They were very active there tho and it was good to be exposed to new thot, tho I remain rather impervious to it. Why don't they, if they are so goddamn w/ it, don't they write great or even good poems. Beside the point. I tried to interest them in you, Olson, Duncan, Creeley, Zukofsky etc—they had had Denny as you probably know. They can't buy Olson—too baroque for 'em I guess that's it. They are interested in you and Zukofsky. There is a man name of Albert [. . .] there who has read everyone and is a "poet:" I talked you all over the place at Lincoln U. too, thinking that you'd be very good for them there, ie, they have an Uncle Tom pres. who they all hate but don't know how to confront. The other man Cleveland, to get back there, is Mac Hammond[121] whom I liked very much. He told me a lot abt "RV" Lang[122] (Corso)[123] who he knew very well—an elegant Harvard dike. Dead dike poetess.

OK—looking very much forward to seeing you soon. Can I really drive our car into that city—will I get hung up trying to park it on the street? Do I remember correctly that that's a hangup?

I had a letter from JH. Prynne ([. . .], Cambridge) asking if it wld be ok to have an Eng. ed of my book, ie, if he could arrange it. I said yes, but we'd ask you as co-publisher. I don't suppose you'd have any reason to object? It's only a vague possibility anyway. He, Prynne quoted Donald Davie (yet) in his letter to this effect "I don't know when I enjoyed reading a collection of poems so much as Edw. Dorn's" Prynne having given him the book. Prynne then says "this is an encouraging comment from an academic of such intelligence (get that!) and standing as him. And I mean encouraging for *us*, in that this nervous and opinionated world here is perhaps now beginning to open up and admit the importance of modern American writing"—so that's from Prynne.

Ok—I suppose you know that Allen has called on Creeley to co-edit w/ him an antho of Amer. prose I suppose to match the *New American Poetry*? I wonder if the vol you are editing will cut into that ground. ie., is that the plan, ie, there isn't any "politics" going on here is there? I was wondering if there might be a fight among the mine owners. Your letter saying what you proposed w/ yr antho came when Creel was here and there was like no comment. I don't know—he wants ms too.

---

121   Mac Hammond, American poet, 1926–1997. Hammond was one of the founding teachers in the State University of New York at Buffalo's important avant-garde, experimental poetics and literature program.
122   V. R. "Bunny" Lang, American poet, playwright, and one of the founders of Poet's Theatre. Lang was close friends with poets like Frank O'Hara, Kenneth Koch, and John Ashbery.
123   Gregory Corso, American poet, 1930–2001. Corso was the youngest of the early Beat poet writers, a friend and contemporary of Allen Ginsberg, Jack Kerouac, and William S. Burroughs.

Anyway, when he was here he was so drunk he did not, needless to say, *see* Pocatello—the only man who came to Pocatello and saw thru it literally—great altercation occurred in "Bannocks" hotel—we went in he, me, two of my local [. . .] smoking friend—man and wife team—and this barkeeper said, I'll give you 3–1 you won't get served here (we looked pretty desperate—w/ Creeley's dirty army coat, he wiping up the bar w/ his beard) myself busted apart—but Creeley started saying things about the barkeeper's weight, looks, relatives etc—so that that flabbergasted man was not hit by the charge that his real reason for being there was to make [. . .], ie until we reached the front entrance at which point he flung himself on Creeley's back and then there occurred perhaps 5 minutes of slowmotion type rolling softly on the floor, much grunting and red faces—much puffing but absolutely no harm inflicted, the audience of bellhops and assorted people being so dumbfounded they all forgot to call the cops who then did not catch us until several bars later. I think it could be said fairly that the eyes of Pocatello were upon us even if ours were not upon it—which is one of Creeley's satisfactions. After everything is said and done, I love that man's public address. It is the only one that ever made sense—ie, Villon and Li Po[124] still live and thrive in his heart and all men are brothers!

Ok, my friend this rambles too much—I hope to hear from you. We will be leaving here about middle of June going by Helene's mother's place northern Minnesota—then in NY about 1st part of July—1st–5th probably—I'll drop card to you along the way—

Much love to you, Hettie, and Babes—Ed

LeRoi and Hettie Jones moved several times in the years they lived together in the early 1960s; in 1962 they moved to Cooper Square, a central point in downtown New York City. In the early '60s, Cooper Square would have been considered something of an in-between space, not quite here or there. Abutting the Lower East Side, the East Village, the Bowery, and the section of Bleecker Street heading into Greenwich Village, rents would have been low and space abundant. Jones talks about this in-between space, describing it as a "halfway house sort of . . . between very fashionable Greenwich Villitch and very hip lower east side." Daniel Kane talks about the importance of this kind of space, locating this area of New York City as "a radical center . . . in developing a politics of joy and resistance" (xiii). For radical, experimental artists, staying downtown but out of the already commodified Greenwich Village, the East Village and Lower East Side were key in "artists' resistance to being co-opted by the kinds of mainstream activity [of] the late 1950s West Village scene" (Kane 2).

---

124   François Villon, French poet, 1431–1464. Villon was known as a thief, vagabond, and barroom brawler, as well as an important poetic innovator. Li Po, Chinese poet, 701–762. Li Po was an important and prolific poet during the Tang Dynasty, known for experimenting with poetic forms.

Particularly for jazz musicians, writers, and listeners, this was a crucial space. New York City was enforcing strict cabaret laws, forcing live music into loft spaces and off-the-radar clubs. Cooper Square and its environs abounded with such spaces, including the Five Spot, which became legendary in the avant-garde jazz scene, as well as "a gathering place for emerging modern artists and writers, from leading abstract expressionists to the so-called Beat Generation literati. . . . [T]he little bar became a coveted gathering spot for New York artists" (Kelley Thelonious Monk *226–27), LeRoi Jones among them.*

E. Franklin Frazier was an American sociologist (1894–1962) who studied and wrote about African American history, culture, and politics. His 1957 book The Black Bourgeoisie *was a major study and critique of some African Americans' middle-class aspirations. Jones, having had his own complicated history at Howard University and with his own rejection of black middle-class respectability, was a supporter of Frazier's work.*

Ed,   [late May 1962]

Glad you finally returned from those cities of light. All that business you speak of must have been tiring, maybe aggravating. But I'm glad it was you instead of me. I mean I've had enough of the middle class spook for the rest of my life. And with the addition of those Mo. crackers, man, it sounds tasty. The Baldwin-Wallace routine is really too much. I mean this president sounds like someone you could kick with complete equanimity . . . and sad thing, or tragic thing is that America has got boots interested in becoming that kind of person, each day thousands more. Imperfect replicas of frigid white folk. And the young ones, not the already demolished wd be or will be drs. and lawyers, but the vaguely suspicious or vaguely bright cd be had if there were people like Franklin Frazier, who just died last week, around to tell 'em what the fuck is up. At Howard Doc Frazier was hated by the rest of the faculty (who were subjects, tres unwilling, for his book Black Bourgeoisie, which is good reading) and the general block headed half white coons of Washington. Oh, well.

The Harvard types sound funny too. V.R. "Bunny" Lang, I know of only from a few works around in *i.e.* and a play of hers I Too Have Lived In Arcadia, and a poem in Measure. She is highly regarded by New York School here (O'Hara &c.) but I never read much, tho I did like stuff of hers I'd seen.

Sure you can drive a car into this burg, and maybe park it right in front of the house . . . since we now live on what is really the Bowery & there is usually some space. Parking is usually the big hassle w/ autos here . . . but there's usually space around this neighborhood. I don't know how to drive at all & I'm not about to learn. (Tho, strangely, I can drive a motorcycle or scooter.) And this is a pretty hip neighborhood . . . halfway house sort of . . . between very fashionable Greenwich Villitch and very hip lower east side. Loads of old Bowery type bars which I frequent more than old Cedar now. Also McSorley's right around the corner (the ancient ale house.) My steady drinking buddy, Larry Wallrich, has departed with his family to Mallorca, so that saddens me quite a bit. He owned the Phoenix bookshop[125] . . . at least the best in this town & a veritable den of iniquity in the backroom. Now, it's all vanished and Larry writes me that "Mallorca is not a drinker's paradise". . . so the exchange has not worked.

Some funny things begin in this season. Spring. Raining and cold today, but mostly nice so far. Yesterday, the weekly poets painters softball game. We won yestiddy 23 to 16. The score wd've been better but Oppenheimer insists he is a pitcher. He walked about 10 yesterday . . . in 3 innings. Gil played center field yesterday and misjudged two balls by about 20feet. We going up Friday to see the Giants when they come in to play the Mets. I'm an old Giant fan, or at least, now, an old Willie Mays fan.

Prynne letter sounds hopeful. He helped with the F.B. obscenity case too, with a really positive letter, unsolicited, which I read for the grand jury. Or, in case you haven't heard, man, we won that ol case! I was in front of the gj for 2 ½ hrs first day, 3 the next. I pulled Baptist cornball—god loves the truth—routine. Whole story will appear in next bear. Great turning pt in whole shit, was federal prosecutor asking me, "What proportion of yr mailing list is homosexual?" Yasss. Filthy motherfuckers, eh? I sd, "What proportion of D.A.'s office is queer?" GJ yukyuked. Then he sez, "Well, now, isn't it true that a great many artists and writers are homosexuals?" I sd, oh yeh? I wasn't hip to that at all. The last big fag bust I heard about was in the state department. Which cooled him out rapidly. At any rate, We won ma.

It's certainly ok with me for Newly Fallen to be published in England. A good deal, I think. I heard about the Creeley-Allen project from Don . . . and I hope it doesn't conflict. I don't see why it shd. We all know each other too well to get involved in that kind of fuck up. At least I hope not. Don and I are very old friends and I'm sure there won't be any diddling around. I want to include a great many more writers than the other project and this book will be hardcover and slick paper. I think the Grove thing will be in the black cat edition of Grove's. The piece of yrs I spoke of was the thing that was in Migrant. Also prose I dug in Measure, the "Skagit Valley." I mean in Migrant 3 (now I see the misunderstanding) the piece called *Ed Dorn in Santa Fe*, which was listed as being the last third of a longer work. I thought that section very beautiful and have always wanted to read the complete thing. I want the ant'y all fiction and I wdn't want to use the Maximus. So, you can let me know one way or t'uther.

The *Poetry* thing was pleasing . . . I don't have to tell you why. Olson and I got a big laugh out of what some feebleminded Canadian wrote to him re/ "The new Jones-Olson *axis*." Whew! I mean somebody ought to give people things to take

---

125   Larry Wallrich traveled a great deal, opening secondhand bookstores in both London and Vancouver after having run the Phoenix in New York.

up their time and energies so we don't have to hear phrases of such splendid irrelevance. At any rate, it looks good for an opening now in that camp. Sorrentino, at my urging, sent poems . . . and they took two of his also. And Duncan tells me that's their policy when admitting mavericks. You may submit twice a year and they'll accept at least two poems. I wish you'd send them something. Also, while on that . . . I got a letter from David Ignatow[126] (know him??). Anyway he's editing another WCW issue, this from Beloit PJ. I was in another collection recently from Mass Poetry Review . . . I guess everybody's trying to honor the old man before he goes or something, which is ok, I suppose? Anyway, if you want to send something:

c/o Ignatow, 660 W. 180 St. NYC 33

Denise sicked him on me.

If you can, get the Gil Evans album where Gil is supposed to be conducting Cecil Taylor's[127] music. Wow. Evans is seldom apparent on the thing which is cool w/ me. But all the Cecil sides (with Cecil's own group) really cut out! We here starting a private jazz club, to try to set up noise in opposition to the silence bastard club owners imposing (Cecil, Ornette,[128] Archie, Oliver Nelson,[129] many wild young heads not working . . . instead you got to hear Art Blakey and his drum and bugle corp or fakes like Roland Kirk[130] (the man who plays 4 horns at once & flute with his nose . . . actually!) Club tentative called The Mississippi Sheiks (after that groovy old time group) will rent loft and get charter like regular old hood organs in village and be open only for members so as not to get busted all the time. We'll be able to pay the younguns at least scale & really be able to hear some good music. Ornette and Cecil have already agreed to play. Archie Shepp (Cecil's former tenor man & a wild Ben Webster-Bird man played two nights ago downstairs in painter's loft on first fl. of our building. They cooked till 6am. But I was layed up here on couch conked silly w/ drugs! Dope! And cheap Bowery wine (Me and Oppenheimer and 5 or 6 other guys went in Bowery type bar and broke the bowling machine but everything was cool because the drunk bartender knew me (he sd!)

I hope Bob survived the great north west and got into Canada! Is he there permanent?? How? But anyway, I'm gonna go outside and follow some young girl

---

126   David Ignatow, American poet, 1914–1997. Active in publishing, Ignatow was for a time poetry editor of the *Nation*, among many other editorial positions.

127   Gil Evans, American jazz pianist and arranger, 1912–1988. Cecil Taylor, American jazz pianist, b. 1929. The album Jones is referring to here is *Into the Hot*, released in 1961 on the Impulse! Records label. *Into the Hot* showcased not just the Gil Evans Orchestra but the John Carisi Orchestra and the Cecil Taylor Unit as well. As Jones points out, the Gil Evans Orchestra was not the featured act.

128   The connections between music and poetry continue to overlap. Many of the writers were deeply involved in music, especially jazz, and many of the jazz musicians were writing poetry as well, Cecil Taylor and Ornette Coleman being cases in point.

129   Archie Shepp, American jazz saxophonist, b. 1937; Oliver Nelson, American jazz saxophonist and clarinetist, 1932–1975.

130   Art Blakey, American jazz drummer, 1919–1990; Roland Kirk, American jazzman, 1935–1977.

or somethin' exciting like that. Or maybe just go in the kitchen and eat. Love to everyone there . . . we all looking forward to seeing yall. Take care too.

Roi

Pocatello, May 27, 1962

Dear Roi—Just a note—I wanted to talk to you suddenly, desperately—wow you put me on to Dubois when I read your Tokenism piece[131]—and was sort of thinking to go to the library for something of his but hadn't until the other day I picked up a paperback *The Souls of Black Folks*.[132] Reading "of our spiritual strivings" I could hardly finish that 1st chapter—I was crying that much, damn I near couldn't make my eyes look anymore but got thru it all choked—I tried, in my excitement to read it to Helene but couldn't do that either.

You've probably known the man's work for a long time—so may not get with my present feeling—of thanks, to you, regret for myself etc.

That old Hebrew use, that pull of those most powerful of the nouns we have—like [. . .]—that pressure of the full emotional sense of the word, like also Dahlberg's[133] opening paragraphs of his autobiography. Well it isn't so much the man's a negro—tho that stuns me too, knowing only Ellison and Baldwin, Wright[134] etc.—~~Wow~~ shit I wish I hadn't been so slow—I could have told, for instance, that very nice kid at Lincoln about such a man as Dubois. Oh well, that's not the point really—I feel I have been gripped where it most belongs by that man, you must be very proud to be of him, no?

Love, Ed

[April 1962]

When you arrive here?!

Yoiks! Somebody must be screwing around with the mails. Maybe Idaho CIA or YAF[135] or some such. It's a gas about somebody picketing the 21st siglo de oro.[136] I've finally been outdone . . . & by a staunch progressive. I figured it was cool enough merely to walk slowly around the 20th w/ the proper signs, like, "I'd rather be anything than anything else" or something. Anyway I sent a letter early in the

---

131   "Tokenism: 500 Years for 5 Cents" appeared in *Kulchur* 5 (Spring 1962).

132   W. E. B. DuBois, *The Souls of Black Folk*, 1903.

133   Edward Dahlberg, American writer, 1900–1977. Dahlberg, an influential literary critic whose work was decidedly nonmainstream and nonacademic, taught for a time at Black Mountain College. Dahlberg was for a time an expatriate in Paris, briefly a member of the Communist Party, and a humanist, proletariat writer in the 1930s and '40s.

134   Dorn is referring here to three important, influential twentieth-century African American writers and thinkers: Ralph Ellison, 1914–1994; James Baldwin, 1924–1987; and Richard Wright, 1908–1960.

135   Young Americans for Freedom, a conservative youth organization.

136   The Golden Age.

week. I wonder what happened? Glad that you did get to Dubois. One of the only *interesting* Negro "intellectuals" & a beautiful man. Only a handful of books have ever been readable, which is tragedy of the great rush towards whitedom. This book I'm struggling to finish (was due Apr 1) is, in part, facing up to that void where the Negro artist has *refused* to be meaningful, or found it impossible, simply because he thot, even art, was merely another way *in*. A social gesture, providing in the end, a means toward social (never cultural) recognition, as an American white man! Only people like Jean Toomer (great member of Hart Crane intelligentsia & Ouspensky-Gurdjieff [137] nut) even found out about The *AVANT-GARDE*. And they cd kill him off easy because he was a fag & a *mystic*. But read his love novel *CANE*, if you ever, or those poems in *Broom*, *Secession*, &c. Even Wright, whose *Black Boy* is a fantastic book was never as *aware* as Toomer, [138] tho B.B. is more moving than *Cane* because it's an autobiog shot, rather than "Western Art." Ellison & Baldwin are middleclass (& O.K., middlebrow) finally, as well in since Ellison means the Academy or at least the appropriation of stale Europe tho they have on Al Jolson vines. Baldwin, my ol buddy, wants, more than anything, to be *respected* (& second, to be loved). He has long ago assumed a public pose. His supreme agony is that he *still* wants to fuck men (which is hardly cool for white house guests!

&me?

I'm going to get busted one day for carrying a gun or nodding in the library. They always beat you . . . "even youse smart ones" sd to me.

Love Roi

Ed,   Sept 6 [1962]

I really dug *Hands Up!*[139] I have already passed it on to Marilyn Meeker at Grove. (She says she "knows" your work & digs it: so, at least, that's a good thing.) I'll probably use the long story *Beauty* & the Black Mt. piece, *C.B.&Q.* I'd like to use the Seattle story too, but I have space problems.

Turning cold here already & sweaters & tweeds out already. I'm MC on a benefit program for Ray Bremser,[140] who is back in the slam again. Money needed for

---

137   The Ouspensky-Gurdjieff System is a set of spiritual beliefs, loosely connected with Sufism.
138   Jean Toomer, African American poet and novelist, 1894–1967. A central figure in the Harlem Renaissance, his novel *Cane* remains his most well-known work; he also has an important body of essays and poetry.
139   *Hands Up!* is Dorn's second full-length book of poetry. Though Jones sent it to various publishers on Dorn's behalf, the book was finally published by his own Totem-Corinth in 1964.
140   Ray Bremser, American poet, 1934–1998. Bremser spent time in prison on more than one occasion; once for being reported AWOL from the United States Air Force and again for armed robbery, for which he served six years. Bremser's poetry was published in *Yugen*; Jones, Ginsberg, and Corso were staunch supporters.

lawyer, so his wife got about 10 poets to read. She is really a thoroughly despicable person . . . she sent me some poems about how sad it is . . . but, of course, how hip to have a poet husband in jail. Wow! Current events.

I've got to split for the place now, but I'll send a longish letter soon. Still trying to get this goddamned book finished, &c. Otherwise, not much is new. Anyway, what's happening in Pocatello? Here, we are trying to keep warm. (You see Cantos 115 & 116 in new Paris Review, plus interview w/ Pound by *Donald Hall*[141] . . . who, by the way, asked about the future of "free verse." O.K., *Kulchur* out & I've got to read that Burroughs-Trocchi[142] again. Hope you got the Bear! Love to everybody,

Best, Roi

—Sending a recent poem—

Hot rod—   [1962]

(a quick list):

a.   Grove just received *Hands Up!* From Don Allen. I called yesterday—they sd some word by tues or wed of next week.

b.   Random House sent (is sending) Rite back to me. But I think there's one more possibility before Sterling. Paul Blackburn's new wife[143] is one of the editors at Pantheon. And she *called* me & asked me to send it up there . . . she having got the word before us mere mortals, that Epstein didn't dig, "It didn't *seem to work*," the book. So, shit, I feel it's just as good possibility as any other.

c.   Coltrane Time is really a re-issue of *Hard Drivin' Jazz* w/ Cecil ostensibly as leader. I've mentioned this record in DB, Metro, &c many times because it was 1st time Trane went that way, & under C's influence. I think it's a wild ride esp J.C. I always dig K.D., who's been forced recently *to work in a record store*!!! & Joe Early makes 180 a week Larry Hellenby 200+, Joel Oppenheimer 125 (which he spends very quickly, to give the impression of knowledgeable bohemianism), shit! As that Spanish cat once sd once in BMR,[144] "It's a hopeless world," or something.

Speaking of Joe Early—he just sent me a pamphlet he & Basil King collaborated

----

141   Donald Hall, American poet, b. 1928. A prolific poet, Hall would be appointed the poet laureate of the United States in 2006.

142   *Kulchur* 7 (Autumn 1962) featured a piece by Dorn called "Notes More or Less Relevant to Burroughs and Trocchi," to which Jones responded at length in his September 21, 1962, letter to Dorn.

143   Sara Golden Blackburn. Golden was a freelance editor and writer and for a time in the 1980s and '90s a member of the board of PEN International.

144   The little magazine *Black Mountain Review*.

on. In fact a whole bunch of them to distribute. Fuck him and his Sicilian wife!! Like you dig that noxious little pamphlet. & like dig the first Max Finstein imitator God has seen fit to lay on our wondering heads.

You hear news of Chas taking a semester job at U. Buffalo. 5000$ for 2 lecture courses. Word from Duncan. I'll have a letter in a few days. I found a copy of [. . .] *Decadence w/ the Dissociation* essays, &c.

Love, R.

Poc Sept 17 [1962]

Roi Jones: I got yr letter and you got mine so now that's straight. This is just a note to say so. I too will get a letter to you this week. Today was the first day of classes. 2 Eng. Comp courses at 8:AM and 10AM Mon Wed Fri—ah I found myself in near catatonia today but my heart was elsewhere etc. I'm supposed to introduce the muthafuckers to "language" can you imagine that? Why language would shit its drawers if etc. I tried to . . .

I wonder if Grove will print me. Doubt it, don't you? Anyway, you already know how I thank you for doing that for me. You know I just couldn't send it "cold." More later. Love to all—Ed

Dorn makes note in this letter of poet Stephen Jonas. Born Rufus S. Jones, Jonas will-fully obscured his own early history; he died in Boston in 1970, but his birthplace and date are unknown, "though it has been reported that he was born somewhere in Geor-gia perhaps in 1920, 1925, or 1927. He was probably raised by adoptive parents" (Selected Poems 1). Jonas was an important nexus for his contemporary poets, being a writer who knew everyone and introduced them all to one another, as well as passing along things to read. Joseph Torra notes in his edition of Jonas's Selected Poems,

> *Jonas constantly gave out lists of books to read; he had steeped himself in the work of Pound and Williams, as well as contemporary poets like Creeley and Olson. . . . It was the Olson reading [the Charles Street Meeting House reading, in 1954] and Jonas's ensuing encouragement that led Wieners and [Joe] Dunn to Black Mountain College in North Carolina." (3)*

After briefly meeting Dorn when they were both in New York City (a place in which neither poet quite felt at home), Jonas wrote to Dorn praising his poetry, comparing him to Mozart: "In this wise you stand shoulder to shoulder with Wolfgang Amadeus Mozart." Dorn's poetry was beginning to gain respected recognition as an important artistic voice.

Roi   Pocatello Sept 18 [1962]

Things are quiet here. I just now returned from down there, where I talked for
2 hours about Indo-European, and I don't know two hours of that shit or any other.
Introduction to language. I'd like to stick a few words shaped like cutlasses on their
throats. They need that old cure of shitting or going blind.

Had lunch, a bottle of homebrew, which we are now making to great advantage.
Now sitting down here. I put on that old lady in satin, Ray Ellis,[145] and she's singing
now like I'll be around. I still want to scream when I think of it, that death they put
her thru.

Wonder what you are doing today. Fall is too very much, I always wanted to be
there at this time. I frankly hate summer. It's the original drag, not a hole to hide in.
It must be easier to have it cool at the top of the stairs, the cat shit, carrying gear
back and forth. I've never felt so cut off . . . all the work I had to do around here.
The class room bit begun . . . now to settle back into my own hopeless rancor? Out
of desperation almost I went on this trip to Missoula over the weekend. Drove up
one day and back the next. 14 hours each way. My eyeballs were square by the
time I finally fell on the bed. In its weird way Montana is very wild, they are the
most relaxed there of anywhere west. But god how one yearns for a friend. Ie, *not*
the friendliness of the stranger.

It's very strange Billie singing in these mountains. I sat w/ my chin on the window
sill and last night watched a fire started by a bug, across the valley, on the other side
of the Portneuf. A nice bright blaze. The poor bastard can't go much longer, the FBI
is after him. This was something like his 7th fire and it finally made it. Beautiful light
fire color. His other attempts were fizzles. They are just fires in the grass. The grass
grew very much, tall, last spring because of all the rain, but now it has been dry for
months and the "fire hazard" is "high."

At night it gets very cold, we have to pile the blankets on. We can see the whole
other wall of the Portneuf Valley across the way and in the folds of the mountains,
where there is more moisture because of a northern exposure where the snow
lingers, there are scrub oak, mountain maple, and other shrubs, they are now
bright deep rich red, looks like blood running down the cuts of the mountain.

I did indeed get the Bear after all, I had just lost it before I could get a look
at it but Helene found it, so forget that request to send it. Indeed I also got a fan
letter from Steven "Steve" Jonas, comparing my work to that of that giant of the
musical world, Wolfgang Amadeus Mozart. "In this wise you stand shoulder to
shoulder with Wolfgang Amadeus Mozart." Something about a quality of music.
Well, who's next. He goes on to say the city is shitty and that's why he didn't dig
come thru to me in NY. I hadn't had that sense of it, unless I don't quite get what he

---

145   Billie Holiday's *Lady in Satin*, orchestrated by Ray Ellis.

means by coming thru. I thot him very interesting. I wonder what happened to that superqueen he had with him.

I reviewed McClure's torture for Kulch but I don't know if they want it yet. I certainly had it there by Sept 15. I haven't yet received the K w/ the notes in it. You said you had it. It must take a couple of weeks for slow mail to get here.

It is damn reassuring to know you like *Hands Up!* There are a lot of things in there, you know, from back when I had the book you did, but which I didn't feel right of that context, but which seem to make it there, anyway it seems unlikely to me that Grove would bite on it because it lacks a certain sensation they've committed themselves to. I guess time will tell. If I can't get the big cruisers to take it I can always try some little press. I would personally like to get it printed. I'll bet that Doubleday outfit wants polite lady poets, no? I could always try Scribner's, altho I don't know I am so gassed by those oddball presses (odbl in the sense they come into this thing late) but I do have a contact with Hutter,[146] but you probably know him too. Well anyway, if it came to that I could write him and you could mail it from there rather than going thru the biz of mailing it back here etc. The point for me is that I want to cause you as little running as poss. Good god you must have your hands full. How's that little Chili, that leetle Jalipeno, zat leetle peppercorn Hettie? You tell her to stop that boosting, I mean I wish she had protection. Helene washed the blanket we took from you, and thinks to send it soon now. So the little kiddies won't friz.

I wanted to write very much and didn't have anything particular to say. There just ain't no news from here you'd be likely to understand. But I'm with you and will come again as soon as possible. Just give my regards to everyone there, and love for all of you.

Ed

Ed,   [21 Sept. 1962 ?]

I been up all night pretending to work, without cigarettes, and nothin' happened anyway, tho I read a great story by William Eastlake[147] called Three Heroes and a Clown, from an old Evergreen. Now it's almost afternoon, and Kellie and Mama just got back from K's first day of school. And she seems gassed, which I hope lasts for a while.

Got the letter and funny little poem, which I dispatched straight way to Groove.[148] No word from them, but it usually takes a while, since BRusset must read

---

146   Donald S. Hutter, 1933–1990, American editor, writer, and publisher. Hutter was an editor at Scribner's from 1957 to 1967.

147   William Eastlake, American writer, 1917–1997. Eastlake's novels were primarily westerns.

148   Grove Press, which was headed at the time by Barney Rosset.

each word of anything published in the joint. A real small time outfit. And the new
ER just like a house organ for Gunk Products, Inc.

Season of Industry here . . . just about finished the book. Sat day (or night)
dreaming about reviews, reviews, and that horseshit. And I decided to frame a
really acid rebuttal to Newyorktimestype critics, though, for all the fuck I know, the
goddamn thing might be as bad as Elisabeth Janeway[149] would say it is. Anyway,
letter will run something like, "Dear Sir, Your blueballed crooked liver mother eats
Sammy Davis," or something conservativer.

I was on the radio just now, on WBAI, a taped re-broadcast of program
symposium I was on with Cecil, Ornette, Gunther Schuller, George Russell.[150] It
sounded pretty good, tho I am always astonished at how high and faggy my voice
sounds. Mostly, all we did was put down a lot of folks. My job was simply to name
names when the musicians got too polite. It's the kind of simple ugly task I like. Like
being a mugger.

Speaking of the "airwaves" Joel—just shaved his beard off—Oppenheimer is
now THE NARRATOR of a radio program, called, strikingly, enough, The Poet In
New York. We already taped one session, O'Hara, Sorrentino, Joel & I. It was o.k.,
again, mostly putting a lot of folks down, tho of course, on this number nobody
bit their tongues. Sandburg really got it for that crumby poem he published "for
WCW" in last week's Times. Don't look for it, if you haven't seen it . . . it'll fuck up
your appetite. It says how much delivering those babies must've been like writing
poems, and that typical SB idiocy. Also, Joel is lining all kinds of people up to serve,
tho, of course, he's a hell of narrator since he tries to talk all the time.

I was supposed to be working with new educational channel, WNDT, as advisor
for long term jazz programs that sounded like they could really make it, for a
change. But now, the fucking television performers union is picketing because
they want all the teachers and advisors attached to the station, like myself, to join
the goddamnd union. Man, what a lotta shit. But I'd feel stupid trying to cross a
picket line, &c. But I'll be damned if I'll join that sappy union. It's like the mafia
or something, they're not going to do a goddamnd thing . . . they just want their
cut. But I'll just wait and see what happens. Also, I may be going into the teaching
racket a little further this year, take a couple of classes at the New School, tho I'm
not sure I'll be accepted because my teaching record is so pisspoor. Hope so tho,
cause we cd use the money . . . maybe to throw out the window on the passing
bums ("beggars," some guy from Denver sd. I said man there ain't no beggars in this
country . . . you got the wrong hemisphere or at least the wrong reel.)

The piece in Kulchur I really like, though, of course, I cdn't disagree more. (Sorry
you have furnished Sorrentino with so many articulate arguments, which I must

149   Elizabeth Janeway, American author and for a time arts critic for the *New York Times*.
150   American musicians Gunther Schuller, b. 1925, and George Russell, 1923–2009.

listen to now, screamed over ale in McSorley's. Like last night the cat says, "I hate people who want to change the world." Ugg. I mean, really, maybe I am square, but I don't see how you can write out of that clutch, I mean if you *really* believed that, and put yourself through LIFE clinging to that feeble stance. Shit, anybody can go to sleep. But I think that somehow Gil must not realize that what he's saying *is* the political act. And one of the oldest dodges in the business. Even The Company of Jesus ain't going that far. Maybe he shd read Huxley or Waugh[151] and find out how to really be pettily elegant.)

But you push, and pushed me, now, with that reading, towards, perhaps, a harder rebuttal. When it takes shape, whatever platform or material it has to use, hell, maybe a fake review of the works of Gramsci, I'll come back waving. There are ideas in the thing that ring, and hurt too, I mean now socio-politically . . . which is how I took the thing, I mean, fuck literature, which I suppose we ought to say perished when Joyce took that "a" out of Daedalus' name. Not ready to pick just yet, but when you said, "Burroughs shd've been a Tman (which is a crazy pun yaknow?)" and "He's against Democracy and with Dulles, Goldwater (?)" I was stung. Because you're right, but only literarily. But man, Trocchi is an 'imported' beatnik (who actually shd've been in Europe trying to get European writing up to the Babbitt stage, i.e., the "local" weakness which is manifest in the whole of European character. Babbitt *was* our strength . . . and we shot off from there.) but like Chas sd in that Kooky piece in Yugen 7 about the "lateral coup d'etat" and setting themselves up as "the elite among the masses" is solidly correct as I see it. Trocchi cd make that same McSorley's statement. "I'm too hip to think about the world." And I'm not opposing Burroughs to this attitude. Burroughs is, make no mistake, a Gestapo. But the thing is placed where it can be gotten to as valid. An entertainer? O.K. With the same intent as Cervantes ending his era, a handbook of disaffection, and not the "phony disaffection" of sitting out in New York's Hudson on a boat. Man there are 7,000,000 right down the street from Trocchi who'll tell you in a second he's a nut. Democrat. But dope, is valid, in that there's only one person out there with Burroughs at a time, and they're all him. Beatniks are never junkies. Never. You could shoot (I mean eliminate) Burroughs, but Trocchi could be *used*. He could be put to work in Random House tomorrow earning 8,000 a week, and still retire hiply to his sanctuary on the Hudson.

Literarily, CB is just a novel. Which is, I think, simply a commercial act. Movies are better, and so's tv. Burroughs comes, ok, out of Joyce. But from the angle, of personae. That destruction that Ulysses made of the 19th century idea of "characters." Like Charles Blip, age 47 ½, a rich landowner, or such. Who is, in fact, *different* from the writer. Ulysses brought in the one mind idea. And with it the virtual anonymity of any personae in the writing. Heroes, Villains, Protagonists by the

---

151   Aldous Huxley, British writer, 1894–1963; and Evelyn Waugh, British writer, 1903–1966.

dozens. A cat like Robbe-Grillet[152] strikes out because he wants his H's, V's, and P's to be description. Emotional adjectives yet. Oh, well, I'm gonna write something not on Burroughs and Trocchi, but with some grim clutch that can include them. Yahh. OK, as not to bore you, I'm gonna stop and take some pills for my cold. I'll tell Di Prima about the bear, &c. You take care, and love to all those other Dorns. (It's 48fucking degrees out here already.) Write when you get time from the academic life.

Love, Roi

Roi,   Pocat Sept 21 [1962]

I wouldn't even bother going thru this for anyone else, but you mother of all people, in the first place, my nomination for pres is Roi Jones and for assistant postmaster Gil Sorrentino. Why assistant. Precisely because he couldn't be trusted to see that *all* the mail goes thru. If you [. . .] a liberal-reactionary, as he is, you've got to figure that everybody from Bill Biculey Jr.[153] to F. Castro is going to put arguments in their mouths. They, are the most promiscuous people in the world. I mean *all* of them! The whole fucking lot. The argument is all the more wasteful between us. I know damn well we see eye to eye. Yet you can sit there and mention people in amounts like 7,000,000, (which is an old census figure anyway) well, jesus christ what's that. Bill Burroughs is a fink and knows it himself and Trocchi isn't. It's quite plain in whose hands rests the capability. Not in Trock's. You have got that internationally reversed because a lot of hate operates for both of us. Like I hate Burroughs you hate T. Alright. That's fine, they are both quite insignificant men, it seems obvious. But I take Burroughs to be the only dangerous one, for the world at large. The world at large being the only context in which I interest myself. Like I am the steadfast generalizer of my time. The particular I take as the dullest of all possibilities. The argument as to why Burroughs is employable by all those factors is as familiar to you as me. The only appealing thing about T is that he's a fuckup. Like I mean a failure. The most notable success on the face of it even, is Burroughs. He even has the gall to put that hayseed Kerouac down, his superior in at least 15 ways. I've seen that documented by the way.

But fuck Sorrentino. Man he comes from gangster stock and that has *always* but always been weird reactionary stuff. It is the most vested of interests anywhere. But can *you* read Burroughs on Bureaucracy and get anything out of it different than Sorrentino? & Hoover? I dare say you're trying to shit me if you can. Did I not in those notes say Sorrentino (yes I gave him that mention because he's the only other mother who's bothered to say *anything* about that creeping parasitism besides Creeley who is so goddamn simple-minded it's appalling, about "sociopolitical"

---

152   Alain Robbe-Grillet, French writer and filmmaker, 1922–2008.
153   William F. Buckley, American author and commentator, 1925–2008.

matters) was WRONG about B's workmanship? And did I not say T knowed nada about the practice of WORK? And do not those cross-wires clean me of my whole intention. And is not the rest simply a record of my disgust. I *detest* Burroughs, the principle subject of those ambulatory notes. A mistake in method perhaps I guess. It meant this to me: There were certain lies in his method. They needed to be able to come along and do it and they didn't, for two years!

For 2 years! Nada nada nada has been said about this man. He is a ghost in our midst. And by the way I don't think he has a goddamn thing to do with Joyce. Really could you? Oh fuck. The only thing that would appeal to me now would be for me and you to go up-town to mug J. Rothenberg. In that apt.

But do you, I hope you don't, assume that I too don't want to change the world. God you don't think that. God I want to throw it away altogether and remake it, altogether, like with the help of the whole world. And that includes GS, as of course assistant postmaster in a little town in Austria.

But that gets us back to the main differentiation btwixt us. Like I couldn't for the life of me *UNDERSTAND* your fascination with that Russian gook poet who visited you in NY and about which you were reporting in that book cat's apt in NY, on 8th st. In a very short while those pricks like him and that international pederast B are going to say to us that we can join em or be like always on the outside. I just wanted to say, before they ask, I'm against em. And if that's a commitment which it certainly is, I'm sure you're going to somehow manage to say the opposite but mean the same, which we two I like to think always do. It is a good necessity. I just hope we don't get caught, isolated from each other, across the river, waving. With nobody to talk to at all. For god's sake don't write a fake review of that cat I've never heard of, write a think on the Burroughs syndrome, like flatten it out.

All love as *always* Ed

By the way, you must be aware the weird "usefulness" Sorrentino puts W. Lewis to. I mean one of the greatest writers of the early 20th cent. he manages to always use for his own "purposes!" That man cld only get published in America by Regnery—a "Catholic" press in Chi.[154] I wish we could talk—our minds are so much alike (if you don't take that as an insult) that we require speech, very fast—like—don't be so fast, movies are not *yet* the equal of the best 1000 novels—!!!!

Oct 4, 1962

Dear Mother Roi—Why don't you write? I'm sorry I wrote that idiot letter to you! I so much wanted to hear from you. All your jazz bit in Kulchur very enlightening. I only just yesterday got the mag due to something sloppy abt the mails. I felt very

---

154   Regnery Press was founded in 1947. According to its own press material, in 2007 it was "celebrating 60 years as the nation's leading conservative publisher."

rancorous and stupid when I wrote that letter, again a sorry state. Please write. I'll give you a letter of recommendation if you want a job as Gov. Barnett's secretary![155] No? If you still want to head up a regiment, I'll join. Love, Ed

Ed,   [1962, Oct 8]

I just ran across the hippest quote, which I right away incorporates into my tome . . ." The negro, with his unusual sense of rhythm, is no more to be called musical than a metronome is to be a called a Swiss music box." George Jean Nathan the editor of the old American Mercury wrote that. Too much.

Sorry to be so slow, but I'm still trying to wrap this muthafucking book up.[156] And feel useless in the attempt. Like all kinds of things I want to say disappear, in favor of other (?) shit, or something. Or sometimes, too many things come into the head at the same time, and I shoot off in futile attempt to, or fuck it all anyway. But I'm just about there now . . . though they tell me I have to hunt up copyrights or some shit for all the quoted blues lyrics. Write ASCAP,[157] and many of the pricks'll probably want loot. And a lot of the shit is public domain or God, I don't remember any *source* for most of it. Or else I transcribed lyrics from old records. A big dripping mess anyway.

Big party season coming up to make things harder, or we not to show? Haven't got data straight from Group headquarters yet. Anyway, group of citizens having birthday party for me tomorrow night. 28, and all used up. Man, we played touchfootball last week and I'm still hobbling around. Some big television actor faggot knocked me on my ass a couple times. Not like the "old days" when you could give 'em a hip then take it away. Now they keeps it.

On the Burroughs-Trocchi debates, you seem right most of the time, or I can agree anyway. Though, it goes back simply (I guess) to fact that I just don't dig Trocchi's writing and was fascinated (or astonished) by Burroughs.' Of course you're right about "capability," and that to me, one way or the other, i.e. directionally, is what any work ought to be. You certainly argue Trocchi right out of the picture as any *force* at all, which I am always ready to agree about. So how can he write, being as you said "insignificant." But Gil, very strange, to have come on in that letter in the Bear saying, "I need love, I must have it," &c. And further cant about Lear. Then to reverse to hating "guys who want to change the world." I dig that anybody that don't is not even junkie hip, since those humble citizens at least want all the dope

---

155 Ross Robert Barnett (1898–1987), governor of Mississippi from 1960 to 1964. A staunch segregationist and the son of a Confederate veteran, Barnett clashed furiously with the civil rights movement. Dorn's letter is, clearly, loaded with sarcasm.

156 *Blues People: Negro Music in White America.*

157 American Society of Composers, Authors and Publishers, which maintains and protects the copyrights of its members.

they can get. Wow, what an erasure of all the possible ways into . . . what? LOVE BEAUTY TRUTH (as McClure wd put it.

And about "putting words" in mouths, &c. If you want to see that principle in droopiest example, dig next Kulchur, Gil's article on painting. I had been reading heavy in Hulme,[158] *Speculations*, *More Speculations* &c. and that gangster's influence on Ezra. Also as further political intrigue to my understanding of Sorel (Reflections on Violence)[159] who I think very important, as far as the "forms" any dissident socializing force may take. As yet there is no other way for me to think about Mississippi, except (Unless I want to come right out and say to all my boys, less go Mao or Che style, to the bush and blow up the fucking bridges . . . which don't have to be that far off, you dig?) I have to play far from actual pragmatic ideas, which is Mao, and go for theorizing ideas of *reform*. Social not military. Though, as I said . . .

Anyway, dig the cut ins on 2nd hand Hulme in the next Kulch.

What's with Bob anyway? I got kinda formal thinking, maybe not sounding, letter from him advising on ant'y. Oh well, I guess he's up to his ass in Vancouver by now. I guess I must've said before I want to use your *Beauty* and the CB&Q . . . maybe the other if we have the space. I oughta be able to send you some advance loot soon. As soon as the Corinths lay it on me. No word from Grove yet.

I just committed my last official middleclass act, bet on that bastid Floyd. And I knew full goddamn well Liston was gonna kick his ass.[160] Now, dig, suppose Sonny Liston was the cat going into the U of Miss. Then I'd feel something. Cause he's the Negro that needs to get in, not any white talking black bourgeoisie horseshitter like Meredith.[161] "What I'm doing will help all Mississippi." Man, you can dig him rehearsing those lines in the basement of the NAACP local. "All Mississippi" don't need help! That's music from the tombs of "credit to your race"-ism.

Anyway, Love, Floyd P.

I FINALLY FINISHED THAT GODDAM BOOK

[10/9/62]

Dear Sir,

What you mean sending me sappy post cards like that. I *dug* letter, and wd hate to think of you *pulling* punches, dig! Anyway I did read a letter earlier today.

Yrs, Sonny Liston

---

158 T. E. Hulme, English critic and poet, 1883–1917. Hulme's writings had a formative influence on Modernism. Ezra Pound championed Hulme's ideas, particularly in *ABC of Reading*. Pound, in turn, was a major influence for the New American poets.

159 Georges Sorel, French philosopher, 1847–1922. Sorel was a proponent of radical, revolutionary social and economic systems.

160 Sonny Liston, 1932(?)–1970; and Floyd Patterson, 1935–2006. Their recent boxing match resulted in an easy, one-round knockout sweep by Liston.

161 James Meredith, b. 1933. Meredith was the first African American student to attend the University of Mississippi, in 1961.

Dear Roi   Pocatello Oct 11, 1962

Thanks for the letter. Your acid wit, like they say, always cheers this wilderness for us. I just took a line of that C'n you gave me. Put it on a mirror as instructed etc. Very heady stuff. In fact that's me on the couch lookin' at you. That's her in the fuzzy orchard. When we got back here in Aug, it was so hot you cldn't stand it. That was the coolest place. The group w/ horse is left to right Paul, Helene's confused brod., Ray, Fred. The horse's name is "big head." The saddle blanket is being put on him. I mean he is being put on w/ a saddle blanket. The little horse in background is "thunder," a little injun pony born in Utah. Big Head is a local horse. Just above big head's head is chink's peak which is much higher than you might imagine from the pict. By road, it is 5 miles up there.

I have no fear that we agree in any case. I knew goddamn well you were loaded against Trocchi, I heard you and Allen argue that warehouse creative bit, a new bit according to Allen, that night I mean in the Cedar when H and I were there, when? It was a year ago last spring, or winter—Feb—it isn't the point but Mr. Creeley has the same emotions you do on that score. I can tell you one thing, I did myself a bad disservice when I forgot to add the notes I had abt how Trocchi went very fucking far off when he did those imitations of Burroughs in that evergreen rev. say a year or a year and a half ago.

I don't know what's with Bob, he's behaving strange. He doesn't write me anymore, just many postcards saying (viz.) he'll write soon. We've written regularly, say monthly, for years. I don't know. I think he's having trouble, but determined, finishing that novel. He's had I think 1 grand, from those people for it thus far, so may be a little pressured. He sent a note last week asking me to read at U.B.C.[162] in January. They'll send plane fare. So I'll see him then and that'll be groovy. Say, I'm thinking you'd be a natural for them to ask to read, and if they haven't I'll ask Creeley why they haven't, it could have to do w/ distance, but anyway didn't you say you might make the west coast this fall? I asked you but you didn't answer. The point I'm trying to make is that *if* you did go there, to UBC, or even the coast, I'd like to try to get them to book you here. Would you be willing to if it were possible? Please when you write answer questions.

This is just a note. I won't expect a quick answer. Good luck w/ the book. Will it eventually be a paperback? Wasn't that Liston Patterson bit too much. I felt kinda bad abt Patterson getting it so soon tho. Was that fixed at all? Poor Floyd. Like man that was unfair. Liston weighed too damn much but you're such a gangster yourself you were probably rooting for Sonny.

                    Ok, my undying love to Hettie Kiddies and yourself - Ed

---

162   The University of British Columbia.

P.S. If Grove won't go for H's Up would it be wise to let those English cats do it if they wld—viz—Davie, Prynne and that guy Victor Gollancz?[163]

I'll be sure to dig those things you talk of in Kulchur. I always read it all anyway. A review of [. . .] by me in there too. You might not dig [. . .] I mean you can always be depended on for a quarrel. In fact you're very damn hard to please!

Preface to a Twenty Volume Suicide Note. . . . came to be considered one of Jones's strongest books, but in this letter he is looking to move forward, claiming it to be full of "apprentice poetry, and sloppy horseshit." As Jones became more and more politicized —and became, ultimately, Amiri Baraka—the critical reception of his work began to change. Critics have often wanted Baraka's work to remain the same as, or at least harken to, his earliest poems; Baraka finds this to be a frustrating request. Baraka has talked about this need for changing art, placing the conversations between himself and Dorn as part of this process and crediting Dorn as a key influence in his own work and thinking.

Jazz musician Ornette Coleman fights the same battle: "'The music industry is mainly interested in my past, never my future,' Coleman told Down Beat *in 1998. 'People always want me to talk about what I've done. I always hope I can do so much* more'" *(qtd. in Anderson 186). In the same way that jazz is often constructed around Cold War ideas of it as "America's art form" (Anderson 187), poetry centered around a particular ideological framework, like Baraka's (particularly in the early '60s), runs the danger of being locked into place by critics or an audience clamoring for more of the same.*

Ed,   [1962, Oct 14 ?]

Just a note because I'm kinda high, and Hettie and I are sitting around playing drunk house, the night before our anniversary. Tomorrow we're going up to see that Orson Welles flick *Mr. Arkadin*, which finally got here from Europe. And even NYTimes admitted it's a brilliant thing. So that'll be the anniversary present (plus I'm finally gonna paint the goddam john). Now that I finished that blues book (though now hungup w/ permissions and shit like that) I'm gonna put another book of poems together. I feel almost a dynamite compulsion on that angle, since that Preface to . . . really weighs me now, with all the pickups, apprentice poetry, and sloppy horseshit in it. Think maybe I can get a halfway decent book together right about now. It certainly is "devoutly to be wished . . ." &c.

Went up to see Albee's new play "Who's Afraid of Virginia Woolf." It is exactly like the mfing title; incredibly clever. I mean this cat has singlehandedly resurrected the embarrassed ghost of Oscar Daddio Wilde, or wow, I'm giving him too much credit, only George Kelly and stuff like Craig's Wife, &c. It's definitely drawing room though,

---

163   Victor Gollancz, British publisher, 1893–1967.

and the dialogue as a newspaper reviewer would say, "crackles." But when he tried to *tell you something* you don't know it's strictly bush. Like one character walks around saying "truth or illusion." Yeh. But Uta Hagen (coming out of a Bette Davis bag) is really great. I met Albee during the intermission (one of O'Hara's friends) and he seems like the kinda cat who'd vomit on you if you punched him . . . just to get the last word.

No word from Charles yet, and I haven't really written him. I guess I ought to get at that very soon. I'm wondering what he's up to. Or, at least, what's on his mind.

Hornick[164] and I, and I guess fellow editor got into a thing the other day. They got this long piece from Corman (about 20 pp?) on Creeley. Nobody bothered to show it to me, figuring I guess that I'd like it, I spose in general line with recurring personnel, &c. But, shit, I don't really think I want to read 20 pages of Cid Corman[165] on Creeley. But Lita, and Gil backed her, said it was a "necessary" piece. Not as necessary as a good enema I'm thinking or an efficient assassin. Fuck. She's giving large cocktail party next month, and I'm supposed to get the music. Hah, she's gonna get the shit scared out of her because I'm gonna get Ornette. (Cecil went to Sweden.) See if they can drink with that fanatic breathing down their bosoms.

Otherwise, not much going on, except when you get a chance get that new Rollins' record *What's New*. It's mostly Latin numbers (that new Bossa Nova fad) but Sonny really starts smoking on a couple of the tunes. It'll knock you out.

Anyway, I'm getting too dopey to write now, so I'll just go back to my cups and spikes (though I'm supposed to be writing a book review for Village Voice on some book called Black Nationalism from Yale, written by some African.[166] Boy have I got some hot words for this patronizing black sonofabitch. Oh, which is something I forgot to tell you . . . I was in a debate, yeh, a debate, with Dan Buckley, WBuckley's younger brother about Cuba, formal thing set up by some happy village conservatives . . . but dig this, I got disqualified. He said I couldn't be "objective," you dig, because I was black. So I called him a mealy mouthed cocksucker. And everybody gasped or grinned, or something. Anyway, I was disqualified and they opened the meeting to the floor. Can you beat that? Wow. "Objective." I thought that word died with WWI or at least Stein. Shit.

Anyway, take care of your objective self, and your objective family. And let me hear something objective from you for a change, willya?

Objectively, Roi

---

164   Lita Hornick, poet, publisher, and literary critic, b. 1927. Like Joyce Glassman, Hornick was far too frequently the target of Jones's decidedly misogynist language. Hornick was known to organize large parties in New York City, most of which Jones and Hettie were invited to and many of which they attended, despite Jones's barbs. Particularly with the women he encountered who held editorial or publishing positions (Denise Levertov can be counted among this group), Jones exhibits resentment and anger at the kind of power over his poetry he perceived them to have.

165   Cid Corman, American poet, 1924–2004. Corman was the founder of the little magazine *Origin*.
166   E. U. Essien-Udom. *Black Nationalism: The Search for an Identity* was published by the University of Chicago Press in 1962.

Dear R.   10/16/62

This man is known in local circles, by the disrespectful as "hardon" Bistline.[167] He must be an Iowan Ray says. He means a pitchfork a pair of biboverals and you got it. He must be quite a drinker if the bar association is that appreciative!

OK. I don't really have anything else to say . . . just fucking around this saturday afternoon. Last night there was about 10 inches of snow, so everything is understandably white today, sorry, but it can't be helped. Listening to Miles'[168] Lazy Susan, remember that. Haven't played this record it seems since we lived in San Fran where we played it every day. It conjures things like Creele's abduction of Mrs Rexroth, Mr. Rexroth's visits to our apartment storming "where is he? Where is the sonofabitch?"[169] And other things like that. Channy trooping in with all her little friends, staring at all the drunks, the kids, naturally, fascinated, pointing, and the drunks were rather high powered even in those days, JK, AG, RC, an asshole name of Leonard Woolf, or was it wolf, or wolfe.[170] I mean how could you care. I don't know why I'm bothering you with all this, but it's just that kind of an afternoon, and in lieu of talking to someone I gotta write a letter. Now they're playing It Never Entered My Mind. And oh yes the orlovesskies.[171] That place just off Divisidero. Not far from that horribly stuffy communal apt of McClures, with that horrible man James Harmon[172] in it.

This book I have barely got started, whew barely. Actually I hope it isn't corn. There isn't much point to it save as a try at the literature say from Guthrie, Shafer, Oakly Hall[173] and cats like that to Douglas Woolf, Abbey, and cats like that. The principle of it will be based on something like, loose, and general what happens when you cross the Mississippi, and why and when did it get that way, and why. The large question, What is the west? will have to be answered at least a try at it. There are certain real assumptions one can start with for example. The west is not a habitation, people don't "live here" in the common acceptation, and never have, on the other hand in a loose sense, it is a place. I think the whole provocative theme of raw and utter exploitation which come right up against us, can be used. Uh, I don't know, as yet it isn't too set in

---

167   Dorn attached a newspaper clipping containing a picture of municipal judge R. Don Bistline; the photo shows him holding a plaque given to him by the American Bar Association for "Outstanding Court."
168   Miles Davis, American jazz trumpeter and composer, 1926–1991.
169   Robert Creeley fell in love with poet Kenneth Rexroth's wife Marthe; she eventually left Rexroth to be with Creeley.
170   Jack Kerouac, Allen Ginsberg, and Robert Creeley. Leonard Wolf, b. 1923, is an American writer. Wolf was a teacher at San Francisco State University in the mid-'60s. While there, he started an alternative to the university, associated with Haight Ashbury, called Happening House.
171   Peter Orlovsky and Allen Ginsberg.
172   James Harmon, American writer, edited, with McClure, the little magazine *Ark II-Moby I*.
173   Woody Guthrie, American folk singer, 1912–1967; Oakley Hall, American writer, 1920–2008. Hall's books were most often about the American West. Dorn's love and study of the West was always important to his work and way of being. Dorn was a western poet, with a deep concern for its representation in literature and song (hence the reference to Woody Guthrie). He was often highly critical of what he felt was the overromanticized, incorrect vision of the West so many artists and Americans held.

my mind, so called. But it is a thing that interests me simply out of long residence and curiosity, and I'll try of course to make it as wildly readable without being unreadable as I can. Ie, I plan definitely to settle on a form of prose that is consistently easy to deliver. My own background reading, ie, the nature of the Missouri, ie, Vestal[174] says it's SPACE primarily, etc, will be secondary and simply used to support or undermine what I think is going on in the liveliest prose about this area I can find. I think I'll arbitrarily start with a piece like Parkman's LaSalle,[175] and work it as much as possible from there. I must confess I am most interested to bring it all Woolf's way if possible, at the detriment probably of Eastlake, ie, in certain respects, the novel, say, not his use of the short story which I find ok. John Hawkes[176] exists like a Kafka to this area. A novel like Warlock[177] for instance I'll probably, if my sense of it satisfies the future like it does the present (how's that you mother) will be simply interesting, for various reasons, for instance the odd tac on the heroine. There will certainly be a chapter putting down the present westerner, but that will be easy as entering a pie eating contest. Nothin but a ball.

Ok. As little as that is, I would be damn glad if you could help me get an advance on same, and I'll be able to send something to you by jan or feb or if bad luck march.

Love to you and fam and all the NY mothers—Ed

This letter was written as the Cuban Missile Crisis was underway, after it had been revealed that the Soviets were building missile bases in Cuba, just before the crisis was to be resolved. Dorn and Jones over the next letters revealed the impact of world politics on individual lives. They express fear and anger, and, once the resolution comes, deep suspicion. They flirt with the idea that the entire affair could have been governmentally orchestrated and that caution is needed on their own individual parts. Dorn articulates the sense that individual citizens seem to matter very little in the workings of international government, taking him further into his always growing position of staying as far away from the governmental machine as he possibly can.

[Oct 24, 1962]
Wed 24

Ed,

I don't know what you're thinking, but Kennedy's speech & the last day's events have frightened me, & mine, out of our wits. Now, the radio says the Russian ships

---

174   Stanley Vestal, American writer and historian, 1887–1957. Vestal was a scholar of the American West.

175   Francis Parkman, American historian, 1823–1893. Dorn is referring to his book *La Salle and the Discovery of the Great West* (1869). Robert LaSalle, 1643–1687, was a French explorer who traveled the Great Lakes region of the United States and Canada, the Mississippi River, and the Gulf of Mexico.

176   John Hawkes, American writer, 1925–1998. A postmodern writer, Hawkes was known for his experimental prose.

177   *Warlock* was a novel by Oakley Hall from 1958.

won't change their course, nor, I suppose, will whatever history has stacked . . . OH shit, I mean what shit. I mean who the fuck are these bastards to kill all of us? What futile bullshit. For what? And pompous motherfuckers like Kennedy sit & say this shit knowing, I suppose, that it won't be their kids who get blown up. Goddam. There oughta be or I oughta start a group of terrorists whose only mission will be to bump off all the self-righteous motherfuckers who don't believe they're gonna die! Anyway, man, I just don't know what to do. I'll probably be in the slam—one way or another—in a couple days—or hours. And the best things I can think to do seem bizarre & crummy. But what?

There's all kinds of picket lines and speech making going on here now. Same old shit. I'm supposed to speak w/ [. . .], "the fighting assemblyman," tonight in front of the U.N. "FOR PEACE." I don't even know if I'll make it. I certainly don't feel like it . . . or anything else. Sorry for this shitty letter. But you take care of yrself, I mean, yourself & send all our love to Helene & children.

Love, Roi

Pocatello, Oct 24 [1962]

Roi—What I meant was—How goddamn dirty can you get—I mean when I heard that cat McElroy (?) came back from Germany, called back from a business trip, that *was* too much. It seems clear the "terror" was the *least* of it, ie, beside what filthy "arrangements" they made. And what abt that election angle? Isn't it just plausible Kennedy & Kruschev made that little scene w/ all their fabulous machinery of arrangement available to them—is that such a simple minded possibility? It seems an interesting question to me because if, and I mean all of us, we're being turned *on*, it just might be interesting to not let it happen again! It just might be. All those coordinated angles—like the pre-packaged shelter food bit flopped like the trampoline craze. This time they were encouraging one to buy conventional canned goods like between that "shelter" date and now. There was a falling out between the promoters of that line that didn't sell, and the chains. Oh shit, that's shit, but that's my point—is one really to take a thing that's blatantly outside one's power, just like they tell you to. I refused then and I still do, to get more than casually involved w/ their shit. And it seems perfectly obvious—the machinery of *their* involvement is theirs—we have none at all—it's just like that interesting ratio of Wright Mills[178]—that the dispenser of opinion, say Paul Harvey,[179] is one man. His audience at noon on wed. numbers 25,000,000. It is as they say nolo contendere.[180]

---

178   C. Wright Mills, American sociologist, 1916–1962. Mills's *The Power Elite* talks about the relationships among the political, economic, and military elite in the United States.

179   Paul Harvey, American radio broadcaster, 1918–2009. His immensely popular daily radio show, *News and Comment*, was a forum for airing his conservative beliefs.

180   "No contest," as in a court of law.

And the gov. can't be sued without they say so. Hail Fidel—I hope he poisons Guantanamo's water. If he of course comes out of this with his neck he'll be doing excellent—if he wrings some guarantee that he won't be invaded he'll be doing good. Ok—this don't add much. How are you? I sent letter & poem yesterday & and had a brief spell tonight—I *finished* another vol. of verse since *Hands Up!* I ain't never worked so much before and that makes it for me more & more—Love Ed

P.S. So dig as I listen to the "news" the area has shifted wherein US interest lies—to India and the blockade has been lifted. And who, have you heard, "started" that? China? India? You'd never know if you didn't know, and, I don't—& who cares fuck them all!!!!!!!!!! I mean man are these issues? involved!? Ha Ha—eat your biscuit and shut yo mouf.

Pocatello Sat Oct 27

Dear Roi—I was gonna write you . . . I just couldn't, I didn't know what the hell was thot there of all this sick horror, I suppose I thot you were more cool and on top of it, but am goddamn glad to hear, perversely, you were put on too. The so called name brand news we have out here is just what you expect, there was not any indication whatever that there were demonstrations, or whatever . . . and we here felt finally embarrassed to see how we had been tricked by that buildup, that it was all too clearly a goddamn plan anyway, one of those crises that are intended to last a decade by both sides . . . and how our patriotism was stirred to the point at least we were very ashamed for our country, for an anti state cat like me, that's perhaps even sentimental. And I felt very regretful for the first time about the few cheap occasions I had taken to mention Fidel in an off light, such disclosure I had taken to be dissenting, had taken to be an above-state sentiment. Well fuck, I know at last I oughtn't to keep a loose tongue about such men, and about such things I don't really know anything about. I suppose that shock of self knowledge if you could call it that came after your put down of my sick poem on Mrs Herrara that woman who cried and got shot. Also Allen's lovely piece in Palante[181] sobered and corrected me. But Helene and I both want to thank you for that gesture, your letter about a common human emergency, thank you and god bless you. It is a horrible thot, I suppose no matter how abstract, to think of not seeing you and your family ever again, if it should be so.

I came home wed after classes and the news at that point was getting pretty fucking banal. I must confess we were thinking as best we could, final thots, or at least trying to figure what those are. I worship my friends, and a tack like the worst devils the world has known propose to take, comes remarkably closer to killing my gods off. And that that must be all there is to it, among other things.

---

181   *Pa'lante: Poetry Polity Prose of a New World* was a one-issue magazine featuring poetry by the League of Militant Poets, including Jones.

I tried to finally think, that it was a very subtle kind of death they had in mind for us all along. Something like the total pre death involvement of the psyche, ie, that what was being outlawed was the very possibility of a private dignified death, say vaguely, what Jung talks of as the necessity of the organism, at that crucial point, to know what is happening to it. Your special terrorist group, to bump off the safe ones makes great sense. A lovely idea, as long as all ultimate estrangements are by death anyway. Unfortunately perhaps for you and others, your structure is not terrorist. You were born with other things to do, and now, no matter how funny that may seem, it isn't. You know anyway the degree of preoccupation the terrorist must have, must be inherited. Terrorists are terrorists at birth.

Oh well. In the meantime we're being attacked by animals, the geese are pulling off my plastic windows. I need a plastic bomb to take care of immediate needs, the heifer is trying these days to stick her horns thru the sides of our shack. Take the enclosed for what you can get out of it and with comes our love to all of you.

Ed

[Nov 1 ? 1962]

Dear Bill,

The adding machine workers are revolting . . . Please come back home with us. Give up your unsuccessful career as a junkie-faggot and return to the fold where they loves you.

Signed, Pataphon Rose[182]

So what is happening there in the woods? Whatever, thank you too for that letter . . . I think the point about depriving "outlaw" was your word all of us of private dignified death was what caught me most. But then the idea that "Terrorists are terrorists at birth" is very true also. BUT, that very idea makes it at many levels almost an irresistible concept, as my birth, &c. Which, you think about it, prepares so extraordinarily for that act. And the entire hideousness, or almost entire, I've been running from all my life is the COP OUT, i.e., of course, the fucking nigger bourgeois cop out compromise. Man, you think what my old man must be thinking now. Because, I don't care what he's into, or who he thinks he is, I know that somewhere beneath all that not very expensive veneer he Knows he's wrong, that he's been wronged, and that his whole life has been a nasty cop out. Who said that about "growing into regret like an old bone." Also, and maybe this is just ego, I feel now cut off in a strange sense, form the poorer Negroes, though probably closer to them in my feelings of social frustration &c., which I need to make as stark as possible. The thing is I know those people Don't read. And that is my frustration, I suppose. Why I

---

182   Patapon Rose is a reference in William S. Burroughs's *The Wild Boys: A Book of the Dead*.

have gone speaking on soap boxes and getting rapped in the face. Because I feel there are things I can say to them which will be of value. Anyway, I will send you a review that Village Voice is supposed to use this week or next, about Black Nationalism, or actually, that's the name of a book by this Harvard African, which I really tried to smash, maybe too severely. Anyway, there are some things in it about all this, said possibly better. But this town is tighter than a drum, tho pressure eased somewhat. Greatest thing was last Fri. when some friends and I had something funny planned, and a uniformed high officer policeman shows up early in the morning . . . 10 or so, comes in (I almost slammed the door it shook me so) and says to me "We have reason to believe that you are a member of a group that plans to demonstrate in Times Square." He then produces a leaflet that sure enough I had helped draft, but there were no names or anything on it! Just a thing calling for Negroes (it was distributed in Harlem) to show up in TS and get their heads bent. The man continued, after I asked him why he came to me, "The point is that if you do show up in TS, in any capacity, *even on your way to buy a hotdog*, you'll be arrested." He left.

Now shit, the motherfuckers are even working inside around me. I thought that FBI shit on the radio (Levine, ex agent . . . you read about it)[183] where the cat says 1/5 of Communist Party aqui are FBI agents, and that they contribute the largest single share of loot to the party! [. . .] Anyway, the other thing we had thought to do was further thwarted, BECAUSE WHEN WE GOT THERE THERE WERE SIX SQUAD CARS SITTING IN FRONT OF WHERE WE WERE TO GO . . . and this was just to make some kind of disturbance. And there not that many people who knew, or were directly involved! Fuckit anyway.

Last week *was* hysterical. Some Reichian cat named Jack Green who puts out a mimeod sheet called "Newspaper" called me a "fellow traveler" in the bar. Sd Fidel was the worst tyrant since Hitler and Stalin. And here's a cat, this JG, who fancies himself a deep intellectual, making fantastically learned comments on The Recognitions, and assuring his blond lady companion that all Kruschev needed was a motherfucking ORGOneBOX!! And this bald stinking cat with droopy socks is calling me a fellow traveler. Wow. It was really all I could do to keep from hitting him. But then man to top that off, after this cat leaves (I did tell him he cdn't come in the bar anymore . . . totalitarian-like he kept saying) Joe Early, the poet, Gil's paisano, comes in with the identical shit, only, & get this man, he says "what are you saying, man, Fidel Castro? Machiavelli said all that for all time." So man, I honestly couldn't resist this time, I had to tell him that he'd stolen that bit of script from you . . . in that Landscapes poem. He denied it like crazy, and was so angry, christ he wanted to hit me. So apparently he went home and, as he said "read all of Ed's stuff and couldn't find it," so I mentioned the Bear, and he went limp. Now

---

183   Jack Levine was an FBI agent under J. Edgar Hoover, one of the first to speak out against the Hoover regime. He eventually lost his job over the testimony he gave in which he accused the agency of using illegal wiretaps.

Now, there Dorn, you got a whole "Anti State" school going on out here don't know their ass from a hole in the pavement. Hee Hee!

To forget that shit tho, Saturday we had a great costume party for Halloween or something. Anyway, we had a live band, Archie Shepp, and Don Cherry sat in, and some fantastic young tenor from D.C., who's name like out of old coon myths is merely "Wrench." I came as Green Lantern, I guess Hettie came as some weird dancing girl. Blackburn's chick had a *real* costume, I mean not just a made up thing, or a lovely thing out of context, but a real honest to gosh Tyrone Power Blood & Sand Costume. Whew. Gil & Joel didn't wear any costumes. Pretty hip shit. But anyway most everybody got blind and staggering drunk and twisted to good music, which is always a gas. I mean I'd rather dance to Coltrane to some Dance Band, even an R&B one. Vicious hangover the next day, though it was certainly worth it.

Against all the other shit kicking around, there's still that basically human act, the drunken party. And I fully intend to rustle a few up in the next few months. Lita Hornick having her annual cocktail party this Sunday. Ornette was sposed to play, but he copped out because the girl he's going with now sys that whole crowd (Kulchur, &c.) "are phoney." Only catch there is that this chick used to go with Sorrentino. INCEST. EXPLETIVES. AMALGAMATE WHOREDOM. SOCIAL INTERCOURSE. Anyway, I got Roy Haynes and his group, so it ought to be a smash anyway. I love to drink those people's booze.

Hey, I forgot you were asking me about a trip? To B.C. to read? When is this? My California thing delayed now, because Di Prima went out there and Hettie would cut my throat if I even hinted at wanting to go. I don't want to see that bitch, but she got the calif. idea from me, and cut out to make my departure impossible. She's living with a cat named Allen Marlowe,[184] a practicing homosexual. You may have seen him in the Chesterfield he-man ads (really!)

Don't worry about the book, I think Grove may take it. They won't give you a party like they gave Gover (1hundreddollarmisunderstanding) at which they employed 6 r&r musicians in green brocade coats, who pumped bad sax noise up the ladies literary drawers, but I do think they will. Hope you got the magazine there by now. How does it seem? Hard for me to know, away from it so long, but having all the material almost memorized. Only goof is asshole printer didn't show me cover proofs and put wrong price on 75 cents instead of a dollar, now we lose money whether copy sells or not. Great, eh? Sorrentino mentioned something about a Western book non-fiction you intend? Well if you get an outline of it, and maybe 30 or 40 pages, maybe I can get my m-f publisher WMorrow to give you an advance. They very generous, and love me because I don't close parentheses. So if you are, do. Maybe can get at least an option on that small amount of pages of

184   Alan Marlowe was one of the founders of the New York Poets Theatre; he and Diane di Prima were married for several years in the mid-1960s. Marlowe was also a figure in Andy Warhol's Factory.

about 3bills, then with completion of say 3 chapters, maybe 7 bills mas. Think about it! It's what we lived on all last year. Oh, and I really do dig that Idaho poem! That *discursiveness* I envy you so much for in the first, 4 pages, up to "the marvelous beauty," &c. and then the thing follows that line, the chick's, more closely, and then the last pages, about page 9, where you start to move away from her strictly, as "like the boxcars on its skin/" is very very moving, and clear, for all that. Yes, it really does move, the whole thing. And the Pound crutch does work. Tho the "this" repeat might focus poem where you don't want it. Anyway it is a marvelous thing. Write. Love Roi

Pocatello Nov 13, 1962

Dear Roi—I've been frantically rummaging some books to straighten me on the China bit. Old stuff to you maybe but stuff I'd never read. To wit Payne's[185] *Mao Tse-Tung* and *China Forever* (the latter I couldn't get w/ much.) and collected works in five volumes. Whew! That Mao's a wild sounding mother. I think I finally understand that India is to be liberated, and not in any tricky sense at that. The maps alone, showing his armies' movements in the annihilation campaign are art and Payne's conclusion that Chiang is a neurosis—wow. And all that reality of the Long March. Anyway—I won't bore you anymore with my catching up. I never read that thing either—*The 18th Brumaire of Louis Bonaparte*.[186] Have you?

?Que tal?—Have you finished indexing and referencing your book?

MODERN POEM

I left for the great outside
My mission was to piss
a final dying fly
buzzed with his November
wings
orbiting my ears. He shit
in the air about my bliss.

Again, what do you think? Helene is sick—ill—I have convinced her she must go to le docteur today at 3.30pm. We're sort of waiting around for that—she's got a *Bad* cold—she grunts and groans. I sent you a card yesterday w/ a big potato on it. This is just still to tell you I'll write soon. Why don't you go to California anyway and ignore Diane di Prima—Hettie will dig that. Let her bake her a poison cake! Like why don't you stop by here we've been to visit you twice! I'll start thinking you're an

---

185   Robert Payne, English writer and historian, 1911–1983. Payne was a good friend of Olson.
186   *The 18th Brumaire of Louis Bonaparte* by Karl Marx, 1852. The "Eighteenth Brumaire" refers to November 9, 1799, in the French Revolutionary Calendar, the day Napoleon Bonaparte made himself dictator by a coup d'état.

inconsiderate man. Otherwise things go on the same here, the weather's gathering its forces for a punitive expedition. We're digging in!

Love to *all* of you

Ed

Jones's notions of himself as an activist and his growing Black Nationalism began to weigh on Dorn's mind, and as Dorn notes here, he couldn't "come up with any relief in [his] own mind about any of it." As Jones began to separate himself further and further from "white" culture, Dorn took issue, believing that Jones's culture was not so different from Dorn's and that these two had more in common with each other than Jones did with the activists and "terrorists" with whom he claimed affinity. Dorn seemed to understand that the driving force behind Jones's politics remained tied to his poetics; he is a poet first and foremost. Dorn's visions of the United States were as dark as Jones's, but he lacked the faith in the literal bomb throwing Jones was professing.

In fact, he didn't think that Jones himself thought this was a solution, believing instead that Jones felt guilty for not having "thrown a few bombs in the right places." And though Dorn understood the sentiment, he did not think it would actually accomplish any real change but really that "throwing oneself against their goddamn walls is one of the most useless *USELESS fucking kinds of suicide ever invented by man." The possibility of watching Jones commit this sort of suicide prompted much thought and discussion from Dorn, and the two would correspond about these ideas over many letters.*

Nov 15, 1962

Dear Roi:

The largest ocean in the world is a strange one.[187] Not literally I mean, but I read it a couple of times . . . and it has deepnesses that look like they wouldn't come of that fragment of form. The whole issue is certainly interesting enough for any number of magazines, ie, more than most could hope for. I think one slight trouble with #8 is that it wasn't around for so long when it should have been that there is a behindness about it, altho how could one say that about such things when there is no known frequency anyway. I don't sabe. It's probably beside the point. As for my own piece there,[188] it's three years old now. It's like reading someone else. But that's rare too, if it's yourself.

Winter kicked in the door and threw shit all over us the other day. In a way it's a relief, you know what's around. I've been thinking about the content of your last few letters these past days, and not coming up with any relief in my own mind about any of it. Certainly, as I said, terrorism is an act of birth, ie, in birth's hands, and you as several other people have an innate right to that. I think it must be

---

187 "The Largest Ocean in the World" is a short story by Jones, published in *Yugen* No. 8.
188 "Some Notes About Working and Waiting Around."

true then that what they say about the "opportunity" factor of say revolutionaries and such, activists of all kinds I suppose, ie, that the time has to be right. The question then becomes when do you know when the time is right? After all. wow, pretentious, AFTER ALL there are one or two revs for every, not even every generation that numbers in the billions, now. So ok, by birth you are an activist, but culturally you're not. Now wait a minute boy! Culturally you're really not. Now I don't give a shit what color you are you got the same culture I got. I've talked to you. You got other things sure, of course that's true, but we understand each other very well I think, and I think it's because you came from a lower middle class liberal background and I came from a lower class conservative background. I mean right here that sociological reality, the lines of dispensation of, cutting across the whole middle patch, name your terms and the connections can be come up with . . . in that sense america *is* the great leveler, like I know goddamn well you're too cool to throw yourself on the chest of say Adenauer[189] with a knife in your hands as say he gets out of the lincoln continental on park ave. And you probably aren't ultimately devious either, which takes care of the hidden aspects of the same act. Perhaps I'm wrong. But I take it your anger, insofar as it can be localized, is poetic, and I am very aware that adjective is in bad odor, but I am pronouncing it here to describe the fact that you ain't cut out for the shit you are one of the most articulate annumbrators (?) of, and furthermore, you mother, you ought, of all people, to know, throwing oneself against their goddamn walls is one of the most *useless* USELESS fucking kinds of suicide ever invented by man. I think you're just feeling guilty that you haven't thrown a few bombs in the right places. Well that's okay. But you gotta face that you were here in the right time in the wrong place when your irresistible captors had other things in mind. And you are as screwed as the rest of us. And further what about this? The poor of your race will occupy you the rest of your life which I hope you don't half cocked end sooner than you ought and that's a very articulate pick out of the whole problem because I have seen your middle class and they're as bad as if not worse than my middle class if only because they aren't even as hip. (But granted the white middle class has been hip for three centuries. oh give me strength!) and the smile on my face isn't even a smile at all?

But it is pretty damn clear that no matter how much I respect Mao if he had had the fbi and the t men on his ass during the long march he would definitely not be around now. For instance Chiang was a fortunate opponent, with his German advisors, and given a general population that dug the whole thing, there's your time, and there's your place. can you seriously argue for yourself a place in the evolution of revo-wow, lution in an utterly captive country where they are still talking horror struck about whether they should give medical aid to farts above age 60?[190]

189   Konrad Adenauer, German statesman who became the first chancellor of the newly formed West Germany in 1949.
190   Medicare was not signed into law until 1965.

Oh no man that would be too far out if you argued that . . . your problem is passion as against sense. Like you are talking about nothing but another and exotic sense of self murder. And I know that can't interest you that much. But I'm getting banal certainly. I do take it seriously. As without question you do. I wish there more to it for our time. I wish certainly there were a true verge instead of a manufactured one. As of writing, of course the whole beat thing, and then the follow up of whatever there was of writing anyway, before that outburst, all of it was so goddamn synthetic, synthetic worries, synthetic gains, reported in synthetic journals. Man there is no satisfaction to be had. Don't you get it, this is not the age of anxiety, of the lost generation, or protest, or much less the beats, those cut ups, but the age of the calculated unsatisfieds. Time dribbles out like shit down a toilet. We don't even have a toilet here. I built too hot a fire in the coal stove and now it's too hot iner.

Helene is sick, poor thing, she couldn't breathe too well, and then besides the miracle drugs i got some decongestant pills which noc her out and allow breathing. She's getting better. This morning I bottled 13 quarts, a six pack, and two cases of home brew. We have a beer tester which tells the temp also and I make 6% beer. Helene is asleep. I have to go get Fred at two-thirty, about a half hour, and take him to the mfn dentist. I'll mail this then. How the shit do I get out of dese mountains. Que tal? Look I will mail this letter anyway, but I don't know if I should. I seem to horseshit more and more these days. A poor fucking 'unemployed' carpenter hit the Idaho Falls bank for 2000 the other day, on the radio they at first said 100,000, and the bastard, who was called by the professional name "bandit" didn't even have a car? He got three blocks and by the next morning was in jail, there was some unexplained lag of time (during which time they must have kicked him silly) and now his bail is get this 50,000 which is half the purported money but many times the real.

Love Ed

And give my love to Hettie and the children please

nov 15, 1962

Dear Roi:

The largest ocean in the world is a strange one, Not literally I mean, but I read it a coupla times...and in any desperate that I ok like they couldn't come out of their hypaneoid form. The whole issue is certainly interesting enough for any number of magazines, ie, more than most could hope for. I think one slight trouble with #8 is that it wasn't around for so long when it should have been that there is a behindness about it, altho how could one say that about such things when there is no known frequency anyway. I don't sabe. It's probably beside the point. As for my own piece there, it's three years old now. It's like reading someone else. But that's rare too, if it's yourself.

Winter kicked in the door and threw shit all over us the other day. In a way it's a realief, you know what's around. I've been thinking about the content of your last few letters these past days, and not coming up with any relief in my own mind about any of it. Certainly, as I said, terrorism is an act of birth, ie, in birth's hands, and you as several other people have an innate right to that. I think it must be true then that what they say about the opportunity" factor of say revolutionaries and such, activists of all kinds I suppose, ie, that the time has to be right. The question then becomes when do you know when the time is right? After all, wow, pretentious, AFTER ALL there are one or two revs for every, not even every generation that numbers in the billions, now. So ok, by birth you are an activist, but culturally you're not. Now wait a minute boy! Culturally you're really not. Now I don't give a shit what color you are you got the same culture I got. I've talked to you. You got other things sure, of course that's true, but we understand each other very well I think, and I think it's because you came from a lower middle class conservative background and I came from a lower class conservative background. I mean right here that sociological reality, the lines of dispensation of, cutting across the whole middle patch, name your terms and the connections can be come up with...in that sense america is the great leveler, like I know goddamn well you're too cool to throw yourself on the chest of say adenauer with a knife in your hand as say he gets out of the lincoln continental on park ave. And you probably aren't ultimately devious either, which takes care of the same act.
Perhaps I'm wrong. But I take it your anger, insofar as it can be localized, is poetic, and I am very aware that adjective is in bad odor, but I am pronouncing it here to describe the fact that you ain't cut out for the shit you are one of the most articulate annumbraters (?) of, and furthermore, you mother, you ought, of all people, to know, throwing yourself against their goddamn walls is one of the most useless USELESS fucking kinds of suicide ever invented by man. I think you're just feeling guilty that you haven't thrown a few bombs in the right places. Well that's ok. But you got a few days more ere it's the wrong place when your irresistable captors had other things in mind. And you are as screwed as the rest of us. And further what about this? The poor of your race will occupy you the rest of your life which I hope you don't half cocked end sooner than you ought and that's a very articulate pick out of the whole problem because I have seen your middle class and they're as bad x if not worse that my middle class if only because they aren't even as hip.(but granted the white middle class has been hip for three centuries. oh give me strength!)

and the smile on my face isn't evne a smile at all?

Eddie,   Nov. 19 1962

Glad to get those two letters. And just now called that publisher, Wm. Morrow, who by the way just sent me a new contract for the second vol. of my proposed history of ex-slaves, the first vol. of which, is finally done. Agent got me 1000$ more of an advance, tho I won't get it all at one time, which is good. So, we probably manage to live 4 or so more months in this controlled squalor, moth-eaten middleclass types. But Joyce Glassman, my contact there at Wm. Morrow, sd yr idea of a book is "Terrific!! We'd love it!!" So, if you can send chapters, say 2 or whatever, but some 30–50 pages or so. And an outline for the rest, or the entire project, I'm pretty sure, so's Miss Glassman, that you can get some kind of option, say until a few more chapters, (usually 30r350.00) then when about 1/3 of book you get some kind of advance, maybe half book, not sure. Advance usually 1000 to 1500 (minus option) and then once you get that in its cool.

Fact is, I've sort of decided the essay, non-fiction routine more in my line, and with the big log I want to roll re/ cullid folks in the u.s. (I.e., what is their bizness? Now that they been here so long, &c. Second vol. about the formation of contemporary black sensibility, most especially the soi disant intellectual and bohemian . . . and the connections, of course, w/ even those descendants of lower class conservative ofay groups . . . I am at least to push this for these next two volumes. The third being, as you might guess, general and specific political history, that is, as it has faced and molded the negro, and as it threatens now to face and mold.

Of course you're right about the fiction of my place as a bullet proof activist, but I do see the need of me taking at least the maximum non-active risks. And in the writing placing it so far, exaggeratedly to the Left, (even the jazz criticism . . . that it correct misconception and lie based on the digested system, and the systematic disregard for economic and finally socio-cultural fact, i.e., even the making of music must have some human reference, and its that I want to make sure of. As this first book is simply saying, "When a man plays this way, or makes music like this, it comes from this other circumstance, the amplifications and ramifications of which are . . ." and so forth. That being, after the initial clarifications . . . and the music part if not merely a gloss, but to me a definite way into a man, a group's, thinking.) But I want now so badly to push *extreme*, and as I see it, the one huge difference between myself and say, Allen G., in that I have a *program* (and I don't don't mean that I am "a Leftist" much more extreme than that name pretends, and certainly less organized, but still a program based on realizable human endeavor. The bombs yes? I certainly wanted that (and still want it For Real, and not as mere thought) but my idea is more complex, and, I trust, more interesting than simple terrorism (vide Che Guevara on the uses of terrorism in his Guerilla Warfare, which is supposed to have scared Gen. Maxwell

Taylor's[191] ass open.) I mean, now, I want to put together a body of work that will at least provide some text that can at least be referred to IN THE EVENT OF the desired explosion, which, and I grow weary at my terror at this thought, Might Not Happen. This country is perfect because it provided an admirable socio-cultural vacuum cleaner in which to suck all its citizens . . . fortunate and unfortunate . . . as I howl when those stupid trotskyites here tell me about "the working class." Oh, yeh? But that is the very meat of it, that even the fucking LEFT, or formal radical commitment in this country is completely bourgeois, as it ascribes an area of society, i.e., all its efforts are pointed at a class THAT HAS NOT EXISTED FOR TWENTY YEARS (and *never* existed at all from that washed out 19th century European Commune point of view). All of which to say that there has got to be another way into it. The simplest social facts have been obscured here, even historically. As contemporary history is the most twisted, re-touched, social lie we got going. No one really knows, that is all the stupid liberal cocksuckers who mention "Hungary, what about Hungary?" at the drop of a hat, even Knows what happened there. I mean, actually; what it meant; its real political significance. I mean it will only take another year before Battista is a *good guy*, and you know it. I at least want to keep shouting as loudly as I can It's A Fucking Lie, however. Do you realize how little really informed thought there is in this society, I mean even among its so called intellectuals and poets. I mean cats like Early can say shit like "Man, China scares me," and be talking only on what he has reflected from the collected works of Pierre Salinger or James Haggerty,[192] Mao's own works, &c., not being "hip enough" to read! The hard hipsters like Sorrentino, Oppenheimer, &c. like to come on about how "stupid the romanticism of the beats is," &c. (as see that incredibly pompous "statement" by Sorrentino in the new *Nomad*, where he calls himself, dig it!, "Aristotelian and Classical") yet, they are equally romantic, believing, even, finally, in Art for X's Sake, &c. Or at least thinking that only intellectual shit like POETRYPAINTINGSPORTSMOVIES can be thought about (ok MUSIC) but not such cheap plebian shit as philosophy, sociology, history (except where recommended by C.O. on Mayans and Hittites, &c.) or political science. Especially not, don't ever mention, Man, what? ECONOMICS. Whew!

O.K., I sound like a blemished recording. But I guess I'm just exercising. Otherwise? Lita Hornick's annual cocktail party. 888Park Ave., my bucolic friend, is where it all is. The $$$. Her old man, who is single handedly martyred because he gives up 5big bills each quarter for Kulchur, is a pajama, or curtain, manufacturer, who got very salty when I asked were his plants organized. I said I was gonna send Dubinsky up

---

191   Maxwell D. Taylor, general in the United States Army and political diplomat, 1901–1987. Taylor was appointed by John F. Kennedy as head of the task force set up to investigate the failed Bay of Pigs invasion.

192   Pierre Salinger, White House press secretary during the John F. Kennedy and Lyndon B. Johnson administrations; James Campbell Hagerty, White House press secretary during the Dwight D. Eisenhower administration.

there and picket the place. He didn't think it funny. Ironically when all the panic was on, and I was thinking seriously of seeing personally the little Caroline got her throat slit if anything happened to my girls, the Hornicks and their group called the YPO (yng presidents organization . . . for men who became presidents of large corporations before 35) were in Moscow . . . on tourist mission. They all put it down, Communism, &c., because food smells in largest hotel in Moscow, and 5000 people show up to the smallest avant-garde production. Crowds, &c. Also, diaphragms right in novelty store windows! The nerve! But Mortie, her spouse, sez he really put those fuggingggggRussians in their place, boy! And, ahem, they are also taking us to dinner next week . . . which means I'll get one fancy meal this wk for a change.

Went to see Zukofsky read 2 nights ago. Some of it, especially long poem from "A" he read last, was marvelous. They're having this series at Mannes Music College, uptown. Denise & David Ignatow! led off a few weeks ago . . . after that was Blackburn and Jackson McLow![193] (the chance! Poit) Zukofsky last Friday, then Dec. 7, Robert Kelly[194] and I read. The two of us coming on the stage shd be a riot . . . that cat weighs as much as Charles (probably more) and is unbelievably fat. But I begin to like his work very much (as that long poem *The Exchanges* in Origin or the longish poem in the new Nomad).

Finally getting the anthology in shape, and trying to use all three of the pieces you gave me.[195] Hope to get a check there in a week or so (tho, at 1$ a page it won't be that much). Definitely have it, check, before Xmas. I also, and the entire household, have vicious colds and Hettie and I, lousy sore throats. The last week has been Hell, especially at night, flat on your back. Anyway, we manage to press on. Tomorrow, Tanksgiving, we are invited to the Kings, also the Sorrentinos. We, together, buying 30bux worth of booze, so even if I don't get enough to eat, I'll be drunk as shit when evening comes. Wish the hell you all were here, tho man, I sometimes wonder how the fuck I cd make out in those woods (Alistair Benjamin[196] notwithstanding)? The first fight I ever had in the service was with some big cat from Colorado, who told me, as I was appointed squad leader, "Squad Leader!!! Sheet, out where I come from we call guys like you Woogies." I caught him just as the first bad tooth poked out in that rustic grin. But then you can carry a gun out there legal like can't you? Anyway, Happy Tanksgiving, and love to all youse, from Radio Free Bohemia.

Roi

---

193   Jackson Mac Low, American poet and composer, 1922–2004. Mac Low was an experimental poet, often using ideas of chance and nonintentional composition in his poetry. Mac Low was influenced in this by avant-garde musicians like John Cage and Earle Brown.

194   Robert Kelly, American poet, b. 1935. Kelly was strongly influenced by Charles Olson and Black Mountain College in his own poetics. He, along with poet Jerome Rothenberg, coined the term *Deep Image* to describe their poetry, suggestive of the deep structures of linguistics.

195   *The Moderns*; he does use three of Dorn's pieces: *C.B. & Q*, *1st Avenue*, and *Beauty*.

196   Alastair Benjamin is a reference to William Eastlake's *The Bronc People: A Classic Novel of the American Southwest*.

Poc. Ida. Nov 26, 1962

Dear Dauphin—That was enough you liked that Fidel poem—I sent it only to you. It never occurred to me to send it to any mag. What mag for instance wld take it? Ans: NONE! Ev. Rev? No. A waste of postage. And these days I'm not at all in the mood to waste anything except what suits me. I'd be pleasured to see it printed tho. But as you know & sd. Palante won't do at all. What a farce that would be—a capitulation before the challenge is even delivered! But did I tell you of my plan to become a commy after having been a Democrat? Pure contrary. Got yr. nice letter for which thks. You keep us going to the mailbox, 2 miles away, otherwise I can't see it's worth it. That Fidel poem was the last one in a small vol. I sent R-G Dienst (abt the size of Nwly F.) last month. He sd. he wanted to print a book of [. . .]. Horrors! You think he'll print it in same style as Rhinoceros? Ok, I didn't want to read it again anyway. Love to all [. . .] more later Ed

Poc Nov 27 1962

Dear Mr. Jones:

You know, so much bragging from that quarter about where it *all is*, parties by lita whornicks etc I thot you oughta have this free ticket to a rally being held here by Dr. Evans—you can use it for the plane fare out too. I've arranged for you to speak if you want to: you can follow M. Tshombe,[197] who is speaking on the topic *"the good neighbor in modern life."*

Enclosed is a poem expressing my very latest thots on the whole gig—P.S. Tell Sorrentino to come over to our side before it's too late!

P.S. Seriously—do you footnote and all that shit, those books for a cat like Morrow—ie wld it be too dull for you to clue me on that?

Love as [. . .] Ed

Friday, Nov. 30, 1962

Roi—Here's the permission. I hope that's all that's needed. I hadn't wanted to make much of the money because I know it must be as you say, not much. But right now a nickel or a dime would make a difference to us. We're sitting here with nada, strictly speaking. I don't get paid, it looks like, until Monday and we're for instance out of fuel. I can probably rustle some of that, but if it got really cold, say 20 or thirty below, it cld be uncomfortable. & the goddamn drag is the given possibility, here I am, supposedly a responsible middle aged man (if I live till 66) & I can't even for certain keep us warm yet. Oh, bullshit, we're trying *not* to borrow money, which we did at times last year, and it's only bitchy, because we have everything we need. It's my own damn fault because my name's not Snotgrass.[198] How abt that?

---

197   Moise Tshombe, Congolese politician, 1919–1969. Tshombe, an anti-Communist, supported an independent Congo, becoming president of Katanga Province in 1960. Tshombe was ousted and driven into exile in 1963, when United Nations forces succeeded in capturing Katanga.
198   A snide reference to W. D. Snodgrass, American poet, 1926–2009. Snodgrass had won a Pulitzer Prize in 1960.

A GENERAL ANSWER

I was handed
something green
they asked me
is this grass?
My answer
had to be no,
Snotgrass!

A cat named Allen Dugan
ate a copy of Yugen
to unstop his ass
they tore it w/ glass
and now, it's shaped Kugen

So, you can use that too. And if you manage to sell it to Mr. Dugan for 5,000, you may keep 4,000. ie, poverty makes a man generous. something you know better than most.

More later, ha. Ed

[Dec. 10 ? 1962]

Sir,

What's happening and why are you there in the woods making yrself totally unavailable to the benefits of democracy? Here, we are swinging democrats in the best tradition. You dig? (lil' word I picked up, along with a lot of prosodic tricks, from Anselm Hollo,[199] you dig?) Anyway, wind is coming under windows and doors and, of course, I'm supposed to fix all of it, being the man and all. But I am also very very sensitive, and like, don't dig manuel, or jose either. And speaking of yr friend Hollo, I'm writing a letter to the editor of Kulchur demanding that a certain slander of Michael McClure be apologized for. Ha, man you ran two poems together. Where you call him "a rank hick," which, on the basis of the shit he had in the issue of K, is a kindly euphemism . . . but the Chamber poem, which is one of his best ever poems, and very good, I think, is not connected to that little shithead poem underneath it, AS YOU MUST KNOW! Goddamn reviewers don't even know how to read, what you gonna do, if you just a poor draggy ass po-ate, Black Bart, the.

Of po-ates, I just paraphrased the hell out of one of yours to my class this week. And buddy when I finished explaining, they really dug, you dig. There were tears in the eyes of one old lady, as her all but palsied mind struggled to grasp your meaning. "Like a Message On Sunday," she repeated, her withered old head, &c. &c. If you had been there I'm sure you wd've understood the poem better as well. But I also read

---

199   Anselm Hollo, Finnish-born poet, 1934–2013. Hollo was a contemporary of Dorn and Jones and a friend of Dorn's.

them Olson, Duncan, Creeley. They found Duncan most difficult to comprehend. Creeley they thought prose, but very intTELLectual. But really they dug very much that poem of yours AND my reading of it.

I wish I cd print all those biographies, and then see where you'd be. Because that'd be the LEGEND OF EDWARD (JOHNNY OR JON) OR JON DORN. POET OF THE MIDWEST. Ahhh. We spoke two nights ago to New Mexico. Larry Rivers in an expansive mood, and sentimentally moved because I mentioned old Arnold Weinstein[200] was staying with Eastlake in Cuba, calld the ranch direct, and we talked, about 5$ worth with Arnold and Eastlake. "How are you? O.K. How are you? What's happening? Not much. What's happening? Not much" for 5 dollars. Since he had the loot I asked him to call Idaho, but none of his friends was staying there so he ixnayed that idea. But I thought it wd have been pretty funny to wake you all up in the middle of the night from the drunkrolling corner of the world, Cedar Tavern.[201] That fucking place almost burned to the ground two weeks ago, and guess who the last persons to leave, under the hysterical screams of firemen and bartenders, all who stood just outside, John Wieners and I were trying to finish our drinks, and really didn't dig that the fire was serious. It was still in the kitchen and really kind of gassy looking. But then these cats started getting hysterical from the door. John and I didn't even realize that everybody'd split. And those heroes waited till they got way outside to start saving us. And when we come out the door, one of the firemen says, "Comeon girls," in honor of J.W. I suppose, since I didn't have on heels. So, of course, I started coming on to the cat . . . lucky there was a shade fireman nearby to explain my remarks. Damn, when you say, "your shiteatin mama the hooker," and the guy stands there not understanding, that my friend, is frustration! But we soon fled when the US Fuzz started threatening. John seems fine, and fey as ever before. A trifle quieter, but now he seems on top of most things, except he always has some no bueno types passing through. The least buggy of which is Jonas, who I suspect, now, of being a boot. He's a very funny cat. He was here, with a friend of his, and he started coming on about why he puts down jews, niggers, &c. As LYRIC expanse, he says, a la Ezra. So we went into that. I saying discursively, I didn't see the difference between lousy nigger and LOUSY SPIC. And man, he turned three shades of shadow. He is cool in his lyric expanse bag when being discursive as to anybody who can't get with Pound, as "that Kike reviewer," &c. which he then goes into doubled up laughter, but then my test didn't really work as he shut right up after that, and merely slumped in the chair popping his fingers with Sonny. Ahhh literature!

---

200   Larry Rivers, American painter and musician, 1923–2002. Rivers was friends with Jones and many in his circles in New York, where he lived and maintained a studio. Arnold Weinstein, American poet and playwright, 1927–2005; Weinstein, associated with many of the New York School poets and painters, was a close friend of Rivers.

201   The Cedar Tavern, located in New York City's Greenwich Village, in several locations throughout its existence, including Cedar Street and University Place. The Cedar was frequented regularly by painters and poets, including, famously, Jackson Pollock.

Of which, I got a very fine 1act play from Douglas Woolf for 1act play issue of K, which is next. Do you have any such? Wd be grateful addition, as I suspect this of being the faggiest of all the issues. Well, we see. But if you have any old Eddie Albee type plays, my dear, please dispatch them forthwith.

Well, we getting ready for the happy season, somehow. A party maybe . . . having sort of open bay Xmas day, with buffet, w/ the Kings, here with Suckling Pig and liquor. But nobody has stepped forward to give big shameful blast. New Years Eve I'd like to get nuclear and radioactive. And we can't have party here, too compartmentalized, need some kind of open loft. Kanowitz[202] the painter around the corner too elegant, says he, "together, we got too many friends," meaning he don't dig all my friends. I have to invite all the ignorant junkies from Harlem . . . who, I aver, are better for parties than make believe middleclass junkies from G.V. or lowereastside. Oh, well, we'll see.

Burning Deck,[203] remember those funny letters we got when you were here. Well they've come out w/ first issue which is not half bad. Has about 4 Duncan poems, something from Creeley, something from Zukofsky. Also, there are pretty good reviews. PLUS, they pay, not on publication, but on *acceptance*. Address: 615 Turner Park Court, Ann Arbor, Mich. Yr anticipated editor, J. Glassman, getting married this Friday, so she'll be in a good mood for a few months. Maybe that'll help some. Hope so. But the cat over her at Morrow, John Willey[204] is a very straight sweet cat; one of the best people I've met in publishing, &c. If there's anything to be done, he'll do it and give you the best deal. Joyce, I think trying to get some loot for you on basis of stories, but sooner other stuff is ready, surer everything will be.

Best to you-all, Roi

19 Dec [1962]

Dear Ida

(which I take to be the diminutive of Idaho??) as Tex)

I suspect the FBI or somebody is opening all my mail, in and out, so I want to say right here I think the FBI eats shit especially JEdgarHoover alias AJ of Islam Inc. alias Dr. Benway, alias Hassan O'Leary the afterbirth tycoon.[205]

Anyway, what's up (as Geo Washington Carver once asked Isaac Newton?

---

202   Howard Kanovitz, American artist, 1929–2009. Kanovitz was friends and contemporaries with some of the leading figures in abstract expressionism, which included working as Franz Kline's assistant for some time. Kanovitz himself expanded his painting to include photography and, eventually, computer imaging.

203   Burning Deck is a small press founded, in 1961, by Keith Waldrop and Rosemarie Waldrop, dedicated to experimental poetry and prose.

204   John C. Willey, American publisher and editor, 1915–1990. Willey was editor in chief at William Morrow, where he had begun his career as an assistant in 1946.

205   Characters in William Burroughs's *Naked Lunch*: Dr. Benway is a surgeon without a conscience; Salvador Hassan O'Leary is a criminal.

I'm writing now especially to see what happened to Fidel Letter. I'm now on editorial board of magazine called *The Minority of One*. It is, I'm pretty certain, the straightest political organ in North America. I've asked that copies be sent to you, especially one, Jan issue, with beautiful explanation of China-Nehru problems. Now they want to add a literary supplement of 10 pages, which means can print poems, reviews &c. I already got two poems scheduled, also poems of Bburns and Lamantia's. I've asked Chas., and some others and hope they will respond with whatever. But I thot immediately of the Fidel poem, but also that you given it to Corman (?) But anything wd be good from you chum, so get on the stick. Also any reviews, short indulgent articles, &c.

Bear looks dead now from this end. Diane got married to a guy named Allan Marlowe who models for t.v. He's the man in Chesterfield ads and was in Look last week with diamonds. He's the biggest queer in western hemisphere, even cuts Hershey bars in the shape of a cock before he'll eat them, yahh yahh bitter roi. Anyway, they came in (dropping me a card to come to a wedding & going away party for them last weekend. At same time I was supposed to go w/ my lovely wife to wedding party for Glassman and her no-talent husband. I copped out and didn't go to either, rather I sat in great bar restaurant called The Ninth Circle and drank slowly to my extinction. Of course I got the cold shoulder around here for a couple of days, but everything seems cool now. Better for conjugal love anyway, like absence makes the hard grow fonder, &c.) But now they going to live in or outside of Lost Angeles in Topanga Canyon. And they also took the mimeograph, the new electric 400$ mimeo which I got up 1/3 of the money for. I am doing a not so slow burn, daddio. I've heard that Diane intends to do Bear from there. I'll see but most likely I will resign, because I had a hard enough time trying to keep my hand on the thing when she lived right down the street. And her penchants, as you might have gathered, are straight up San Francisco types, McClure, Kirby Doyle,[206] &c or New York lady poets like Frank, Ashberry, Berkson.[207] Sorry to see the thing go, if I had a mimeo here I'd do it on my own as I started to do before, before Diane offered to help.

That's wild about the trip to Canada mit ganzen familie.[208] Bob mentioned Allen and Charles as well. Didn't no Allen planned to get back so soon. Thot he was pushing even further East or south. Sounds good tho.

---

206   Kirby Doyle, American poet, 1932–2003. Doyle's poetry was included in Donald Allen's *The New American Poetry*; he was part of the San Francisco poetics scene, associated with poets such as Robert Duncan. Doyle emphasized the spoken over the written word and counted the lyric sensibilities of Olson, John Keats, and Emily Dickinson, all of whom he loved, as part of his poetic influence.

207   Frank O'Hara. John Ashbery, American poet, b. 1927; Ashbery's work has been continually honored throughout his life. While at Harvard he became friends with poets and writers such as Frank O'Hara and Robert Creeley. Bill Berkson, American poet, b. 1939. Berkson studied with Kenneth Koch and became friends with O'Hara and others in the New York poetry scenes. Berkson has also curated art exhibits extensively. The reference to "lady poets" is, ostensibly, because both O'Hara and Ashbery are gay, Berkson being included in the list because of his friendship with O'Hara.

208   "With the whole family."

The Billie record sells for about 12 or 13 dollars. Very steep. Discount houses wanted 8 1/2, but worth it. One good thing about writing reviews is the loot aspect. And speaking of Kulchur, we got to do something to pep that weak sister up. This last issue was really not too much. Corman's article was old business and dull, McClure's simpleminded mule shit . . . I mean elf-light? Whow! and I told you what I thot of the big think piece on painting. I was thinking maybe we could start to write a culture gossip column or something as "C.Y. Cream, editor of Fuggit, the best selling stroke book, was recently seen with a white girl. What's happening C.Y.?"

Deadline for me to turn in new Morrow book is Nov1 1963. I'm sure I'll be late, and I don't intend to start until after my introduction for the Prose book is in, and I finish a full-length play I want to do. Warm here now too for a change, and I finally got the heat situation somewhere approaching normal, and finished painting the john. Went to a groovy concert for Stefan Wulpe's[209] birthday last night. Compositions by Feldman, Brown, Shapey, Varese, were lovely, and some others not so lovely, but good anyway. Tannd Lenny Bernstein was there, also Suzy Parker,[210] who is a beautiful woman. I wrote some of the lyrics for Wulpe's piece, which included a singer and narrator, written for octet. It was pretty funny, and the audience demanded an encore. My fee was a bottle of wine and cab fare. Anyway, stay on yr toes!

Love, Roi

Poky—Dec 22/62

Dear Jones: It looks to me like you had it. But really that *is* sad news abt Bear. I liked that little sheet very much. And wldn't trust that di Prima donna as far as I cld toss her fag hubby. Oh well, the West Coast needs a mag bad. I guess that's the xtian attitude. But there ought to be a way you cld sue those Bastards or "detain" them or "incarcerate" their asses. Just their asses. The rest cld go free.

You got that wrong abt Chas & Allen & *me* at Vancouver.[211] This shot is just to read in Feb. What you have in mind must be a writers conference—and I didn't know abt Allen, but I knew Chas was invited. That's summer '63 as of the poem for Fidel— you may certainly consider it available. Cid wrote back saying #1 he didn't like it, ie, it was too "tough guy" (wow!) #2 Fidel himself he (Cid) was sure wouldn't like it

209   Stefan Wolpe, German-born composer, 1902–1972. Wolpe taught at Black Mountain College from 1952 to 1956, where he was director of music.

210   Suzy Parker, American model and actress, 1932–2003.

211   Dorn is referring to the 1963 Vancouver Poetry Reading, part of the University of Buffalo's summer courses. Jones mistakenly thought Dorn would be part of that series. Fred Wah notes, "The July–August 1963 Poetry Conference in Vancouver spanned three weeks and involved about sixty people who had registered for a program of discussions, workshops, lectures, and readings designed by Warren Tallman and Robert Creeley as a summer course at the University of B.C."

either, #3 it wasn't even "for Fidel" but seemed to make a play for my own obscure "purposes"—so, I guess he don't like it. Wouldn't you say that? I think I made some minor changes in a later typing—I'll send again.

I think you're right abt making Kulch visible—that last issue was straight shit. By the way did you get my apology to MacClure? You didn't say—or are you trying to come on impolite? What is this I hear of a new bk by Gary Snyder—what kind is it? Did Totem do it? I want to invite you to join w/ me in liberating the word asshole. Later we might get around to liberating the artifact itself. A good title cld be "step into my orifice said the fag to the dike." Ok. You stay straight over the holidays. Oh, yesterday I got a letter from Don Allen in SF. He wanted to know, after 2 yrs of being asleep at the switch, if I'd send him CB&Q & other prose for a Grove Blk [. . .] bk. Is there a sort of rivalry between Corinth and Grove over this prose anth? They think to make it a text book & Creel is assoc. ed. Let me in dad. Of course I'm explaining to him that you have already made that scene—

Love Ed

[Dec. 1962]

Dear Sorehead,

I have decided not to denounce you, &c., as I get a sense of deep gnostic pleasure, or got, reading your anguished note. Actually, if we are faulting, &c., that has literally to be placed at the editor's feet, i.e., Sorrentino, who possibly should have spotted the thing, but then he doesn't give much of a shit about McClure. But all of this is out of proportion as I was merely bullshitting in the first place, and had no real intention of carrying past *your* attention, and had no idea you would get so raised up about it. But "the hell of one man's making, &c." chuckle chuckle.

As to my goofs in Yugen, or elsewhere, it is just unfortunate I am such a lousy editor, even tho it is true that my dear wife is the proof reader here. But fuck all that. I think the only person who will dig all the hassle about that poem (and what you said about those lines was true past anybody's denial, and for you to say that the oversight "cuts" that, is not even close, and I suspect you know it is McClure. There's no real reason for you to go to sackcloth and ashes, why not can the whole apology?

My last word forever on that subject. But strangely enough this morning when I got your letter, I also got some poems from a man named Kenneth L. Irby[212] in Cambridge who has certainly been reading you, tho the poems are not derivative in any crude way, but seem, or at least seem to me, to have derived a certain impetus or tone from you. Also, and possibly I am merely tricked into seeing a similarity, his "subject matter" moves along very parallel to your own, as one poem, a very good

212   Kenneth Irby, American poet, b. 1936. Irby's poetry is associated with the Black Mountain School, and he was friends with Duncan, Creeley, and Dorn, among others.

one, called *The Grasslands Of North America*. He sounds young, because his ideas are so strong and miss so consistently, though they ring anyway, if you can hear that. As: "The grass that is in/ my backyard, caught/ in the same winds as/ over and over were/ the far-reaching green prairies"

"That same country as entered/ the first time it was ever seen/" per example. But I am going to drop him a note asking to see more. Also, we wd like to get another Yugen out, I suppose to get back on top of everything, or at least I feel that you were very right in feeling the issue was almost old news, though I think what actually was missing was the sense of coming attractions or The New, which maybe some of the others had. But I wd like to have some poems or whatever from you.

Good to have this time off, you bet, from all that horseshit education routine. Ha, your classes are being possibly cut, and mine enlarged, as a bunch of screaming G.V. ladies are signing for the course now I am official teacher, to get, all the beatnik apparatus, from the horsies mouf. But again, predictably enough, the money compels. Tho one good thing could come out of it if KKoch stays on my team, that is the possibility of my arranging and heading up a series of big paying jazz concerts at the school in the same fashion as the poetry reading series, the partial schedule of which I enclose. I wd, of course, run the thing down from most modern to trad. and figgish (as the english wd sigh). Like first concert Ornette, then Ben Webster,[213] then Cecil, then Lightnin' Hopkins, then Coltrane, then Coleman Hawkins, then Rollins, then Eldridge. Like that. Get all those swinging mfs in it. I heard Webster a few weeks ago uptown, and wow, he sounds possibly more "beautiful" than he ever did before, so sure and so consistently *there*, and now, of course, completely Webster. 5Spot still under construction and they're straining to open by newyearseve, but I doubt it which is too bad, since they wd stand to pick up a lot of loot. But I hope Koch, who is getting to be big time academic voice, e.g., you see who heads up the poetry reading series, and I told you he got me and O'Hara jobs at the place, which I, at least, very badly needed, tho Frank gets a pretty good check from the MuseumdeModernArt evvy week. Will back the bean! I also send for general delectation program from concert we went to this week that was pretty good, i.e., the pieces by Brown, Feldman, Wolpe, Varese, Shapey were very good. I did some of the words, lyrics, for the Wolpe piece. ByeBye

Roi

IV

1963

Events both good and bad filled 1963, but almost all seemed momentous, indicators of a quick-paced time of change. The links between the personal and political were every-where: when John F. Kennedy was assassinated on November 22, it prompted poet

---

213   Ben Webster, American jazz saxophonist, 1909–1973.

Bob Kaufman to take a ten-year Buddhist vow of silence; he would not speak again until the end of the Vietnam War. The assassination of South Vietnamese president Ngo Dinh Diem at the hands of a CIA-backed coup d'état marked the ever deepening United States presence in world affairs, as it increased its military power as a means to its own ends. This year also saw the March on Washington and the death of William Carlos Williams, key turning points in the American spectrum for poets like Jones and Dorn in both politics and art. Howard Brick, in his study of the sixties, Age of Contradiction: American Thought and Culture in the 1960s, *notes that "American thought and culture grew turbulent and rife with contention; the realm of ideas and arts became more subject to instability than the foundations of American social structure itself" (22).*

In the letters from this year, there is an expression of growing dissatisfaction and a desire to change place, as each poet struggles both against his own personal problems (most acutely of poverty) and against the increasingly frightening actions of the United States and its interactions with the rest of the world. Along with the upheaval of world events, Jones's black radicalism was growing, bolstering his public presence, while Dorn's stay in Pocatello as an overworked, underpaid part-time college instructor was beginning to wear him down. Dorn was struggling to make ends meet, and he could not always be sure of money for necessities like rent or heat. Both poets, at the same time, were beginning to find more public reception for both their poetry and prose, and the reviews, thoughts, and commentary around American art they had been sharing with one another through their letters was finding newer, public spaces in magazines, newspapers, and books.

N.B. There are many missing letters in the archives from Dorn to Jones in 1963; for this year, the conversation is reconstructed primarily from Jones's side of the correspondence.

《 》　《 》

Edward,   [Jan 12? 1963]

Speaking of Corman, I just got all those poems back w/ letter, a tasty morsel of which I will quote, dig: (here he's talking about that poem *Hegel*) "I keep wondering too how much violence the big city engenders. So that your:

> Cut out
> the insides

becomes a paradigm for everything. My own feeling would be, why not take one's 'insides' out for a walk, some place where there is earth again, water moving, a galaxy of trees, maybe mountains, etc. Something where one isn't trained on the inside of one's head all the time.

Man that cat's a hick and what's worse a square. Between he and that Scottish

cat Ian Finlay[214] with his "wee's" I remain unimpressed. But fucking that, I just
got ahold of something crazy, i.e., Sonny's[215] new album. *Our Man In Jazz* . . . the
breakthroughs we heard at the Gate. One side is 25minutes, his old *Oleo*, which is
demasiado.[216] So pick up if you can, or if it's difficult I'll try to get a cutrate version
out there. Let me know.

Not much else here. Supposed to hear from Grove soon, I'm told. They held or
are holding soon, their "what shall we publish" meeting. Sorrentino called, at my
urging, and they gave him rather optimistic report, i.e., they dug mss, the editors,
and now it was up to Barney Rosset, the one man dipstick. My book's over there too,
so we all should hear soon. I feel optimistic for some reason.

Ground getting out from under my feet at Kulchur. I asked Duncan for play for
the play issue, which was my idea, &c. But LeSuer,[217] drama ed, was "in charge." He
turned play down, it was, I suppose, of a rival faggotry, and he didn't dig. He also
turned down Joel's musical, which I'm going to see next Friday. So only play I got
in actually was one of Doug Woolf's and my own. The "panel" idea seems to have
completely backfired, tho I hope still to keep at people to charge the thing up. Got
a review from Charles on the WCWilliams' book Contours Of American History,
which I hope you get to read. His other book is now in paper, and is also more than
worthwhile to get into: The Tragedy of American Diplomacy. I wish Gil wd get to
more people and ask them for reviews, &c. Hope, also, you continue to send some
things. *The Politics of Luxury* continues though I've many hitches and restarts. Also
a determined laziness and willful uncertainty about what I'm doing. It will probably
be a long piece, full of all the bullshit and non-specific invective I'm always capable
of, but also, I'd hope, crammed full of some kind of *new politics*.

O.K., I'll get back to my devices, and leave you, for a time, to your'n. YAWN.
Hungover and grumpy today. FUCK CID CORMAN TED ENSLIN[218] IAN FINLAY GAEL
TURNBULL AND ALL THEM JAPS AND ITALIANS THEY GOT GOIN FOR EM. RIGHT????
AS ASTRA[219]

                                                                            Roi

214   Ian Hamilton Finlay, Scottish poet and art historian, 1925–2006. Finlay's work combined the ideas
of art and text, as in his *Rapel*, wherein both typography and content form the effect of the work in its
entirety. Finlay would later begin inscribing his poetry into stone.
215   Sonny Rollins.
216   "Too much."
217   Joe LeSueur, American writer, 1924–2001. LeSueur lived with poet Frank O'Hara from 1955 to 1965;
he wrote a memoir, completed in 2001, called *Digressions on Some Poems by Frank O'Hara: A Memoir*.
218   Theodore Enslin, American writer, 1925–2011. Enslin is most closely associated with *Origin*
magazine, put out by Cid Corman, who Jones is also referencing here.
219   *Ad astra*, "to the stars" in Latin. This phrase is commonly used by the U.S. Air Force, of which Jones
was briefly a part in the 1950s.

Ed,   14 Jan [1963]

Today is first in about 5 that I've been up off my sagging ass. I had infected throat, &c. that took about 5 days and 2 big shots of penicillin. So you can see how fucked up I was. I think overindulgence, &c. getting too potted too high and walking around coat open at night helped. Last Monday some guy from uptown I've known much too long shows up w/ Fee[220] nickel caps of H!!!!!, I mean free. Seems de nummer hit or something, but whatever I got really sick blind stoned, and then walked around drooling on bar tables or something. Anyway next day I woke up with what I thought was just drug hangover and sorethroat. Gil, Selby, and I had planned to visit Doc Williams, and they came over so I went along anyway to Rutherford N.J. That man still managing to hang on, tho this day he did have much trouble talking, and he was really boiling and likewise frustrated about that. Only clear word he managed at will was *Shit!*, and appropriately put. But he seemed to enjoy our visit, tho now I begin to feel a little dumb . . . like suppose I left some of my deathray germs. I mean they really knocked me on my ass . . . deliriums and everything. Oh well he's stood everything else.

   Anyway glad to hear from you. (Just found your letter of Dec. 28, dropped behind the stairs). And all sympathies, &c. Irby wrote me a letter that he owed you a great debt, i.e., poetically, but I spotted that out long back. He seems straight enough thru the mails. But then so do you.

   That Yale cat with his inherited letter style is something else again. He sounds positively ugly thru the mails. He wrote back how he liked one long poem I send wd use I suppose, his one objection was to the title, which he thought "vulgar and obscure (?)." Title was *Rhythm & Blues*. You think the cat's a bigot? By god. More literatitalk: Grove set to have their big "Acceptance" meeting end of this week, or so the scuttlebutt sez that I got wind of. My agent prowls around squeezing this kind of info, I presume, much like Nick Charles or Nora Charles anyway. Point is that there may be some further information, resolution, very soon on the book. My book up there also, but I told them no matter what their decision I'd like to add about six poems. Still trying to get somebody to distribute our books. People that distribute Totem/Corinth refused to distribute the books we'd done alone. Dig this, the cat's supposed to be a Socialist, but he turned me down because poetry don't make de bread. Ferlinghetti also refused, but sd he will take some on account or what the fuck. Everybody seems like they got their eye on something don't smell so good. Like my friend K. Koch, who is now standing his fat syrupy ass in front of the jazz series, i.e., "he don't quite know if it wd be *right*" for the New School. I mean man you know the "associations" w/ that kind of music, No? Dope and Darkies I suppose. Well, he's might right, cause that's exactly what I intended,

---

220   A sly reference, maybe, to Fielding Dawson, who was commonly called Fee.

maybe even stand for. Further, he was one of the people I named as sponsor for the Guggenheim. At my house Christmas day he sez, "Roi, why don't you send me some of your recent work so I can see whether I can write the recommendation for the Gugg." I almost fainted! Wowee. That cat's flipped right into the Phd mambo. That Dr. Koch shit has completely aborted his finer instincts I wd say.[221] But I guess it don't really matter since I won't get the thing anyway. But the act, hopeless to say, did infuriate me.

I don't know anything about an "overlap" agreement with Don. Wonder what he's talking about? What stories are you sending him? I know the idea of the other ant'y has set him smoking and turning. He wrote me he's working his ass off. Getting all my shit straight . . . he's also my editor on the Dante book, which I hear is supposed to be out by April. That's certainly good news. But I hope there's no fuck up or scratchy conduct on this ant'y scene. Books themselves, from what Don tells me, won't conflict since Corinth's is hard back review type, and the Grove thing is Black Cat high distribution, &c. But I better query Allen. He also sd he wants to cut the NAP second edition to about 25 or so people! There were 44 in it first. He also asked me for a private list of who I thought shd be in it. But I'll never go for that, you bet! "Discrete list" was the way he sd it. Anyway, I hope something's going with Glassman. She's really a lighter than air weight as far as her mental processes, I fear. A real dumbbelle. She seems very vague, and not quite sure of anything. Not even her new husband, who is a real flip number. She really got into the bush leagues. I mean this cat lies about working. You see the cat in the bar and he says, "Yeh, I worked half a day, thought I'd knock off." He's a painter, like. But then you see somebody and they'll tell you they saw him in the bar the other half of the day too, and so on. Anyway. Luck there, hope it all works out toward some loot.

About the Bear, &c. I'm just very sorry the thing is stopped as I looked forward to it, and am deeply put on by its absence. Diane is, of course, very impressionable, so there's no telling what will be in the Occidental edition. Maybe I cd find a free mimeo free this & that I cd do it here, single mano, but without that mailing list, &c. it'd be in a deep hole. As far as the gossip shit about my jealousy, and what not. It's me saying that my jealousy cd be assuaged with the striking of a simple combination to the head of Senor Marlowe who is not only a rotten queen but owes me in excess of 150.00 dollars american money loaned to him for a jazz theatre project. He has paid me 10.bucks of it back. But all of Fagville has it that I'm boiling because he *stole* Di Prima. O.K., I do not go for the idea of her married to this cat, because I was deeply involved with her, for sure. But she is a rare and consistent opportunist, and saw possibly the way out of what she considered even uglier emotional stress. The Daring

221   Poet Kenneth Koch received his PhD from Columbia University in 1959.

Bohemian tac broke down, unfortunately with the wrong companion, &c. But I admit to being very furious at the whole business and have sworn to break Marlowe's back, which I probably won't do . . . which is the height of the self-hate frustration routine. Anyway it is making for some kind of international intrigue, which, of course makes Hettie mad as shit at local fags—of whom Diane was considered Elizabeth I—play the whole bit as chief romance of west, with "Two Poets" and their beloved Di Prima being deprived of her real love and life by "a plain unfeeling joosh[222] girl." Well I have had to straighten one motherfucker out about that, by the numbers. And am willing to provide better information to any cocksucker who thinks thus. Moreover this Affair rages as good cocktail talk, and will probably until something of equal conversational valence shows up on the scene. Anyway, I just hope Bear comes out if it's going to, and that it's worthwhile.

We trying to hold on here, scraping loot from wherever. My first dept. meeting was a real bust. I fucked up from the git-go. Saying why are we discussing this shit, no real writers are coming out of this writing dept anyway. Which shook up everybody except Mrs. Boyle[223] (yass she's there sans daughter) and a model type name Anatole Broyard.[224] My hard's in the high lands. But now I swear to be a good boy, tho I pondered sending strange things in the mails to you . . . for your head. But thought possibly there was too big a chance for you to get in difficulty??? Let me know as the bush scene here is veddy veddy hip right now. But maybe you got more reliable sources much closer?? That shit you told me about Corman merely confirms what I thought of the cat. But I sent some things to him about same time as I got your letter and I haven't heard as yet. For sure if he writes me some blockhead letter like yrs I will disappear badslave style. Anyway, in the same way as it used to please me to say FuckGod! or walk through downtown Washington singing Parker's *Squirrel* with lyrics that went "You better get yourself a white girl . . . A colored girl ain't no good," so all the good cracker citizens wd be hip that a complete fool had just passed, Now I figure to get in a more mature position to do something equally outrageous. And literarily, straight at you like a junkie headhunter, I am writing *The Politics of Luxury* in which I am out for all you cats. So polish your SuWord or your assgike I'm bound to be satisfied. Poetry, by the way, took 3 poems more! [. . .]

Fat Roi

---

222   Jewish.

223   Kay Boyle, American writer and activist, 1902–1992. Boyle had lived for a time in France (where she had a daughter with Richard Brault, whom Jones references here), where she was involved with several experimental literary magazines. Boyle was an outspoken Leftist who faced serious charges under the Truman administration. At this point in 1962, she was a writer in residence at the New York City Writer's Conference at Wagner College.

224   Anatole Broyard, 1920–1990, author and literary critic for the *New York Times*.

Hombre,   28 Jan [1963]

I am in the middle of writing Donald Allen about the story. I can't understand why he'd want to do it again. Also, today, I'll be checking w/ Wilentzes about what they think, &c. I'm just lowly editor without that kind of real power. Lumpen-publisher type. But I'll let you know as soon as there's words, quick time.

I am sorry to have come on so coarse, &c. But that pressure burns as ever, especially here in the hot-bed of nuevo fagdom. Also I go in so many directions, frequently playing the dervish with the uncareful sword. As I wrote that fool Corman, who wrote me *again* protesting that I call him a hick. But I have sd, and mean, at least, to stand by it, i.e., *risk* is something I need. It is as traceable as distortion, which I stand by too, that is I don't *expect* to be right, but it does profit my energies when I am. Moreover it's the swing itself I dig, if I feel it. Ditto I think you go by that. But I *do* feel close to you, whatever I say or however. But that's not the point I expect. The Politics of Luxury is mostly for me, though, I will publish it when it's finished. I expect, when you see it, you will at least want to write me a heavy letter . . . for which, &c. &c. I am always turned on. My trouble, as you guess, I know, is that I am too securely on top of everything local. The people I know remain too statically that, and even their disagreements seem tepid to what I could arrange as a catalyst. It was simple when I was younger, "Your momma eat red shit," could always serve, and when I improvised, like "Red shit eat your mamma," it *was* abstract for the local talent, and they revered me for it. But shit, I thought this was the big time. Too often it's the bush. You and some others stand against it, and it'd be corny to go on with that. But you know what I mean. Air Air, "in the violent city."

I do hope you are getting some satisfaction from Glassman-Johnson. Great that you don't have to put up with her idiot husband. And, god, I hope they take to the novel. I didn't know you were into that. What I hope is that it's a best seller and you make eighteen billion dollars and come back to newyork in a silver cataract. Then you cd have debates with Norman Mailer and the white man's burden, Jimmy Baldwin. Hoooo! Then I cd get invited to boss cocktail parties and tell everybody I know the host. Man, I dream of it. Hurry!

Other than my dreams . . . we went to 5Spot last week, for first time. It's a great room. They still don't have all the cabaret shit, so they can't have horns or drums. But they did have two groups that were something else. One was Tommy Flanagan, piano; Jim Hall, guitar; Percy Heath, bass. The other: Walter Bishop, piano; Les Spann, guitar; Sam Jones, bass. Mingus[225] sat in w/ Percy, and Bobby Timmons, who nodded out at my house earlier, on piano. Junk scene very curious hereabouts. Many new junkies, and weekend bandits turning up, including some close friends of mine. I am butt of many jokes, since I have automatic thermostat somewhere that gets me very sick when I've had what amounts to a habit-beginning portion.

---

225   Charles Mingus, American jazz musician, 1922–1979.

So when I get sick I immediately get sick, and that's that for a long time. Visions of sugar plums, &c. like I remember so many people, in that cold way I have, who I actually loved, who are, for all intents and purposes stone cold daid. But these cats are very protective, and do not even like to see me turn on. But the industry, goes on.

We were on our way out to Larry Rivers' house for long weekend, but Lisa, at last moment, fell out of her chair and loosened all her top teeth, breaking her lips. Trauma trauma, and that cooled the trip out. Which bugged Hettie much more than me. God knows when the next opportunity will come up. We even had a parlor car reserved to booze in and play cards on the way out. Ah so. But the little one's better now, lips unswollen, teeth getting stronger, I imagine. Diabolic shit though.

Well, I'm going over to Wilentz now, I'll let you know everything as soon as. I may get to teach a straight up propaganda course calld American Poetry Since 1945. I submitted outline, but they may not go for it. I put your book on required reading list. You dig how objective I begin. You take care of them Americans and I'll take care of these. Amour.

Roi

[1963 Mar 10: Though the letter is dated March 10, it is later, since Jones refers to a boxing match that did not take place until March 13th.]

Hey malo hombre,

What's with those thin assed letters? Sorry I'm so slow on this end, but we've been up to our assholes in financial difficulties as they wd say at general dynamics, and we've been doing weird things trying to keep from pawning the girls. They both have tonsil-adenoid troubles, and we've been advised to get them out immediately, which is supposed to cost mucho dinero. So, let me weep on your shoulder a few seconds, baby, because all this shit is driving me in the sand and this morning too, a little bitching hangover about to drive me a little deeper in my own stews. You sound equally cool. Which is groovy I thinks, because it means we are sensitive young men dying in the service of Art. But Spring here too, this cool bright sunday. And things ain't ever as bad as they seem.

Het and I went to a real old fag party couple of nights ago. We were thinking how gassd you and Helene wd have been there w/ us. It was a party for Edwin Denby,[226] you know him . . . very sweet cat aged 60, H.D.[227] contemporary, and

---

226   Edwin Denby, American dance critic and poet, 1903–1983. Denby was close friends with New York painters like Willem de Kooning and would have encountered Jones and Hettie at various gatherings such as this one.
227   H. D. (Hilda Doolittle), American poet and writer, 1886–1961. H. D., whose poetry was avant-garde and most commonly associated with the Imagists, was a formative influence on avant-garde twentieth-century poets, including Ezra Pound, William Carlos Williams, and Robert Duncan. Duncan would write a monumental work of poetry, essay, and memoir entitled *The H. D. Book*, written in 1960 and 1961 and published in small pieces and through underground presses until 2012, when it was released in its complete form, edited by Michael Boughn and Victor Coleman.

poet, also ballet critic. Well every important fag in the industry showed up. At one time Virgil Thompson, John Cage and Aaron Copland[228] are standing next to me talking . . . they all queer . . . and I'm thinking. Woowee, mama, melican culture is too much. Chile, I cain't tell you how badly I wanted to take my ole dick out and wave it around screeching here it is yall, here's what you all need jammed in yo sweaty jaws. But you know how shy I gets. But there was plenty of food (some of which I brought back to our little cave for the tots) and plenty plenty liquor served by 3 taciturn coons in white coats who kept feeding me liquor cause I asked them where the coolest place to get a haircut uptown and they all came on like haircut geniuses to let me know. Also, we leaned in the corner and shot at the guests. For truth, there was only about 4 straight cats in the joint, excluding the waiters and I. But also, they had a very hip puppet show, then a groovy film, so you see how you can benefit in the company of them which favors unnatural sex. Only straight cats I talked to all night was Larry Rivers, who's a pretty straight cat all around, and some painter named Kanovitz, who argued w/ me all fucking night about "modern music." Ugg. Per exempla: "I don't think that's really avant-garde." &c. &c. Horseshit rhetoric.

And speaking of fags, K's [229] about had it. Gil just quit as Books editor. Lita refused to take Joel in his place. Bang. 10 won't be so bad, but after that. Screeeeech! Girls, whose pecker shall we dingle this number. Hope you got a copy of 9. Back matter is pretty good. Gil's poetry chronicle got a lot of folks angry which is always a good sign. And I agree w/ him about all, except I think Voznesensky[230] may be a good poet, Anselm Hollo notwithstanding. I've read other translations of him, and he might come through.

Those Deep imagists descended on us just last night. Ugg. Just as I was about to get real high w/ some of my dirty junkie pals, Rochelle Owens[231] and her husband George Economou[232] show up w/ a cat named Armand Schwerner[233] (Rothenberg's doppelganger) and his big boobed wife. Man does she have a big ass and a set of huge gongs. I wonder how come she got hooked up w/ Schwerner. But every time

228   Virgil Thomson, American composer, 1896–1989; John Cage, American composer and poet, 1912–1992; Aaron Copland, American composer, 1900–1990. Thomson and Copland, in particular, were great supporters of Denby, helping to establish his influential dance columns.

229   *Kulchur*. Gil Sorrentino was the poetry editor at this time.

230   Andrei Voznesensky, 1933–2010, Russian poet. Voznesensky was a well-known, well-liked poet and public intellectual, earning the disdain (and a threat of expulsion from the country) of Nikita Kruschev.

231   Rochelle Owens, b. 1936, American poet. Owens was involved with Off-Broadway theater, including New York's LaMaMa Theatre. Owens figured in the early and influential poetry readings at New York's Le Deux Megots (central to the development of the New York School of poetry) and at the St. Marks Poetry Project.

232   George Economou, American poet, b. 1934. Economou was, like his wife Rochelle Owens, involved in the New York poetic scenes, later becoming a university professor.

233   Armand Schwerner, Jewish American poet, 1927–1999. Schwerner's works form some of the more avant-garde, experimental poetry of the time. His most famous work, *Tablets*, is a work of poetic reconstruction (i.e., re-creations, new creations) of Sumerian inscriptions.

she opened her mouth noises came out and that put me off. Otherwise I thought to leap on her like the cat man.

Floating Bear was real shit, seemed to me. If that's the tac Di Prima's going to keep, whew, I wish at least she'd change the fucking name so as not to scrape all memory of the old thing's function away. Well, the hell with that. Plus she sent me some goofy letter asking me to be the, diggit, east coast editor. Man, that's all I need. But I wish there was some way to put the thing out here. Same deal; small quick mimeo, which I always thought was very valuable. Oh, well, who's got the bread, now that the machine got took.

Joel, Gil, Bro. Antoninus,[234] and I went out to William's funeral. Oddly enough, the service was handled quite well. The minister quoted at length from the work, and never copped out about WCW being a poet, and an unpopular one as far as the formal culture of US was concerned. Place was full of local folks too. But when we went out to cemetery, only the poets and close family remained. Townspeople fled. But minister read two poems . . . one A Tract, which was a gas in such buggy circumstance. All kinds other poets were there too; Denise, Zukofsky, Blackburn, Oppen, dopey Bly,[235] Ignatow, J. Laughlin,[236] Rothenberg, some others. A reporter asked Celia Z.[237] and I were we "some of Wms New York friends?" Also, were there "any international celebrities on hand?" She said, you looking at one, and pointed at yrs truly. Which broke both of us up. So Celia named everybody on hand, making us, very quickly, for the Rutherford Standard, international etcetera.

I guess you heard by now that Wm Stafford[238] won the Nat. Book Award for poesy! Whew, they really digging at the bottom now. I knew Bob didn't have much of a chance, but shit, not this creep Stafford. Horseshit. But I hope you get a chance sometime to see a television broadcast of the proceedings. Probably not. But Dr. Robert Oppenheimer[239] spoke, and he was really beautiful. I mean he put every shit faced asshole in our establishment right down. Even called the Nat Book people the "national book club" . . . and took several very good shots at JFK, one in which he said he'd been talking w/ a Russian scientist about the world &c., and the Russian seemed puzzled about the way the world was moving, &c., as to whether or not there would be one much longer. Oppenheimer said, about this Russian, "Poor man, he was so confused . . . but that's only natural . . . he didn't have the

234 Brother Antoninus (William Everson), American poet and printer, 1912–1994. Everson was an anarchist and pacifist, closely associated with the San Francisco Renaissance.
235 Robert Bly.
236 James Laughlin, American poet and publisher, 1914–1997. Laughlin was William Carlos Williams's publisher at New Directions.
237 Celia Zukofsky, American writer, 1913–1980; Celia was the wife and oftentimes poetic collaborator of poet Louis Zukofsky.
238 William Stafford, American poet, 1914–1993. Stafford, a pacifist and conscientious objector during WWII, was a close friend of Robert Bly; hence, Jones's derision.
239 Robert Oppenheimer, American physicist, 1904–1967; Oppenheimer is most well known today for his work on the atomic bomb.

advantage I did of having read JFK's national goals program," &c. A real heavy blast that shut that whole audience up. Also Opp kept calling for some kind of mind and morality to come back to science and scientists instead of "being willing or unwilling dupes of evil ignorant men who run this country." Whew. Man he was gorgeous! Hettie and I almost wept watching this old man perform.

Speaking of older men, have you heard from Chas. recently? I wrote him couple times, but only brief word, and now none for some time. I wonder what he's up to. Probably I'll send him a note soon. I did get a review out of him for Kulch tho, hope there's something coming very soon from you, buddy. You want to review the gentle Italian's book, i.e., Gregorian Corset's[240] "Long Live Man." A title I think sums up G.C.'s cool right in a nutshell. Long live man. Wow, what a fucking naïve slob. And he's so gassd w/ himself for not knowing anything, it's murderous. Yeh, how come you don't do that. I'll get if for you if you like. Or anything you want to review or do, please come through, Ace. No word from Grove at all, but I know Rosset just got back from Europe. They sure take a long ass time to get things settled.

Now I think I'll go watch the Yanks on television and get drunk again. Only thing I know to cool my hangover. Oh, man, I went up to see the fight Clay-Jones,[241] last week, w/ A.B.[242] and couple other cats. We had a grand time. All the fucking celebrities. We sat, for 2bucks, up in heaven, but we could see, and some cat next to me gave me a piece of groovy barbecue. Sugar Ray[243] stole pre-fight show, with impeccable natty suit and gleaming process. He is the coolest cat in America next to you. Clay won the fight, as close as it was. He has a lot going for him, if he wasn't so fucking cute. He don't even put his hands up he's so hip. He just backs away. But he ain't ready for no Liston. Sonny wd break his face quick quick. Patterson's young brother debuted too. He washed his opponent in 2nd round with that leaping hook. I got some good bets spread on second Liston-Patterson routine. I say Floyd will last 5, and I got a cat to give me 3 to 1 saying he won't. Good bet I think.

O.K., you stay loose and active. Drink a lot and stay in people's hair. That's the only way to get any satisfaction out of the literary life. Otherwise it's a dull clump of feathers. Let's start a magazine called The Noble Cocksucker. Or something hip like that. WE PRINT THE TRUTH ABOUT NOTHING!! DISTORT OR DIE! And have hip pictures of ourselves on the cover w/ guns . . . naked and pissing in Jackie Kennedy's ear. Man, it would sell! LOVE, Roi

---

240   Gregory Corso.
241   Cassius Clay (Muhammed Ali) vs. Doug Jones, March 13, 1963.
242   A. B. Spellman, African American poet and music historian and critic, b. 1935. Spellman was a close friend of Jones, and both were active and influential in writing about jazz and African American history.
243   Sugar Ray Robinson, American boxer, b. 1921.

[Mar. 1963] [#1]

Thank you for that lovely lovely poem. How come you don't publish a bunch'a new poems in some magazine so's I can get a chance to see the new work??

Har,

Fomentor Prize[244] is only won by fags or foreigners. So take your money or your choice. Maybe effeminate cats from Idaho qualify, but that'd be stretching it quite a bit. Quite frankly I'm against the whole thing. I'll send you a million dollars soon as I get my check. (It's late again.) And, shit, from what I heard, the F prize is in the thousands, and is given from Mallorca, so once or twice a year all the really hip publishers can fuck each other's wives in the tropics. Barney Rosset usually brings a colored girl. He replaced the one I took from him with another one made up to look like the old one. Actually he wants me to jump at this one cause he's got her ass stuffed with nitro . . . but I'm not going for it, I know a phoney when I hear it ticking. But luck to you, hombre. Fuck Mrs. Johnson,[245] completely (if you can stand chicks with dirty teeth and anonymous figures) . . . she don't know her ass from anybody else's. Last I saw her (three days ago) she said editors were still mulling things over, but it don't sound very cool to me. She mentioned that if the thing did fall through she would try her own publisher (where she published her little masterpiece "Come and Join the Dance") *Atheneum*, whom she claims are fairly knowledgeable types. But try anything, tho, for sure, I think the Morrow loot wd be much better than Grove. Rosset being a saver.

My book at Morrow (Blues opus) which, by the way, just had its name changed to BLUES PEOPLE: NEGRO MUSIC IN WHITE AMERICA, which ain't bad, but . . . well, they, Morrow, may throw a party on publication date, pushed back to Sept 25, to sort of set the thing up in the market place. Well, if they furnish the loot, I'm gonna get some hard type music in and blow the block up. Cedar is moving over to where Jazz Gallery used to be. Closing ceremonies on Mar 31, a freebee drink bout. And that's where this book party might be if everything comes off.

I just sent a letter to Di Prima saying I'se through w/ that funky ol animal. Tho it is sad, &c., and now I think, especially after seeing the first west coast or W.C. issue, that there will be a kind of vacant stare where something used to happen. Wild Dog[246] sounds like a good thing. Who's doing it? Will there be nude photos of junkies? Make it a fan mag. Does poetry day entitle poets in the state to request anything of their feller citizens? That must be a groovy state. But I'm thinking serially about moving to Kenya. Har! Up on that exclusive plateau the british

---

244 The *Prix Formentor*, or Formentor Prize, was an international literary prize based in Spain; it ran from 1961 to 1967 and was then reestablished in 2011. The Formentor Prize was awarded for unpublished works; a second prize, the *Prix International*, was awarded to already-published, primarily avant-garde works, as a way to grow support for authors outside of their home countries.

245 Joyce Johnson (Joyce Glassman).

246 *Wild Dog*, the little magazine started by Dorn out of Pocatello.

used to cool themselves out on. Beautiful weather (I read a book) people from temperate climates can really swing. And now, there's something about ranches, &c. being available. If I could get a gig there, or be invited permanently (har) but just a teaching gig, or something, I'd sweep out of here velly smartly. Really, it seems a heavier preoccupation with me day to day. I keep seeing that bombsight over this burg. Wow, a ranch! I saw television program about Jim Shoulders[247] and his groovy place, and how his little daughters ride around on horses and shit like that. As soon as Kenyatta and M'boya[248] cool the brits out, I may make the move. Bring my own ice making machine, get my driver's license and a pilot's license for quick trips up country and to look in on cool friends in Tangier and Algiers (I know editor of new Algerian Magazine, Revolution Africaine . . . I'm supposed to contribute article each month on jazz for them . . . eng lang. edition . . . small pay . . . but shit like that might make the whole thing possible.) I CAN'T STAY IN THIS COUNTRY MANY MORE YEARS. Or at least it doesn't seem to me like any of the pressure, &c. will slack off, and we'll get into some ugliness I won't be able to take so quietly. And I don't dig jails at all. No bueno. What you think, white hunter? Why don't you all come with us, and we make settlement high up on escarpment overlooking new africans. Coolest of all is that it's an eng speak colony (oops!) state, cause I don't really dig the idea of having to speak something else or whatnot forever. Shit on that. Took me too long to learn this thing. O.K., let me know immediately, Ernie's waiting out at the plane with his hunting gear. Again, I'm hungover and up too early in the mewnin.' (Confidentially, wd you fuck Jimmy Baldwin if he made it worth your while???) LOVE Roi

Ed,   [Mar. 1963 #2]

Sorry about the Morrow drag, and I feel especially involved since I did suggest, &c. that you get connected with them. But Glassman had, of course, built it like the new world and I went for it. Apparently they are willing to go out on limbs as far as non-fiction, i.e., ideas that they are only vaguely aware of, because as far as their readers are concerned my book is about "jazz," which is now cool. But if they had to be literally responsible, in their minds, for some of the stances found in that book, it would not see the light of day. I mean to show you just what hold they have on what's in the thing, Glass Joyceman asked me if I thought maybe Martin Luther King wd write a blurb for the cover! I wanted to shove a mackinaw down her throat and pull it out at the other end. That book cd be called or subtitled "Why don't MLK

247   Jim Shoulders, American professional rodeo rider and rancher, 1928–2007.
248   Jomo Kenyatta, Kenyan statesman, 1894–1978. Kenyatta served as prime minister during the time of British control and maintained it afterward; after independence, he served as president of Kenya. Thomas Joseph Odhiambo Mboya, Kenyan politician, 1930–1969. Mboya was an essential figure in Kenyatta's administration, a key figure in organizing Kenya's independent state.

eat my ass" or something similar. Shit. But she also told me she had this scheme for Atheneum. Did she mention that or was that more bullshit for me? I do have another idea though, if you're not punchy from them already. If you want to try the Grove lottery or the Scribner's that's cool, and when or if they show their ass, why don't you let me take the book plus as many stories as you can gather together, (as book if necessary, but with option for single use, &c.) also some outline if possible for non-fiction book . . . cd be short and in exposition, not Aal, &c. but statement of intention and where information is to be gotten, &c. Then I would take all this material, plus some kind of letter from you saying what's what with you, and I would take all the material to my agent. Sterling Lord,[249] who is very groovy cat, plus lots of people working for him. Man, I think it would be a very good solution, with much possible results. They the ones pushed up my price, hence status at Morrow. (Morrow having good shit kickers idea of the higher the advance, &c. the more we got to push the book, so now they give parties, &c. and all that horseshit. But it does ensure to a certain extent that the fucking tome won't just disappear into the pavement. Also they send all stories around and around, and not to just those big goofy mags, but to many places you might do yrself. Of course, with the poems, like myself, you still on your own, &c. Don't nobody want none of them. (Ha, though Barney's lady called recently and wanted to know if you or Gil had had first books . . . which is dumb because I included yr book with the mss. They wanted to know because they wanted to submit one of them to the Lamont Poetry Award, which Ed Field[250] won last year. But poet cannot have had a previous volume. But that at least means like they considering it with some degree of seriousness??) But Lord seems to me a good idea, really. Selby with him and Kerouac and some other cats, oh your favorite author Red Neck Bill[251] is also with them. But they try to do straight with you, and man with a novel and a book of ss and an outline of a nf book, you would be cool with them. And of course they "know your name," &c. so it wouldn't be a cold appearance, &c. Think it over. I'd be, of course, glad to do the thing. Let me know, &c. what you think. But I definitely advise it.

Virgil Thompson I meet at two pink parties and he is as gay as a ladybug. In fact fags tell apocryphal stories about him, e.g., ". . . and then Virgil said to him, 'My dear you will just have to stop sucking now . . .'" or some such. But I am having a copy of my book sent in advance in a couple months to him for possible comment. Also to John Cage. Maybe them highassed cats will dig the book and Morrow is hot for some kind of blurb, only I got to suggest who they ask . . . so it wouldn't have to be Moishe Tshombe. But why don't you stick a rock up VT's ass and see what happens, maybe he's got some loot up there. Hell it's worth a try.

249   Sterling Lord was Jack Kerouac's editor, publishing the seminal *On the Road*.
250   Edward Field, American poet, b. 1924. Field is a Brooklyn-born poet who has long resided in Greenwich Village.
251   William Burroughs.

I'll send a Kulchur out there. Tho Lita H's in L.A. at the Beverley Hills Hotel (that is until this sat, then she and her fleabit new monies will be staying near you, friend . . . at the Arizona Biltmore. Why don't you drop down, shoot the shit for a few hours . . . maybe he won't recover.) Sho, I'll be the WD correspondent. Flash, Mr. and Mrs. America and all the ships at sea, Stanley Gould,[252] noted junkie just got stomped in the Cedar tavern. You do mean all the news that's fit to print, don't you? Like who won what, who's being published where, &c. What junkies are trying to kick, and why they can't, &c. By the way, god, I saw your boy A Trocchi on the television, from Angloville, where he was demonstrating shooting up techniques for a documentary on DOPE. Wow, now really, man, Happy Bill[253] would never get involved in no shit like that. At least I don't think he would. Trocchi sits there grinning in his fucking accent, sticking the fucking needle in his arm, and saying, dig this man, "You see, I taken it, you don't see me turning into a wild man, do you?" Whew! It would have been a literal groove if he had od'd right on the t.v. as Happy Bill would say, "it was tasty."

How long wd such correspondence be? Could I tell about the nuns raping the Congolese troops, &c.? Is this a Hearse publication? If not, why not?

Dig especially on that side *Eos*, especially the rhythm section behind Ornette. Sweet. The other record is mostly corn, but grooves in spots. Cross Breeding is another wild tune. Oh, the Sullen Art, interviews book is out,[254] and you'll see it soon I guess. You had one of the only intelligent sounding things in it. And of course Bob. I sounded like a fucking dullard. And Gil is so fucking pompous it's impossible to read it without getting annoyed. But book serves some use, though I wish the included interviews were longer and that Duncan[255] had not pulled out (I hear) at the last minute.

Glad you are keeping some stuff coming to K. Wow, what a dazzle that's getting to be. Hope you will at least have a review or something as often as possible. And that spring poem, if I didn't say already was really very lovely. Also, there's a cat in Argentina, who prints a magazine called Eco Contemporaneo.[256] He reprinted my Cuba piece, also he prints American poetry, bilingual, but it is essentially an Argentine mag. Well he wants a few poems from Americans, or actually 4 poems by 4 Americans. He's got a poem of mine and one of Joel's. I thought maybe I could send him the Spring poem since he wrote me this frantic note about wanting to make a quick deadline. Shall I send??

Idaho sounds like it is tightening your head by now. Maybe you ought to start

---

252   Stanley Gould, 1926–1975. Kerouac was friends with Gould; he shows up under various pseudonyms in Kerouac's *The Subterraneans*, *Book of Dreams*, and *Big Sur*.

253   William Burroughs.

254   *The Sullen Art: Interviews*, edited by David Ossman, 1963.

255   The rumor was correct; Robert Duncan does not appear in *The Sullen Art*.

256   *Eco Contemporaneo* was an Argentine magazine that ran from 1961 to 1969. It was started by the writers Antonio Dal Masetto and Miguel Grinberg.

yelling May Day, and make your break? Not for a minute to paint a rosy picture of goofsville here, but simply to point out, and I know I don't have to, that this is at least a communal desperation, well in the sense that you can at least bitch in concert, tho that very fact can get heavy after a while. Very. And you know, for the most part, what kind of work you'd find. Library or publishing, &c. That kind of horse shit. Gil's thinking of taking a job as a bartender at the new Cedar (if it happens though I think he will fast get sick of that shit . . . but it is a kind of no bullshit genre or work though he will be in the place of the largest and most extravagant kind of bullshit, possibly, en el todo mundo.) And of course there's no sense coming East to go to Jersey. That shit hole. But you also must see that I'm going to get out of here in a few years. A few years? Whenever the fuck that is, I don't know. And don't put Kenya down, Man.[257] It's a definite possibility, as I have had to wonder about a social cannibalism for a long time now, not that that shit could ever drive me out of here. Come from very old family, all Americans. But that bombsight, and the terrifying wrongness of this place, is actually frightening. Plus Kenyatta's a goddamn vegetarian. Remember I got some half-white kids, but then that takes care of most of North Africa, i.e., all those mulatto countries. But if Idaho is getting too heavy it might be time to shake it loose. If we had say 500 dollars together I would say start our own fucking bookstore in town here or something. I told you I was gonna do it last fall, but my so called partner pulled out at last minute, and we lost a beautiful location 2nd ave and St Marks, cross roads of new faith, w only 65 buck rent. I'm still contemplating it. Fucking Ferling took himself out of financial harm's way. It's a very solid thought. All love, Roi

Jones continued to be moved by Dorn's work, excited that Dorn understood and exhibited so many possibilities for what a poem should do or say. Dorn had just sent him "Mourning Letter, March 29, 1963," a poem about striking coal miners in Hazard, Kentucky. The miners had recently been striking against "starvation wages and the failure of operators to contribute to the United Mine Workers welfare fund, forc[ing] most of the mines in eastern Kentucky to close" (Russin). The poem starkly captures not just the events but the larger sentiment of despair of the workers and the cruelty of the mining companies: "The mine owners' / extortionary skulls / whose eyes are diamonds don't float / down the rivers, as they should / of the flood / The miners, cold / starved, driven from work, in / their homes float though." In this letter, Jones connects the poem about the miners to Dorn's interview in The Sullen Art, *published by Corinth Books in 1962. The book is a collection of interviews conducted by WBAI Radio's David Ossman with various poets, including Dorn, Jones, Robert Creeley, and Allen Ginsberg, among others. On being prompted by Ossman to talk about his poetry being political, Dorn said,*

257   Dorn, as was his manner, would call Jones to task for his unrealistic or romantic visions about politics and nations: Dorn felt that Jones's desire to move to Kenya was both of these and told him as much.

For one thing, I don't know a thing about politics, and I think that gives me the greatest right in the world to be a zealot about it. People who congregate in a square in London and make a march on the atomic works are not really concerned with politics either. Everyone knows the machinery of politics goes on far above our heads, and I don't think there's anything we can do about that. There is energy there to be had, to be put in service of mass statements about this torture, the condition of the world, and I think poets are in a very good position to keep insisting—to lead the way with whatever vision they have. (Ossman 86)

ed,   [Apr. 1 ? 1963]

Here's first installment of Wild Dog column. When's that thing coming out? Hope this makes it. Also, hope you dig my latest pseudonym.

Hey, that was a very lovely poem you sent me on the miners. Makes that interview-speech in The Sullen Art look very much to the point. As you have taken your own clear swing, and it rings with more than social statement. And of course, you know that's what interests me most at this point. I come to think that finally, a poem has got to be about *something* . . . and I mean that as an amateur phenomenonologist. All questions now of "modernity" to the side it seems that in order to completely address the poem to all the possibilities of expression . . . what actually exists has to be taken into account, and "at the point of" and "in the time of," &c. As this German cat name Zuckerhandl[258] about music saying, a picture of a tone as "wave lengths of different dimensions and shapes" can be represented, that is everything that characterizes the tone as an acoustical phenomenon . . ."is represented in a particular feature of the picture." Like pitch, loudness, color, and all that can be represented. In such abstract fashion, as it were. The one thing that could not be gotten in such a fashion is "the dynamic state of the tone." Yeh, which is like saying everything but the way it really sounds.

So it seems to me about, say, someone like Denise that she represents all the exact intelligent registrations a poem ought to have today, but there is simply no dynamism of *purpose*, save that beat up horse shit of "the mind," &c. which leads directly to AESTHETICS. Of which it is not my place to put down, simply it becomes a useless habitual boredom, which makes it more difficult to see what's really goin' on, &c. UNLESS, the term itself can be revamped, or refilled ?? Aww shit and marbles. I guess maybe tho that's almost like saying Christian soldiers all over again. But fuck it, one has to, I assume at this point, leave the responsibility to one's ideas, and get emotional about them anyway, even if finally in some "other" context they can be represented as wrong.

---

258 Victor Zuckerkandl, Austrian musicologist, 1896–1965.

I mean I don't think Hitler is absolutely the worst man that ever existed, &c. And very simply because he can be put down by anybody. And here's something I may be still working on:

LETTER TO ELIJAH MUHAMMED

When your talking is murdered, and only very old women
will think to give you flowers. When history is the homework
that presses you, silently, at your dying, in your blood
some briefer hatred digs long shank claws, what will it be like
to be more than that? What will it be to adore the nature
of your killer's affliction?
In whatever epoch of new understanding.
New faiths new religious zeals. The lone saver is knowing exactly
how far to trust what is real. I am tired already
of being so hopelessly right.

Anyway, now Sam, We are getting all revved up by Spring, after the long slow clinging winter. Now we feel like romping, which is always trouble. I'm supposed to see Joyce tomorrow. She didn't send the book so I'm going to pick it up. Then the plan is to take it right to Hutter at Scribner's? Donald Hutter?[259] I'll call him and make some kind of assignation just as soon as I get the mss.

Otherwise all kinds dumb shit continues. The Npaper strike is over and the fuckin times just went up to a dime.[260] Which news I will cover in the next WDog. Now it looks as if the cat that took over my friend Larry Wallrich's book shop will let me use the electric mimeo if I wants, to put out a thing like the bear. What you think? Think it's still a useable idea? I sorely miss the Bear, &c. Maybe I'll call it The Caliph, or *Arithmetic*, or/ *Sheiks*. What you think? Let me know Dusty, how's Doris and the Wauchopes?[261]

O.K. (O, man did I tell you about the cat who was here who wanted me to sell that bulletin board I have?? Wow, what the fuck is happenin' in the world?? Look, I'll let you slide right now. I got to get in the wind, as the junkies around here say.

LOVE, ROI

259　Donald Hutter, American publisher and editor, 1933–1990. Hutter worked for several publishers throughout his life, including Scribner's, Dial Press, and Henry Holt.

260　From December 8, 1962, through March 31, 1963, there was a general newspaper strike in New York City. Initiated by the Newspaper Guild, the strike affected nearly all of the major New York City newspapers, stopping production for a full 114 days at newspapers like the *New York Times*, the *Daily News*, and the *New York Herald Tribune*, among others. Alternative media, however, stepped into the spotlight; the *New York Review of Books* was started during the strike.

261　This is a reference to T. S. Eliot's *Fragment of a Prologue*.

Hi,   4/17/63

Thanks for those two veiny dogs. They look like they never been fucked by nothing, except maybe oaths. Sitting on my ass now, after writing that goddam introduction to the fiction book. It's arch as hell, but so what? Pretty soon I'll walk it over to Eighth St. book store, then maybe hang around there an hour and "charge" a couple of books we can't afford. Shit, there's nothing like having a goddam charge account in a book store . . . it's the only one I got.

(Basil & Gil)

Guess by now you could have heard about our/illfated bout at McSorley's Old Ale house. Shit, that was really stupid. The three of us stood round mcs's for 7 hours, from about 3 until 10, getting completely out of it . . . some magazine, Post I think, was doing a "spread" on the place and was buying free beer to keep the cats looking like they were really going at it. We were closest to photog, so we took about six out of every batch. Later, I, we, got into a verbal kind of thing with some blue suited ivy looking cats who were whooping it up. Like the cat asked me, "How you like our singing boy?" So I sd, "Fine, mister," and threw some pennies on their table. You dig, really sociable like. Anyway, they leave, and then we go to stagger out, me & B to my house for dinner, Gil to his own dinner. Whereupon, we encounter these cats out front. Gild sd something to one of them, like, "You're a prick," and baby it was on. There was about 12 of them, and it turned out about 4 or 5 of them were like in another group . . . they were off-duty cops. Man, they kicked the shit out of us. I mean literally kicked. No fists much. But I backed against the wall street fighting style, and there was a cat on one side kicking me in the shins, I mean calm like he was jerking off. Finally, during this long 5 minutes Basil gets sent sprawling on the ground so I broke out of my corner because some cat was getting ready to really do it to him. I blocked the cat off, but fell to my knees, and when I did that some cat on the side delivered a size 10 shoe right at my eye. My whole head was swollen and lacerated, like they say. Now it's all cooled down, and I've only the black eye to show for it. All my students were very curious. I told them it was an old battle wound that keeps coming back, sort of like stigmata. Anyway, we've all been pretty sore for the last week, and I've been wearing dark glasses all the time. Oh woe woe! And the season's changing.

This fri or sat (20th), I've got a short article coming out in The Saturday Review; the middlebrow's Esquire . . . or whatever it's got to be around now. If I can get some extra copies of article I'll certainly send it. It's a "symposium" *The Problem of the Negro Writer*, part of a speech I made, before the P.E.N. club, international writers' organization. I met Marchette Chute (the chick who does popularizations of Shakespeare) and James Ghoul Cozzens[262] . . . that's the kind of groovy in-the-world

---

262   Marchette Chute, American biographer, 1910–1984. Chute wrote biographies of early English writers: Shakespeare, Chaucer, and Ben Jonson. James Gould Cozzens, American writer, 1903–1978.

cross section that makes those kind of things. Lucky that came though . . . means I can maybe pay this month's rent.

Cedar's closing is a big void in my life. And that other place up the street, Dillon's is grim as shit. But new Cedar is supposed to open soon in the old Jazz Gallery. Dining and dancing, probably.

This morning John Wieners and Michael Rumaker came over, and we shot the shit for a while. Michael just in for his monthly fuck . . . he's working in a real estate office up in Nyack, New York, one of those terrible little towns upstate New York.

Hey, that Woolf piece is really something . . . in fact I quoted parts in my introduction. Lita assured me the piece wd be done article style in the front. K doesn't have to completely fold. Shit, as long as we can get some good material in, I don't see why we shd completely exit. Though Bob Creeley seems to think the towel throwing in is in order, but then he never did much to see that K was anything to begin with. Which is a mighty drag; anyway we see the way the struggle will move. Gil jumped prematurely, more from an outraged social sense I guess than any "literary" consideration, tho they are heavily linked. I'm digging a new tenor man named Chas. Lloyd[263] who is imitative but wild!

Love, Roi APPLE CORES WILL COME AGAIN!

Edward,   April 17 [1963]

So what's happening out there, for God's sake? I mean what're you doing and why? I hoped you dug that groovy tie. It had a western flavor I thought wd go well with the scarps and drops of Idahore. No word yet from Scribner's?? I want you to know I had to put on my fucking good suit (only suit) and a tie, go uptown and deposit that mss. But shit many to say it again, that was really a fucking beautiful book. Really and truly, I can't tell you how much I dug that. Now, I guess, the long wait sets in. Well, Ted W. of 8th St. book store, says if it's negative at S&sons he'll put in a word with that cat at Random House, Jason ??? I can't think of his last name. But that's some help, but I hope it won't be necessary.

Did I tell you about that article I have in Saturday Review? It's in the April 20th issue. Can you get that out there? If not I'll send it. Really it's part of a longer essay, but they wanted it cut to 1000 words, which was not bad. Let me know what you think. That fucking SR to have so much middlebrow prestige don't pay much at all. I got 100 bucks for that, or am supposed to get it soon. It will go out immediately to pay this here fucking rent.

Now we're thinking of how to get out of the city this summer. I've got to teach all of june, and most of July . . . or rather from June 17 to July 26, but we thought

---

263   Charles Lloyd, American jazz musician, b. 1938.

maybe in August we could go out in the woods. But the rent for the houses, &c. plus the racial angle make our choices very narrow. I'll have a few dollars after the summer semester, but not really very much. So I don't really know what to do. But shit another fucking summer here might not kill me, but it wd go a long way towards that end. I know the kids would dig the country, &c. or beach, as we could secure someway. There was an old lady in my class who offered her summer place on fire island, which I immediately told Hettie about . . . but now it turns out the chick only wanted to get fucked. She came on first about how she and her old man don't use it much, and how they might even be on their way to Europe. No such luck or fact. She figured I'd be there alone, it turns out, and she could rush in breathless and nude and throw herself on the raffia rug. Shit. As if I didn't have enough fucking troubles. So that whole thing collapses.

A cat named Kanovitz, a lousy painter, but a very nice cat, has tenuously invited us up to his new quarters in Provincetown. His old lady owns a jewelry store around the corner from us, and she's opening one in Ptown. They bought a big ass house, with a separate apartment for house guests, &c. But I despise Provincetown. It's like an open air Cedar, and worse. Plus those fucking cops and shit up there are unbearable. But if it's the only thing left, we may have to take it. But shit I hate staying with people who don't have any kids . . . and have set their lives around that. They will have to get irritated with ours and their bullshit. I mean it will quickly get tiresome for them . . . the yelling screaming and general administration necessary to keep the girls in running order. You know what I mean. People shd only take kids to houses where they'll be "understood." Genteel tolerance is like very cutting after a while.

Last Saturday I'm standing at the phone, this is early morning, talking to some fool and all of a sudden this girl, Dorothy White, who lives around the corner, is banging on the door. She comes in almost hysterical and tells me her husband, an old friend of mine, Bill White, a painter, is going out, heroin O.D. style. I had to rush around there half dressed and pack his head in ice, and all the other survival mechanics of dope. He came out, and then I walked him around for a few hours, but it was really scary for a time. Man, why don't these cats cool themselves out? He's really a very sweet cat, and could be a good painter. I met the cat in the service, and he moved from D.C. to right around the corner about 1½ ago. But he's got some no bueno friends. The ugly bohemians George Oppen[264] writes about in the next culture. Oh, well, there's not to much I can do about it. Took him to a hip fag dr. tho. Love to all yall. Roi

Wasn't that *Letter 27* of Olson's a gas, in the Yale Lit Mag?[265]

---

264   George Oppen, American poet, 1908–1984. Oppen was associated with the Objectivist poets and was a friend of Louis Zukofsky, with whom he started a publishing house called To Publishers, which published works of William Carlos Williams and Ezra Pound.
265   "Letter 27" was part of Charles Olson's *Maximus Poems*.

Jones wrote this letter from New York City's Bellevue Hospital, ill with a bout of hepatitis contracted after shooting heroin. The oldest public hospital in the United States, Bellevue has a notorious public reputation regarding, especially, its psychiatric facilities. Jones's description of his ward is at once a horror show and a social critique, noting "all the horseshit & indolence of any 'charity' institution." Jones witnessed the realities of very poor white men; while he expected the dire circumstances for African Americans and Latinos, "the old white poor person is terribly shabby & unnerving." R. G. Kelley describes the conditions inside the hospital for Thelonious Monk in 1957 that Jones was experiencing firsthand in 1963:

> *Surrounding the red brick building on the corner of 30th Street and East River Drive was a ten-foot-high "spear-topped, wrought-iron fence." Attendants often acted like prison guards, and with 650 patients jammed into a 630-bed facility, the overcrowded conditions were reminiscent of [New York City's old complex of jails] the Tombs. . . . [Paranoid schizophrenic was] a catch-all phrase frequently applied to black patients and nonconformist artists. The list of alleged paranoid schizophrenics who passed through Bellevue in the 1950s is long and distinguished, including Bud Powell, Charles Mingus, not to mention Gregory Corso, Norman Mailer, and Allen Ginsberg. (*Thelonious Monk *214)*

Ed,   Tues May 8 (?) [May 9, 1963]

I guess you know by now the horseshit that has virtually plowed me (& us) under. It's a stupidity past any I thot myself capable of. Oh well! Shit & eat shit!

But hepatitis. The ass sucker's sickness. That is the limit! Dirty needle, for sure. And the hoot is that I had stopped fucking around w/ that shit for about 2 months before it happened! Bitter fruit.

Anyway, it means, most practically, 3–5 wks in bed. 3 in this wild hospital. A city hospital of which no genre more hopeless exists! All the horseshit & indolence of any "charity" institution. The sloth & terrifying poverty. Old men scream here all night. I had forgotten. But I'm here, they say, for at least 3 wks. And after that, a [. . .] clean cut [. . .] wearing resident sez, "You drink too much, sir. I'm telling you for your own good." Me, who's practically a teetotaler. But I plan, after I get out of here, to get to some specialist & see just how much my drinking will be or *can be* curtailed.

Otherwise, of course, my family is humming & confused. & the kids, now suddenly ain't got no old man! What kind of dumb shit is this now. I'm really a stupid shithead. This is one of the dumbest things I think I've ever done.

Anyway, we see what the hospital holds in store. There's about 20 other cats on my ward. Old men. 30 years of P.R.[266] & Negro cats. White men tend to be old & nuts. The all night screamers. Poor old city white men. Where have these cats been all their lives? In what hopeless furnished room or whatever. A poor Negro or Puerto Rican is one thing. Their culture is reactive, is to a large extent formed, because of the need to exist & *grow* in such conditions. But the old white poor person is terribly shabby & unnerving.

There's an old cat next to me who moans night and day about his death, in the most unpleasant, sentimental terms. & I'm sure he's right.

I'm still very sick. Can't eat much. Very jaundiced—eyes and skin. Can't move around too fast. But I'll beat this shit in for now. Meanwhile, let me know how the real America is. But maybe W.D. will have to get a new correspondent? We'll see how I feel . . . I'll try to let you know.

All love

Roi

[May 14 1963]

Tues.

Edward,

Glad to hear from you, especially in this poor folks' rest home. I am getting stronger now, tho my eyes still have that sickly yellow squint. One good thing, I've had plenty of visitors. So many in fact that one of the head whore nurses found it in her soul to send some home one day for smoking. But I rattled her ass . . . called her some names that froze her right in her smelly tracks. I bet she'd never been called a "stale eyed cunt" before. It was my poetic inspiration forging through. Even Ornette Coleman came yesterday. All the beards & black-white combos thrill the other patients . . . & they stare reverently even deferentially at the diversity of my entourage.

Otherwise, I'm reading my frail ass off. Even read old Thos. Mann again. What an arrogant pompous bourgeois he was. Criminally fastidious!

Lunch is just being served. And I find now I have a constant ravening hunger & immediately gobble everything down. My poor mother came yesterday, bringing me loud silk yellow pajamas & staring at the derelicts in my ward, murmuring "how depressing these sad men are." Now you know where my poetry comes from. The good black bourgeois soul. Ah well, it is tender & irrevocably sentimental. For one thing, I miss the girls pretty badly, children under 12 are not permitted to visit. And I will be here at least another week, possibly two. Even when I get out I'll have to take it very slow, for maybe another month. I hope I'm strong enough to take on those summer classes. We need that loot very much.

Mormons, and especially lil' Mormon girls, give me a pain in the ass. I hope

---

266   Puerto Rican.

the Muslims ravish them all or send them out on 42nd St. peddling their stingy holes. Ah the purity of ignorance, &c. What she needs, of course, is a good non-blackboard fuck.

Maybe Scribner's will come through. I really hope so, too bad that Rossett is delaying the acceptance of the poetry book (I'm sure he'll take it) that wd be a little loot for you, pitiful tho it may be. Look at this word: MONEY & figure John Dillinger wasn't so dumb. He dug, at least, the limitations of the republic.

Paul Blackburn brought me a long skinny notebook, so I scribbling couplets of quatrain & unintelligible notes about the structure of the instinct, inspired by a book I am reading now by Max Scheler[267] called *Man's Place in Nature*. More phenomenology.

I begin to think in this hospital that my days in N.Y. (America) *are* numbered. A year maybe two—who knows. But I right now feel I must get away quite soon. And last night, again, I had a long dream about having a farm in Kenya. And watching my little girls grow up to marry the chiefs of state. While their daddy writes large boring books of abstruse social philosophy. It's a warming thought. I think I'll renew my flying license, in order to hop over to Tangier or Peking & maybe even to Idaho. The great international future. Come stay w/ us on the veldt. We can hunt tigers & get drunk. (Tho I'm off the booze for a *year*!) Oh well we'll see what happens. In the meantime keep a stiff upper lip & keep our Mormons clean. Tell the little girl I said go lick a leper's ass.

Love, Roi
24 Eckert Ave.
Newark, New Jersey

My dearest Eddie,   25 May 63

Good to hear from you. And from Pocatello Heights! Wow! Is it run by the Hilton people? Sounds like a place Rubinosa or one of those international studs wd hang out. Hah, I'm not doing so well. Right this second I'm in my tiny (2) room at my parents' house in New Jersey. Man is it dull here. Tho, of course, my parents are very sweet to me. And my mother tries to make me gain weight (I lost *10* lbs the 1st wk I was sick—now I weigh about 122). But I'm getting a great deal of reading done—maybe too much. (Eastlake's new book *Portrait of the Artist w/ 26 Hosse* is not so much. He's just a stylist when he's weak). And I'm still very weak, tho my eyes are just about back to their normal pink. My old man's off on a bowling tournament so I'm trying to subvert my mother, telling her filthy stories about the gout. The Ala. routines are getting closer to what I think will be the final form of

---

267   Max Scheler, German philosopher, 1874–1928.

social dispatch. (The taxicab cat w/ the knife in his back!) Stupid tragedies, set in motion by Bull Connor[268] & [. . .]. King[269] can't hold the poolroom cats back much longer if B.C. & co are gonna play ofay all the time. As a So. African exile told me that those cats, Afrikaners, may not make the Olympics!

Hettie and kids coming over here tomorrow—only a few miles away—but another country for sure. I'll probably be here another week or so—I'm supposed to start teaching 17 June. I hope I can make it. But I've got to—weak or not.

Enclosed, latest installment of "A.C." ⟵ a harmful object I lost the guy's address or I wd have sent it straight to him.

No word from Scribner's yet? I wonder what's taking so long? Still I somehow feel better that it is taking a little time. Probably a lot of people reading it.

Larry Wallrich & I to do some publishing this fall. He's out in Mallorca. Any small 32pp books you want out? Maybe 3 or 4 stories or something? Small collection of poems. Essays? I'm not certain of exact set up as yet. But I shd know very soon. But let me know what you think. (Other projects too, he's proposed but this sprawling on my back all day has slowed things down miserably. It's enough to drive anyone buggy!)

Anyway, I'll be here in the sticks until the first so probably when you write I'll be back in the Apple but most likely still on my back.

We trying to get away for August anyway, but where? Prices are too much or else there's those hip northern restrictions—even tho I got yellow eyes & don't many coons ever have them. No Go tho!! And then there's places that even I wldn't go (But I haven't found them yet. Oh well probably we'll have to stay where we are, which is something after Bellevue!

Love, Roi

Ed,   [June 7 ? 1963]

Got the note from Hutter saying he was sorry but he "cdn't offer Mr. Dorn anything," whatever that means. Euphemism is like scalded (or scaldt) shit. I was certain they wd take it, but why I cant tell you. So N.D.'s[270] the next go? Wilentz tells me he wants to read the book, & on "my recommendation" he's got this cat Jason Epstein[271] interested at Random House. So we'll see what happens with Laughlin first.

Thot heavy news by we got still heavier from here! *Hettie came down w/ the*

---

268   Theophilus Eugene "Bull" Connor, 1897–1973. Connor was the infamous commissioner of public safety in Birmingham, Alabama, during the civil rights movement in the late 1950s and early 1906s, known for his extreme bigotry and violence toward African Americans and their white sympathizers.
269   Martin Luther King Jr.
270   *New Directions*, with editor James Laughlin.
271   Jason Epstein, American editor and publisher, b. 1928. Epstein was one of the founders of the *New York Review of Books* during the New York City newspaper strike in 1963.

yellow sickness Tuesday!! After the M.D.s sd everything was cool; the Bellevue cats. So now we are completely fucked. And no $$ to boot! Also we got to send the kids away to N.J. till Hettie gets well enough to get back in the saddle. I waited till my frustration & hopelessness subsided a bit, before I wrote. Like, after all, who the fuck am I to command so much specific evil from wherever? So everything here is low & grim & like this paper, muy amarillo. O fuck! Will we survive? You Bet!! So the two of us will be locked up here together for a couple of weeks anyway. Alone & we can't even fuck. That's the heaviest blow! I'm much better tho—getting a little stronger, but still wobbly. Hope I can get ready by 17th when my first class begins. So we're both teetotalers for 1 whole year! And I swore off dope. What's left?

If you see D Goodman Levertov in Idaho tell her Caliph say for her to gobble de goo! Her version of New Y. is Mitch's falling face and the empty markets of her hairless pouch. Or something "controlled" like that. Boy I'm so tired of Denise—why are almost all lady poets full of shit? Is that the prerequisite? Dennie needs to be raped by Peter Orlovsky every tuesday for a year! That wd cool her out.

But still good to be home & listening to funny Monk! Hey, a cat just got home from Ibiza (one of the Balearic groups,[272] at Majorca, &c.) & he say he had a huge pad for 9 dollars a month. But electric cost him 20 a month. But he is a painter, & they like to see too much anyway. Fuck them anyway out of spite, rich bastards. I mighta ask de Kooning to lend me a grand till Sonny Liston become atty general. But Ibiza sounds groovy, tho probably boredom wd get to be their chief product. But 9 dollars a month!! Food also is dear I suppose because they have to import almost everything! Maybe altogether 50$ a month. But where the fuck wd I get even that? Damn! But on less than a grand perhaps you cd spend the year? But really I'd be reluctant to go to an island of irresponsible turds like that one must be. Everybody "having fun" & being hip. It'd probably give you a venereal disease just thinking about yr new friends. But I *do* think that our splitting is coming closer. Because I've ceased almost to believe that any significant *change* is possible in this country. And any idea of "romantic" socio-political utopias aside, the rise of the city is always more healthy than the crumbling. That "insect doom" is finally, I hope, going to be strictly local, i.e., western. And yr book can outline that collecting bag of terror, more heavily, and more lyrically than I've seen done. People think that N. West[273] was nutty or pessimistic. He at least didn't say "Everybody." But I am.

Hope, by now, you heard from Liter the Mosquiter about yr story & essay. I haven't seen the story yet . . . but she told me over the phone that she wanted to use one at a time! to give more room for Les Girls. Anyway, Anselm Hollow wrote me that you (& G.S.) are narrow. But he really razzed Gil (in new K. (comparing him to Goebbels! Yeh!

272 The Balearic Islands off the coast of Spain in the Mediterranean Sea.
273 Nathaniel West, American author, 1903–1940. West was a contemporary of William Carlos Williams.

Speaking of T Monk, he's right up the street now, possibly for the whole summer. I haven't been yet because of yellow tone but I'm gonna be jam up in there liquorless or no.

We spotted a place up near Charles. Cape Ann. Little 5 rm house for a couple hundred for Aug. till Labor Day. May w/ another couple Basil or Gil, we might be able to swing it. Private beach, &c. Man we, collectively, needs that water & sun. So we see.

O.K. love to Helene & the kids. Hettie & I gonna sit here in separate beds w/ very hot pants. Oh, well, it's all scientific & in the public interest. Stay well & keep in shape!

Love, Roi

19 June
1963 YEAR OF THE
GREAT SICKNESS

Eddie,

Ok, here I am back on the machine,[274] but still weak as a smoke ring. And maybe even still a liddle beet yaller. Hettie now almost completely re-covered, white that is. She had just a gentle hint of the plague so was only dumped for a couple of weeks. Here I was taken sick on May Day and I'm still shaky. That's how bad I were. Dr. No sd I shd've died, yes for real, but nobody told me, which is the coolth of naïve singlemindedness. But let's see what happens in the future. No, absolutely no kind of alcohol, not even in medicine, for the rest of the ano.[275] Shit, that's a real goddam torture. Parties will be very selectively screened, where before I'd go any damn place cd run out a drink. Dullness appears vedy vedy quickly w/o juice. I may even have to reshuffle my closest friends. As, for instance, who cd stand X without the saving veil of grog, that maybe gently boosts the conversation?? Oh, well. And now I'm even afraid to smoke, illegally, that is. Since I did so this last weekend and maybe had a tiny ill effect or two. The paranoia that comes with this shit is fantastic. I'm always looking at my eyes upon arising, during the day several times, and before going to bed, just to see if the yaller is coming back. Also check pee at each instance to see if color is maintained, also the stool. It's silly shit.

Lita the mosquiter is head of big (& bigtime) benefit people have gotten together to give us. Tho the theme of starving roi jones is certainly annoying and embarrassing. Like shit after all who needs to give a damn. And here in Ithaca we all strong hard asses for sure. So far people to participate in Regime party: Cecil Taylor & group; Don Cherry & his big band!; Joel, Paul, and Frank O'[276] will read;

---

274   His typewriter. Jones had been handwriting letters for most of his sickness, too weak to sit at the table to type.

275   *Año*: year.

276   Joel Oppenheimer, Paul Blackburn, Frank O'Hara.

Larry Rivers will give a speech (and maybe an old spike) also bigtime bdway cat Jack Richardson[277] will do along with movie star Gaby Rogers & O'Hara, a scene from his bigtime recent flop Lorenzo! (all this at O's bidding) plus a supper club singer Anita Ellis. Shit man we shd video tape all this shit and sell it as a package to NBC. I got to make the program, it sounds so groovy.

You see we really do things up here in ol' Apfel. No fuckin twiddly biddly shit. Just zoom zoom right into the heart of American Exchange and hip craft for the ominous money Lords. Oh, well. Everybody means well (you know what they mean).

But see the new issue Lit Issue of Esquire and turn red and bit the pages. Man those people are the real lumpen shit eaters of our time (except for poets who are inspired by Martin Buber[278]).

HOORay for Poetry. But shit it'll be at least end of the year before the poems show. They took some of mine in DECEMBER and I haven't even gotten proofs yet. Gil sent them things they took in NOV. and he still don't have proofs. A further note to Rago revealed that it will be some time before the poems show. So. But good that there is some knowledge or recognition from that side.

Lita didn't show me Clay but she sez for sure it's in, I hope, next issue. They shd print essay and that piece same time to assure some worthwhile inside. I gave her a very vitriolic review of a book on black nationalism. Probably too loud and fumey to make much sense. I also gave her peculiar piece called Expressive Language, which I hope you dig if you ever get a chance. A hopeful addition to semantic philosophy but taken from attitude of seeking to weight cultural references by the meanings specific culture gives to words, &c. Very short and maybe fragmentary, but at least a preface to something I'm very much interested in, and the seed of which was the heavy duty hypothesis under jazz book. Meanwhile Morrow's got quotes from Rexroth and Langston Hughes for book, getting more I think.

Man, I can't understand all the bad luck and adversity, &c. we're having. That's weird about the kids. What kind of virus do you think? The Asian kind seems at least easy to identify? What have we done to be so singled? And to boot my sweet grandmother died . . . and with her my last link with the old south.

I got the book back from flitty Hutter, and took it over to Wilentz. Of course, if there is no go I'll zip it over to No Directions. But T.W. sez his connections might be valuable . . . so no matter how screwy it might seem, I don't see any reason why it shdn't be tried.

I was on television the other day w/ Cannonball, John Killen (shade novelist),

---

277   Jack Richardson, American playwright, 1934–2012.
278   Martin Buber, Austrian Israeli philosopher, 1878–1965. Buber engaged with various forms of existentialism.

Ossie Davis (the actor).[279] All bullshit, about Negro problems. And all I wanted to say was EAT MY PUSSY, YOU BLACKGUARDS! But the euphemisms didn't begin to get that across.

Just back from teaching wed afternoon, now evening, and I stopped off at the 5 spot where Thelonious Sphere Monk is packing the place nightly. I'm trying to get him to get young musicians in opposite his names. He digs Cecil (who in fact 3 Sundays ago filled the place for him on a one day gig). But he says Cecil ruins his pianos, and he can't afford to keep buying expensive boxes. He says Barry Harris[280] is a good cool musician, knows how to treat pianos. Anyway I get free 7ups there, and starting two days from now am gonna try to sit up for two sets.

But right now Louie is singing "From the Tables Up at Birdland to the Place Where Louis Dwelled." Poor Little Cats That Have Lost Their Way . . . &c. So take care of yoself, and read the paper. Love to Helene and all dem other Dorns.

Roi

Lil' Brother Montgomery singing:
"I love you mama
But you don't mean me no good."

Hey sporty,   [June 1963]

Yeh, that's wild about Buffaloes. More I think about it the more I marvel. Only possible goof is Big Kelly's ol lady, Jobie, who's a little literal, specially about wife duties, baby she's always on the spot . . . qualifying Heavy's statements as fast as he makes them. But Bob's a good man, despite (or because of?) of it. Otherwise, pure nut! And I am slowly getting my health back. Had a couple beers night or so back, feel fit, but strange twist this is. I don't conk out now in the middle of things, but now when I get in the sack I sleep at least 8 hours which was always a lot of sleep for me before. I ran 4, 5 hours per night as usual. A curious balance this way, I'll just have to AdJuSt!

I haven't written Chas yet. I'll do that this afternoon. Still half-twisting behind publicity gimmicks for that book. I figure maybe I shd just cut my landlord's throat, then the book will really sell. I also just got a deal to go to Calif., U. of, at Berkeley, for some kind of conference, &c. with many mediocrities, eg, Mark Schorer,[281] Ellison, &c. But four days, all expense cooled, plus 100 papers . . . which altogether is some qualified groove, No? Speaking of names, I got invited to a gathering of international

279   John Oliver Killens, African American writer, 1916–1987. Killens was a founder of the Harlem Writers Guild. Ossie Davis, African American actor and writer, 1917–2005. Davis was a well-known civil rights activist.

280   Barry Harris, American jazz pianist and teacher, b. 1929.

281   Mark Schorer, American writer, 1908–1977. Schorer was well recognized, the recipient of three Guggenheim Fellowships and a Fulbright professorship (in Italy).

coon intellectuals last night, at Senegalese mission to UN. They putting on a festival
of negro arts in Dakar in 1965, Alioune Diop,[282] the poet in a two or three hunnerd
dollar suit (really) talked in French, which pissed me off in the first place, and the
whole thing turned out to be a shuck. They just want to put on a little minstrel show,
including us minstrels, for benefit of European ofay. Money, get this, will come from
some US foundation. I raised question(s) in middle of talk, like Are yall interested in
getting Negroes to this O-ffair? Because then, how will they get there? World Eco
set up forbids, &c. All my shit. Finally, I asked just what kind of festival *is* this going
to be. For rico touristas or what, of which, then, baby, there ain't too many black
ones. They skidded around the first few questions, but then a white man, or two,
one a stone upper east side international queer, right out of the1.rivers-f.ohara-e.
albee[283] set, got very upset and asked me whether or not I cd read. Referring to some
fucking brochure they had printed up. It turned groovy for a few seconds, some other
prominent negroes taking my cue to ask their own assinine shit. Baldwin and that
whole prominent clutch were there. Jimmy strangely embarrassed when talking to
me, and he wd only talk to me, having put down, by ignoring, all the other also rans
for his honor. But he walked all the way across the room to grin and take my hand,
and then got very embarrassed when I questioned his activities. Weird. But fuck
ALLLLLLL those cats. But a wild thing, when we were leaving, I w/ a yng cat I been
traveling around NY with, for protection, we stood for a second on corner of Park Ave
and 66th st., probably the chicest part of this world, I say to some them french cats,
Hey let's get a cab quick (to my friend) man, I don't want to be in this neighborhood
after dark. Some fool start to explain how this is really quite a good. . . . . So fuck
ALLLLL of them.

   When's this New Review gonna come? I get missiles from Don from time
to time, but no definite word. Be glad to see that. There's goddam little else
around. I got a copy of NorthWest already. From you?? or from them? Anyway
I got it, and man those are nice poems of yrs there, but specially that last one
Explanation . . . but I liked the Chronicle very much too. The whole book looked
good, glad to see the Snyder. That 2review thing of Creeley kinda hokey, and that
annoying fool Corrington[284] naming great poets, X,X,X and Thomas???? Wow. Oh,
well, fuck him too. Did you see last sunday's trib book review? Hentoff[285] gave
me a very good review. We all ready to go get drunk Friday. My mother bringing all

282   Alioune Diop, Senegalese writer and editor, 1910–1980. Diop was the founder of the important
intellectual magazine *Présence Africaine* and a central figure in the Négritude movement. Négritude was
a movement started by black intellectuals in the 1930s, bound by an ideological base of a powerful black
identity and a rejection of French colonialism and racism.
283   Larry Rivers, Frank O'Hara, Edward Albee.
284   John William Corrington, American poet, writer, and lawyer, 1932–1988. Corrington and his wife,
Joyce Corrington, were television screenwriters as well.
285   Nathan Irving Hentoff, American historian and music critic, b. 1925. Hentoff has been a longtime
newspaper columnist.

her lovely ladies from Nwk (man, you have never dug anything until you dig black society ladies . . . they's really something . . .

But ok, I got go now. Enclosed a directive, and a little confessional poem as well. Take care of everybody there. Now I'm gonna go on some kind of indirect health kick so I'll be at full strength by July. But we'll see . . . love to all Idaho Dorns.

Roi

Edwardian;   [July 12? 1963]

Sorry for the pause, but life here, reasonably healthy has also got, very quickly, more than normally hectic. The school shit (where tomorrow I am reading from your book . . . Wow, wait till I start explaining those poems. Shit. Will they be as smart when they leave that class. But that's a good class, interested types Poetry Since 1945 only draws the good guys. But not so much luck in the other class. Runt heads and hip Ivory leaguers. Murderous, ja ja. But over the 26th, and then I hope we can split. At least, in that direction, is the fact that a new play of mine is being done up at Westport, Conn. Rich ass suburb, Aug 11, and we can stay there in de lady house for the week, pool &c. (viz. Hip Bob C.), and lounge like ugly americans. Shit, if I'm good, maybe I'll get to fuck a man.

Speaking of such act, Kulchur met today, and we are to have an INTEGRATION CIVIL RIGHTS INDIVIDUAL RESPONSIBILITY issue! And not at my insistence. Them other guys thought it up by themselves. Tho, of course, it might make room for something to happen. Would you consider writing something from 4–7 double spaced mss pp on such subject(s), in whatever form you find inarresting?? What you think? They are sending letters to all kinds Well known birds and beasts in hopes of getting their cocks nibbled. What the fuck is Tinassy Williams[286] gonna say about such subjects (he one of the asked . . ."Makes no difference what color a man is if he's got a big dick. PUSH HARDER, OLD MAN!" Or whatever. But you can see the lengths (ha ha) they'll go to. And the list reads like JBaldwin, Styron,[287] Lowell, Virgil Thompson (who walks around in a top hat waving a little wand), and other such maggoty intellects as set their hinies to music. But I am after you and Chas and Bob to get in this gangbang as well. The idea (and it is sickening that it gets to Ohara and the rest, only because it could follow the "french tradition" of intellectuals' manifestos, &c.

Waiting now to hear from Wallrich about the Books. The Idaho Out and

---

286   Tennessee Williams, American playwright, 1911–1983.
287   William Styron Jr., American writer, 1925–2006. Styron and Baldwin were friends and would, in 1967, gain notoriety because of Styron's novel, *The Confessions of Nat Turner*, which faced a tremendous degree of criticism for its depiction of the slave Nat Turner as a racist stereotype. Baldwin would publicly come to Styron's defense.

Gloucester . . . sound like good combination, how many pages you think? My idea now, since distribution is the core of this problem, is to use Yugen distributor, by making books issues of magazine. And then when the returns come back, send them ourselves to bookstores, interested, simply as books. This wd get them more spread than heretofore, except the Totem/Corinth which are pushed by mustachioed hustlers in paper suits. So the mag-book idea might work. But each issue wd be entirely devoted to the work and given the title you give, with the yugen nailed at the lower obscure page edge, just for the distributor's sake, &c.

    Proofs from prose ant'y starting to show. So more weight on the big, drive jones back in the sack push. Also trying to work on some new things,,, like that new "non-fiction" book, number 2 in the series, i.e., after the music one, now I want to get to the intellectual political and social enforcements behind yng negro intellectuals. As a reason for some final socio-political statement. To be? Eat Me! Barry! Also, I am going to D.C. next month with the crowd to raise hell during the filibuster. So we'll see what happens. But further, I've come to see what the possible limit of responsibility is. That given a social structure that is committed to lessening or making nearly impossible ignorance as its total and indigenously manifested cultural responsibility, one is then able to hope that even ignorance would be a personal preference . . . which does not lessen individual performance but wd heighten it by the necessary rise it would need to *be* individual. Beatniks are corny because they haven't risked enough. Right out of Oscar Wilde, like, how can you call yrself hip when everyone else is so unhip??? What is the measure??? Dig? But more tomorrow, when I get up and pee. Love to all of Idaho. !! Roi

Eddie,   [July 18? 1963]

Oh, boy, sorry to hear you up against it too. You sound stripped and tied. Whatever it is, I hope you can somehow cool it (a pitchman's contemporary blessing, in the face of whatever . . .). Right at this particular moment I am waiting for a phone call from Lita the mosquiter, about, dig, the check which Julien Beck[288] just turned over to me from that benefit, just BOUNCED. And I've several checks on top of that, like rent, &c. that will soon come back on me like boomerangs. I swear to Jesus if I see Beck today (The Living Theatre's limp dicked impresario) I will mash his nose. What a crud! Stealing an invalid's loot. God I'd like to kick his old ass . . . really have always wanted to, but now, of course, I have a reason. But what to do until some loot can be got out of him??? That, right now, is the question. No loot will fall out of his ear no matter how many times it is struck . . . I suppose. But Gee whiz Loopdeeloop,

---

288   Julian Beck, American actor, poet, and painter, 1925–1985. Beck was the cofounder, along with Judith Malina, of the Living Theatre in 1947 in New York City. The Living Theatre based its philosophy on Antonin Artaud's idea of the Theatre of Cruelty, meant to shock audiences out of complacency with its art.

people always told me Amerrykins was honest as the day was long. Shit, another dead miff. Anyway, we'll see.

Now, to boot, I discover that the check the cat gave me was in no ways good. He hadn't had an account in that bank since 1962!! Oh, man. And gloom gloom!

Now more good news. I took my book of poetry away from Grove, because the way it looks they were gonna sit on it indefinitely. Court costs, &c. they say, cutting down their releases, and they have, at this date, 180 books contracted, which they have, somehow, in the next 3 or 4 years to get out. My Dante won't be released until, get this, Spring 64. But I will get the rest of the advance when the 18 mos contract runs out in Oct.

I begged that they publish Hands Up! And more word he said, a little later. They already sent Sorrentino's book back, with a handy little rejection slip as courteous as a fart.

Anyway, I guess something will happen w/ yr book soon. One way or the other. If they decide to give it back I'll take it on up to Atheneum w/ mine, tho I don't see any reason why they shd take either book. Do you?? Except my agent seems to think it's the best bet. I was thinking about Wesleyan also, but T.S. Eliot is gonna be their new advisor on poetry, &c. So baby you can about predict the odds, &c. But if you're laying 6–1 I'll still take Floyd.

The Kenya thing now seems more and more a possibility. Since now, there's a good chance I'll actually be offered a Univ. gig after Dec. 13 so sez a guy who is now architect in charge of public housing for sd state. Wow! is right. And don't you make any cracks about Mau Maus,[289] &c. I just had that fucking argument with Joel Oppenhustler. Also, and this is going straight into that corny Luxury essay, the idea of repression to whites in a black state is the first idea that comes into all of yall's head (conscious or unconscious) can't you see the insult involved there?? Especially after all the cool moderate shit that's been going down in all these white states to non-whites therein. You cdn't make it in Kenya because of antiofayisms???? Wow, to give the same disease to niggers as possesses your own, like that v.d. the ships brought in. Without a try, even. Bang. Bang. (the local coon paredon just wiped out some cats trying to eat w/ them in Nairobi!) SHIT! Not everyone is as unsophisticated as local us culture heroes, e.g., George Wallace, Beckwith,[290] and the boys. It is cooler somehow to be here with Allen Ellender, &c. than risk your ass under the sure to be oppressive regime of Tom M'boya??? Wow, like where's all that shit come from?

---

289   The Mau Mau Uprising took place in Kenya from 1952 to 1960. The Mau Mau were an anticolonial group fighting the British Army in the years leading up to Kenya's independence.

290   George Wallace, American politician, 1919–1998. Wallace was at three separate times governor of Alabama and a staunch segregationist who infamously said, "Segregation now, segregation tomorrow, segregation forever" in his inaugural speech as governor in 1962. Byron De La Beckwith Jr., American Klansman, 1920–2001. Beckwith was a known white supremacist, convicted of assassinating civil rights leader Medgar Evers. Though the murder occurred in 1963, Beckwith was not convicted until 1994; trials in 1964 had resulted in hung juries.

Gasp! But anyway, stay away from those boys. They's corrupting your better judgments. Dean of Men from NYU came into 8th st. today to buy City of Night.[291] That's why it's a bestseller. It happens in the best cellars! I read that fuckin Sousa poem in my Poetry since '45 class and a lady wept. A beautiful lady too. I shld've sd I wrote the thing then maybe she'd have dropped her drawers, as we used to say in N.J. Drop down honey! Yugen will come out, I swear on my grandmother's expensive bed. (And she is dead.) Oct. I feel, shorter, but happily, with the same cliquish biases (so sez P. Blackburn the intelligent man's liberal.

But dig, a cat refused to sell me a Jackie McLean[292] record right on 8th st. a german cat, because he didn't think it was uplifting. Let Freedom Ring, was the side. He sd "You people will never get your freedom. Jazz is shit. If you wanted to do something with the freedom thing why didn't you make a movie." Then he walked away. He was the clerk in the store. You dig?? When I finally got in gear, the other fag, went and got a cop, and he took me out on the sidewalk. I'm sure the same shit wd happen to you in Kenya????

But fuck all that noise. It's too hot in this room. Everybody's sweating. Including our new little baby sitter, whose about 16, and looks like she must shit caramels. Ummm! But 1 more class this week, then 4 mas next week, and all through for the summer. I have some very boss grass, to help the nights along. Also a few cakes of Burroughs' candy, to keep a lull on things.

Social life there seems absolutely wild! Why don't you get Denise in town for a few and liven things up? Maybe she could pee in an indian's mouth.

If I was in Idaho I'd have that whole place jumping like Mintons. The call to arms wd be DRUGS OR DEATH! Or maybe even FUCK KENNETH KOCH. Something complex like that. I dig digression. Maybe we cd picket a stable, get them black hosses in with the spotty ones, and all. Shit man we cd go down hard on the Indians! I got a groovy zip gun. Whizbang cha cha cha!

But look I'm already getting ready to get HigH, so I better duff until next time. Dig? Like take it easy greasy, you got a long way to slide. Yass Yass Yass!

Love, Roi

31 July [1963]

Dear Funky Louie,

I'm just using weird stationery[293] today because I feel like it. How's everything out there? We rattling along here. I still haven't got all that money from Julian Beck

---

291 *City of Night*, by John Rechy, published by Grove Press in 1963. *City of Night* followed the travels of a young male hustler as he moved across the country, written in a stream-of-consciousness style that was meant to highlight the colloquialisms and idiosyncrasies of local language.

292 Jackie McClean, American jazz musician, 1931–2006.

293 Jones's letter is on Corinth Press stationery.

of the Lebende Theatre.[294] He writes me notes telling me what a bad boy he is. Meanwhile a junkie I know, have known 20 years, just burned us for 60 bucks in checks. I'm acting like the most gullible asshole east of the pecos. I depend on you to take up the slack west. I told you Diane di Prima & her consort moved almost next door to us. They live at 35, & last night they had a party (for dancers only) & put some queen up to calling the house here asking cd *I* come. Of course Hettie answered the phone, & this cat made a pt. of asking only cd *I* come. I'm gonna burn that fucking shack to the ground. O.K. Fuck that. I hope you working on that Black & White Idaholes. It wd. shake up Wall St. I saw Cecil Monday night at 5 Spot. Trane and a lot of other musicians were there digging & Cecil *performed*! I'm getting him to contribute something to our "symposium" too. Hope something came out of all this instead of a few faggot hog calls. Bulletin of the month, maybe year, is that I received a few days ago a letter from Denise saying, & I quote, "Have seen some beautiful poems of yours around" . . ."Seems to me you have developed while Gil Sorrentino . . . has stood still." WOW. What gives? Why put me up at Gil's expense? What's the pt? What you think? Maybe she think I am dynamite Jack in sack? Available for Bar Mitzvahs & weddings! Oh, well, this literary life is too much for me. I tink I go to woods. Ant'y getting ready. A blurb about it yesterday in Times. Mucho activity here at old Corinth. Page proofs maybe soon. Oct 23, publication date—even NY Times says, but maybe books by 1 Oct. No more word from grove, but it does look bad. Miller case is using their capital, or what capital Rossett intends to allot to his little project.

I saw the Patterson-Liston coming attraction. Man, Sonny is the real article. His first jab dropped Floyd into the ropes, & the very next punch, somewhere to the body, was the 1st knockdown. Whew! The one punch that Floyd threw—very hard & square on the chin—stopped Sonny about .00025 second, then he proceeded to do him. I was at the Americana Hotel—special press showing—a friend of mine got me in too. Floyd like a rag doll. O.K. this is jes' a note; we all have awful colds now. Anything for a laugh, dig? I'm going to get a haircut & smell the lady barber.

FUCK GOD! Love, Roi

Jones and Dorn had spent, and were still spending, much of their letter-writing energies on informal reviews, both of one another's poems and prose as well as of the other authors they were reading. By this time, their literary exchanges were crossing the boundary from their personal correspondence into the public arena, appearing in a flurry of reviews in various magazines and newspapers. Jones, who was becoming more widely known for his political beliefs and activism on behalf of African Americans, was being asked more and more frequently to write about not only African American literature but also its history, politics, and culture. Jones would accept these requests,

---

294   The Living Theatre.

but on his own terms, offering his own usually far more radical take on things than what his editors necessarily expected or wanted. In this letter, he writes to Dorn about one such assignment, for Poetry *magazine; at this point, he was not sure if* Poetry *would accept, or if he would even submit, the review. Called "A Dark Bag,"* Poetry *did print it, in the March 1964 issue.*

Jones reviewed eight books in one seven-page article: American Negro Poetry, *edited by Arna Bontemps, and* Poems from Black Africa, *edited by Langston Hughes, were among the works. Rather than patting magazine editors on the back for their inclusion of black writers and works, Jones called it "flashy moral presumption":*

> *In such a gathering, unless one has special vested emotional interests in hoping for something different, as I admittedly have, there is usually not much hope of running into anything of a strictly literary persuasion. We can be pretty certain when faced with a batch of books by black men, anywhere, of being told quite a few definite truths, a great many of which we must already be familiar with, if we are vulgar enough to be "modern" people, and not fools, or Madox Ford Anglicans. For instance, in each of the three anthologies listed here one will find poems that tell us the black man has been oppressed and generally misused, usually by the white man. Very few of these poems, however, tell us what that is like, at least, very few do with even the intensity of Kipling telling us what it is like to do the oppressing, or know people that do. And in such cases, where what we are faced with is the act of "protest," certainly a picket sign, or a pistol, would do much more good. . . . I mean there is no point in this being poetry, especially. No poetic point has been made, though granted the moral fact is clear enough before the writing. So clear in fact that editors of literary magazines find room from time to time to publish or review such work, as a gesture in the direction of flashy moral presumption. But, unfortunately, it is usually like listening to muffled sounds in a closet. ("A Dark Bag" 394–95)*

Headward,   [August 1963]

Sorry to let lapse like that. But things here are not as cool as they cd be, I mean with me, and the no-drink has, of course, sent me looking for other less socially sponsored stimulants. Fuck all that, however. How're you, & all yours? And the Creeleys? And all your nomadic visitors??

Did I get it straight that Grove sent the HU[295] back?? What word? And the

---

295 Dorn's *Hands Up!* manuscript.

novel, you got that back too?? I gave my address to Random House, they were supposed to return the book to me, so I cd take it over to Atheneum. Anyway, Joel Oppenheimer, America's answer to the Gobi desert, has now got a project going mit Sorrentino, whereby they'll be able to get out a few books thru "some lovely cat" (oppenheimerese) who works in a type shop, &c. This is the poetry. And this wd happen immediately like. So if you did get the HU back, please re-send it, if you can stand the whole fucking business again.

Finally, Grove decided to publish my poems, this Spring. Before the Dante. I don't know what's happening w/ them, but that's, so far, that. Kelly tells me you were supposed to send the Idaho Out to him for book. He's hot to do it. Are you?? I think it wd be a gas. You know we spent some time with them a few weeks ago. They're all right, even though Bob does have an Olson stereotype he's got to work out. (I mean he actually sees himself *physically* aligned, &c. And stays out of New York, for much the same reason Chas dreads the city.) But it was good to get out of Mafia country for a few days.

(Wd publication by the Kellys fuck up the North West R. thing, or vice versa?) But whatever, I think a little book from the Trobars wd be very nice.

Otherwise I am shot full of doubt, frustration and general unreasonableness. About what?? You name it. Is it the wall full of bedbugs I found two days ago, that were eating the shit out of Kellie and the rest of us, or the fact that landlord has not yet fixed the broken windows in the kitchen and the kids' room? I doubt it. Must be some other shit then. Trying to finish that review I was supposed to do for Poetry. First four pages out of projected seven was pure polemic, of course, trying to nail Rago's balls on a fender for sending me the chronicle, of dead black poetry, in the first place. Fuck him, tho. I put him down, and still found some good work in the books to boot. Only now the fucking review is much longer than he asked for. Don't know whether to send it, and see what happens or start cutting. Fuck him I'll just send it and tell him if he don't print it as is his mother will turn black.

Did you see Bob Creeley's Island yet? I'm very anxious to see that and now Dapper Don Allen has asked me to review that for his new project The Seasons, which I'm sure you must know about. Speaking of the fair sex, I went to a party two nights ago that O'Hara gave for John Ashberry who's in town from Paris for a few days. He seems a nice enough, extremely cultivated lady. Anyway that party was something. Billions of fags. Hettie and I and a few other heterofinks were there for conversation pieces, but that was all. Plus H &I cdn't drink, po kids. I had to keep ducking out to take a few pokes on a dynamite joint I had. No good tho, pot high always makes you feel superior to alcoholic queens. (A cat on the radio is singing, "Why do fools fall in love?") (Now another cat's singing, "Oh, I want somebody to tell me what's wrong with me . . .") So even that invention is hip to humans.

But anyway what the fuck can I do to cheer you up?? You want a ticket to the big D.C. minstrel show the 28th? A. Philip Randolph and his 200,000 nuts![296] Plus 4000 combat ready marines in case the shit ain't funny. Dig?

O.K., I got to get back to that fucking review (I'm sittin here la la waitin for my ya ya, another radio quote.) Take care of yourself, enclosed cover of a new bestseller. It'll outsell City of Night, at least on Cooper Square, O.K. O.K. man, shit, why don't you take it easy. For Real??? Your boy, Slick

Dear hippie,   Oct 16 [1963]

letter ought to be incoherent . . . I'm doped up to the gills &c. And Hettie marching around looking grave and concerned. The works. But good to hear from you tonight, that is rereading yr letter and realizing I hadn't written, & all that. Thanks for compliments on BP,[297] waiting now for reviews. I saw a couple of real lukewarm asswipes on The Island . . . which is draggy as no reviews at all. But Herald T. reviewing mine this weekend, complete w/ another photo I understand. Which means I'm on FeeD's[298] shit list. Well he been on mine's a long time, so it's time for equitable titty mix I guess. Speaking of Herald T.,[299] do you think you wd mind reviewing books for them. Their new Book Week literary supplement is supposed to be coming on literate. They already got me to review one book, some lump of shit called Fiction of the Forties . . . a real loser, but I might have put it down too hard, and might not get another book, which wd be where things usually go I guess. But it might just be some available loot. Guys name there is Richard Kluger, Editor, Book Week, c/o New York Herald Tribune, 230 W. 41st St. NYC 36. But shit, I enclose an info sheet from them for general delectation. But write this cat, some general kind of shuck sheet, with all yr qualifications, &c. Where published. Teaching. Your preferences, as far as the kind of books you want to review. I think maybe they pay 35 to 50 bucks a review. That's pretty good change the way Jones &co need. But see what happens; write this guy very soon. He's sort of put out the word he wants "yong" reviewers. Gil wrote him, and I think he's gonna get in on it too.

Any word from Joel yet?? Totem/Corinth doing three books this spring. Olson's essays, a play of Duncan's and Gil's book. Let me know what happens. Some good news though. Poetry Center in SF wants me to read there March 3 & 4, but they say only 200$. Don't they have to pay carfare in addition to that? How'd New York Poetry Center work that out w/ you? I don't want to make any money, but I can't spend any. I surely wd like to go out to the coast tho. Is Salt Lake City the closest

---

296　The March on Washington for Jobs and Freedom, August 28, 1963, in Washington, D.C. A. Philip Randolph, African American civil rights activist, 1889–1979, headed the March, which was organized by African American civil rights activist Bayard Rustin (1912–1987).
297　*Blues People: Negro Music in White America.*
298　Fielding Dawson.
299　The *New York Herald Tribune.*

airport to Pocatello? I cd stop there on way back and stay w/ yall for a few days?? What you think? But I ain't gonna make it unless they give out more dough.

Went up to Birdland couple nights ago to hear Trane. I'm doing liner notes for his next album, which they taping up there. One of those Live sessions. He calling one of the tunes on the album Blues People. Now that's a real deep gas. And man, this cat, Trane, is really something. He was telling me how he'd been reading all my stuff, &c. like that, and its real revelation to find out one of yr idols keeps track of what you do. He wailed his ass off that night too. He promised to come downtown to this party they giving for me next week at the school. Morrow got in cahoots w/ the school to put this clambake on to push the book, but it ought to be a good thing anyway. Roy Haynes[300] quartet gonna play, with a whole lot of sitting in. No cocktails, but barrels of beer.

At any rate I'm keeping very busy running, and teaching, and now & then, even trying to write. But look I'm too high to go on right now, so let this be short note like. More very soon. But take care of yrself please, somehow I feel your just about all I got. Love to evybody, we all fine here, or talk like it anyway.

LOVE
Roi

In the mid-twentieth century, the university system in North America experienced a rise in attendance and funding in the flush of Cold War prosperity and the push to solidify the image of American power. There were differences, though, between governmental desires for the university and artistic or radical desires. While a greater range of poets and artists (many of whom would never have been considered worthy of university positions in the past) could hope for steady incomes to support their art and benefitted from this public outpouring, there was a cost. In the depth of the Cold War, teaching at a public university came with a caveat: all potential professors had to sign a loyalty oath to the Constitution of the United States.

In 1950—a year marked by the start of the Korean War and the announcement of Senator Joseph McCarthy's "list" of Communists working within the U.S. State Department—poet Jack Spicer refused to sign at the University of California, with the result that he was refused by and ousted from the California university system. Spicer went on, through a friend, to work at the University of Minnesota, which was not requiring loyalty oaths, for two years instead. Jones and Dorn would benefit from the growing support of universities and colleges in 1963, if only briefly, with short-term positions at the University of Buffalo (SUNY) under the auspices of Charles Olson.

Oct 20/63

Hey baby, if the world don't stop treating us so good I'm gonna be a goddamn

---

300   Roy Owen Haynes, American jazz drummer, b. 1925.

convert. That Buffalo bit is nearly too good to be true like they say. I was away the other night when H called you but she told me about it. At that point I was across town casually wasting my time insulting one of my colleagues. Then at 3am or 4 was it, I went with a hunter to the top of a mountain when he shot a deer, me watching. Thus carrying my role of observer of the West to the silliest extreme yet. It was a rather lovely doe.

What's cooking? I always wanted to be an assistant professor in New York. I didn't have exactly that city in mind, I was thinking more of Scarsdale. Like a great place to take your scars. We went to a "department" party last night. I beat everybody, the last man on my feet, boilermaker grown crusty and permanent in my hand. Whew. This is sunday, my only day of work. If I have the date right. I just finished a review of your book for Don Allen's *New Review*. He asked me, otherwise I think it's bad policy to review books. I can't see that interest as anything if not at least an essay. Or not that, but a longer more attractive piece of writing.

I'm sending you a copy of the northwest review. Don't know if you'd have it. They did three poems and are going to do Idaho Out. Did I tell you that? I hope it won't make any difference to K. I don't know why it shld. This guy, van Aelstyn[301] who edits it was at Vancouver and dug Charles the most, says he's going to do an Olson issue, the whole works. The damn thing's like a book, a very substantial nicely printed quarterly with donors and university money back it. So that sounds great. It makes it. Shit they're all screaming at us now. And funny, it gets not to depend on the hip outlet so much, which worried me knowing I'd never be able to keep up. It might still be possible to convince officialdom [. . .] to get a job in South Africa.

Know abt any good books? What's going on there in lil ol NY? I'm keeping my eye one *time*. I hope *time* is money. Well anyway—see you next summer—oh wow isn't that *some*thing!

Love to all

Ed

Pocatello, Sunday Nov 17 [1963]

OK mother if I see that frowny picture of you starin out at me much more I'm gonna stick pins in it. Hasn't anyone ever told you to smile. Wipe that. Saw Hentoff's piece on BsP in Nyhtbrs.[302] Pretty paternal. And did you lie about Pee Wee Russell?[303] It is a good shake tho. We get the damn thing pretty later out here so I haven't yet seen the panning of the Moderns, Hettie mentioned it in a letter to H. I like it very

301   Edward van Aelstyn, who served as an editor of the *Northwest Review* while he was a graduate student at the University of Oregon; he later helped to found *Coyote's Journal*.

302   Nat Hentoff reviewed Jones's *Blues People* in *Book Week*, October 1963. The review may have appeared in other venues as well. Dorn's "Nyhtbrs" is the *New York Herald Tribune* review, to which Jones referred in an earlier letter.

303   Charles Ellsworth (Pee Wee) Russell, American jazz musician, 1906–1969.

much, useful, as Creeley wld say. For one thing it gives me a chance to like Russell Edson, a prick I find it hard to do, or not very often am able etc. What a likely place for an American Kafka to spring from, Stamford. Thinking back he was almost my first exposure to the world of shit, only he was eating it with a grin, a thing I had to reach middle age to "appreciate," and come to think of it I've known him even longer than those other two stalwart shitslingers Fee and Joel. And your intro there is about the best wrapup of the scene, that historical capsule treatment of what's what in America I've ever seen. The.

How's your balls hanging these days. We haven't written each other for a while have we. I told Creel that you had two props to go west sometime this winter the Duncan reading and the Berkeley conf. and he sd he'd try to get you to stop off at UNM. A good thing. I hope it doesn't, won't, interfere with your stopping by here which I want you to do more than I wld care to say. The New Mexico thing was finally a drag for me. I had seen Bob too recently and there are so goddamn many other people I "know" there too, I must confess except for a couple of times talking to Bob, I was bored to shit. Ken Irby was there in his 150 a month pad, he's nice in spite of his thick skull. Or because of course. A couple of the Vancouver coterie who followed Bob. Oh my. Oh my. I was flown back, again, by the hip Berlins in their bonanza a trip of the kids shitting in open pails, Lucia barfing for fifty miles at 15000 ft.[304] He and myself forgetting utterly vitrified on quite boss New Mex grass. Thus the world as such melted happily away and we crept finally up on the wonderful string of the Wasatch Mtns, storied peaks, the sublet cutoff, and also Laughlin's spread at Alta. Oh my. Take a look. Your friends are down there somewhere. and then when we got here the weather fucked up and they cldn't get off the ground for five days. They left not speaking to us, or to one another but Helene and I spoke. She said hi to me and I said hi back. There is something about Poky that turns people on. In quite different ways. But in any case it brings the out out in them.

As for those mss I don't know where either hands up or rites of passage are, I take it when you say you have one you mean that novel (which by the way douglas woolf, one of my heroes didn't dig at At All, and said, en effet[305] it was about the worst fuck up he'd ever seed. Either he's bugged or he's not joking. I think I'll tear a couple of pages out a wall to wall. Selby is I suppose the greatest prose writer in all three hemispheres.

Red wine will not flow
nor october be orange
cast from your lips,
                    until
I have seen you

---

304 Lucia Berlin, American writer, 1936–2004. Dorn encouraged and mentored Berlin as a writer.
305 Indeed, actually.

is the way I started a poem yesterday. I guess I'll have to throw it away. So I don't know where hands up is either. The lovely printer must have used it for fancy shit paper in his toilet. Wipe your lovely ass on a Dorn poem. A torn poem. oh my.

What's happening? Where is it all. When I came back they hip hit me with mucho paper work I wldn't have assigned naturally. So that's what I been under, midsemester to boot. So write and I'll do likewise, I need that touch again. I'll be able to say something next week so it ought to go.

love to all always,
Ed

Dec 1/63

Roi—

Dig I saw Olson's poem in Poetry[306]—Gravelly Hill yah it's great—You sent me $25 last year. Why don't you forget the rest $6 isn't going to get me laid or anything useful like that—the clan increases in Buffalo—last news was that J. Prynne is going to make it from England & Mr. Creeley from N. Mex. So, sport, why don't you get w/ it and write me a goddamn letter, I've writ you two, and how abt coming west— still possible? Had long sloppy drunken call from Joel Oppenheimer Thanksgiving night—he wept lovely printer ain't gonna print our books—do tell! Oh my. So write you miserable etc Love Ed

[Dec ? 1963]

Ed,

Look I realize how much shit all this criss-cross yes/no shit is. And especially to you, out there in anyplace. But, goddam all I wanted and want now was to get that book, or those books, published. And I guess you must know that. I don't know what to say at this point. I've cursed at Joel, and made him claim he wept, &c. All that grim social hysteria, to no visible end at all. For what, finally? But I thought that Grove wd do the whole thing *better*, whenever. Better, meaning, with more benefit to the author, as far as any further question past the actual writing, which, for chrissakes, *is* done. I mean it seemed and seems to me that once the writing is finished, you *can not* afford to say fuck it, even though it might seem the most honest approach, &c. But anyone who claims they do not give a fuck about publishing, once they haven written is full of shit, no? It's like jumping in the English channel and then claiming to be a tourist. Oh, man, you know what I mean.

So now, suddenly it looks like I am vulnerable vince, because I don't have any

---

306 Volume 103, October 1963.

trouble publishing. Well, fuck that! That's what Oppenheimer thinks, and if he says it to my face he's gonna get hit, so help me. Look, what I meant was that there was no reason in the world for you to be playing apprentice. Kelly is not that. Kelly, as I was, and still am doing, is merely filling a gap. He has a certain means and method nowise available to Lovely Louie the poetic printer. Man, that cat's even got to read the stuff to see if he digs. I just didn't think you had to at this late date, sit still for that game.

But shit, Fielding MushFace Dawson calls me up the other night and says, "Oh, man I just saw Creeley's picture in the Times" (An ad Scribner's made) "God, it really made me sad." And you yrself sd this shit about the society to promote obscure reference. Goddam, Dawson, who 5 years ago had some cruddy drawings in Vogue, now has the fucking gall to say something like that. And out of the most childish spite imaginable . . . i.e., just because BC didn't stand up to Dallen[307] about the stories in that Grove book. Whew. Adolescents running around all over the place, and just because they stop masturbating they think they entitled to have opinions. Well fuck them, squarely.

But look, whatever you want is jake. See what happens, if the cat fails, I'll take the book back to Grove and make the explanations, &c. But it's strange, how many shots everybody claims. E.g., when we were getting ready to do Joel's book for Corinth "The Love Bit," he calls me up suddenly one day and says, I'm sorry man, but let me take the book up to Atheneum, there's word they'd like to see it. And this, after that book was promised. So where's all that small publishing spirit gone in such instance??? And as far as publishing, &c. even if Grove don't want the book, it can be published thru the Corinth machine, w those snakey royalties, &c. If you want that. I just figured from the go to make a larger move this time that's all. But let's just drop the whole fucking subject for a while and see what nature does.

Of publishing tho, we're doing Chas' essays as soon as Duncan passes the mss on. He's doing an introduction. Did you get the blues book yet? I made a mistake I guess in sending it the cheap way, but I was busted at the time. But let me know.

I'm trying to get into the other book now, but much trouble w/ school starting, and you know what that is. Also radio interviews for book, and an article I'm doing on or called VIOLENCE.[308] But Allen G. just sent me a poem for the Kulch Civil Rights shot. He's back in the halter he says after 3 years. Wow. All notebook until this he claims, and this poem is a motherfucker. It don't have nothing to do w/ CR, but just AG's usual comeon about sucking cocks, but it's a beautiful obsession the way he sees.

I really don't know what I'm doing. Right now, just trying to find time and space to get something in. Scribbling away in scattered notebooks, with no hope of ever finding the material again. Book will be straight shuck I'm afraid.

---

307   Don Allen.
308   "What Does Non-Violence Mean?" in *Midstream*.

H & I had our first drink the other afternoon, since May. Great Gibson, but it put me very quickly to sleep, and I'm still twinging in the hip. But soon, I'll be back. No yellow from it. No discolored pee. So some progress.

Cecil Taylor in Bellevue now w/ that same shit. Podners on the same dirty needle. Or at least starving &c., on the same sections of Occam's Razor. Now he can't play for a few weeks after he gets out, and he's been in there for three weeks already, almost a month.

Look, tho, more very soon, I'm going to see John Wieners' play which opens tonight at a hip church in Greenwich Village. Yes, yes. Look, again, man, you better ease up a little some kind of way. I know it sounds goosey of me to say like this, but still, sit still a little, or something. You worry me. But love to everybody in your house. It's filling up ain't it???

Love Roi

[Dec 1963]
16–17

Dear Eddie,

I haven't written because I'm a big prick, or a little one anyway. It means also I've been out, running around like a nut, hard at the drinking thing already . . . sticking my head, and other parts of my body in places they don't belong. Too, I haven't written much of anything, which is why I haven't been at typewriter and have been putting off writing in general. Whatever that means. Today I have a terrible hangover headache, and no sleep, and Gerrit Lansing[309] is coming here in about ½ hour, so you can see what the gentle afternoon holds. Otherwise, not much happening. Turning very cold, and I've got to stuff cracks and like that. Stupid mistakes cropping up in everything I touch. Hell, and I wanted to make this a "light," happy letter.

But the big cut was, of course, the Kennedy thing.[310] Which put me, and I suppose, really, everyone, way off in the dark. That is I had to stop "thinking" for a while, and start pondering, which is evil stuff. Man, these are weird times, no? Went to a UN party last night, for the Kenyans, and got raging drunk. Drunk enough to make a nearly successful pass at some diplomat's daughter, "Hey, mon, don' squeeze my titty too hard now . . ." &c. Actually I sneaked off to the party claiming to go somewhere else, then I had to think up another "story" when I got home this morning 06hundred. A real charmer I turn out to be, from the stupidest pages of history.

Anyway, what the hell are you doing? Are you happy to be called Robert Frank[311]

309   Gerrit Lansing, American poet and editor, b. 1928. Lansing was a friend of Olson's.
310   John F. Kennedy's assassination, November 22, 1963.
311   Robert Frank, American photographer, b. 1924. Frank took often stark black and white photos of American life, particularly in *The Americans*. Jones notes here reviewers comment on the similarity of Dorn's poetic style and content to Frank's photos.

of the typewriter (Tribreview)?? Why don't you use color sometime Bobby?? What do you make of the Buffalo project?? How you think we live, in what kind, what's that word??? accommodations. If there's one thing I want to be right now it's accommodated. But it does sound great, and it's the one thing right about now that I do look forward to.

My mind has been working pretty strangely, in and out, not fastening on much. Find myself reading Tractatus again, just to get as far away from a constant Human reference as possible. I feel like jerking off, getting high, getting drunk, or sitting long times in dark places, but that's about all. Sir, you think these symptoms are promising? You think maybe I can get a good job behind it all? To show you just how silly I can be in the last month or so . . . just last saturday (this is tues.) I almost killed myself off with an overdose of heroin . . . Hettie and some friend of mine who happened to be here had to walk me around the better part of an hour, also the ice down the back treatment, &c. So today, sitting in front of the desk, rubbing my prick, I said to myself, Wow, I'm really a good guy, haven't had any shit in a couple of weeks. And for two or three seconds I actually believed it! Huh. What do you make of that buddy??

-Wed—

And so last night we went off to a party given for millionaire paint man Larry Rivers. Allen G. was there and his shadow . . . but mostly very glittery like those peanut diamonds in loaf shit. And one cat there who I really like, a funny painter named Alex Katz,[312] a hardnosed City College jew who don't take no shit . . . we spend our time arguing which is the only salvation, about the legitimacy of what I suppose is human. His point that he is only responsible to the intellectual world, and therefore has no feelings nor should he about the rest of the creeps. But the point is at least Alex knows what the fuck he's saying. He's not trying to be cute, or make some hopeless point. He believes all that. "Aw, man," he said, "everything else is just subject matter." Which is, I suppose, right. But I ain't going for that, even if it means absolute inquisition terror death murder beating. No. Each piece of shit that goes on in the world *does* hurt me. It must. Even as abstract . . . even simply as an idea, which is all I got, I know. But it all does matter. But what can you do surrounded by such shit. I just strike out wildly, and I suppose, badly. So what? Some other painter says, "I get my best ideas in bed reading." I said, "I know." I'm writing another letter tonight. Just to get this off. Love to All

Snowing here now. About ½ inch, & cold. See all the "new" publications, eg, *Set*, *"C," Signal*, &c. John W's got some good things. Any word from Joel? He gave me his seat at the Giant-Redskin football game. What are you doing? *Merry Xmas*

---

312   Alex Katz, Brooklyn-born American painter, b. 1927. Katz's works are most often associated with pop art.

V

1964–1965

The group of letters from 1964–1965 proved to be the final stretch in this early period of the Jones-Dorn friendship. It includes only one missive from 1965, Jones's brief note to Dorn informing him of his unwillingness to participate in the momentous Berkeley Poetry Conference and asking Dorn if he would like to go instead. By now almost completely entrenched in black radicalism, Jones perceived an event like the Berkeley Poetry Conference as unacceptable to his politics. Indeed, Charles Olson stated in his now famous and much debated performance at the Conference,

> *I was asked to read. I never read in a coffee house in my life. I never spent an hour in jail. I'm the White Man; that famous thing, the White Man, the ultimate paleface, the noncorruptible, the Good, the thing that runs this country, or that is this country. And, thank god, the only advantage I have is that I didn't, so I can stand here among men who have done what I couldn't do, can't do. All I have done is what I have done alone.* (Muthologos 133–34)

This is the last letter from this period: after the death of Malcolm X, Jones rejected the Village scene and moved uptown to Harlem. The former LeRoi Jones would emerge after several variations as, finally, Amiri Baraka, a man incensed by the conditions of Blacks in the United States and throughout the world. The year 1965 also brought great changes for Dorn, who would spend the next five years teaching at the University of Essex in England.

In the midst of growing civil and political unrest (leading toward the Civil Rights Act of 1964 and the Voting Rights Act of 1965), these years at the same time saw new recognizance of the arts by governmentally backed institutions: the National Council on the Arts was developed out of the National Arts and Cultural Development Act of 1964; the National Foundation on the Arts and Humanities Act of 1965 created the National Endowment for the Arts. With poetry perpetually fund hunting, the creation of the NEA was an especially important development, but as per the usual, the actual funds, competitive to get already, were more so for anyone marked as too radical or troublesome. There were ideological complications, too, even should a non-mainstream poet choose to apply for and accept government-sponsored money.

How to maintain artistic and theoretical autonomy while also being able to function, literally—where and how to find money for printing, circulation, space rentals, and so on—was a perpetual question needing constant answers. Very few would attempt the business model (rather than the nonprofit model) of Lawrence Ferlinghetti's City Lights Books, a situation that enabled him to sustain City Lights Press without government funding. Baraka would face this dilemma upon establishing the Black Arts Repertory Theatre/School in Harlem, accepting government funding while pushing against the boundaries of the attendant government regulation.

“ ”   “ ”

Eddie,   [Jan 5? 1964]

How're you doing these early sprung days? Too bad about the trip, but what'd
you expect? I went up to Boston-Cambridge for similar literary business. Read
at Harvard and Wheaton (all the little unopened plastic snatches, covered w/
thready blon' hair). Met yr ol friend Ellie (Yes!) Dorfman. Ugg, baby, she's like a
cementsmell. Old and hairs sprouting out her nose. You really pickem.' She's talking
about last year or two years like it was off into the dead past of the West . . . in that
moan she thinks is a voice. Anyway Wieners showd up for the or after the Harvard
reading. He's gotten fat, which means he's happy, &c. or at least, cooling it. Smoked
a lot of bush which I brought. Around two or three in morning JW asked cd he stay
there at apt with ED. She flushed and sd, "I'd rather you wdn't." Wanted John to go
all the way out to Milton, Mass. Miles away. Ugg, she's the shit face of the world.
May no one come in her tweedy box.

Anyway, now there's things poppin' around here. My play, Dutchman, supposed
to open at Cherry Lane theatre, Mar. 24. But last week we find out that leading man
has signed to be in JBaldwin's play, Blues for Mr. Charlie. So, what? I realize actors
have to be opportunists, &c., because they're so basically phony anyway . . . and
usually thick as god's own stone. But play's supposed to come in w/ the Beckett
"Play" and a play by the SpanishFrenchman, F. Arrabal[313] called Two Executioners.
(He wrote The Automobile Graveyard.) Now we're struggling to find a replacement
for the actor right away. No luck so far, but this morning (Sun.) we got to go at it
again, letting people read, &c. Looks like 50/50 chance at this pt that the thing will
get on . . . but I'm all hopes, I'll tell you.

I've definitely got Wilentz to think about publishing H.U. as soon as I get the
mss. I don't see Joel, so it's difficult, even though he left his own poems with me,
because he was too tired to carry it around, last time I saw him at 5spot. The day of
that massive reading, w/ Allen, Peter, Gregory, Franko,[314] Arnold Weinstein,[315] Joel,
Gil, & many etceteras.

Speaking of litrachur . . . I just read a very inaressting review (w/ sporadic
putdowns) of Dahlberg's by rwFlint.[316] Some very good pts in that. I'd like to
see ED's face when he sees that (Hey how come yr initials are the same as
dahlberg's?????)

Abt my pop art speech. What I say is this: Something's gotta happen . . . is
happening now. I'm just looking, and I've already seen the things I genuinely dug,
as p.a., if that has to remain a useful nomenclature. To me it's simply a genre, like

313   Fernando Arrabal, Spanish playwright, poet, and director, b. 1932.
314   Frank O'Hara.
315   Arnold Weinstein, American poet and playwright, 1927–2005.
316   R. W. Flint, reviewing Edward Dahlberg's *Because I Was Flesh* and *Truth Is More Sacred*, in the *New York Review of Books*, March 19, 1964 (Vol. 2, No. 3).

anything. And as "social art," it's alone . . . for this time, leaving Levine Shahn and followers of Grosz[317]. . . but it *is* corny. But it also makes you see, more "clearly," what is around. But to me most art is just petrification. What led to the art, that "process," or verb force, is what I wd be beholden to, were I beholden to anything. So "pop art" like "beat," of course, don't mean *anything* . . . and that's what I'm saying. Individual confrontation irrespective of genre . . . or something. And I was not putting down Obermayr . . . I don't know him . . . I was saying something.

End of the month I journies to Buffalo, with a cat named Harvey Brown,[318] who was a student there, Creeley and Olson reading, and I'll stay around another day, to see if there's going to be anyplace to live. I'll let you know my findings. Time's awastin'. . . . I'd like to be sure about that place.

Delayed mailing this so now the play thing seems to have cooled itself out. Got an actor Sunday morning. He's in The Blacks now, name Bobby Dean Hooks,[319] but he'll go. Grove now wants to publish the four plays . . . big opportunistic pricks, and they are very angry that Morrow will do two of them. Big meeting this aft up at agent's but I ain't going. They got it. Big hysterical Rossett, behind as usual, now getting nasty. Sent word maybe I ought to take all my books to Morrow. Dig??? Ohhh, that foul wd be faggot. Anyway, what're you doing?? I'm trying to write another play now . . . abt the army. A big hairy tragedy. Hey, Morgenstern's Gallows songs[320] now published hardcover by U. of Calif. A gas!!—Best to you & yrs We all send mucho love—Roi

[Jan 1964]

Thirsty

Edwardian,

Sorry for lull, but I'm steeped in insignificant insignificant bullshits. From friends and foes. (what fo?) Also frozen for a couple of weeks where I cd not write my name to paper . . . those reviews, pictures, &c., froze me, literally, where I cd not think straight. Till finally, I remembered that all that shit wasn't me . . . that I was still here to touch secretly where nobody not even Newsweek wd know about. But shit on that. Great about your auto. Look, what you think we ought to do. How long you expect to have that car? Maybe we cd put in some money and you cd get

---

317 George Grosz, German artist, 1893–1959. Grosz was part of Berlin's Dada movement; he was known for his striking—and brutal—caricatures.

318 Harvey Brown founded Frontier Press. He was a great supporter of many jazz musicians, having started a recording company to promote musicians such as Don Cherry, Ornette Coleman, Clifford Brown, and Clifford Jordan. Brown was, as well, Olson's benefactor for a period, from the time they were both at the University at Buffalo, State University of New York.

319 Robert Hooks, African American actor, b. 1937.

320 Christian Morgenstern, German poet, 1871–1914. Morgenstern's *Gallows Songs* (*Galgenlieder*), a book of humorous verses from 1905, is among his most well known. The edition Jones refers to here was translated by Max Knight and published by the University of California Press in 1964.

a station wagon, and take that back w/you?? I mean so's we cd go up together, &c. What you think? Is that at all practical. I guess not. Oh, well. But let me know.

Shit, man, you too selfconsciousmodest. WD[321] is as good as anything out now, . . . ain't it? What else is there. Maybe brief dedication wd be cool. Think about it. I still haven't gone up to Buffalo. Harvey's car broke down . . . no, it was stolen . . . and he's trying to borrow one . . . but now other complications . . . anyway I'm gonna write Chas this afternoon. *Hands Up* shd be out by time we come back from Buffalo, I think. That's the plan. I'll give you final words on that, next letter. What about cover, &c. You got any ideas? You mention Fielding. But he's doing Idaho Out. Cassias X??[322] I got article coming out on he, Sonny, Floyd, and Jack Dempsey, in *Nation*, soon I think. I'll send you a copy. Have to make it w/ articles now . . . enclosed letter I got from your moll DLevertov re last group of poems I sent. By the way it's all right for you to use those 2 poems if you want . . . just let me know for certain. But for cover how about getting somebody to draw wild hands, naturally UP, as interesting drop behind lettering &c. Is that corny?? Maybe somebody cd make it less so. There's a pop guy named Joe Brainard[323] who's pretty good . . . he cd write you??? What you think???

Now we trying to get The Baptism back on . . . it was done w/ Ohara's play at Writer's Stage a couple times. Want to redo it, same cast. But places we have auditioned the show wanted Baptism but not Frank's play. So now that puts me in dumb position. Baby, all this is straight out of cheap fiction, no? Either I play 25cent hero or 25cent heel. Shit. What you think?? Say something about this.

Gary Snyder in town. We all, w/ Allen, Peter, Ed Sanders[324] (a groovy yng cat . . . editor of Fuck You/A Magazine of the Arts which is very good mimeod shot, privately handed around. You haven't seen it yet??? If not I'll get ES to send it. Some interesting yng cats coming in now, like Sanders, John Keys, George Montgomery, who also edits something, also mimeod, call Yowl. You see Carol Berge's "Vancouver Report," a Fuck You publication. Man is she cruising for a bruising. She put down Rbt D very handily, I think, as some kind of faggot or something. This chick is sick, and ambitiously thus.) went to a groovy party, made so by our presence, as lower class poet types. Party given by Popfag Andy Warhol, in a loft with dig this Aluminum Foil wall paper . . . john completely decorated thus, with toilet plungers painted silver. Gag. He had the party catered

321   *Wild Dog.*

322   Cassius Clay (he would become Muhammad Ali in 1964).

323   Joe Brainard, American artist and writer, 1941–1994. Brainard was most frequently associated with the New York School poetry and theater scenes and was good friends with poets such as Kenneth Koch and Frank O'Hara.

324   Ed Sanders, American poet and musician, b. 1939. Sanders was the founder of the radical *Fuck You/A Magazine of the Arts*, one of the founders of the band the Fugs (with poet Tuli Kupferberg, 1923–2010), and founder of the Peace Eye Bookstore in New York City's East Village. A longtime radical activist, Sanders has also been recognized by more mainstream institutions such as the NEA and the Guggenheim Fellowship.

by Nathan's of Coney Island, w/ hot dogs, hamburgers, cornoncob. Whew. Booze.
A juke box! No money, just press yr choice. Some people there . . . how they
know artists?? . . . in black tie and long dress . . . look at Allen, Peter & me like
we some kind jerks. But when the music started I asked one of them bitches to
dance . . . and when she put her nose up I took it as my cue and started twisting
my ass off. She retreated into the shadows of her husband's wallet, and I followed
say. Hey, bitch, can't you even dance? Party got firmly off the ground. Reading
at Gug was ok, Duncan the most impressive. Bob coming on strong only at last
couple new poems. Denise read her cunt poem, and another I liked, otherwise
she don't move me as good as Sal Hepatica,[325] another lady poet. Everybody
shouting about breakthrough . . . but when's AG gonna be asked to read at Gug or
YMHA or you, or me, or Snyder, or Whalen, or Ed Marshall, or Wieners, &c &c &c
&c. Jack Marshall, Kathleen Fraser, Raphael Rudnick and Harold (Paul Blackburn's
ghost) Dicker reading at Y monday!! Man they scraping the catbox. PB intro them
as promising yng poets. Aggggg! Hey we might have a chance to get to Germany
and England this winter, with play. I'm trying to make them take Hettie & girls.
LOVE TO YOU ALL—Roi

*In September of 1963, Charles Olson began teaching in the English Department at the
State University of Buffalo in upstate New York. The poets he considered important
both for their writings and their friendships, many of whom had studied or taught
with him at Black Mountain, always remained in the forefront of his mind, and he
quickly appointed teaching jobs for both Jones and Dorn during the summer semester
after he'd just begun at Buffalo himself. This is the "Buffalo dragnet" Jones is referring to here.*

   In late 1963 Jones published through Corinth Press The Moderns: An Anthology
of New Writing in America, *a collection of prose Jones found to be "the most interesting and exciting writing that has taken place in this country since the war." Walter
Allen, an academic literary critic and novelist, reviewed the anthology in the* New
York Review of Books, *a newspaper steeped in the niceties of the literary canon. The
review, unsurprisingly, slammed it with willful misunderstanding and an abidance
of the "rules" of various poetic traditions, taking Jones to task for manipulating the
boundaries of standard definition. In 1963 as well, Jones's history and critique of jazz
in the United States,* Blues People: Negro Music in White America, *was published
by William Morrow & Co. Ralph Ellison reviewed it, also for the* New York Review
of Books. *While Ellison's review was much more supportive than Allen's, even sug-
gesting that other jazz writers follow Jones's lead in questioning the many prevalent
assumptions of jazz criticism, he found fault with Jones's overt militancy and attempt
at critical theory: "Read as a record of an earnest young poet-critic's attempt to come*

---

325 "Sal Hepatica" was a laxative and antacid medicine.

to grips with his predicament as Negro American during a most turbulent period of our history, Blues People *may be worth the reader's time. Taken as a theory of American Negro culture, it can only contribute more confusion than clarity."*

Blues People *is a testing ground and at that may not be as fully polished or neat as Ellison may have liked, but the truth of the critical discomfort (not only for Ellison) may be closer to the fact that the book also proposes discomforting theories about what it means to be African American, or American at all. There is a caricature of Jones on the front cover of the issue of the* New York Review of Books *in which the review appears. Jones's immediate thought is to Harriet Beecher Stowe's* Uncle Tom's Cabin *(his "UT of UT'C" here).*

Ed,   [Feb. 7? 1964]

It was very wild to hear from you like that, in the middle of everything that seems to be cluttering and weighting me down. I don't know really what it is, things zoom along at a weird clip, and I'm not really sure what is actually happening. Last night saw Allen G, Orlovsky Corso and I went up to somebody's house to see movies, saw a flick Genet made. It was terrible. Dicks being waved all over the place. I think Allen would've liked it, but I kept saying, it was shit, it was shit, and he, I think, was convinced. Because it was so well made and obvious . . . anyway Salvador Dalí was there, but I didn't get to meet him, though Allen and them other cats started pumping his hand. Allen knew him from some other place. He's old and starch faced, but easy enough and very open. That Flaming Creatures shit was on the bill again, and it's the 3rd Fucking time I've seen that lump. Anyway, then we went to some cat name Harry Smith's[326] house, who's making flip films that cut most of the famous flip/collage . . . shifting speed image cats. Cat uses Monk &c. as background, also, weird natural sounds, wind, storms, &c. very spooky effect.

Seeing Allen quite a bit, who's always good to be with. He's working on some movie now of Kaddish, with Robt. Frank. Also see a lot of Frank O and his crew who are mostly gaylights. But shit, I'm so tired of mediocre error, and that shitty little string of gradual compromise. Like Oppenheimer telling me "Man I don't want to write for a living . . . just give me a job like any other cat and I can make it". . . and then the cat, at first offer, starts writing little dirty novels for a paperback house. Like the old whore said about integrity, how you know till somebody ask you??

Anyway, just junkies and fags, and nuts of other kinds, plenty of musicians, with their flashy ego, that's about it. And baby don't that just isolate you from old strong man crowd. Yes, and then, of course, the need to be constantly, and never

---

326   Harry Everett Smith, American archivist, ethnomusicologist, and filmmaker, 1923–1991. Smith put together the recovery project of *The Anthology of American Folk Music*, a six-album compilation of blues, folk, and country music from the 1920s and '30s. Smith was also an experimental filmmaker, creating works with abstract imagery and sound.

reasonably, vituperative, as you pick up on. But that's just for my own benefit, getting all that shit together, so I won't have to ask as poor Allen in the cab last night, confronted by Corso as a neo-junkie, "Where's poetry going?" Where am I going, or You, I asked him, and you too. Where? That's simple-minded enough to need some answering. But "we going?" seems a better emphasis.

Your new house sounds and looks like something you needed. Looks like a lot of space. But I know that moving shit must be a drag. The thought of it chills me stiff. Wonder what changes required for the Buffalo dragnet. You on a break now? I've got two weeks now one till classes resume. But look, this Summer, let's try to stay together, at least close somewhere. I don't know nothing about Buffalo, but a cat was telling me, also giving me addresses of clubs, gin mills, &c. which seem hip enough to scandalize us properly. But shit, man as long as we got to be there . . . and I got a fucking 9:30 class! In the filthy morning! And that Modern Poetry class w/ Hopkins Yeats Eliot Auden, &co. I read a book of poetry written by head of the dept, Albert Cook. Wow, that cat is really wrapped up fine. He can spell his ass off.

Guess you saw Walter Allen's little piece in NYReview about Moderns? How' you like them apples?? An Englishman for the Americano shot, ahhh, and then yesterday to see what Ralph Ellison in new issue of that sheet has to say about Blues People. Ahhh, he really reamed me. Poor fucking bourgeois nigger, as he says, "middleclass Negroes . . . whatever that means . . ." But he writes a long thing just to say you young prick shut the fuck up about failure . . . none of my people was ever really fucked up . . . or something, I'm not sure. Also, there's a big caricature of me on the cover of the review. Why? I don't know, but distorted like UT of UT's C, if you know what I mean. Only the banjo has been changed to protect the innocent. Pretty evil . . . but what do you do then? I guess I shd write some kind of cool letter putting him straight. But for what? It's just major drag that's all, but what else?

That's strange you heard about that play so quick. Now they're signing contracts, I guess I'll get to sign one soon. Money is pretty bad . . . something like 200 dollars off broadway option 200 more when play is produced, and min. of 50$ a week while it runs. So that's the messenger level, 50per. My old man always told me if I fucked around I'd end up discrediting my race, like messenger salary. Shit, my old man gave me three pairs of his old pants last night, so you see the kind of hip charity you can get into calmly, even heroically. But hey nice pants.

You not sending to Niagara Frontier?? Will be a gas to see the Northwest with your things. I want to write a novel now, have already started w/ three chapters worth, about 60pages. But I'm hung with this Bohemians thing, which has gotten out of hand, and at a stone wall. If I write it it will be a simple political tract calling for Fire, thass all. So what?? Anybody can do that?? But enclosed is the General poem which might be interesting in spots. Got proofs from Poetry today on a long review I wrote for them on books by Africans and domestic woogies.

Tonight Gil and his double Joe Early read at 5Spot. Now I'm just off in left field because I didn't like show up to introduce Blackburn (Fuckhim!) and Zukofsky. I just cdn't make it, failure or treason included, which was Louis was to read, and did read, and I didn't want to hear Blackburn, at all. And for sure I didn't feel like introducing no fucking body. In truth I was trying to fuck some junkie-widow with two kids, and forgot the time. But I didn't get to fuck her . . . she's too hip, it seems, for the casual. And I'm much too weak to propose anything other than what she could casually get. So. But Hettie and I are pretty tight and responsive. It's just that I just can't shut up when Somebody expresses an interest in my fingers or my ears, or even those turned up suede shoes I been moping through the snow in. Women are just too much for me. I go down every time.

But you sound not wholly unacquainted with such horseshit of "modern living." But wow, to go through with all this shit and still have some motherfucker call you Beat. Wow! But those hip types you describe there sound like they need something stuck up them, maybe an automobile or a german policedog. They all over here too. You shd see some of the rich faggots that come to O'Hara's house. Wow. Slick and pretty, and baby so sure that everything's cool as it is. I met Virgil Thomson, who really wants to run his tongue up my hole I guess. A slurpy fairy he is, but ingratiating I suppose. Types and diagrams, we got them all.

I'll send you the carton of cigarettes . . . don't send money . . . I owe you some cash . . . I'll just deduct and send change, &c. I'll do it by the weekend . . . this is monday. Weird funny business recently. Remember the magazine, Revolution, I sent you. Well you might have guess that StateDept lists it as commie propaganda, &c. Well now they really got something to go on. Two weeks ago a member of the editorial staff, one, Mohammed Babu, cut out, and went off to Zanzibar, for the toppling, where he is now Foreign Minister! Now you can dig what them assholes are saying in Washington. Great! Great! Anyway, it all draws closer and tighter, which is the groove, and I am going all out to help Barry Goldwater get into office. But I'm afraid there are evil forces working against this man who must be the truest legacy of what the pioneer spirit has become in this hemisphere. No? At any rate, get the shit on, is the way we used to say it. Let him get in there and then see what happens, like Atlanta everywhere, or something. But he won't make it. Too bad. Another pure product of America getting fucked around.

It was warm for a while, then rainy, then very snowy, now just cold and bland. We got the floor painted, finally, and the halls, and the bathroom floor. Now if I cd just get up the strength to finally put up the fucking shower curtain, we'd be out there in pure blissville. I see where Wild Dg getting ready to go again, I hope the Sheik can get it up again, not sure, not certain I can keep that tone, but what the hell, whatever tone, might be interesting. As Denise says that's not New York anyway, so what the fuck. She and Diane di Prima reading *together* next monday evening. I'm not sure whether or not I'll be allowed to go. I hope they take off their clothes and do the cunt trot, I love them both so dearly, that is to say, I wish they would leave me the fuck alone. Love to you all

I owe you more letters . . . Roi

Pocatello 2–17–64

Hello Keed—That non-violence shot you sent from midstream was the closest to it I've *EVER* clapped eyes on and I want you to know I thot so. So. Wow. Send *Apple Cores*! Pronto! In fact cld. W.D. reprint small section from the N.O. essay? Haven't yet dug caricature on NY Bk Rev. yet but go to lib. this evening to look. What does Ross mean by space-time nwacence?[327] Did I ever write a poem like that. Did you see news of our Buf. Endeavor in poetry Feb? They got a bloody grovey[328] name for it! What chance is there to get copy of Artaud tape.[329] Forget cigs. Send tape. Help! I go Feb. 28 to Eugene Ore—the univ. to "Manuscript Day." See poets like James Baby Schevill, Earl the Fink Birney[330] etc. Big Deal! Take my best student. Crit. much poetry. Will see however Northwest Rev. studs. Right on Obermayr's pop art. He learn that whole art of thinking right out of Veblin which can be interesting if limited. Don't be too hard on us hicks out here—we's just tryin. I mean if Sorrentino can . . . So why don't you settle down and stop being so cool. What's this abt—Kulch?

Love Ed

Ed,

[Feb ? 1964]

By all means get the copy of NYReviewofBooks with the caricature of me on it, and that review of Ellison's. Oh, yeh. And this week now a review in Partisan Review by a psychiatrist! Concern by the quarterlies. Ah, yes, that is an advanced state of decay.

Otherwise, thanks for new WD. I donno about Obermayr's piece. It's right, in a sense. But now I'm inclined to look more closely at PA. After all it's just another style . . . the world's not ending . . . something there too, just like everyplace else. Hopeless, or maybe not so hopeless, part of that way of working is that usually you're late and not as heavy . . . ie nobody can actually be funnier than the real thing eg a letter in the mail this morning from the Associated Blind, asking for donation, &c. In the brochure they send, staff bars, &c. . . . the music for a song called The

---

327 Nonsense.
328 Groovy.
329 Antonin Artaud, French avant-garde playwright, poet, actor, and director, 1896–1948. Artaud's work and life were highly influential in the development of Beat and avant-garde literature in America.
330 James Schevill, American poet, 1920–2009. Earle Birney, Canadian poet, 1904–1995. Both Birney and Schevill's poetry garnered many official awards, praise, and popularity, possibly leading to Dorn's derisive tone here.

Song of the Associated Blind. No Pop Artist is that hip already. But the recent surge do make cats like Jap Johns[331] seem classic. But it does make you look and consider all the swill and shit in the country and see its possibilities *objectively*, as shape and information, which can be pretty comic at least. Most of the cats I see I despise because of the faggybaggyhippyinsidegreatnews camp. Like Andy Warhol, who, I understand, has got the next cover of Kulch as well as four inside shots. Lita has been playing editor recently with a vengeance, not even informing us Eddytors. Well fuck she. I, for one, ain't gonna stand for that kinda shit. It's me ducking out I guess. I don't really know. I don't think I want to be involved anymore, especially not in any deal where she da brains, &c. Also, I lost interest in being great hip jazz editor at no dollars . . . I'm becoming so pissy and lazy and shit headed that I don't want to do nothing anymore it seems. Today, up out of bed around 10, mark a few papers, sit around, then off to see Dean about a raise, to which he assented, then teach, then to book store to see T. Wilentz and bullshit with Spellman, then up to Cedar for two drinks with painter Ray Parker,[332] then to ChuckWagon for two more drinks with painter Ray Parker, then to Five Spot for quick bullshit to pay off my old tab, then home to eat and fall asleep in chair digging television, then in my study to fall asleep in chair, then suddenly awake at two oclock in morning, dragged and with absolutely nothing accomplished, and because it's so late and everybody else asleep (now there're a little uproar from littlelady room) I don't even get to make it with my old lady, the final putdown of the day. Writing? I've got one half finished short story next to typewriter, also one just started tape transcription, that will be an interview with tenor player Archie Shepp . . . a two chapter finished novel behind the typewriter, and notes, only notes, for the next non-fiction book. So that's where I am . . . lost and fucked through by the alky, which now, because of the old woman, acts on me like an immediate mickey finn, but I does continue.

Of Wilentz, &c., I asked him again today about Hands Up, and, of course, they are, or at least Ted is interested, and wants to speak to Eli (the cat who think he da big brain of universe . . . cat also responsible for all the fuckups in The Moderns, like typos, &c. and no proofs to authors, &c.) but I am pretty sure he will say yes. Now if I can get the mss, we be in to something. If I see Wil'Man Of Borneoppenheimer, I will clue him that perhaps something else can happen. Unless he is stiff working with the LovelyP. Newly Fallen on the way, I only sent 8 because that's how many fit in the envelope. You want more?? Also we have plenty P.V. You want them sent where?? Let me know. Man, I thought you was teaching Joni J. I don't know those other cats. At any rate, it's now 3am of a wet snow and I think I'll get off this line so's I got an excuse to go out and mail it, and also drop in fivespot to see Charlie Mingus for a second and see if there's any familiar addicts about, as well as any

---

331   Jasper Johns, American avant-garde artist, b. 1930.
332   Ray Parker, American avant-garde artist, 1922–1990.

familiar ladyholes. If there are neither, I will retire to this little room and turn out some more deathless prose I suspect, and with now school tomorrow, probably sleep till noon, then rise and get my ass up to the hawaiian barber. (He says he's glad he's a hawaiian, he says it enables him to go both ways as far as haircutting is concerned . . . straight and nappy . . . white and black. He is a natural moneymaker in these parts cause that's only kind we have. All to you you fucking american. And yr americanische family. Roi

[1964]

Roy: Just this afternoon read the rev. in NYBRev. of the Mods. Oh, that's a mean, dirty one. So much cleverer & informed than the rev. in [. . .]. I note w/ delight that altho he doesn't like you he devotes 1/5 pgs of his time to your intro. alone. He turns out to be not such a clever man after all. But that game is very early given away—he didn't read it—i.e., is much more interested in his own pitch as to what mod lit or writing is. And he's English. The whole shoot is English infiltration—looks like a syndicate out of New Statesman. I wonder now indeed if that anthy will ever be reviewed except to be put down. True Diprima is worthless as is Edsan but there is a man here who like the thing a lot, Eugene Dawson—a Lawrence expert. I wonder if Kulch, say, wld be interested in a review from him and if you cld get a rev. copy sent to him—c/o Eng Dept, Idaho State University, Pocatello, Idaho. I've seen work of his and it looks good. What you think? By the way how's it going now. Don't get bugged, just stay cool dad. Do you ever have access to a tape machine? Cld you send me a tape of you reading? If you cld I cld sure use* it and beside I'd like to have it anyway. Ok keep straight & write—Love there Ed
*poetry class

Feb 22/64

Rer—Did you catch that strange wop anthology? Oh wow *that* beautiful stretch from Emily to Roi. But isn't that cover more American than it's possible to allow. Just great. Jesus! I mean they're so cool I wonder why Paul Harvey[333] isn't included, or is he, I'll have to look. Many shades there—that's too much. I haven't heard of many of them—How abt that chant for children—Horne I believe—crazy shot— anyway I dig it for its difference. Nobody can accuse it of being "standard."

What's happening now—what the hell you up to. I read *The Burning General* again last night—it was under a pile of papers on my desk. Great poem—that end is so damn fine. I wanted to tell you again if I hadn't.

I leave next wednesday for the University of Oregon to attend "manuscript day"—take a "promising" student (ie, I hope she promises) and there will be the

---

333   Paul Harvey, American radio broadcaster. Jones references him here because Harvey was known for his dramatic on-air speaking manner, something akin to what would later evolve into slam poetry.

guns of the great northwest there—Carolyn Kizer from Washington. Also James Schevill from San Fran State. Oh wow—I'm walking into a nest of shitkickers. You, also Natl Bk award winner William Stanford from Portland.[334]

If a house in the country as you said is best in Buffalo—have you looked into it? How about transport? It's an every day shot isn't it. That sounds complicated. What abt a car? Tell me what you know—I wrote that prick Cook and he didn't bow to answer.

Joel has *Hands Up!* Just ask him for it if you see him—I sure wld be pleased enough if the Brods Wilentz went for it.

Later & you write—Ed

Ed,   [Mar ? 1964]

Ok, they say, OK, Hands Up is scheduled . . . so by late summer it shd be out. But, as usual, there are some strings. First thing, Eli Wilentz, who is the final word on such activity, says mss is too long! I have been arguing, ie for the inclusion of one more form, but he wants to stick to max of 48 printed pages (that including covers, &c.) like my book or Whalen or Snyder, &c. He sez, since other book we're doing, will be Gil's, two 48's make exact 96pp form, which is, maybe 50$ he wd save. Thass right, *maybe* 50$. The idea of it, without all the other human associations, ought to make you shit. It shore does me. I mean if you ever think of what you're doing as meaning full, then the whole weight of the insolence and ignorance of such men does really make you stagger, if only momentarily . . . too brief a thing to register anywhere else. So, now, I have the ms. (Joel wdn't give it back to me . . . he dropped it off at store, which is his substitute for hari kiri I suppose. Oh, the shit involved in living. Blah, blah . . .) But what you think. I'm supposed to be going over ms now, to suggest possible cuts, &c. But I remember from our first reading that I liked the whole book. Which makes me I guess too uncritical as an editor, but I'm going back there today to say I don't believe the book ought to be shortened. What you think?? Have you copy of ms there (I hope??) Look it over, tell me what you want done . . . if anything. If you don't think it shd be shortened or whatever just tell me . . . and I'll just have to try to face them (ha) down with it. They've also decided they don't want to do the tiny Olson essays (from Kulch, Yug, F.B. &c.) say it's too small a vol. They want a large one. They also don't want to do the Duncan play I gave them, Maiden Head, which is, among other things, really embarrassing, since I assured Duncan it could get published. Wow. What's happening?

---

334   Carolyn Kizer, American poet, b. 1925. Jones notes that he's walking into a "nest of shitkickers" here. Kizer, Schevill, and Stanford were all widely accepted poets, winners of national awards; Jones stands as the outsider in this group.

Me and another cat off to Buff and environs next week. Creeley shd be there too?? I'm gonna look around. I find out I got a fucking 80clock class at that fucking place. Man, that shit begins to look less and less appetizing. How many days a week will we be at it? Shit . . . seems like real hard ass work to me. I'll get the Core thing to you in a little while. Just have to get properly inspired, to that kind of windiness. Some good things happening though. BluesP sold to French and Eng, though shit of that is no loot until initial royalty payment which is end of may. When do we get paid from Buf, end of term?? I'll bet so.

I'm supposed to be writing a review for *Poetry* on Zukofsky's "Bottom." Wow, that fucking book is over 400pp in one vol. and the other vol is a whole score for Pericles, by Celia. Damn . . . I don't know why I bothered to take that thing on. I read at it up and back to Harvard, and only go through 160 or so pages . . . the reading is that thick, and redundant. But the whole book is tautological, ie, he's only saying one or two things, and using the whole world (or his ww) of "culture" literature, &c. to cement it in. EYES EYES EYES EYES EYES EYES EYES EYES EYES . . . is what he keeps saying, and behind that, I's. But you know those shots from BMR.

Otherwise, it's suddenly cold again, after fake spring. Hornick taken over K completely now. Just got a note from her telling me I'm just a contributing editor . . . so aside from loose jazz shots, and the stuff she's got all ready, she can kiss my ass, I guess. I still feel sorry the whole thing got away completely. (See A. Warhol cover of new # 13). But what can you do. Everybody else drifted away, so what cd be done was, or became, very fitful. I still think occasional stories &c. cd be sent. Why don't you send her a long story or something?? What are you up to?? I'm going out and buy a paper and a sandwich right now. Then sit down to prepare this afternoon's class, which will cover James Wright, Robt Bly, Wm Stafford, Jack Gilbert . . . you see where I am. OK, let everything go the way it ought to. Love to your groovy family.

Mar 21/64

Roi—That's very damn good news for me altho the objections you suggest are true enough—but for christ sake I ain't got no "choice" really—the mss you have shld be what I got a carbon of, as I have 65pp in mine—the title poem is last & Vaquero is first. Ok. It seems to me 65 mss pp wld go into 48 typeset but I guess not? I'd like to see the whole thing used because it *is* a book, even, say if anyone might not like certain poems. But these are the ones I'd remove in order of descending preference:
2 the reception
5 comparison
1 every cat needs a home etc
4 a wild blue, yonder
3 For Ray
7 an inauguration poem
6 Late in the [. . .]

Surely all those wldn't have to be removed to reduce it to a 48 pager—or how about 40—8 pagers—a 9 inch shelf of fuck books by America's only hip farmer boy! That finally might attract them more. Suggest it.

Ok—thanks again, always and continually. I'm damn sorry that business w/ Joel has to be that way—it took me months to write him a *not* nasty letter and still make my point that I want him to yield that ms. Fuck argument & neurotic Jews and people who like Whalen write me nasty letters saying the poetry in W.D. is no good! I guess some people imagine they have to *say* something to you, or me or anyone. Oh Euripidean drag! Oh my mother's cunt! That passage from which I emerged!

As for cover I'd like to know if Dawson is doing the cover for *Idaho Out*, he said he had it from *Kelly*—I supposed that was why—I dig his cover more than *any* other but 2 wld be a little too much. Otherwise I guess I'd dig a photo—of Cassius or Elijah Muhammed punching Rockwell Lincoln.[335] I have a snap shot of my three children which wld be great but probably considered too gauche by the Willentz brothers. How do you spell it.

And as for the teaching "load" at Buffalo—I got that straight and it makes me laugh my ass off that you didn't—your scrawny skeleton's gonna rattle man. That's a five day week they got going. 3 semesters—we're the middle one—what do you expect—even *one* 8 wk semester is concentrated. Oh yea! I *told* you it was a *working* proposition— Creeley didn't believe it either when I was in New Mexico—Bobbie for instance thot it was gonna be one big "party." Oh my my. That's why I was bitching about the bread.

Helene's fink bro is remaining ominously silent abt that apt and tho it isn't out yet I think we ought to start thinking of alternatives at least. I suppose apartments will be scarce as hens teeth this summer there because of the world's chamber of commerce fair. And we did damn well want to get something "free" because I'm sure Buffalo will pay in August.

Have you seen Miguel Grinberg![336] You *never* mention that. You got the 2 copies of dog? You may not dig Carol Bergé I shld think not, who could, but can't you get a hold of her weathered snatch & find out something? I sent her a card at 641 E 9th apt 10-R, nyc 9 hoping it wld get there. Another fucking thing Whalen says (god what a *uselessly* bitter man) "I particularly liked stories of Miss Berlin and Miss (gawd!) Dawson. Also the news from Mexico, which must have been one of the most solemn non-meetings of minds since the League of Nations, Geneva, Switzerland, Summer of 1936." Well what the shit does *that* mean. I know what he thinks it means! Why doesn't he join CORE[337] or masturbate on an unintegrated playground.

---

335   George Rockwell Lincoln, 1918–1967; founder of the American Nazi party.

336   Miguel Grinberg, Argentine poet, b. 1937. Grinberg led an association of poets across the Americas called "The New Society." He was close to many of the Beat poets, including Allen Ginsberg, with whom he spent time in Cuba in 1965. Grinberg was one of the founders of the magazine *Eco Contemporaneo*.

337   The Congress of Racial Equality, a civil rights organization founded in 1962 whose emphasis was a nonviolent end to segregation.

So screw the simulacrum spring—there never was a straight spring here anyway. The Colchester (new University of Essex) business looks settled now—I'm told all I got to do is apply and I'm there. Of course we ain't on the boat yet—it's maybe like that apt in New York.

I had four photocopies of that nonviolent piece made at school and sent one to William Wroth (asst. ed of Northwest review[338] and a very sharp guy—from Rhode Island dig!) and one to Raworths—I think that's one of the greatest statements since Spengler! So shit abt that. I read it to my freshman comp class who were writing themes on civil rights, ha hee. They thot wow! I never thot of that! And several want to [. . .] order that mag. When their potato raising parents find out about that I'm going to be pulled up by my roots, no! Ok playwright—give me the word on all this and don't put off *covers* too long we're gettin' ready to go w/ #7—

Love to Hettie and children and you—Ed

Eddie,   [Mar ? 1964]

Just getting your letter, after mailing one. But I thought I'd get back to you or something. And thank you for such a deep communication. I'd almost forgotten exactly what I admired, but that brought it back real enough. Deeper connexions was what I wanted once, and now, again, I see the need for them. Wow. And last night I sat very drunkenly watching Gil and JEarly read up the street. Very honest cats, I suppose. In ways that I could never be, of what I was doing, somehow. I know who I am, though that territory is not completely explored . . . but I still do the name of it. What the fuck. They ARE honest. But Gil was smoking big cigars and JE cigarillos, honest! There were only a handful of people at the reading, and as Gil remarked, "It's just like the Cedar bar." And indeed it was . . . only the Cedar, as you must know, was torn down a year ago. So what is the honesty in that observation, unless he was right, and the aura of those times still does hang about our heads. But not for God sakes, no, not mine. I would agree with anybody about anything, my personality, haha, is like that . . . just to get whoever or whatever off my personal back. But the way I really am is exactly that too, except to function oppositely. Shit. I don't agree, never, with nobody, no matter what, unless I like them, and then I listen, and do from time to time, agree very much. I'm not at all sure what this is about, except that reading last night was boring and tweaky. So earnest everybody was . . . it's easy to see why I haven't seen those people more often of late, ie, since maybe the hepatitis shot, which turned the whole thing around, and brought, very heavily for a time, the drug scene down on my tender head. But fuck that too, junkies are dumber than most people, or at least

---

338   Wroth would also go on to coedit *Coyote's Journal.*

they're bigger liars. I was hanging out with Elvin Jones[339] and this nutty painter friend of mine Bob Thompson,[340] which is like, if you listen to Elvin play, hanging out at the Olympics or participating in the motherfuckers. Trane is playing at the Halfnote and after the last set the three of us lit out into the snow with those cats screaming at the tops of their lungs . . . man did we love each other that night, I mean completely, and at a real point of ecstasy. They woke up some other cat up, named Miles Forst,[341] another painter . . . this at 430 in the am, and of course the cat was fucking his old lady, hence the light. But we go right the hell up in the cat's house, duplex w/ studio included, and wife is sitting in next room with overcoat on and boots, with nothing but panting flesh underneath. A really sexy scene. So we put on, or rather those cats put on or made Miles put on his records and take out his bush and those two cats took turns rubbing up against the cat's wife. She is the daughter of rich southern (I mean the deep south, baby) family, and her admiration of the "classless" society is not a little sensual. She was rubbing her ass off. Finally when Forst did get up enough nerve to tell them cats (530) it was time to split, and took them both in next room to tell them why . . . she falls headlong across my knees. I almost shit on myself. Naturally, the cat comes back in the room seeing me prying his old lady off me takes it most unkind. So out in the street those two cats just raise hell with me, accusing me of getting us all kicked out in the snow. Then we went to Bob's house and used up all his skag . . . and that shit always makes me sick, always. But we finally ended up standing on corner, Elvin and I, talking till 8:00 Am, and I was so exhausted and high and drunk by that time I slept till evening. Completely dishonest but wow we got into something other than just standing around being suffering fucking artists. Man those cats suffer on the run, which is what I dig, and take I suppose to be the truest playback of my sensibility. But not that earnest mediocrity . . . that calmness and stealth. Fuck that. Like that fucking Bear as you mention, those fucking poems are four years old, I didn't even know that dumb whore had them anymore. She just printed those to get at me and pinch Hettie's twat. That cover especially delighted my ol lady, you bet! But what could I do after the shit had gone down. I stewed, cursed, as usual, just got out of it, but I would never never say anything to DP and her fag about the unpleasantness that caused me. Nunca![342] Fuck them, they'll never get no jollies at my expense *outside*, because I *know* I'd have to strangle that Marlowe, may yet have to if they keep it up. That sheet shd be called The Camp Journal. Allright. I'm going an buy a coat.

Love to Everybody, Roi

---

339   Elvin Jones, American jazz drummer, 1927–2004.

340   Bob Thompson, African American painter, 1937–1966. Thompson was friends with a number of the Beat poets, including Allen Ginsberg.

341   Miles Forst, American painter, 1923–2006. Forst was a New York–born painter, associated with the abstract expressionists and avant-garde artists of the mid-twentieth century.

342   Never!

Deah lee rory** April 5/64

How they hangin now? Just got w.d. out again and I think Wagnon is mailing them this afternoon. That shot of yours looks good this time up front, a counteractive at last to the runaway south of the borederos. I wish we had a Cannuck worth something, Bowering[343] is such a dull bullshitter. And I didn't know he'd go someplace like Calgary! The fink. I thot Inago was hopeless. Who is a Canadian with more sense. Do you think your friend Oscar Peterson[344] wld contrib. "reflections on how I got my piano via the underground railroad." But it seems the best issue in some ways yet. I'd like it if you cld suggest what possible steps to make it a sharper instrument than it is, I am aware it is too *fucking* random so far. I got the Selby prose, is he good for more later? How does he feel about making the lil mag scene, cld you send his address, or ask him to, and am I right in assuming *he* isn't one of those you don't see much anymore.

In the rumpus room of the Hotel Whitman downtown cowtown Pocatello there sings a very young lady named Carolyn Astroskii, impossible moniker, wife of the famous local and very hip tenorman Tony Astroskii, from the wilds of New Jersey, your home state, however she's indigenous. She is very damn good sounding, sort of the best parts of Anita O'Day, Chris Connor and oh say Julie London,[345] but with a much better voice than any of those, and none of their vices. A great pleasure, for instance she sings *It's Alright w/ Me* better than anyone who ever lived, she plays bass while doing it, oh god you'd shit your pants. But she plays plenty bass too. W/ her are drums, good, piano, good, and a cat who gets a little Dixie on clarinet but who also plays tenor and baritone sax, better. All local cats. Cut on out here and we'll make that sound some night.

You haven't said what you think of the play, its reproduction etc. You must be utterly tied up, I don't expect to hear from you really. It looks less and less like we'll get that apt in NYC, Helene's brods. She's going to call him this afternoon I think. And if not, then that puts another complexion on the first part of the summer for us. We might have to do what we feared all along, ie, not rent our place here at all and just go to Buffalo and make the shot there, come back and forget certain other niceties, like seeing the apple. But it isn't settled yet.

I thot I had written you about Betty Olson,[346] but when Hetty called H, it seemed, no it was true, she hadn't known, I can't understand how that was. The

---

343 George Bowering, Canadian poet, b. 1935. Bowering attended the 1963 Poetry Conference in Vancouver.

344 Oscar Peterson, American jazz pianist and composer, 1925–2007.

345 American women jazz singers Anita O'Day, 1919–2006; Chris Connor, 1927–2009; and Julie London, 1926–2000.

346 Betty Olson, Charles Olson's wife, had died in a car accident. According to Tom Clark's *Charles Olson: Allegory of a Poet's Life*, she was severely depressed at the time, and Olson suffered guilt over the incident, worrying that he'd neglected her in a time of need. Ralph Maud also notes how devastated Olson felt at Betty's death (*Harbor* 214–17).

day after it happened Mack Hammond[347] called me from Buffalo. Well, it is too goddamn final to even think of. And so utterly quick and shocking, good lord, just as their lives after all the hopelessness of those years seemed to get straight.

Hey write, ok. Anything further on *Hands Up!*? Did you see that Granta, the American section edited by Crozier,[348] I asked him to send you a copy. He was wanting to know who might like one, and I thot it odd you weren't there too. Have you echewed (is that right?) those comabridge connections? It amounts to little enough anyway. God there's no doubt of that. What about that white fundamentalish (?) cat who was stabbed by the mugger in Harlem, who was he what was his scene? Write immediately.

Love to all—Ed

[1964 Apr. 9]
Thurs

Ed,

God, I don't know what the hell to do about Betty. I want to call and write Charles, but shit, what do you say. Fucking Dan Rice[349] called me up, tho I wasn't here, to ask why I hadn't written Chas, or rather that he thought I shd. But the stretcher is that the first time he called, he just calld for the address, and didn't even tell Hettie what had happened.

I know a cat named Mike Strong in Toronto who was a pretty good yng poet at one time, tho I haven't seen anything, but I think he'd make the canadian news sparkle, &c. All I can see to make the d. more interesting is to get some more practicing poets into it, as well as the just started. Edward Marshall, Lorenzo Thomas,[350] Mack Thomas (prose), Susan Sherman,[351] Ed Sanders, cat I know named John Marlowe, are some good bets. Lt's address is 161–21 199 Drive, Jamaica, 34, Ny., although I told him a while ago to send. Mack Thomas, I will send something of his with this, though you might not go for it. I will say it ain't his best, but I'll see what you think.

---

347 Mac S. Hammond, American poet and professor of creative writing at SUNY Buffalo, 1926–1997.
348 Andrew Crozier, British poet and editor, 1943–2008. Crozier was part of the independent publishing scene in England, associated with J. H. Prynne, who was helping to bring Dorn to England.
349 Dan Rice, American painter, 1927–2003. Rice was a close friend of Olson's and attended Black Mountain College. His work is most often associated with abstract impressionism; he lived in New York City throughout the '50s and into the early '60s.
350 Lorenzo Thomas, Panamanian American poet, 1944–2005. Thomas was associated with Umbra, a collective of black writers and poets formed in the early 1960s in New York City. Umbra was a radical literary group with an interest in creating a space for a distinct African American literary consciousness. Writers of Umbra include David Henderson and Ishmael Reed.
351 Susan Sherman moved to New York in 1961 from California and became involved in radical, feminist literary movements. She was an editor for the *Village Voice* in the '60s and worked with Carol Bergé running poetry readings at the Metro Café.

Kulchur looks now for sure, past anybody we know. LHorny is all over, and strong like a bitch. She de man, now. But I hope to send some things from time to time, have, in fact, a goofy essay on esthetics, &c, I'll probably send in a little while.

Play, Dutch-man, now seems like it might have a successful run. Good reviews in general, some glowing. Clurman in Nation is wildly enthusiastic, ditto Newsweek, Newsday, NYPst, Trib, NewYorker . . . so it looks pretty good. I hope anyway . . . we have things . . . specially me . . . cd do with the money.

Letter today from woman up at Buffalo, saying 350 for six weeks, for 4 bedroom place. Very dear. I thought maybe we'd only have to spend 150 or so for the thing. You set now?? How's it look?? Write that fucking broinlaw and find out where everything's at . . . wd be a groove if you cd come in early.

I went up to Bennington last weekend, they had some kind of "arts festival." I read. Cecil Taylor played. Anna Sokolow danced. Panels on jazz w/ MWilliams, Teo Macero (who also played his warmed over Pres licks), and Billy Taylor's group as well as Hall Overton's group w/ Teddy Charles.[352] I had a chance to argue with Bernard Malamud up there (who's a fag, by the way, even though he's married . . . or at least I think so). Also met Stanley Edgar Hyman, who's a hopeless alcoholic . . . and his hideous wife, Shirley Jackson, the novelist.[353] They have a son with a blonde mustache who wants to be a jazz musician.

Thing on Hands Up now is that I been trying to convince them not to cut anything, but Eli is stubborn. It looks like I'm going to have to cut it down, as much as I hate to do it. The cat just won't budge man. I don't know what to tell you. But if it's alright with you . . . I'll just prune it till we get under the limit.

Weird thing is that I got a letter from Charles the day I heard about the thing happening to Betty. Letter was postmarked the day the thing happened. Very weird. Letter from Charles baiting me on my social attitudes, &c. which I *was getting ready to sit down and answer* when the word came, and froze solid.

Creeley, Duncan, and Denise read next week. We already got tickets. Hope it's good. I think maybe I ought to give a party or something after the reading. Shit. World shifts so fast. I've been giving out interviews and shit for the last week. Seeing pictures and words about me, the sense of which I am not even yet hip to. I mean I don't even know what I feel about all of it. When something good happens to you you figure you deserve it, or something. Two more plays have been optioned for the fall . . . The Toilet, and another thing called The Slave. Also, now, there is talk of Spoleto, for Dutchman, and BBC and CBC broadcasts. So we'll see what happens.

---

352   Anna Sokolow, Jewish American dancer and choreographer, 1910–2000; Teo Macero, American jazz saxophonist and composer, 1925–2008; Billy Taylor, American jazz pianist and composer, 1921–2010; Hall Overton, American jazz composer and pianist, 1920–1972; Teddy Charles, American jazz pianist and drummer, 1928–2012.

353   Bernard Malamud, American writer, 1914–1986; Stanley Edgar Hyman, American literary critic, 1919–1970; Shirley Jackson, American writer, 1916–1965.

At any rate, I'm now working on long play . . . but bogged, or not bogged just now no time at all to do anything but answer the phone and stay very high.

Reading the other night with Joel, Denise, Frank, Paul, Allen at NYU to raise money for Metro café fight against evil. Allen was the show. Later at someone's house I had to hear that stupid Joel tell Allen, "I really like yr poetry now man . . . it's improved . . . jesus . . ." Who does that think cat he is? Wow. You've improved. That elite horseshit, but now so it gives advantages where there are none. Do you think Joel thinks of himself as having some shit for AG?? Whow.

Selby in the junk bag right now. Though I understand he's cleaning up right now. I'll get o him. It's 345am and Ives is on the box . . . I'm looped and twisted right about now, played basketball earlier.

Love—Roi

Edsel,   [April 10? 1964]

Jesus, Joel is more hopeless than I thought. God! I mean, really, to *stay w/ you* on his vacation? Are you going to spare yrself the tragedy of this particular human relation/ship?? Really it's too pathetic even to beat him with. But I keep saying to myself what kind of life does this cat fancy himself as leading?? Have you any ideas?? Got a note from somebody up at Buff saying six weeks of a 4bedroom place for $350. Wow, that's pretty steep don't you think? We'll suck around for something else. Have to sublease this place as well. Man this Buffventure getting more complexcated as we get further in. Wrote you last night . . . still a little staggery from all night session. Got to have lunch with a cat this afternoon, so off to wash my sucio self. Thought better about *that* Mack Thomas piece . . . I'll get another. Keep yr head up.

Roi

April 11/64

Dear Roi—I know there's nothing you can say to Charles not a letter or phone surely. But can't you get away for a day and go see him? I'd do that if I lived as close as you. That seems much more the point. The night I got the call from Buffalo I, we, Helene and I sent him a telegram, a night letter. I'm sorry now I didn't call you and Hettie but you know we first assumed that people in New York wld know of it first and never dreamed anything like Dan's behavior wld occur. But Dan can be goddamn vacant at times. Anyway I'm sorry for that and certainly understand your being upset.

The address of brother Jack's apt is 1374 1st Ave New York City 21 apt 4c and as I told you on a card I sent 2 days ago—we leave here the 3rd of June arrive there the 5th and will have all that time there until time to leave for Buffalo. We're taking train. It wld be magnificent, to say the least, if we could all go to Buffalo together, don't you think?

All those names you sent re—better poesy for W.D. are useless to me w/ out addresses. Look! I'm aware you don't have any time and it seems best to let all that wait a month & ½ til I get there and can get that straight. I get buggy when I don't hear from you for a long time but dig that it's alright. It's alright w/ me. Oh shit. You know I wrote you a gang of letters last mo. in one I told you poem for poem what I'd rather have cut from *Hands Up!* Some, 2 or three I'd like, even, to pull out—you sound as if you didn't get this letter. I wonder if you're getting all your mail, man. The six or so deletions I suggested seemed to me wld make it reduced to 48pps. *and* if Lena Horny gets too horny W.D. wld dig *very* much to have the essay on assthetics you sot.

What objection cld Charles possibly have as of yr social attitude? Years ago I remember him coming on that shades were not the *only* minority group but that seems beside the point now.

Look—April is the first anniversary of W.D. We're planning to do 50pp and make it April May and June issue since we won't be able to come out in May and June anyway. I thot to dedicate the issue to the memory of Betty Olson. A lithograph cover which can be done here easily but we'll have to have a lot more material!— I'd like something straight from you & beside the [. . .] John shot or the [. . .] John not at all, or different in *tone* for that issue—whot you think? Tell me. I thot to get John Wieners to write a thing, something abt Betty—they were *very* close in a good sense. Very touching, really. I don't know, Jesus Christ! A remembrance or something like that. What do you think?

Also, can we use that poem you sent on back of letter. 2 actually—*The Burning General* & *Major Bowe's Diary*? I like them very damn much and hope they aren't taken elsewhere already.

I'm writing this letter in bed—sick—damn intestinal flu. I went 20 miles over to Twin Falls (Twin Balls as we calls it here) Thursday night last & got some bad water me thinks. That's very fucking funny what Joel said to A.G. Indeed! Joel is, I'm afraid, getting a bigger drag even than he used to be. Called Helene on horn the other night & jawed for ½ hour abt how he cld teach *my* classes "free" in Buffalo when I was tired—this to counteract Helene's demur abt his staying w/ us. Gawd! I don't at *all* know what to do abt him. Can you still hire assassins in Manhattan? I mean, no joke, he was serious. What is his hang up. Why doesn't he just write point fuck & shut up? He makes me almost anti-semitic.

That 350 pitch for 4 bedroom seems outrageous. But I don't know. Some [. . .] cards w/ listings that came to us via the Eng dept. One had *2* living rooms (what the fuck! live twice) for $400. Shit that sounds like a "keep the money at home" policy. Hammond is charging us $150 for 5 wks w/ 3 bedrooms but since I know that cat it's prob a "decent" price. Those prices are a fraud but Helene thinks they're probably "nice" places. Oh shit.

Bennington sounded a gas. The music must have been anyway.

By the way I got a letter from Charles the day it happened too asking what the fuck was up w/ those South American types no word or hint of the event of that day. Oh wow. there is something very sanely bitter abt that. Write & answer questions—

Love from all here—Ed

Helene says "Roi Jones is a most immaculate libertine"

April 25/64

For instance we're now thinking of renting our place for whole summer—ie—June–Sept 1st otherwise known as Labor Day—and therefore what wld we do . . . For instance what do you have in mind w/ that Atlantic coast beach gig Het mentioned—? Cld we all make it—that wld mean *we'd* have abt 3 wks to kill—we cld tour. How abt going to Vera Cruz—Mexico D.F.? Or, Maine? You name it Buster. We'll get there in our car—or maybe we cld all fuck around Province Towne? But seriously if you ever *do* write me a letter again—explain what you intend après Buffalo will you—because we're worried about that interim and we sure as hell, as you, don't want to return to New York—Maine couldn't we all tour Maine—I've never been there in my whole life. We could take turns fucking Theodore Enslin[354] in his red shirt in his rustic cabin w/ Denise chained to the table, forced to watch— like a reverse Erskine Caldwell!!![355]

If you don't get that C.J. bit for W.D. here soon I'll burn a cross on the roof of the Hartz Mtn Birdseed Co in full view of your pad man! And tell Hettie she'll be sorry she ever bought that abolitionist package—OK—The best, grandest of all holidays is coming up—*MOTHUH'S DAY*—I'll send you a wire—make it—

Ed

April 26/64

Hey man, I damn well owe you an *intense* apology—for that horseshit call last night—my god, Helene said later I *was* hysterical. I'd been on some powder and drinking my head off—later a friend stopped by and I was actually she says,

354 Theodore Enslin, American avant-garde poet, 1925–2011. Enslin was associated in the 1960s with the little magazine *Origin*.
355 Erskine Caldwell, American author, 1903–1987. Erskine's novels focused on the American South, and his 1958 *God's Little Acres* was deemed pornographic and obscene. Erskine was arrested and tried for obscenity; he was exonerated at a jury trial. The novel's plot contains a multitude of sexual entanglements, to which Dorn is referring here in his unfortunate and vitriolic scenario involving Enslin and Denise Levertov.

Jew-baiting—Oh wow am I bugged w/myself and bugged period—man if we don't get the fuck outta here soon I'm gonna be done *for good & sure*. Your letter, and the mss. came today—it was a great relief to get it and assuaged my tremendous guilt of last night—I mean just the exposure to it—look—you make it w/ or w/out whoever's play goes—what the fuck good will it do anybody else finally if you *drag* simply because the world won't Gugg a given package—You got to do for you or there damn well ain't any point for *any* of us. Ok the cover idea sounds good to me. Pop 'Hands!' up. I ain't got *any* ideas as of now and Fee is, has done IDAHO OUT's cover. So this car is a swinger dad and we'll take a long ride after Buffalo—dig—See you in a month get C.J. the Miss Sheik here quick—Love Ed

April 28/64

Roi—No I have not seen F. You, a Mag. of the Arts and wld like to velly much—But tell Ed Sanders this: Lockwood Memorial poetry lib's* "poetry curator" wrote me last month asking if I had a file for which he implied he'd pay advance premium bread. Maybe he shld look into it?

Ed.

(By the way Raworth did Gloucester Out a beautiful lil "chap" book. He's [. . .]. I'll send you a copy as soon as he sends me some.

   P.S. Stop worrying abt the car, we'll all make it fine cos it's very roomy & sta wgn's a drag anyway. They're *wagons* dig!

   P.P.S. Also [. . .] 180 [. . .] Buffalo sent a letter I believe soliciting poems from Ed Sanders they wanted, if it was the same form letter. To see off 25pp dig they must think I'm that cat's agent!

   *NY State at Buffalo

   Got, and dug, key poem, [. . .] prose.

S+P's D   May 17 [1964]

E.D.

J.O. finally got the ms to T & EW.[356] They seem very much disposed to do it, in fact, I think, for sure, they will. I'll know for sure tomorrow (they say) . . . & I guess I shd have waited until then to write—but screw that. I think it's cool. You got any cover ideas &c.? We gonna have big wild party next week. And one when you get here!! I feel better!!

LOVE LEROI

---

356   Joel Oppenheimer; Ted and Eli Wilentz.

Pocatello
May 19, 64

Dear Rory—Getting things wound up here and a real sense of going at last but I don't know who or how good thatsagonna be. There keeps being a bad as well as good side of the ledger. For inst. cat. came from buffalo summer sessions and looks as grim as it sounded. Theys putting the work on us poor folk baby. I figure well to get out of there short of 8 hours a day. And I get this asinine letter from some cunt in California, Wilmington who'd been to the great Vancouver president and she wants to know ohhhh, jackoff, is it going to be a "repeat" of *that* luvvvvly summer, I just love poets and poetry, I've published too little I know but here they are and then the list. Consummatum est. I'll ram a one volume Shakespeare up her miserable cunt if she gets close!

Dig they give us 1½ hour for lunch. I wonder if there is a Y nearby.

But I got this word from Professor Donald Davie yesterday in the mail and he's cooled the University of Essex bit thru the Fullbright and it looks now to go with no hitches. If I ever do leave these shores I'll lasso the Statue of Liberty and drag that bitch out to the middle of the Atlantic on the way by. Oh shit. The end of things are here, here. And it is about time. Lotta people around here might get very busted for smoking various wild growing weeds namely one. All uncool. Culture types shld never fuck with the stuff. A Bircher[357] plot it is said to be to embarrass what they think to be a too liberal administration at ISU. And it makes sense, ie, that rumor. I am clear as far as I can see because I always put them down as yokels and we never had much to do w/ that scene. Time, however, will tell. In any case there is a lot of political shifting and it looks like the good guys are in for some shit.

Hey, it won't be long now we'll see y'all. Oh god. Pray we make it down that highway alive. More than 2 thousand miles all the way. I'll get various words to you in meantime. C.J. came and I was damn sorry it wasn't in #8, but that great poem of yours rides there at the end anyway, and I did dig the way it comes on w/ Lawrence and goes out w/ Jones.

Drop note soon so I hear from you before we leave.

Love to all kids and grownups, Ed

Jones had, by this point, earned himself an increasingly public reputation, both as a poet and as an activist for black Americans. While these arenas only sometimes over-lapped, Jones moved fluidly through them. As he continued to write poetry, expanding his ideas and experimenting in American poetics, he was at the same time continuing his work as an activist, historian, and chronicler of African American culture and

357   A reference to the John Birch Society, an extreme right-wing political advocacy group.

*political life. The public responded to both things: he was frequently invited to confer-
ences, lectures, meetings, and public talks about everything from Beat poetry to Black
Nationalism.*

*In this letter, Jones casually mentions two very different experiences without artic-
ulating just how wide the degrees of separation are in American culture. In Asilomar
on the Monterey Peninsula, he took part in a conference sponsored by the University
of California at Berkeley Extension concerning black American cultural life with figures like Arna Bontemps, Gwendolyn Brooks, and Ossie Davis, an event at which
James Baldwin and Ralph Ellison were also to have appeared. Their failure to appear
led* Newsweek *to note, "Jones . . . carried the day." From Monterey Jones went to San
Francisco, where he met up with Donald Allen and "old heads" like Philip Whalen,
Michael McClure, and Gary Snyder, finishing the day by going to a baseball game
with the poets Jack Spicer and Ron Loewinsohn. This group of poets was key to the
core of the Beat/San Francisco Renaissance/Black Mountain radical New American
poetics. That Jones shared history with, and was an integral part of, these spaces in
mid-twentieth-century American culture speaks to both the confluence of varying
circles of cultural influence as well as Jones's own rising recognition in the public eye.*

[Sept. 8, 1964] Day after labor D.

What's happening gen'ral . . . all our travels look like they've come, finally, to an
end, and I'm a happy mfer about that. We just got back from Southhampton about
two hours ago. Hettie drove. I navigated. She had rented a cottage out there, way
off the fashionable section, near only a thin rocky beach, but some of the hiprich
took her to their breasts and informed her about all the hip waterholes, 12ft waves,
niggermaids & Bentleys. That scene. LarryRivers & the rest, but even chief faggots
of the art world, &c. Really.

My california thing was a gas, completely, wishd I had some clippings to give
you actual word from bird, but the conference, first, was very strange. Baldwin
& Ellison didn't show, so as Newsweek put it, "Jones who is no Ellison or even
Baldwin, carried the day." (Aug 24.) I'm gonna show Jimmie that clipping, let him
get to that. Lot of yng beautiful kids there, from south, and local, like SF, Berkeley,
Oakland, & LA, and they hung out in my quarters all the time, except when I
was speaking. Wild informal casual lit/political discussions, complete with short
speeches (by the hipper in attendance) to some there, not completely with the
social growl these kids insist on. But very good, to see, and get started. Hentoff was
at the thing, and Rexroth (who I talked to a great deal, saw him later in Sf) Arna
Bontemps, Gwendolyn Brooks, Ozzie Davis (who got very tuff, for the occasion)
sociologist named Horace Cayton, coauthored good book Black Metropolis, was
there, and an old beatup alcoholic, but very strong. Many parties, chicks walk
around with stacks of 45's in their purse, dog monkey frog fish, you name it.

Then I went up to Berkeley, and in an out of SF w/ Donald Allen, who took me all over, and was very pleasant. He got me copies of all that 4Seasons material, now out in three lovely little (dated) pamphlets. But still nice proper cute, like Don. (Has Harvey Brown of Niagara Frontier written you about publishing *Rites* as a separate project? We talked long time about it. He sd he cd get it out quick. You interested?) Saw the old heads, Whalen, McClure, Snyder . . . who's divorcing now, or being divorced . . . he was in good shape, living on the beach, headed, when I saw him, up the Washington Mts. Don arranged a reading which went off better than I'd hoped, and crowded. Went to see Giants w/ Spicer & Loewinsohn . . . Spicer really a derelict looking cat, I was surprised, like our neighborhood is full of cats look like him. But he was good to be with, and gave me his new book, The Holy Grail.

After reading, in Spicer's Bar . . . Gino & Carlos . . . I made a wild scene, pulling this cat Andy Hoyem's old lady's drawers down in the middle of the bar (She came up to me, I didn't know her, and says she used to like me but she don't now, because I come on as "a forthright yng man," not a poet (?), she sd I was "getting in a mould," so I unmoulded, jes for her. Richy Brautigan came to her aid, and I took his gold spectacle off and threatened to kill him, then Joanne Kyger,[358] Gary's ex, came up, and I punched her in the face, she falling against the bar, & screaming, her escort, a little fag, came out of someplace crying, I didn't have the guts to punch him, finally, with all these people surrounding me, and Jack S sitting on his stool looking benign, excited, drunk, interested, two spook boys came in, thought the white backlash has me, and whipped out they swords. It was sweet, the whole bit, like out of JK's untermenschen.[359] I can't wait to see it get mentioned in literary contexts. Dig?

Hands Up at the printers now. Eli says end of the month we'll have bound copies. You get in on the big wave in fall publishing. What's happening w/ the Knopf thing, you still got a lot of manhours to put in?? NewSchool gig starts 21 Sept, so I still got some time, tho that's only 1 day. But like the dean, or new dean sends me letter asking me who I think *shd teach the writing courses*!!! I'm sure I'll get Gil on this semester, and Joel next, if he wants it. Paul too, if possible. I'll be a whorehouse.

I finally finished the goddam long play, just couple days ago, now to retype. It's 108pp or so, so that's a sweat, but man I'm so happy I cd shit. When they get it printed up I'll send you a copy. Very anxious for you to see.

Creeley sent me a letter other day, listing some readings to be had out yr way if I come . . . I might go to Calif in Oct, for twothree days, readout there, and come

358   Joanne Kyger, American poet, b. 1934. Kyger was deeply involved in the San Francisco poetry scenes at this time. She had been for a time married to poet Gary Snyder, accompanying him to Japan as he furthered his studies in Zen Buddhism while she herself expanded her own studies in Buddhism. Kyger's *Japan and India Journals* are an account of her travels with Snyder from her own point of view as a writer and a woman (she'd become Snyder's wife in Japan because social mores at the time would not allow for them to live together as an unmarried couple).
359   "Subhuman." The term *untermensch* had been used by the Nazis to describe "inferior" people as part of their racial ideology.

through nmexico, but really, right at the moment I'd rather not. I'm tired of being outside apple. I'll write soon. Let me know what happened to youall, and how's all those??? Love from us

Roi

2

Oh, I meant to tell you I spoke when I came in nyc 2weeks or so ago, w/ Bill Epton the cat who is being charged w/ criminal anarchy.[360] They havn't revived that charge since 1909. 55 years ago. So we spoke up at Hotel Teresa w/ some other cats. About 100 cops in and out, plus 2 cars of ofay cats, probably tourists, sitting in alleyway. Lloyd Sealey, newblackcapt. Was sitting outside, & I peeped him. Funniest deal tho, was inside, suddenly the speaker, says be calm, folks, please. I want to make a little announcement. He says then, "Biggest Uncle Tom around is here . . . or one of the biggest . . . anyway a model UT." Then he announces that a capt Bard or Brad, a spook plainclothes dick was in audience taking notes. Speaker asks him to stand up and take a bow. The cat did. Very wild.

I'm including Epton's letter so you can see what's happening. How'd you like that Philly square dance.

I was on a tv show last week w/ Allen, WDSnodgrass (yah), Sandra (fuck me baby) Hochman, Norman Rosten (who read a poem about kissing some chick in an abomb attack, it began, really, "come live w/ me and be my love." No, I'm not bullshitting a tap. He really read that shit. Program will be on in San Francisco in a month, but it might not get out there. Peter Viereck[361] was also on it. Allen & I were drinking beer out of these coffee cups & the camera started spinning to me, also in middle of show, I had to leave the set to pee. Engineers just about committed suicide. Ok, tho I'll talk to you soon.

LJ

Dear Roi,   Pocatello, 14 Sept [1964]

I wrote a letter 2 weeks ago, a long rambling thank you letter for all that I know you know I dig about that stay w/you—and it got there alright. Right next door 28 (Fort Square) Cooper Square. Never made that damn confusion til I was both places— equal points of strength for me EAST. Ok. It came back & I was glad. It isn't good to reread some letter you've sent off. Wow!

---

360   William (Bill) Epton, American activist, 1932–2002. An outspoken radical agitator, Epton made public speeches during the Harlem riots in the summer of 1964 that tested the limits of free speech. He was consequently arrested and was the first person since the "Red Scare" of 1919 to be convicted of criminal anarchy: the jury concluded that Epton's speeches maintained the momentum of the riots. Epton wrote a letter to Jones at this time (referred to in this letter to Dorn) asking for his support and help.
361   American poets: Sandra Hochman, b. 1936; Norman Rosten, 1913–1995; Peter Viereck, 1916–2006.

I sent the mss. I hope you got those. This poem enclosed is the one I'd like you to put in for the one sent abt page 61 in the book. I hadn't kept a copy & didn't know the real words until *The Nation* came.

I haven't been exactly morose since returning, but cool & thoughtful like they say. The hold of the land stays for me, here, but the bigness gets more quickly hopeless. I start 2 courses, not one, shortly, but feel on top of that. Letter from Creeley just after we returned saying he was very very disappointed with Vancouver. God damn.

How is it there? A confused question I know the answer is probably simple. Give my love to Hettie and my deep undying thanks. Please send me a note. I didn't have any expectation you'd write but I am anxious to see your hand at least as a reassurance.

At Buckwell they fucked me around. The biggest drag I have yet to experience in my life. 15 people at the reading including Helene & myself. And man— unbelievable—the town was DRY—ie *no* beer even. More later. Love, Ed

One of Dorn's major sticking points was the issue of race as identity. At a time when naming one's identity through race affiliation was on the rise and was directly tied to civil rights, Dorn refused to play what he thought of as identity politics. In this letter Dorn takes on this problem, tearing through writer and critic Leslie Fiedler (1917– 2003) and 1964 Republican presidential nominee Barry Goldwater (1909–1998). This is an interesting point given his deep friendship with Jones, for whom race and identity were inextricably bound. While Jones was engaged in an overt battle to recoup and create the cultural identities of African Americans, Dorn's dealings with race ran to disruption rather than coherence. Dorn understood identity and race as distinct yet complicated matters and held no patience for either racism or simplistic theorizing. But while Dorn's sensibilities were nuanced and demanding, he was at the same time greatly sympathetic to the plight of those subjected to the marginalization and violence of racism.

He was particularly concerned about the decimation of Native American peoples, writing several essays and one book, The Shoshoneans *(with photographer Leroy Lucas), about this issue. Dorn and Jones were continually challenging each other's ideas in this matter, but when Jones felt it necessary to leave his white friends behind, despite Dorn's own hurt at the temporary loss of his friend, he spoke out in support of Jones's decision. Though the two were still in regular contact at this point in late 1964, the momentum was building in both the microcosm of their friendship and the world they lived in toward major change.*

Sptmbr 20/64

Dear Roo: I haven't written all this time because I haven't been able—I've thot of doing it every day but you know . . . I've been in a stupor sort of, since we got back. I've read a lot and that's kept me going but I haven't so much as written a letter. I will write lots of things, I always do this, lay out for so long before I come on. I re-read everything I have of yours. (By the way, in that New York hold up of our auto *Blues People* was stole, and I could order another copy from here, but damn it was Signed, you did it, and I felt the loss of that particular book anyway sharper than the rest—cld you send me another, signed, jesus, cld, you, do, it, all, over again.?) ((I am sending you a *present* you won't believe)) and then as I told you on the horn I read Native Son for the first time. Oh shit. Les Fiedler is a lucky motha I had neglected that. Him with his Jews are black too shit. But Boris Max is a Jew. Oh yeah. Yes that book makes it very much for me the first for a long time of that kind of shit. And I see sets in it of a lot I cldnt recognize until I read his fragment of autobiog in Post by the way. Strange writing, like he really did it himself. But when he's talking politics and the "Race" problem it is impeccable, except I see he buys that bullshit like everyone else too, that Goldwater really *Means* what he says, is at least *Honest* has principles etc. Well no man can be completely right. But he comes so close it is a shame to see that. I don't see why the stupid demos don't knock that prop out from under that obviously lying bastard. I mean the idea he shld be able to use 'honesty,' or 'principle' words? The world hasn't changed as far as this place is concerned. Things were pretty much as we left them. South Hampton sounded like it was ok. That must have been a great interlude for Hettie at least. I can see with terror in my eyes her driving that 1954 Chevy down to the sea, madness, a kind of post-buffalonian grip on the wheel. By the way I showed Ray that thing you wrote about pulling the chick's pants down in SF. He laughed his head off. And then asked if I thot you really did it. I had to tell him yes. Oh wow. Well. We all lived that one vicariously. Thank you. Drew wanted to print that letter as a CJ installment but I sais nix. ie, I thot that might not be what you meant by literary context. But it wld have been a pleasure. By the way he

Sptmbr 20/64

Dear Roo: I havent written all this time because I havent been able--
Ive thot of doing it everyday but you know...Ive been in a stupor sort
of, since we got back. Ive read a lot and thats kept me going but I
havent so much as written a letter. I will write lots of things, I always
do this, lay out for so long before I come on. I re-read everything I have
of yours)By the way, in x that new yourk hold up of our auto Blues
people was stole, and I could order another from here, but damn it
it was Signed, you did it, and I felt the loss of that particular book
anyway shapper than the rest-cld you send me another, signed, jesus,
cld, you, do, it, all, overagain.?) ((I am sending you a present you
wont believe)) and then as I told you on the horn I read Native Son
for the first time. Oh shit. Les Fiedler is a lucky motha I had neglected
that. Him with his jews are black too shit. But Boris Max is a jew. Oh
yea. Yes that book makes it very much for me the irst for a long time of
that kind of shit. And I see sets in it of a lot I cldnt recognize until
now. A lot is prophesied by that book. Malcdm shldnt be a "suprise"
I read his fragment of autobiog in Post by the way. Strange writing, like
he really did it himself. But when he's talking politics and the "Race"
problem it is impecable, except I see he buys that bullshit like everyone
else too, that goldwater really Means what he says, is at least Honest
has principle etc. Well no man can be completely right. But he comes so
close it is a shame to see that. I don't see why the stupid demos dont
knock that prop out from under that obviously lying bastard.I mean the idea
he sld be able to Use 'honesty', or 'principle' words? The world
hasnt changed as far as this place is concerned. Things were pretty much
as we left them. South Hampton sounded like it was ok. That must have beeer
a great interlude for Hettie at least. I can see with terror in my eyes
here driving that 1954 chev down to the see, madness, a kind of post-
buffalonian grip on the wheel. by the way I showed Ray that thing you
xxxxxx wrote about pulling the chicks pants down in SF. He laughed his
head off. And then asked if I thot you really did it.I had to tell him
yes. Oh wow. Well. We all lived that one vicariously. Thank you.
Drew wanted to print that letter as a CJ installment but I sais nix.
ie, i thot that might not be what you meant by literary context. But
it wld have been a pleasure. By the way he here the other night and
said he'd sent you a wire as of CJ. I am going to be a sort of consultant
to it from now on. Glad to see it, WD, move on to fresh hands. He sld
make it new in salt lake. I saw a very beautiful thing of olsons,
a new "West poem,,, the only one to really make it so far, finally that
series gets started and relates to his form of poem, not just his
form of learning, leaning ok, and reading.
                    Did you dig the pickture
of Race Newton in the Sept esquire mag? He looks good. Some pictures of
Burroughs, the articlex isby him. of course you have.
                              Harvey Brown
has not written me yet bout that novel.I wld x feel very unprotocally
writing him. I hope he does.It wld be a good think to have it that way,
fanally xx afterx all this. I have been doing a lot of thinking. That
course here in cont lit, for what it means, has turned into an almost
exclusive shade lit course. This is prob the only university in the
country with such a specialty without Calling it that, ie, it goes as
whats happened! All shot up I come to consider a very good novel,
sans detective shit at all. As a form of writing it goes that well. not
quite so Big gold dream. I almost give up trying to lay hands on
The real cool killers and crazy kill. 3rd Generation is a Great book,
there is no fucking shit about that. That ending by the way is very tricky.
I figure he took Charles thru those scenes and dumped him right in the

was here the other night and said he'd sent you a wire as of CJ. I am going to be a sort of consultant to it from now on. Glad to see it, WD, move on to fresh hands. He cld make it new in Salt Lake. I saw a very beautiful thing of Olson's, a new "West" poem, the only one to really make it so far, finally that series gets started and relates to his form of poem, not just his form of learning, leaning ok, and reading.

Did you dig the pickture of Race Newton in the Sept *Esquire* mag? He looks good. Some pictures of Burroughs, the article is by him. Of course you have.

Harvey Brown has not written yet bout that novel. I wld feel very unprotocolly writing him. I hope he does. It wld be a good thing to have it that way, finally after all this. I have been doing a lot of thinking. That course here in cont lit, for what it means, has turned into an almost exclusive shade lit course. This is prob the only university in the country with such a specialty without *Calling* it that, ie, it goes as what's happened! *All shot up* I come to consider a very good novel, sans detective shit at all. As a form of writing it goes that well. Not quite so *Big gold dream*. I almost give up trying to lay my hands on *the real cool killers* and *crazy kill*. *3rd Generation* is a great book, there is no fucking shit about that. That ending by the way is very tricky. I figure he took Charles thru those scenes and dumped him right in the middle class basket, with no relief at all. I talked to Helene about it. She was disappointed in the end. But I convinced her that the end of *that* book finally made that literary responsible ending what it was all along, to be left just there, the motherfucker plays out and starts thinking about the "legitimate" responsibilities he was all along avoiding. I never saw a "lesson" like that. Concurrent with the element of "hope," there is the most blasé and devastating slap in the face for everyone except the writer. Well that's it, I mean that is *precisely* modern and it. But that's a real fucking piece of writing. I never by the way saw any technique like that. For whole long stretches of space in that thing a paragraph is a story in itself, self contained and moving, there must be more happening there per page than anywhere ever. Do you know him at all, have you ever written to him? I mean why isn't he more actively included in our scene, niggling as it is, why isn't he more here. Dig I *know* why tacitly he has to be in Paris. I am now trying to get hold of if he hollers let him go.

I got Ray Charles singing Just for a Thrill and I got another new album. Now's the Time, Sonny Rollins. Ron Carter on part of it on bass. Also, a Morton Feldman Earle Brown record. And the Hopkins thing with Happy Blues for John Glenn in which there is the line—Ain't no livin man can go around the world three times!

Sept 21

1st day of school. It looks worse this year in one way, more crowded, pop explosion etc. But I personally am cooler so that offsets that. I gave the librarian of the university hell this afternoon for not having any of your books except that anthology. He's square, not malicious. But what's the difference? I checked out another McLuhan book that looks inneresting—*The Mechanical Bride*, Vanguard, 1951. Today in the mail came a slip from Fee with Different People printed on it which you must have, for Aram, w/ the line . . . dialed the number of his friend the famous Negro writer . . . that's *got* to be you. Cld you please very much please, send me the add of Ed Sanders, it isn't on his mag. Today I got also, from you, the slip from the Post Office, and the Yellow Kid gallery sheet. That keeps me up. By the way, I have to say it, your long and detailed letter brought me back to consciousness and I don't know I'd have made it otherwise. No shit. You may not quite believe it but it has to be truer than you cld imagine. Naturally. Thank you very mucho. I haven't, hadn't, done much actual work on that book but I will, it is a dreary time for me in that sense. I feel very much that I'm "out of it" and that it is my own stupid fault, etc, no one to blame but the way I thot *I* was. *Lonely Crusade*, Chester Himes, I picked up today at the lib Knopf, 1947. I'd never heard of that. It must be an earlier one. Haven't read it. Yet. Looks like work in a war plant. 1943. Hey isn't that Revolt domestic workers revolt too bitchy. Jesus! 'Culture and cleanliness ins not their stick!' . . . It wld be hard, goddamn hard, to get past *that*!

All the local art dickers are looking forward with rancid baited breaths to the arrival of Stan (the man) Brakhage[362] in December to preview no less his film Dogstarman which I hear via Kelly is finished. It will be glad tidings to have him. He's going to stay with us. What tires me of course is that once these cats fasten on to something they think it is the whole world, aesthetically, nada mas. So films are what they talk about. Now, they talk about films if someone were persistently goosing them, say, or if they were being run off the end of a splintery plank. Now I've written I will again soon, you write, I've been looking for reviews of Dutchman & Slave in the nytimes bkrev sec but none so far? And Why don't those morrows have ads everywhere. Creeley went thru NY on his way to England, where he is now, did he stop, or if he didn't he may plan to do so on his way back. Marilyn Schlimeck said Charles is back in Buffalo with a winter coat of . . . love to you Edward Fard, the Master[363]

Oct 1st [1964]

I just dug in the National Guardian you're speaking at the Manhattan Center the 15th. I remember your talking about that during that phone call. Oh shit it's cold here. It's going to freeze tonight, not much just getting down to 25 degrees. I just sent off a package to you /is to show my concern for you, and even if you never use it, it /meant as an instrument of your own protection and a reaffirmation of

362   Stan Brakhage, American experimental, avant-garde filmmaker, 1933–2003.
363   Dorn's "Edward Fard, the Master" is a reference to Wallace Fard Muhammed, often referred to as Master Fard Muhammed, the founder of the Nation of Islam. Elijah Muhammed took over in 1934 after Fard disappeared.

my continuing belief that you *should*, on every occasion, whether public, private or that limbo one calls "being with friends."

A Warren rept awaits everyone. Gee, we saw the Burton Hamlet. He is brilliant to a degree, or as Blind Snooks[364] says, up to a certain extreem. A well advised piece of modern legerdemain. By changing the character, once that is settled, one cld see a strong feminist case there. In a way it is "extremely" dirty. He has by way of a casual management of deep terms managed to take all the tragedy, out of it. So there remains the attraction, sparkling, "brilliant," of all one wants, existential certainly, completely, that fashionable question mark. Hard and cold one is not allowed to identify with any relief, like if I had that dress I cld have a jazzy silhouette too, by the way the voguish fotografy was farther over than the beatle shot) It goes clean out. Right back to what we feared, the 'problems' of the very successful, a capitalization of first order. The solidifying of those gains lame brains expected, hoped, were dwindling. I think it sets back thinking forty years. Ie, he'll be able to insist, via any vehicle, he was the man who married Liz Taylor. To the whole world. Electronovision. That production seemed delicious, wow, taste up the ass. That stark set of Gielguds. And dig they even had a neurotic hip "New York" type chick playing O'feelya. I suppose you saw it? The wit is superb, like that evoking the ghost 4 times on the platform. But Claudius is like the banker down the street, a very simple goodnatured trouble in de conk. No cunning at all, he simply "realizes" he done bad. Some bullshit former singer, Alfred Drake? Oh my! And Laertes is a little too simple. But this gets the focus exclusively back on the kinda flashy Hamlet he was. A sort of 'interesting' J. Paul Getty, whose ships are far too scattered to keep track of, oh, problems, problems.

(He damn well did infuse his whole body in it tho, I thot the damn performance, there, was very wild. The welding of gesture and speech, a whole language . . .

Hey thanks for sending that picture of my hero Hank Thorow.[365] I got him up above my desk here in this dusty place. I ain't got nothing else that's true. I guess you ain't going to san fran and I guess you won't be coming up here. I got that film culture finally with Brakhage metaphors. It looks good. I dig him and the films and what he *says*, I'm anxious to look at it.

When you think of it and can, tell me what I ought to know.

Ed

We're very concerned to hear how Kelly checks out w/ the doctor—I read Hettie's letter to Helene—Christ—she is such a beautiful child that that seems the point—all of it, in any case, no matter what any "test" can say. Hettie's worry is understandable but tell her that it is everyone who shares in such a concern and to not feel alone in it—Love—Ed

364   Blind Snooks Eaglin, American guitarist and singer, 1936–2009.
365   Henry David Thoreau.

Originally published in 1963 for Midstream *magazine and later collected for a book of essays called* Home: Social Essays *by LeRoi Jones (1966), "What Does Non-Violence Mean?" was an incendiary article denigrating the philosophy of nonviolence as an effective course of action in the civil rights movement. Jones, as was usual when he had new work published, sent the piece to Charles Olson, who, it turned out, disliked both the article and Jones's "social stance," as Jones heard through poet Frank O'Hara. Even by 1963, when "Non-Violence" was written, Jones's attitude had become increasingly militant against the white world, American and otherwise, and against the edicts of nonviolence as espoused by Martin Luther King Jr. Never a believer in the pacifism of King, the Southern Christian Leadership Conference (SCLC), the early Student Nonviolent Coordinating Committee (SNCC), or the NAACP, Jones followed, rather, the early teachings of Malcolm X (albeit without any adherence to the Nation of Islam). While the article's critiques are often well-founded—after all, physical violence was being regularly perpetrated on African Americans with very little, if any, support from the government (which is precisely what King hoped to achieve, institutional intervention)—his counteroffer was fraught with many difficulties.*

The question of violent action is a deep human concern without any simple answer; Jones was (like Malcolm) bound to cause vehement responses from his audience. In any nation-state, violence must be officially mandated to be considered allowed: i.e., the armed forces, police departments, the FBI, the CIA. The militancy of Jones and others incited the degree of anger it did in great part not because it was violent per se but because the violence was being brought in from outside regulated channels. Olson's own personal beliefs never tended toward violence, and Jones's beliefs as poet and man were dismaying to Olson, coming especially from someone he considered a friend and whose work he respected. However, Olson's position was ambivalent; in both his poetry and personal letters, he also indicates his support of radical action such as Jones was advocating, as well as of Jones himself.

Eddie,   [Oct 1964]

Sorry to be so long, but getting back into this town is full time. And with the fucking school shit also starting, I'm up to my ass. Very cool for this time of year here, but today I ran up and down for two hours playing touch ftball out front, turned a knee, and sweated my ass off. Before I forget, I'm editing a special poetry edition of Kulchur coming out about Feb. So please send me a group of poems as soon as you can. Harvey B. in Buffalo now, I talked to him on phone, he says he'll get to you soon, but UB or Sunyab has him screwed around, and he's trying to get straight. But he was very hot to do the book. And I'm sure Chas is putting word to him. Apparently, according to O'Hara, who went up to Buf to read, Chas kinda bugged at me, for social stance, &c. He, FOH says, really didn't dig the NonViolence piece which I sent him when it first came out. Also he's bugged, it seems, because I never answered his letter putting down sd stance. Shit. But I'll see him 13th Nov when I go up to MC master Univ in Hamilton to read. I'll find out just what's shaking.

Yeh, Fee sent me the little gem. I think that cat's mind is among the simplest devices known to man. JesusXX! But Chet Himes, wow. That 3rd Generation is really something. So much shit happening to one family, like those evil weights dogging everyone in Thos Hardy, and the paragraph thing, like one par all shit breaks out, then another, all's pleasant, even hopeful, then bam, the motherfucker falls down a goddam elevator shaft, or hits people w/ his car . . . &c. Just on and on. Lonely Crusade is supposed to be a bitch. I never read that. Let me know. I'm rereading If He Hollers Let Him go, which I remember as being fantastic.

I told you I finally finished the long play. Got it mimeod. I'll try to send you a copy soon. Bar-Wilder-Albee, who produced Dutchman, have looked at it, and sd "It's wildly disappointing . . . very sloppy . . . not up to Roi's usual standard." So that's completely broken my back for last few days, I mean really. Of course, my rationalization is that those cats only liked one thing of mine really, Dutch, because they had a chance to produce all of them. Anyway, Harold Clurman's got it now, and I shd hear something about that tomorrow (Monday. Leo Garen still fucking around with Toilet/Slave, just getting around to reading people. So play definitely will not open until after election. Some other things happening tho. Chance I might put together series of 15 jazz programs for Nat Educational TV, which wd be a gas. Last idea I got is to put together a big band like Cecil, Archie S, Tchicai, Cherry, Ayler, Coleman, couple drummers, two basses, etc, see what happens. Cecil already's got some big band charts, so if the thing goes through that might be a wigola. Oct 7 I turned 30. So now I'm in yr groove. XXX is the word.

Since Dr sd no drink, or only 1 per day, max, (tho beer's ok, and champagne, oddly enough) I've been getting high too much. No grass but that other thing. Hettie's very, and now I'm starting to be. But I figure I'll be cool if I can just get back to work, and get people to stop bugging me. Hard now even to go into nightclubs like 5spot or local scene, always somebody's got something to ask me, usually a favor.

You see WmWorthy's article in Esquire on Red Chinese Negro??[366] Very ill advised, putting halffacts into Gestapo's heads, tho they already knew most, but still giving popular affirmation of things that wd look simple for JEdgar to come up with. Don't know what's on that cat's mind but, he did a dumb thing. Cool weather cooled city off a bit now, tension visibly eased. But far east is like occupied slobovia. Cops stop you on corners on foot or in a car, spot checks, want id. Section now called Peking, because all the Progressive Labor types live over there, and there are jillions of "advisors" walking around with their electric sticks.

I didn't get a chance to see RickB. May not get one. I did see Hard Days Night the middle of which I dug very much, also crowd chasing scenes. Those cats are

---

366   William Worthy, "The Red Chinese American Negro," *Esquire* 62:4 (October 1964).

pretty hipslick I suppose. San Fran thing finally didn't seem like a good idea to me. I'm just getting back, and can't begin now to see shooting off for longish stay. Too much to do. Thought, like I sd, sometimes I really wanna blow this burg, or not so much that, but just be left alone to fuck myself up in quiet.

Kellie now has pills to take every night. But she still goes off into those things. Today I watched her trying to fight one, but it's like she just floats off, away. I think she'll be alright. These kind of things usually show up in puberty, or thereabouts. Also she's pretty much aware of what the pills, and Doctors are for. She sd, "so I won't go to sleep." But now, happier, both of them are in nursery school during the day, so H &I have the days pretty much to ourselves, she playing my secretary, which is damn cool. I'm applying for a Guggenheim again, 2nd time. Allen G is too. I applied to write a "Verse play," so as not to go strictly for poesie and fuck Allen up, or vice versa. But shit certainly Allen shd have had one of those fucking things by now. All the grants and shit given out in this fucking country every year, very seldom does anybody worth a flea's nut get anything. Saw where Rockefeller gave 450,000 to playwright to small stage companies. Like hip church groups &c. Lst playwright to get 5000 or 7500 for to learn to write a play is, are you ready, Philip Roth. Lowell and Bellow got grants last year or two years ago of same amt to do same thing. Bellow's thing on Bdway now, may not last too long. Lowell's will open soon. So they'd rather "make" playwrights, &c. or anything else, rather than give money to somebody outside the grove. But that sure ain't telling you anything.

Got Duncan's Roots & Branches haven't had a chance to read it. But you got to get JWieners' new one, Ace of Pentacles, man there are some very very beautiful poems in that book. Like even when John gets "cute," he really is, so the poem means that, and moves anyway. Very strong. Be glad as hell when yrs appears. The W's are getting ready to move their store across the street, hence the lag. Last time I asked TW sd, "Any time now," so take heart. Spengler's[367] abridged "Decline," now remaindered. I had only plucked at it before, but now I'm really making the effort. I think it's something else. Whole section called "Soul-Image and Life-Feeling" is so overwhelming but on the other hand, straight, German style, as "For everything that our present-day psychologist has to tell us—and here we refer not only to systematic science but also in the wider sense to the physiognomic knowledge of men—relates to the present condition of the *Western* soul, and not, as hitherto gratuitously assumed, to "the human soul" at large. A soul-image is never anything but the image of one quite definitive soul." But you can see the combination mystical/socio-political reasoning has got to be my stick. After all it is America's spirit that is oppressive finally. The rest of it can go to shit.

Got a letter and huge ms from Max Finstein a few days ago! I haven't read all the

---

367   Oswald Spengler, 1880–1926; German historian and philosopher most famous for *The Decline of the West* (1918), in which he espoused a cyclical theory of the rise and decline of civilization.

poems yet, but they seem generally "better" than those of a few years ago, ie, there seems to be some flourish or extension rather than that constant maniacal crossword, product of RC's dead eye. He remarked in his letter about all the "upset" people that SF incident produced. Wow and that scene is so much hetero vs homo, spose you haven't decided, or just, as AG once sd, "I'm AG and I sleep w/ anybody I want to"??? Wot happens, then? Though to be sure I'd much rather have humped those chicks than lumped 'em. The boys I am content with lumping. Oh, well, such choices. But now that I'm 30 I feel old enough to rot at any second, so I care less of a fuck about what anybody says, I imagine . . . tho right now I'm probably the most paranoid creep in all christendom. Also, just recently I've started feeling deep curiosity, maybe more than that, about child next door. Diane's brown war baby. This might sound shitty, but I can't stand the idea of that child first of all growing up in and on an all ofay scene, since, no matter liberal opinion, she ain't. O, fuck that. Anyway love to you & yrs. Tell me what's happening out West? What about those cats in Phoenix??

protecting LBJ
Roi

Pocatello, Oct 19/64

Dear LJ—I got some time this afternoon so here I am. I just took Helene and Paul up the street to the dr. Paul has some pain in his back, nothing I'm sure but he's been complaining about it for too long now. Wow the afternoon is lovely smoky smells in the air, the air bright and crisp, not at all cold but warm with that fall edge to it . . . to answer your last letter I did finish the *Lonely Crusade*. It is truly a bitch, so much so in fact I still ain't out of it yet. I read it over the weekend and still think about it. It ranks with Native Son I don't think there is any doubt. It come 7 yrs later and shows that. I have a lot of notes on it and Native Son and you, mostly as of Slave. I'm writing a piece on the whole show and will send you that so won't get too lengthy here, more because I'd like to say it more there, for you. I haven't yet got ahold of If He Hollers but see it is in paperback and have ordered it for this class in cont. lit. But Wright predicted Luther McGregor in Lonely Crusade to such an extent Himes cldn't have done anything else. And Lee is the man finally. Himes makes it possible for a Negro to write a novel, as a writer, so, the next great shot *can* have a proper ending, which Himes wasn't given to do. I love that art, that frankness, of such a penetration, into Lee's entire mood on the street, at work, and in bed, that I can't say how much. Himes is a great man. You know Roi, Baldwin is an asshole in Notes of Native Son. He shld have his head kicked. I remember this summer you said it was time to get off Jimmy's back. I wish you hadn't said that to me because I'd like you to get on his back, like Tutuola's[368] half-bodied baby, say

---

368   Amos Tutuola, Nigerian writer, 1920–1997. Tutuola's books often centered around Yoruba folk stories.

like put the backlash of the psyche in some other shade's hand. Christ it still bugs me that I hadn't read any of that shit this last summer. Reading O'Neill. Emperor Jones. Uhuh. Oh no. I just got all the plays from the library. That's a lot of shit. Speaking of that it wasn't good of course to hear the news of those cats putting down your play. I will be very anxious to get a copy of it when you can send. And speaking of them, they must be fags. Speaking of fags, I have to assure you that Gregory Markopolous[369] was the toughest fag to grace these parts now or ever. He was invited by the local film society to show a film and lecture last week. He was passing thru Salt Lake City on his way back to apple from L.A. The lecture was the simplest thing you cld have heard and he was stingy with the film, there was about 10 minutes of something called rushes (?) anyway some garbled shit that wasn't finished. Oh he *was* a drag. And dressed hip? Umm. Very Saks 5th ave. These people around here are still so nervously shocked they won't quite admit they were screwed. I heard from Harve Brown so I'll send that "novel" to him. This is a half assed note but I didn't want to let writing you go again like I did last time. I am so fucked up behind work here I cld kill myself just to get out of it. But I did want to admonish you, you motherfucker, to take CARE of yourself, every day in every way. Take heart anyway, with the gains of the past year behind you you ought to get a guggy with no trouble. Ought is never it I know, the way those sonsabitches seem to operate. But you shld. You shld. I got a record by a cat name of Black Ace (BK Turner)[370] you must know of him, plays a steel bodied "national" guitar. He had a theme song in the 30s which he came on with "I am the Black Ace," that *is* too much. Arhoolie F 1003, called Black Ace. And this other guy, Mance Lipscomb,[371] I dig very much, got a picture of him, a sharecrpr, very nice looking man. OK. Cecil Taylor live at the Café Montmartre is the best sound I got that way you must know that too of course, Trance, Call, Lena, D Trad, That's What, Copenhagen Nov. 23, 1962. We are all fine. Helene and P. back P. has to have an Xray. Doct doesn't think it's serious but wants to check. Which makes me think of Kelly, and glad to hear she seems straightened. We miss all of you very often. That damn buffalo seems far over the hills now, thank god, but still being there together I think of as good even in moments of despair. Love to all of you. Ed

Oct 23/64

RJ. By the way I got [. . .] today, a magazine of how to write like WcW's w/ out even trying, or for the blind, lame, and half. I dug that sickeningly unctuous "admonition" of Denny's there also. Oh God! Doesn't she ever get tired of being "right." Fiedler, and your other friend Norman Podhoretz, I noticed are going to speak at the YMHA

---

369   Gregory Markopoulos, Greek avant-garde, experimental filmmaker, 1928–1992.
370   Babe Kyro Lemon Turner, American blues musician, 1905–1972.
371   Mance Lipscomb, American blues musician, 1895–1976.

on the mod nov. I guess I mentioned I'd seen that in the *N.Y. Times*. This is the second card I've written you tonight why didn't I write a letter? Love again, Ed.

P.S. I will say the mag has 'bout the hippest cover of any I've ever seen. I mean they were consistent. They put things on the cover. Six bits! Love to Het, too, and Kelly & Lisa. Hope everything is straight there. Ed

After this final letter from this period, the friendship between Jones and Dorn would suffer separation but never total loss. With Dorn in England for the next five years and Jones in Harlem and then Newark, the two nevertheless kept abreast of one another, each supporting the other's decisions despite any trepidation they might have. This friendship is the truest kind: neither man would pretend his politics, morals, and beliefs could be separated from those he associated himself with, and each would be willing to walk away from even those he loved if he felt too much compromise was being asked of him. As Baraka has said on more than one occasion, "Dorn would rather make you an enemy than lie to you." Baraka's respect for Dorn's willingness to lose a friend if necessary went both ways. Jones would, and did, make enemies rather than lie, and it is this sharp and unwavering sensibility that underlies this strong friendship. Hettie Jones noted in her autobiography that in 1964, after dedicating The Dead Lecturer *to Dorn, "Roi was to tell me, soon, that Ed Dorn was the only white man who understood him" (212).*

[1965]

Dear Ed,

Do you want to go to California in my place? I don't really feel like making that, so if you want to, and feel like substituting and all that bullshit, &c., then you're definitely welcome.

Let me know and I will write to Dick Andrews. Thank you for that poem, it was deep, and I appreciate it, and to know that feeling exists.

We are at work most of the time on the theatre/school. Blk Mountain is a useful concept in forcing this into some usable form. Classes and workshops this summer, political theory/consciousness + the art, remedial education axis, for what the communities dictate.

It has turned very hot today, but I have on a felt slouch hat, tweed jacket, twill pants, and a heavy red cotton shirt. I am also going to carry a heavy trench coat and briefcase, but the temperature is 85 degrees. I have no idea why I don't change clothes.

OK,
take it easy. I'll
see you
Roi

Dear Ed,

Do you want to go to California in my place? I don't really feel like making that, so if you want to, and feel like substituting and that bullshit,&c., then you're definitely welcome. Let me know and I will write to Dick Andrews. Thankyou for that poem, it was deep, and I appreciate it, and to know that feeling exists. We are at work most of the time on the theatre/school. Blk Mountain is a useful concept in forcing this into some usable form. Classes and workshops this summer, political theory/consciousness + the art, remedial education axis, for what the communitiess needs dictate.

It hasturned very hot today, but I have on a felt slouch hat, tweed jacket, twixll pants, and a heavy red cotton shirt. I am also going to carry a heavy trench coat and brief case, but the temperature is 85 degrees. I have no idea why I dont change clothes.

OK,

take it easy. I'll
see you

LEROI JONES

27 Cooper Square
New York, N.Y., 10003
February 4, 1965

Dear Friend,

The Black Arts repertory theater/school as its name indicates will be a repertory theater as well as a school. It is my intention to set up in Harlem a repertory theater where the most meaningful dramas of our time can be staged, in repertory, in this largest of Negro ghettoes.

By repertory theater/school is meant that The Black Arts will also set up and continue to provide instruction, both practical and theoretical, in all areas of the dramatic arts. Acting, Writing, Directing, Set Designing, Production Management workshops will open aimed at gathering young Negroes interested in entering the professional theater world. The Black Arts will in turn make use of these "students" in its own repertory company.

The Black Arts will also make use of much of the already "established" Negro theater talent, as well as providing a place for new talent to come to maturity. As a school, The Black Arts would create an impressive learning situation to develop and stimulate an interest in contemporary theater, theater techniques, in a black community.

As Director of this project, I intend to surround myself with the most intelligent, serious and socially responsible staff (permanent and visiting) possible. I also intend to use the best material around. Young Negro playwrights like Lonnie Elder, Adrienne Kennedy, Douglas Turner, who are already known, but whose work has not yet received the attention it deserves, will be among the contributors, while still younger Negro playwrights like Nat White and Charles Patterson have already indicated their willingness to promote such a project. We have commitments, already, from a great many theater people, e.g., actors like Robert Hooks, Lou Gossett, Al Freeman, Barbara Teer, and hope to have more commitments as we move.

We have figured that the minimum budget for a project such as this would be close to $1,000 per month. We already have some pledges of financial help, but we are in desperate need of more. The Black Arts will be housed in a once elegant brownstone in the center of Harlem. The theater, classrooms, dressing rooms are being designed by a young architect, himself passionately interested in theater arts. If we could raise one year s budget, i.e., $12,000, we would be well on our way to achieving what so many people think of as "only a dream." I hope you can help us.

Sincerely,

LeRoi Jones, for
THE BLACK ARTS
repertory theater/school

Attornies:

Lynn, Spitz & Condon
401 Broadway
New York, N.Y. 10013
(212) CA6-5226

LJ: tl

LeRoi Jones's Black Arts Theater letter (right) was enclosed with the above letter to Dorn.

VI

1981

There is one final letter extant in the Dorn/Jones collections, from 1981. Here, Jones in this short note praises Rolling Stock, *Ed and Jennifer Dorn's little magazine, and asks for Dorn's help regarding his conviction of resisting arrest. Though Baraka notes that he and Dorn continued writing letters through the 1990s until Dorn's death in '99, these letters have not yet come to light in either personal or public archives.*

1) Get to Jeffrey
2) Ask Roi for report on writer's conference[372]

Ed   July 27, 81

Good to see *Rolling Stock*. Irony is that wife & me want to do a similar—in newsprint but a little different viz poetry, dram music reviews. This (RS) gives us heart. I'll tell you how I like it later!
I'm asking if you are coming to The Writer's Congress sponsored by The Nation magazine Oct 9–12. If you are I'd like you to do a reading w/ a few of us to raise funds but mostly consciousness around my case.[373] Let me know. All best (if you can find it)

                                                                                    Amiri B

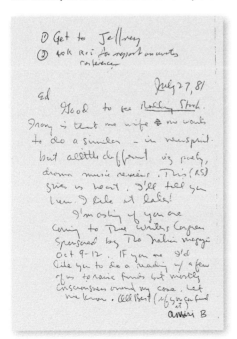

372   These notes (numbered 1 and 2) at the top of the letter are written in Dorn's handwriting, notes to himself after receiving the letter from Baraka.
373   Baraka was convicted of resisting arrest in November 1979; he had now made a motion to reduce the ninety-day prison sentence he had been given.

References

Selected Works by Amiri Baraka (LeRoi Jones)

Baraka, Amiri (LeRoi Jones). *The Autobiography of LeRoi Jones*. Chicago: Lawrence Hill Books, 1997. Print.

———. *Black Music*. New York: William Morrow, 1967. Print.

———. *Blues People: Negro Music in White America*. New York: William Morrow, 1963. Print.

———. *Conversations with Amiri Baraka*. Ed. Charlie Reilly. Jackson: U of Mississippi P, 1994. Print.

———. "A Dark Bag." Book review. *Poetry* 103 (1964): 394–401. Print.

———. *The Dead Lecturer: Poems by LeRoi Jones*. New York: Grove Press, 1964. Print.

———. *Digging: The Afro-American Soul of American Classical Music*. Berkeley: U of California P, 2009. Print.

———. *Dutchman* and *The Slave*. New York: William Morrow, 1967. Print.

———. *Ed Dorn & the Western World*. Austin: Skanky Possum & Effing Press, 2008. Print.

———. *Home: Social Essays*. New York: William Morrow, 1966. Print.

———. "The Largest Ocean in the World." *Yugen* 8 (1962): 58–59. Print.

———. *The LeRoi Jones/Amiri Baraka Reader*. Ed. William J. Harris. New York: Thunder's Mouth Press, 1991. Print.

———. *Preface to a Twenty Volume Suicide Note. . . .* New York: Corinth Books, 1961. Print.

———, ed. *The Moderns: An Anthology of New Writing in America*. New York: Corinth Books, 1963. Print.

——— and Larry Neal, eds. *Black Fire: An Anthology of Afro-American Writing*. New York, William Morrow, 1968. Print.

Selected Works by Edward Dorn

Dorn, Edward. *The Collected Poems: 1956–1974*. Bolinas: Four Seasons Foundation, 1975. Print.

———. *Ed Dorn Live: Lectures, Interviews, and Outtakes*. Ed. Joseph Richey. Ann Arbor: U of Michigan P, 2007. Print.

———. *From Gloucester Out*. London: Matrix Press, 1964. Print.

———. *Geography*. London: Fulcrum Press, 1965. Print.

———. *Gunslinger*. Reprint. Durham: Duke U P, 1989. Print.

———. *Hands Up!* New York: Totem-Corinth, 1964. Print.

———. *Idaho Out*. London: Fulcrum Press, 1965. Print.

———. *Interviews*. Ed. Donald Allen. Bolinas: Four Seasons Foundation, 1980. Print.

———. "The New Frontier." *Kulchur* 11 (1963). Print.

———. "New York, New York." *Views*. Ed. Donald Allen. San Francisco: Four Seasons Foundation, 1980. 45–50. Print.

———. *The Newly Fallen*. New York: Totem-Corinth, 1962. Print.

———. "The Outcasts of Foker Plat: news from the states." *The Wivenhoe Park Review* 1 (1965): 51–62. Print.

———. "Some Notes About Working and Waiting Around." *Yugen* 8 (1962): 38–50. Print.

———. "Strumming Language." *Talking Poetics from Naropa Institute Annals of the Jack Kerouac School of Disembodied Poetics*. Eds. Anne Waldman and Marilyn Webb. Boulder: Shambala, 1978. 83–95. Print.

———. *Views*. Ed. Donald Allen. San Francisco: Four Seasons Foundation, 1980. Print.

———. *Way More West*. Ed. Michael Rothenberg. New York: Penguin, 2007. Print.

———. *Way West: Stories, Essays & Verse Accounts: 1963–1993*. Santa Barbara: Black Sparrow, 1993. Print.

———. *What I See in the Maximus Poems*. Ventura: Migrant Press, 1960. Print.

———, and Leroy Lucas. *The Shoshoneans: The People of the Basin-Plateau*. New York: William Morrow, 1966. Print.

Bibliography

African American Review: Amiri Baraka Issue 37.2–3 (2003). Print.

Allen, Donald, ed. *The New American Poetry*. New York: Grove, 1960. Print.

Allen, Walter. "What's New?" Rev. of *The Moderns: An Anthology of New Writing in America*, ed. LeRoi Jones. *New York Review of Books* 1.10 (1964). Web. 12 Mar. 2008.

Anderson, Iain. *This Is Our Music: Free Jazz, the Sixties, and American Culture*. Philadelphia: U of Pennsylvania P, 2007. Print.

The Atomic Café. Dir. Jayne Loader, Kevin Rafferty, Pierce Rafferty. Prod. Jayne Loader, Kevin Rafferty, Pierce Rafferty. Archives Project, 1982. Film.

Baker, Houston. *The Journey Back: Issues in Black Literature and Criticism*. Chicago: U of Chicago P, 1984. Print.

Baldwin, Kate. *Beyond the Color Line and the Iron Curtain: Reading Encounters Between Black and Red, 1922–1963*. Durham: Duke U P, 2002. Print.

Barney, Stephen A., ed. *Annotation and Its Texts*. Oxford: Oxford U P, 1991. Print.

Benjamin, Walter, and Gershom Scholem. *The Correspondence of Walter Benjamin and Gershom Scholem, 1932–1940*. Ed. Gershom Scholem. New York: Schocken Books, 1989. Print.

Blackstock, Nelson. *COINTELPRO: The FBI's Secret War on Political Freedom*. New York: Pathfinder, 1975. Print.

Brick, Howard. *Age of Contradiction: American Thought and Culture in the 1960s*. Ithaca: Cornell U P, 1998. Print.

Brotherston, Gordon. *Book of the Fourth World: Reading the Native Americas Through Their Literature*. Cambridge: Cambridge U P, 1992. Print.

Butterick, George, ed. *Charles Olson and Robert Creeley: The Complete Correspondence*. Santa Barbara: Black Sparrow Press, 1981. Print.

Byrd, Don. *The Poetics of Common Knowledge*. Albany: State U of New York P, 1994. Print.

Campbell, James. "Edward Dorn." Obituary. *Guardian* 14 Dec. 1999. Print.

Carson, Clayborne. *In Struggle: SNCC and the Black Awakening of the 1960s*. Cambridge: Harvard U P, 1981. Print.

Cassady, Neal. *Neal Cassady: Collected Letters, 1944–1967*. Ed. Dave Moore. New York: Penguin, 2004. Print.

Cento Magazine. "Edward Dorn: 1929–1999." Web. 5 Dec. 2007.

Churchill, Ward, and Jim Vander Wall. *The COINTELPRO Papers: Documents from the FBI's Secret Wars Against Dissent in the United States*. Cambridge: South End Press, 2001. Print.

Clark, Tom. *Charles Olson: The Allegory of a Poet's Life*. Berkeley: North Atlantic Books, 2000. Print.

———. *Edward Dorn: A World of Difference*. Berkeley: North Atlantic Books, 2002. Print.

Clay, Steven, and Rodney Phillips. *A Secret Location on the Lower East Side: Adventures in Writing, 1960–1980*. New York: New York Public Library and Granary Books, 1998. Print.

Collins, Lisa Gail, and Margo Natalie Crawford, eds. *New Thoughts on the Black Arts Movement*. New Brunswick: Rutgers U P, 2006. Print.

Cruse, Harold. *The Crisis of the Negro Intellectual*. New York: New York Review of Books, 1967. Print.

Davidson, Michael. *The San Francisco Renaissance: Poetics and Community at Mid-Century*. Cambridge: Cambridge U P, 1989. Print.

Derrida, Jacques. "This Is Not an Oral Footnote." *Annotation and Its Texts*. Ed. Stephen A. Barney. Oxford: Oxford U P, 1991. 192–205. Print.

DiEugenio, James, and Lisa Pease, eds. *The Assassinations: Probe Magazine on JFK, MLK, and Malcolm X*. Los Angeles: Feral House, 2003. Print.

di Prima, Diane. *Recollections of My Life as a Woman: The New York Years*. New York: Penguin, 2001. Print.

———and LeRoi Jones, eds. *The Floating Bear: A Newsletter. Numbers 1–37, 1961–1969*. La Jolla: Laurence McGilvery, 1973. Print.

Duberman, Martin. *Black Mountain: An Exploration in Community*. New York: E. P. Dutton, 1972. Print.

DuBois, W. E. B. *The Souls of Black Folk*. Chicago: A. C. McClurg, 1938. Print.

Duncan, Robert, and Denise Levertov. *The Letters of Robert Duncan and Denise Levertov*. Eds. Robert J. Bertholf and Albert Gelpi. Stanford: Stanford U P, 2003. Print.

"Edward Dorn." Ed. Burton Hatlen. Spec. issue of *Sagetrieb* 15.3 (1996). Print.

"Edward Dorn: American Heretic." Ed. Eirik Steinhoff. Spec. issue of *Chicago Review* 49.3–4 & 50.1 (2004). Print.

Ellison, Ralph. "The Blues." Rev. of *Blues People: Negro Music in White America*. New York: William Morrow, 1963. *New York Review of Books* 1.12 (1964). Web. 17 Jan. 2007.

Engelhardt, Tom. *The End of Victory Culture: Cold War America and the Disillusioning of a Generation*. Amherst: U of Massachusetts P, 1995. Print.

Faas, Ekbert. *Towards a New American Poetics: Essays and Interviews*. Santa Barbara: Black Sparrow, 1978. Print.

———, and Maria Trombacco. *Robert Creeley: A Biography*. Lebanon: U P of New England, 2001. Print.

Fanon, Franz. *The Wretched of the Earth*. Trans. Constance Farrington. New York: Grove Press, 1963. Print.

Fariello, Griffin. *Red Scare: Memories of the American Inquisition*. New York: Avon, 1995. Print.

Flint, R. W. "Dahlberg's Wisdom." Rev. of Edward Dahlberg, *Because I Was Flesh* and *Truth Is More Sacred*. *New York Review of Books* 2.3 (1964). Web. 4 Apr. 2009.

Franklin, H. Bruce. *Vietnam and Other American Fantasies*. Amherst: U of Massachusetts P, 2000. Print.

Fox, Willard. *Robert Creeley, Edward Dorn, and Robert Duncan: A Reference Guide*. Boston: G. K. Hall, 1989. Print.

Frazier, E. Franklin. *The Black Bourgeoisie*. New York: Collier Books, 1957. Print.

Gilbert, James Burkhart. *Writers and Partisans: A History of Literary Radicalism in America*. New York: Wiley, 1968. Print.

Ginsberg, Allen. *Howl and Other Poems*. San Francisco: City Lights, 1956. Print.

———. *Spontaneous Mind: Selected Interviews 1958–1996*. Ed. David Carter. New York: Perennial, 2001. Print.

———, and Neal Cassady. *As Ever: The Collected Correspondence of Allen Ginsberg and Neal Cassady*. Berkeley: Creative Arts, 1977. Print.

———, and Louis Ginsberg. *Family Business: Selected Letters Between a Father and a Son*. Ed. Michael Schumacher. New York: Bloomsbury, 2001. Print.

Gosse, Van. *Where the Boys Are: Cuba, Cold War America and the Making of a New Left*. New York: Verso, 1993. Print.

Grace, Nancy M., and Ronna C. Johnson, eds. *Breaking the Rule of Cool: Interviewing and Reading Women Beat Writers*. Jackson: U of Mississippi P, 2004. Print.

Greetham, David. *Textual Scholarship: An Introduction*. New York: Garland, 1994. Print.

———. *Theories of the Text*. Oxford: Oxford University Press, 1999. Print.

Hanna, Ralph. "Annotation as Social Practice." *Annotation and Its Texts*. Ed. Stephen A. Barney. Oxford: Oxford U P, 1991. 178–84. Print.

Harrington, Michael. *The Other America: Poverty in the United States*. New York: Macmillan, 1962. Print.

Hazel, Robert. "Embodied Knowledge." Rev. of Edward Dorn, *The Newly Fallen*. *The Nation* 194.3 (1962): 64–65. Print.

Henderson, Stephen. *Understanding the New Black Poetry: Black Speech and Black Music as Poetic References*. New York: William Morrow, 1973. Print.

Hoffman, Daniel, ed. *Harvard Guide to Contemporary American Writing*. Cambridge: Belknap Press of Harvard U P, 1979. Print.

Howe, Susan. *My Emily Dickinson*. Berkeley: North Atlantic Books, 1985. Print.

"In Remembrance of Ed Dorn." Spec. issue of *Big Bridge Magazine* 3.4 (2007). Web. 12 Mar. 2007.

Johnson, Joyce. *Minor Characters*. New York: Penguin, 1983. Print.

Jonas, Stephen. *Selected Poems*. Ed. Joseph Torra. Hoboken: Talisman House, 1994.

Jones, Hettie. *How I Became Hettie Jones*. New York: E. P. Dutton, 1990. Print.

Joseph, Peniel. *Waiting 'Til the Midnight Hour: A Narrative History of Black Power in America*. New York: Henry Holt, 2006. Print.

Just, Ward, ed. *Reporting Vietnam: American Journalism 1959–1975*. New York: Library of America, 2000. Print.

Kane, Daniel. *All Poets Welcome: The Lower East Side Poetry Scene in the 1960s*. Berkeley: U of California P, 2003. Print.

Kaufman, Bob. *Cranial Guitar: Selected Poems by Bob Kaufman*. Minneapolis: Coffee House Press, 1996. Print.

Kelley, Robin D. G. *Freedom Dreams: The Black Radical Imagination*. Boston: Beacon Press, 2002. Print.

———. *Thelonious Monk: The Life and Times of an American Original*. New York: Free Press, 2009. Print.

Kerouac, Jack. *Selected Letters: 1940–1956*. Ed. Ann Charters. New York: Penguin, 1995. Print.

———, and Joyce Johnson. *Door Wide Open: A Beat Love Affair in Letters, 1957–1958*. New York: Viking, 2000. Print.

Killian, Kevin, and David Brazil, eds. *The Kenning Anthology of Poets Theater, 1945–1985*. Chicago: Kenning Editions, 2010.

King, Martin Luther. *Where Do We Go from Here?* New York: Harper & Row, 1967. Print.

Klein, Herbert. *A Population History of the United States*. Cambridge: Cambridge U P, 2004. Print.

Knight, Brenda. *Women of the Beat Generation: The Writers, Artists and Muses at the Heart of a Revolution*. New York: MJF Books, 1996. Print.

Kubler, George. *The Shape of Time: Remarks on the History of Things*. New Haven: Yale U P, 1962. Print.

Kurlansky, Mark. *Non-Violence: The History of a Dangerous Idea*. New York: The Modern Library, 2006. Print.

Kyger, Joanne. "*Communication is essential.*" *Joanne Kyger: Letters To & From*. Eds. Ammiel Alcalay and Joanne Kyger. Lost and Found: The CUNY Poetics Document Initiative 3.7 (Fall 2012). Print.

———. *The Japan and India Journals: 1960–1964*. Bolinas: Tombouctou Books, 1981. Print.

Lhamon Jr., W. T. *Deliberate Speed: The Origins of a Cultural Style in the American 1950s*. Washington, D.C.: Smithsonian, 1990. Print.

Lytle, Mark Hamilton. *America's Uncivil Wars: The Sixties Era from Elvis to the Fall of Nixon*. New York: Oxford U P, 2006. Print.

Malanga, Gerard. "Charles Olson: The Art of Poetry No. 12." Interview. *The Paris Review* 49 (1970). Web. 15 May 2010.

Malcolm X. *The Autobiography of Malcolm X*. New York: Ballantine Books, 1964. Print.

———. *Malcolm X Speaks: Selected Speeches and Statements*. Ed. George Breitman. New York: Grove Press, 1990. Print.

Mariani, Paul. *William Carlos Williams: A New World Naked*. New York: McGraw Hill, 1981. Print.

Maud, Ralph. *Charles Olson at the Harbor*. Vancouver: Talonbooks, 2008. Print.

Martin, Douglas. "William Epton, 70, Is Dead; Tested Free Speech Limits." Obituary. *New York Times* 3 Feb. 2002. Web. 10 May 2010.

Mayali, Laurent. "For a Political Economy of Annotation." *Annotation and Its Texts*. Ed. Stephen A. Barney. Oxford: Oxford U P, 1991. 185–91. Print.

McNally, Dennis. *Desolate Angel: Jack Kerouac, the Beat Generation, and America*. New York: Delta, 1979. Print.

McPheron, William. *Edward Dorn*. Boise: Boise State U P, 1988. Print.

Meltzer, David, ed. *San Francisco Beat: Talking with the Poets*. San Francisco: City Lights Books, 2001. Print.

Middleton, Anne. "Life in the Margins, or, What's an Annotator to Do?" *New Directions in Textual Studies*. Eds. Dave Oliphant and Robin Bradford. Austin: U of Texas at Austin P, 1990. 167–83. Print.

Moretti, Franco. *Graphs, Maps, Trees: Abstract Models for Literary History*. New York: Verso, 2005. Print.

Mullen, Bill V., and James Smethurst, eds. *Left of the Color Line: Race, Radicalism, and Twentieth-Century Literature of the United States*. Chapel Hill: U of North Carolina P, 2003. Print.

Nielsen, Aldon. *Integral Music: Languages of African American Innovation*. Tuscaloosa: U of Alabama P, 2004. Print.

Olson, Charles. "A Bibliography on America for Ed Dorn." *Selected Prose*. Eds. Donald Allen and Benjamin Friedlander. Berkeley: U of California P, 1997. 297–310. Print.

———. *Call Me Ishmael*. San Francisco: City Lights Books, 1947. Print.

———. *Charles Olson and Frances Boldereff: A Modern Correspondence*. Eds. Sharon Thesen and Ralph Maud. Hanover: U P of New England, 1999. Print.

——. *The Maximus Poems*. Reprint. Ed. George F. Butterick. Berkeley: U of California P, 1983. Print.

——. *Muthologos: The Collected Lectures and Interviews*. Ed. George Butterick. Bolinas: Four Seasons Foundation, 1977. Print.

——. "Projective Verse." *Selected Prose*. Eds. Donald Allen and Benjamin Friedlander. Berkeley: U of California P, 1997. 239–49. Print.

——. *Selected Letters*. Ed. Ralph Maud. Berkeley: U of California P, 2000. Print.

——. *Selected Prose*. Eds. Donald Allen and Benjamin Friedlander. Berkeley: U of California P, 1997. Print.

Ossman, David, ed. *The Sullen Art: Interviews*. New York: Corinth, 1963. Print.

Parkinson, Thomas, ed. *A Casebook on the Beat*. New York: Thomas Y. Crowell, 1961. Print.

Pells, Richard H. *The Liberal Mind in a Conservative Age: American Intellectuals in the 1940s and 1950s*. Middletown: Wesleyan University Press, 1985. Print.

——. *Radical Visions and American Dreams: Culture and Social Thought in the Depression Years*. New York: Harper & Row, 1973. Print.

Perkins, George, ed. *American Poetic Theory*. New York: Holt, Rinehart and Winston, 1972. Print.

Petro, Pamela. "The Hipster of Joy Street: An Introduction to the Life and Work of John Wieners." *Jacket* 21 (2003). Web. 22 Feb. 2007.

Posnack, Ross. *Color and Culture: Black Writers and the Making of the Modern Intellectual*. Cambridge: Harvard U P, 1998. Print.

Rasula, Jed. *American Poetry Wax Museum: Reality Effects, 1940–1990*. Urbana: National Council of Teachers of English, 1995. Print.

Raworth, Tom. "Edward Dorn." Obituary. *Independent* 16 Dec. 1999. Web. 10 Feb. 2007.

Reiman, Donald H. *The Study of Modern Manuscripts: Public, Confidential, and Private*. Baltimore: Johns Hopkins U P, 1993. Print.

Rexroth, Kenneth. *American Poetry in the Twentieth Century*. New York: Herder and Herder, 1971. Print.

——. "Disengagement: The Art of the Beat Generation." *A Casebook on the Beat*. Ed. Thomas Parkinson. New York: Thomas Y. Crowell, 1961. Print.

Rigney, Francis J., and L. Douglas Smith. *The Real Bohemia: A Sociological and Psychological Study of the Beats*. New York: Basic Books, 1961. Print.

Rothenberg, Jerome. "Pre-face." *A Secret Location on the Lower East Side: Adventures in Writing, 1960–1980*. Eds. Steven Clay and Rodney Phillips. New York: New York Public Library and Granary Books, 1998. 9–11. Print.

Rukeyser, Muriel. *The Life of Poetry*. New York: Current Books, 1949. Print.

Rumaker, Michael. *The Black Mountain Book*. Asheville: Black Mountain Press, 2003.

Russin, Joseph M. "Kentucky Coal Dispute Still Bitter: Desperate Strike Brings Violence." *Harvard Crimson* 13 Apr. 1963. Web. 5 Jan. 2008.

Sauer, Carl. "Foreword to Historical Geography." *Annals of the Association of American Geographers* 31.1 (1941): 1–24. Print.

Saunders, Frances Stonor. *The Cultural Cold War: The CIA and the World of Arts and Letters*. New York: New Press, 1999. Print.

Schiffrin, André. *The Cold War and the University: Toward an Intellectual History of the Postwar Years*. New York: New Press, 1997. Print.

Scott, Peter Dale. *Deep Politics and the Death of JFK*. Berkeley: U of California P, 1993. Print.

Scully, James. *Line Break: Poetry as Social Practice*. Willimantic: Curbstone, 2005. Print.

Selections from El Corno Emplumado/The Plumed Horn. Ed. Margaret Randall. Lost and Found: The CUNY Poetics Document Initiative 2.1 (Fall 2010). Print.

Sherman, Paul. *The Lost America of Love: Rereading Robert Creeley, Edward Dorn, and Robert Duncan*. Baton Rouge: Louisiana State U P, 1981. Print.

Small, Ian, and Marcus Welsh. *The Theory and Practice of Text-Editing: Essays in Honour of James T. Boulton*. Cambridge: Cambridge U P, 1991. Print.

Smethurst, James. *The Black Arts Movement: Literary Nationalism in the 1960s and 1970s*. Chapel Hill: U of North Carolina P, 2005. Print.

Smith, Dale. "Edward Dorn Out: Forms of Dispossession." *Exquisite Corpse: A Journal of Letters and Life*. Web. 3 Oct. 2009.

Smyth, H. D. *A General Account of the Development of Methods of Using Atomic Energy for Military Purposes Under the Auspices of the United States Government: 1940–1945*. Washington, D.C.: Superintendent of Documents, United States Army, 1945. Print.

Stansell, Christine. *American Moderns: Bohemian New York and the Creation of a New Century*. New York: Metropolitan Books, 2000.

"this pertains to me which means to me you:" The Correspondence of Kenneth Koch & Frank O'Hara. Volumes 1 and 2. Ed. Josh Schneiderman. Lost and Found: The CUNY Poetics Document Initiative 1.2 (Winter 2009). Print.

Thomas, Lorenzo. *Extraordinary Measures: Afrocentric Modernism and Twentieth-Century American Poetry*. Tuscaloosa: The U of Alabama P, 2000. Print.

Von Hallberg, Robert. "This Marvellous Accidentalism." *Internal Resistances: The Poetry of Edward Dorn*. Ed. Donald Wesling. Berkeley: U of California P, 1985. 45–86. Print.

Wah, Fred. "Vancouver 1963 Poetry Conference & Miscellaneous Readings/Lectures." Slought Foundation. Web. 5 Feb. 2008.

Waldman, Anne, and Marilyn Webb, eds. *Talking Poetics from the Naropa Institute: Annals of the Jack Kerouac School of Disembodied Poetics*. Boulder: Shambala, 1979. Print.

"Wanted: An American Novel." Editorial. *Life* 12 Sept. 1955: 48. Print.

Ward Jr., Jerry W. "A Black and Crucial Enterprise: An Interview with Houston A. Baker, Jr." *Black American Literature Forum* 16.2 (1982): 51–58. Print.

Watson, Steven. *The Birth of the Beat Generation: Visionaries, Rebels & Hipsters 1944–1960*. New York: Pantheon, 1998. Print.

Watts, Jerry Gafio. *Amiri Baraka: The Politics and Art of a Black Intellectual*. New York: New York U P, 2001. Print.

Wesling, Donald, ed. *Internal Resistances: The Poetry of Edward Dorn*. Berkeley: U of California P, 1985. Print.

Whalen, Philip. *1957–1977 Selections from the Journals: Philip Whalen*. Volumes 1 and 2. Ed. Brian Unger. Lost and Found: The CUNY Poetics Document Initiative 1.4 (Winter 2009). Print.

Whitfield, Stephen J. *The Culture of the Cold War*. 2nd ed. Baltimore: Johns Hopkins U P, 1996. Print.

Wieners, John. *Selected Poems 1958–1984*. Santa Barbara: Black Sparrow Press, 1998. Print.

———and Charles Olson. *"the sea under the house."* Volumes 1 and 2. Ed. Michael Seth Stewart. Lost and Found: The CUNY Poetics Document Initiative 3.3 (Fall 2012). Print.

Wilford, Hugh. *The Mighty Wurlitzer: How the CIA Played America*. Cambridge: Harvard U P, 2008. Print.

Williams, William Carlos. *The Autobiography of William Carlos Williams*. New York: New Directions, 1948. Print.

———. *In the American Grain*. New York: New Directions, 1925. Print.

Woolf, Douglas. *The Hypocritic Days*. Palma de Mallorca: Divers Press, 1955. Print.

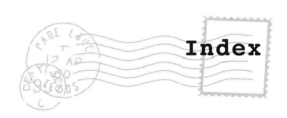

Index